Spinning the Dream

Assimilation in Australia 1950-1970

Anna Haebich

Anna Haebich is a scholar of international repute, known for her leadership in multi-disciplinary and cross-cultural approaches to historical research. Her multi-award-winning book *Broken Circles: Fragmenting Indigenous Families 1800-2000* was the first national history of Australia's Stolen Generations. Anna's career brings together university teaching and research, centre directorship, museum curatorship, visual arts practice, and work with Indigenous communities. Her research interests include histories of Indigenous peoples, migration, the body, the environment, the visual and performing arts, and representations of the past. Anna is Professor and Director of the Centre for Public Culture and Ideas at Griffith University and is a Fellow of the Australian Academy of Humanities and of the Academy of the Social Sciences in Australia.

For the 'grannies'

Little Tooda, Sahnimah, Jonathan and

Jasmine Anne, Jonathon and Amelia Rose

Abbreviations

ANIB	Australian National Information Bureau
ASIO	Australian Security Intelligence Organisation
CPA	Communist Party of Australia
FCAATSI	Federal Council for the Advancement of Aboriginal and Torres Strait Islanders
ILO	International Labour Organisation
NAA	National Archives of Australia
NLA	National Library of Australia
UN	United Nations
UNESCO	United Nations Educational, Scientific and Cultural Organisation
WA SRO	West Australian State Records Office

Contents

Spin

1. [verb] **a.** turn or cause to turn or whirl around quickly: *the girl spun around in alarm.* **b.** give a sensation of dizziness: *the figures were enough to make her head spin.* **c.** give (a news story or other information) a particular interpretation, esp. a favorable one. **2.** [verb] draw out (wool, cotton, or other material) and convert it into threads, either by hand or with machinery: *they spin wool into the yarn for weaving.* **3.** [noun] a particular bias, interpretation, or point of view, intended to create a favorable (or sometimes, unfavorable) impression when presented to the public: *he tried to put a positive spin on the president's campaign.*

Phrases and phrasal verbs

spin one's wheels (informal): waste one's time or efforts.
spin a yarn: tell a long, far-fetched story.
spin something off (of a parent company): turn a subsidiary into a new and separate company.
spin out (of a driver or car): lose control, esp. in a skid.
spin something out: make something last as long as possible: *they seem keen to spin out the debate through their speeches and interventions.*

Origin

Old English *spinnan* [draw out and twist (fibre)].

Oxford American Dictionaries on-line (2005)

Introduction

More than any time in history, mankind faces a crossroad. One path leads to despair and utter hopelessness the other to total extinction. Let us pray that we have the wisdom to choose correctly.

Woody Allen[1]

The good old days were not always so good in Australia. They were not so good if you happened to be an Australian Aboriginal. Or, indeed a woman. Or an Asian confronted by the White Australia policy. Or a homosexual Australian. A homeless person. A person with little English.

Hon Justice Michael Kirby AC CMG[2]

Nostalgia for an assimilated nation haunts current public debate on national identity and nationhood, and spills over into related issues of race, ethnicity, Indigenous rights and immigration. Commentators on both sides of Australian politics deny that the pages of government are being turned back to the assimilation policies of the 1950s, and they are right, of course. We celebrate cultural diversity and acknowledge Indigenous rights, cultures and histories. Yet while the word assimilation is rarely mentioned, more than a trace of its essence remains in official pronouncements on national values, citizenship and the practical integration of Aboriginal communities. This paradox of public denial of assimilation and hidden allegiance to its tenets can be explained in terms of 'retro-assimilation'.

From the perspective of retro-assimilation, current visions of the nation can be seen as yet another example of nostalgia and clever marketing. Retro-assimilation mixes 1950s dreams of an assimilated nation with current ideas of nationhood using today's spin to create an imagined world based on shared values, visions and agreements where all citizens will be treated equally and the same and share fully in the benefits of Australian society, once they agree to cast off their differences and *become* the same. Like other retro products this imagining uncritically exploits the surface of the past without regard for original meanings and significance. Retro-assimilation has strong appeal in today's climate of social turmoil, transformation and global threats: we are irresistibly drawn to its retroscapes, its nostalgic memories of safer and simpler times.

As we respond to the rosy glow of this imagined past, few recognise the deliberate tactics of promotional campaigns in the scenes of happy Australian families and responsible citizens juxtaposed against the bogeymen of war, terrorism and other alien 'isms' encapsulated in such expressions as 'of Middle Eastern appearance'. Like all quality retro products, retro-assimilation has a time-tested lineage. It dates back to the 1950s when the Menzies government avidly promoted the vision of an assimilated nation of Australian families living the 'Australian Way of Life'. Many senior conservative politicians grew up surrounded by these images and fifty years later some remain in their thrall. In a world of retro-assimilation the past is a grab bag of clichés used to sell the present. Nostalgic memories peddle solutions for current issues or camouflage unpalatable political agendas. While this may be ethical for designers and marketers, it makes for dodgy politics when governments adopt retro tactics to manufacture anxiety about threats to national security, to encourage complacency about the treatment of refugees, and to undermine Indigenous rights of sovereignty and self-determination. Our national history deserves to be respected as more than just a marketing ploy for the use of later generations. The retro past never really happened.

This book is a response to the urgent need to set the record straight on these distorted imaginings. At first glance the word assimilation looks familiar and straightforward. Many Australians recognise it as the policy adopted in the 1950s to transform Aboriginal people and new migrants into Australian citizens. They also know it was officially abandoned in the 1970s in favour of policies of multiculturalism and Aboriginal self-determination. From this time assimilation became something of a 'dirty word' among 'people of progressive opinion',[3] yet for many ordinary Australians it retained a nostalgic appeal of memories of simpler times when we were one nation, united by race, culture and our dreams of Dad, Mum and the kids nestled cosily in our suburban homes.

Assimilation's meanings, its application and genealogy, are far more complex than our potted policy histories suggest. Even during its heyday in the 1950s, politicians, bureaucrats and academics argued over what it meant and used it to push often-conflicting agendas. Today Indigenous Australians assert that rather than referring to a distinct policy governing a specific slice of time, assimilation has persisted as core doctrine in policy-making over the generations from first contact to the present. Political historian Tim Rowse suggests that assimilation is 'built into the very fabric of Australian society' and that 'we cannot say that it came to an end'.[4] Academic historians now address assimilation as a global ideology and strategy, one that swings in and out of fashion in colonial, national and international contexts from the Enlightenment to the present, with antecedents stretching back to the Roman practice of the Latinisation of invaded peoples.

Attention to the influences of these broader global intellectual and social movements and shifting political and economic imperatives brings new perspectives to the study of the post-war vision of an assimilated Australia. Constructed as an inevitable unilinear process of cultural and structural absorption into the host society, assimilation is in fact a powerful act of national imagining. It has been the dominant vision of nationhood and the preferred model for incorporating disparate migrant and Indigenous peoples into united settler democracies like Australia. The threads of assimilation are interwoven in our national history with colonial Indigenous policies, with early twentieth-century nation building and the mid-century dream of a unified world family, and with our own vision of a modern assimilated Australian nation in the 1950s.

Forged from successive waves of immigration into Indigenous lands, Australia is a society where whiteness — defined in terms of Anglo-Celtic culture and ancestry — has determined rights of citizenship, status, and belonging. We are the heirs of an unequal triangulated relationship where 'settler Australians' — defined here as the generations of migrants of Anglo-Celtic ancestry and their descendants from colonial times to the present — have been privileged over other immigrant groups and over Indigenous people. For generations our core British-based institutions and their networks of power and privilege have worked to advantage the settler Australians who fitted the ideal Anglo-Celtic racial and cultural profile. They are represented as the principal actors in our national histories. They are the citizens who *truly* belong. This hegemony of whiteness dominated visions of a White Australia in the first half of the twentieth century. Assimilation operated side-by-side with segregation to render Aboriginal people invisible in the national landscape and 'coloured' migrants were barred from entering the country. Immigrants from European nations were discriminated against in selection and resettlement programs according to shifting hierarchies of preference shaped by changing race stereotypes and national enmities. They might find acceptance as Australian citizens but they could never *truly* belong.

The race-based discriminatory practices that upheld this White Australia were seriously challenged following the Second World War by the new international discourse of universal human rights and racial equality promoted by the United Nations. Reeling from the horrors of race genocide during the war, Western nations sought peace and security in new visions of cultural homogeneity and a united attack on racism and the biological explanations of race. Nations like Australia that excluded people from participating as citizens according to distinctions of race and ethnicity now faced the threat of international condemnation. It was in this new world that Australia moved to embrace assimilation, largely in response to international pressures to meet the new expectations of modern nationhood. There was also a new public sentiment of humanitarian concern at home.

In these stormy seas the vision of an assimilated Australia appeared as a safe haven for an anxious nation. The dream was of a modern, prosperous Australia, united by culture rather than race, which could stand tall in the world for protecting the rights of its citizens. Assimilation was heralded as the mechanism to sweep away racial and cultural differences and divisions and to absorb all Australians — Indigenous, settler and immigrant — as equal citizens sharing a common way of life. And while the vision of assimilation fitted international imperatives of opposition to racism against minority groups, the paradox that its promise of universal equality came at the price of their cultural obliteration was conveniently overlooked.

The Australian government had more pressing considerations. As it embarked on the nation's first mass immigration program to include a significant proportion of European migrants, it was eager to reassure its citizens that Australia would remain essentially white and British. The vision of an assimilated nation also glossed over contradictions between Australia's status as a settler nation and its negligible performance on Indigenous rights and sovereignty — a performance that attracted international criticism in the United Nations General Assembly. Drawing on new models of advertising and political spin from the United States, the government sold its vision of a new White Australia to the public. It created carefully planned propaganda campaigns using images of European migrants and Aboriginal people living the Australian way of life to persuade settler Australians that they would quickly assimilate. Given the widespread public ignorance and misinformation about migrant and Aboriginal people, these claims went largely unquestioned. Clever marketing diverted attention from the continuing inequality and discrimination, despite the government's glowing promises of a better life for all.

Assimilation promised equal citizenship rights to Aboriginal people through the abolition of discriminatory laws and practices and improved living conditions, symbolised in images of Aboriginal families living in conventional suburban homes. In return they were required to abandon their distinctive cultural values, lifestyles, customs, languages and beliefs and conform to the national way of life. What was presented as 'benevolence and tolerance' for individuals became in fact 'intolerance aimed at collectivities, their ways of life, their values, and above all value-legitimating powers'.[5] As anthropologist W. E. H. Stanner pointed out at the time, for Aboriginal people this was yet another instance where they were being asked to 'give up something as the price of good relations with us … [with] no promissory note of good to come in return'.[6] No wonder then that many began to 'suspect that the old, old story [was] being told again'[7] as the snail's pace of reform and the miserly services drew families into new webs of welfare dependency and a 'Groundhog Day' nightmare of never-ending preparation for assimilation.

From the beginning the vision of an assimilated Australia had its critics, at home and abroad. Settler Australians soon found that the reality of a new culturally diverse population was irrevocably changing Australia's social and cultural landscape. They could find consolation in being the beneficiaries of the nation's new prosperity, but for European migrants the promise of a happy life in their own suburban homes proved a difficult goal, while for Aboriginal families it was an impossibility. Institutionalised racism at all levels of society made this outcome inevitable. A growing chorus of Aboriginal voices and their supporters, such as Aboriginal leader Pastor Doug Nicholls, West Australian parliamentarian Bill Grayden, Aboriginal activist Charles Perkins, and Aboriginal activist and poet Oodgeroo Noonuccal (Kath Walker), protested first at government delays in delivering on promises of citizenship and better living conditions, and then at the process of forced cultural assimilation. A new pan-Aboriginal protest movement emerged, drawing inspiration from the long history of Aboriginal activism at home and from new international models in the United Nations, decolonising countries in Asia and Africa, and the civil rights movement in the United States. These leaders were developing an alternative vision of Australia as a nation that acknowledged Indigenous rights and cultures, including the right to self-determination.

The conflicting visions of the nation have come down the decades into the present with their own distinct historical trajectories, their champions and detractors. They continue to divide Australians and render elusive the possibility that their differences can ever be resolved. Maori academic Makere Stewart-Harawira asserts that there can be no closure to this 'continuous unresolved contradiction and ongoing provocation' as long as settlers continue to assert control over territories and resources, and Indigenous peoples refuse to surrender their rights.[8]

The central focus of this book is on imaginings of assimilation in the 1950s and 1960s — the period acknowledged as the high point of assimilation in Australian history and, for many citizens, the benchmark of Australian nationhood. While the book makes little direct reference to more recent immigrants from the Middle East, Asia and Africa or to refugees or current Indigenous issues, it hopes to provide the critical framework with which to assess these and other histories. Certainly, for some readers there will be 'aha' moments as they recognise in the historical examples the progenitors of the present-day spin on national policies for Indigenous people and immigrants; on initiatives promoting Australian citizenship, values training and mainstreaming of government services; and on the official stereotyping that undermines the human stories of the most vulnerable people in our midst — refugees, Indigenous people, and the growing underclass of Australians living in poverty.

That Indigenous and migrant histories are considered together might be construed as courting controversy. But the intention is to tease out and compare variations in assimilatory pressures of nation building on Aboriginal people, new immigrants from Europe, and settler Australians. Of course this in no way denies the prior and continuing rights of Indigenous people and the significant historical and cultural factors that differentiate them from ethnic minorities so that they can never be constructed as 'another tile in the multicultural mosaic'.[9] However, this approach allows us to compare the treatment and experiences of these different groups who were subject in varying degrees to the assimilatory pressures of nation building at the time.[10] In particular it helps to expose how the tradition of preferential treatment of settler Australians and new British migrants, established earlier in the century, continued on in the new White Australia of the 1950s and 1960s. This comparative analysis highlights the government's discriminatory treatment of Aboriginal people *and* non-British immigrants in its implementation of assimilation. It also reveals how Aboriginal disadvantage was compounded by government failure to extend to them the economic benefits that were boosting the material prosperity of other families around the nation.

The book is divided into four sections that explore separate threads in the history of assimilation in Australia, drawing together the varied perspectives of Aboriginal history, anthropology, cultural history, migrant history, the history of representation and my personal experiences of living in migrant and Aboriginal communities. Through local case studies, comparisons with other settler societies, and analysis of transnational influences, the discourse of assimilation is addressed in its articulation and implementation, its legacies, political strategies and resistances, and its persistence in political agendas.[11]

The first section, White nation', situates Australia in relation to mid-century global tensions and explores how these shaped the new vision of an assimilated nation. Chapter one begins by peeling away the retro clichés of the 1950s as a golden time of prosperity to expose an anxious nation gripped by a mix of contrasting forces — global change and personal conformity, optimism and fear — that resonates with tensions today. Subject to increasing international pressure to adopt new models of modern nationhood, the Australian government looked to assimilation to deflect criticism of its race-based policies of nation building. The second chapter analyses the bold imagining of an assimilated nation that promised settler Australians that dramatic change would be contained within the parameters of a modified White Australia. To convince the nation, the government looked to the new industry of political and advertising spin and its tools of mass persuasion. Of course, assimilation inevitably brought change. With the entry of one and a half million British and European immigrants between 1947 and 1961, and the government's attack on racial segregation, Australia's demographic, social and cultural landscapes were irrevocably altered. While the requirement to assimilate weighed heavily on

Aboriginal people and immigrants, successful assimilation also depended on settler Australians developing more enlightened attitudes and behaviours.

The next section, 'Selling Assimilation', is a comparative study of federal leadership in selling the assimilation of European migrants and Aboriginal people to the nation through promotional campaigns and its practical programs of change. Part nation building exercise and part spin, the campaigns also sought to convince overseas critics of the government's commitment to positive change. Chapter three critically compares the official discourses of migrant and Aboriginal assimilation as optimistic narratives leading to modern family life in the suburbs — a rapid trajectory for migrants disappearing into the Australian suburbs, and a more gradual path for Aboriginal people. The more lavish attention devoted to migrant campaigns — despite the urgency of Aboriginal conditions — reflected the strategic economic importance of migrant labour for the nation. The fact that Aboriginal people outside the Northern Territory were a state responsibility was no excuse for the federal government's failure to adequately provide for a national campaign to mould citizen attitudes. Chapter four compares federal models of migrant and Aboriginal assimilation and is framed by my experiences growing up in a migrant community in Wollongong and my husband Darryl Kickett's experiences growing up in a Nyungar community near Narrogin in Western Australia. Both communities suffered inadequate provision of much-needed services, resulting in great hardship in a time of unprecedented national growth and prosperity. An explanation for this neglectful approach that has resonances today was the federal government's conviction that special treatment would encourage ethnic and racial 'ghettoes' that would obstruct the process of assimilation. Also familiar today, federal/state bickering over funding responsibilities blocked urgently needed housing and essential services for Aboriginal families living in appalling conditions around the nation.

With the contours of the differential treatment of Aboriginal people, European migrants and settler Australians in the assimilating nation established, the next section, 'Assimilation in Nyungar Country', shifts the focus to the implementation of Aboriginal assimilation. While European migrants were pushed out to survive in mainstream life, the majority of Aboriginal people remained under strict control as state authorities prepared them for assimilated living. The example of Western Australia and the experiences of Nyungar people provide a case study of how one state attended to its obligations to deliver equal citizenship and quality of life to their Aboriginal charges. Chapters five and six deliver a damning account of the obstacles to improvement created by endemic racism, government intransigence, bureaucratic inertia and public and stakeholder self-interest. The accumulated effect was to impose stifling expectations of cultural homogeneity on Nyungar communities while failing to deliver on assimilation's promises of legislative reforms and improved living conditions. When assimilation was finally dropped as state policy in the early 1970s, Aboriginal people could claim equality under the law and equal rights to government services but they remained severely disadvantaged. Tragically, the government and the public blamed *them* for this outcome. Chapter seven tells a different history of Aboriginal people engaging with assimilation, through an account of the history and activities of the Aboriginal-run organisation, the Coolbaroo League, which operated in Perth from 1946 to 1960. This micro perspective highlights the potential for human creativity and adaptability in all nations as people negotiate their way around assimilation in ways that the authorities would never have imagined.[12]

The final section, 'Cracks in the Mirror', looks at ways in which assimilation was refracted in popular culture and public debate, and how an explosion of interest in Aboriginal cultures and histories contributed to the undermining of the vision of an assimilated nation. Chapter eight explores the seeming paradox that the government's program of assimilation coincided with the fashion for appropriating Aboriginal cultural motifs to express national identity and for use in commercial design and the visual and performing arts. Rather than erasing Aboriginal cultural difference this kept it firmly in the public spotlight. The story of Beth Dean and her 1954 ballet *Corroboree* is examined as a case in point. Chapter nine looks at iconic representations of assimilation in popular culture and the media — *They're a Weird Mob*, *Jedda* and *Fringe Dwellers*; press accounts of the life of Albert Namatjira — and in academic research. Public pessimism about the possibility of Aboriginal assimilation was expressed in the popular trope of Aboriginal people 'caught between two worlds'. The media captured attention with accounts of Aboriginal activism — the 1965 Freedom Rides in New South Wales, Oodgeroo Noonuccal's poetry, the rise of Black Power, and the setting up of the Tent Embassy (1972). The entry of Aboriginal voices into public discourse challenged the closed loop of white imaginings and began the dramatic change in representation of Aboriginal people and their cultures and histories witnessed from the 1970s. Assimilation now symbolised outmoded approaches to cultural diversity and nation building. Governments formally abandoned polices of Aboriginal and migrant assimilation at different times during the 1960s and early 1970s, however assimilation did not come to an end, but continued on 'in one form or another' in government practice and as the imagined ideal of one nation for many Australians.[13]

Assimilation was a seductive solution to the threat posed by global change to White Australia. While the imagery and rhetoric of assimilation created the impression of a new nation of equal citizens, the mechanics of it reinforced the inequalities of the status quo, and its marketing — through the powerful images of Australian life and Australian families — distracted the public from the fact that there was no level playing field, only players who always won and those who rarely could. Confronted by our own global fears and anxieties we remain susceptible to the repackaging of this phoney dream as a solution to today's dilemmas. But where will this leave us? If nations who do not know their history are destined to repeat the past, what happens to those who pin their hopes to the retro marketing of a phoney dream?

Clockwise from top left: Living the Australian Dream (1959) [Courtesy National Archives of Australia: A1200 L33480]; The Doomsday Clock (1947) [Courtesy Bulletin of the Atomic Scientists*]; Portrait of Professor A.P. Elkin, Aborigines Welfare Board (1955) [(ML REF: GPO 2 frame number 06649) with acknowledgement to the Government Printing Office collection, State Library of New South Wales]; Vincent's powder*

White Nation

Part I

advertisement (ca. 1951–1960) [Courtesy La Trobe Picture collection, State Library of Victoria]; Winning the Australian dream, Pix *advertisement (1950) [Courtesy* Pix/ACP *Magazines Ltd]; The Queen's visit to Australia,* Pix *cover (1954) [Courtesy* Pix/ACP *Magazines Ltd]; The Bomb and you,* Pix *cover (1957) [Courtesy* Pix/ACP *Magazines Ltd].*

1. Anxious World

> *How richly people have always dreamed of this, dreamed of the better life that might be possible.*
>
> Ernst Bloch[1]

> *Societies are mechanisms for the generation of hope … the caring society is essentially an embracing society that generates hope among its citizens and induces them to care for it. The defensive society … suffers from a scarcity of hope and creates citizens who see threats everywhere. It generates worrying citizens and a paranoid nationalism.*
>
> Ghassan Hage[2]

> *Humanity is forever involved in two conflicting currents, the one tending towards unification, and the other towards the maintenance or restoration of diversity. … In different spheres and at different levels, both currents are in truth two aspects of the same process.*
>
> Claude Levi Strauss[3]

In 1959 crowds in Melbourne, Sydney, Adelaide and Brisbane thronged to visit the most popular blockbuster photographic exhibition of all time. Billed as 'The Show You See with Your Heart', *The Family of Man* opened at the Museum of Modern Art in New York in 1955, toured thirty-eight countries and was viewed by over nine million people before it was 'retired' in 1963.[4] At the time the exhibition was praised for its hopeful message of peace for a disillusioned and shocked world still reeling from the horrors of global warfare and confronted by the new threat of nuclear annihilation. Today *The Family of Man* is acknowledged as an iconic expression of the vision of universal humanity and equality that sustained the hopes of an anxious world in the mid-twentieth century and is on permanent display at the Chateau Clervaux in Luxembourg and listed on the UNESCO Memory of the World Register.

Peeling back the layers to find the *real* 1950s is not easy. Like visitors to *The Family of Man,* we have been seduced by the veneer of civilised optimism glued over a world of crises, threats and unprecedented change. This veneer helped shape the popular view of the 1950s as a 'decade of normality' wedged between the violence of the 1940s and the political protests of the late 1960s — a time of stability, conservatism, peace, circumscribed gender roles, restrained sexuality and a conservative mass media. However, this was a strange normality: shockwaves from the war had forced a 'desperate flight into normalcy' and a determination 'to move on and not look back'[5] as nations and individuals quietly drew an 'amnesiac veil' over war-time horrors and complicities.[6] In such a time, many people found security and stability in the metaphors of family and universality popularised in *The Family of Man* and promoted by the United Nations. We can now look back on the decade as a social and psychological turning point, a pivotal period of global upheaval and dramatic change that transformed the world and determined the shape of events to the end of the century.[7]

Australia was swept along in these changes. No longer a Cinderella satellite of Britain, it had to carve out its own place as an independent nation on the world stage. There were also dramatic political, economic and demographic transformations at home. Historian Nicholas Brown describes a period of 'complexity, frustration and transition'.[8] In this context Australia was pushed to reconsider its unifying race-based vision of nationhood — a White Australia built on the twin pillars of Anglo-Celtic racial origins and cultural heritage — and bow to the newly emerged international democratic model of nationhood that advocated human rights and equality for all citizens. The government was driven by fears of international censure of its discriminatory Aboriginal and immigration policies and the threat of repercussions such as exclusion from vital economic, political and defence alliances. What emerged was the vision of an assimilated Australia where a common culture rather than race was the driving force of nationhood. This promised security and hope for an anxious nation and, for some, suggested the realisation of humanitarian ideals fought for in the war. However, as we will see, this new program of assimilation remained embedded in race ideology and practice, so that criticism at home and abroad continued on in tandem with implementation of the policy.

Mixed messages

The 1950s provided a peculiar mix of contrasts — rapid change and conformity, exhilaration and fear — that resonates with today's global climate of turmoil and transformation. *The Family of Man* exemplified the mixed messages of the times. Curated by Belgian photographer and US resident Edward Steichen, the exhibition contained fifty-three black and white photographs depicting family groups from sixty-eight countries around the world happily caught up in their daily activities or celebrating the joys and achievements of family life. The focus on the commonality of human experience was reinforced by relevant quotes from world religious texts. Together these served to reduce the marked differences of nation, culture and race in the images to mere surface trappings of a common human core while distracting viewers from memories of the recent past when the world tore itself apart over distinctions of race and culture. The exception in this seamless narrative was a single large colour photograph of a nuclear explosion — a stark reminder of the horrific potential for world destruction. Steichen's biographer and contemporary Rosch Krieps recalled that the exhibition's mass appeal came from its optimistic promise of peace by virtue of the essential oneness of all races and cultures.[9] Publicity for the exhibition reinforced this message with iconic photographs, in particular showing rival Cold War leaders US Vice President Richard Nixon and Soviet leader Nikita Khrushchev sitting amicably together at the 1959 Moscow exhibition opening.[10]

Not all viewers were convinced by the exhibition's veneer of optimism. For Melbourne writer and peace activist Elizabeth Vassilieff the exhibition was a reminder of the terrible choice that faced humankind:

> … on the one hand the assertion of faith in people's capacity for goodness, their dignity and worth, in the vital energy of the Family of Man, in the potential even of the bodgies, the widgies, the tramps, the crims, the beasts of the world, in the human capacity for moral indignation, rebellion, struggle, in the concept of justice and freedom for all in the world now; on the other hand, contempt for the Family of Man, historical pessimism, resignation to evil, and the abdication of responsibility, leading to universal death from a war with nuclear weapons.[11]

French critic and theorist Roland Barthes visited the exhibition in Paris in 1956 and attacked its veneer of universality, achieved by 'denying history … eliminating difference, overlooking the scars of life in particular social circumstances, and inundating the viewer in sentiment'.[12] Gender stereotyping and US hegemony could be added to his list. Barthes' sentiments have echoed down the years in continuing criticisms of the exhibition's 'sentimental humanism' and opulent images that, like the specious multiculturalism of more recent Benetton advertising campaigns, mask the challenge of the heterogeneous, the complex and the contradictory. Cultural analyst Eric Sandeen describes Steichen's vision of universality as an illusion that is 'continually challenged by the relentless fracturing of the globe among competing interests and communities, and the consolidating power of multinational capital and globalising media'. This, rather than the mute silence of Steichen's exhibition space 'is the cacophony in which we live and through which the images must be read'.[13]

In creating *The Family of Man* Steichen had hoped to arouse an imagined sense of global community that would 'incite people into taking open and united action against war itself'.[14] However, *The Family of Man* was not universal and nor was its message confined to peace. The exhibition was a product 'Made in the USA' within a particular historical context. Developed in a prestigious New York museum, it was bankrolled by the Rockefeller family and created by a largely US curatorial staff with the vast majority of its images taken by US photographers. Like the Billy Graham crusade that also toured Australia in 1959 — preaching Christianity, anticommunism and the American way — the exhibition provided ammunition for America's Cold War cultural diplomacy campaigns, although this of course had not been Steichen's intention. Masterminding this darker side was the US Information Agency, which funded the exhibition's ambitious touring schedule to promote America's new status as a superpower and to spread positive images of US democracy in the wake of the bad publicity from its communist witch hunts and persecution of civil rights activists.[15] The underlying domestic ideal promoted in the exhibition was of the American family with its familiar constructs of religion, patriarchy and gendered family roles that challenged communist ideology with an image of a 'classless society with the family as its nucleus'.[16]

Such public relations doubletalk that communicated its messages through the potent symbols of family and nation was typical of propaganda of the 1950s. When the Australian government promoted its new vision of an assimilated nation it adopted these same measures to sell the concept. Like visitors to *The Family of Man*, Australians would also be seduced by images of happy families — British, European and Aboriginal — all joining in the Australian way of life, the veneer of unity covering over the mass of tensions, contradictions and inequalities that characterised the changing Australian nation in the 1950s.

Age of anxiety

For poet W. H. Auden, the 1950s were an 'age of anxiety'.[17] Beneath the complacency and conformity lay the velvety darkness of anxiety and fear. The United Nations and the *Family of Man* exhibition pumped out comforting messages of universal brotherhood and equality and the ideal of an international family of nations, but the political and economic realities were different. That decade had unprecedented global migration, extraordinary economic development, undreamt of prosperity and a new world of consumerism and advertising and political spin. Despite the creation of the United Nations with its promise of world peace, reports of new theatres of war escalated, along with political terrorism in decolonising nations and racial backlash sparked by the civil rights protests in the United States. Overshadowing everything else was the spectre of a world split by the competition between capitalism and communism and the terror of atomic global annihilation through the Soviet and American competing will to power. Even outer space was threatened by this deadly conflict. Fanned by US doctrine at home and abroad, a scenario of fear and delusion was created, with Janus-faced paranoia about enemies at home and abroad that is familiar to us today in our own age of anxiety.

Today we grapple with the black dog of depression; the personal devil in the 1950s was anxiety. The prescription drugs of choice today are Prozac and Zoloft but back then the 'miracle cure for anxiety' was Miltown (Meprobamate) a tranquilliser known popularly as the 'peace pill', 'happiness pills' or 'emotional aspirin'. Miltown was 'an overnight sensation', the first psychotropic wonder drug in medical history that 'fulfilled the promise of better living through chemistry' by reducing 'tension, anxiety, depression, menstrual stress, psychosomatic symptoms, and insomnia'.[18] Within a year of its launch in 1955, one in twenty Americans was prescribed Miltown, over a billion tablets had been sold and the monthly production of fifty tons could not keep up with demand. The drug promised to relieve post-war tensions in gender expectations, as well as threats to patriarchal authority in the home by reconciling wives and mothers to domestic life and a restricted 'new femininity'. It was widely prescribed for mothers to bolster their role of maintaining peace and stability within the haven of the family.[19] Miltown became the panacea for the anxieties of American life, its calming effects helping to prop up the increasingly precarious vision of a nation of happy families.[20]

In Australia mothers relied on the analgesic properties of the aspirin, phenacetin and caffeine in headache powders like Bex, Vincent's Powders and Aspro to get them through the day. Advertisers promised to 'soothe away' the effects of 'modern tension, "nerves" strains, pain & headaches'[21] — it was only later that the harmful effects of addiction and overuse causing serious damage to the liver and kidneys and even death were made public. These products could be purchased at any corner shop and their widespread use gave rise to the iconic 1950s housewives' remedy of 'a cup of tea, a Bex and a good lie down'. According to Hugh Mackay, the anxiety of the times penetrated the heart of the Australian family to shape the nihilistic view of the baby boomer generation: eat, drink and be merry because, with the press of a button, the world could be annihilated.[22]

Anxious nation

Australia, like many other nations, was in a state of high anxiety following the war as our leaders struggled to carve out a respectable place within the changing boundaries of empire, nations and alliances. For a nation finding its way on the world stage, this was a demanding new era of international standards of conduct and scrutiny under the United Nations, and an expanded global media — including an emerging press in decolonising states — that accelerated the speed and spread of criticism and brought a sharp critical edge to reporting. In this climate Australia's race-based immigration and Aboriginal policies were a liability rather than a positive statement of nationhood and allegiance to Britain. Our outmoded domestic policies threatened to blow out into scandals that could irreparably damage Australia's international reputation and our leaders sometimes seriously misjudged world opinion — an infamous example being the refusal in the late 1950s to condemn South Africa's apartheid system.

Significantly, as historians Sue Taffe and John Chesterman point out, the international climate provided the impetus for concerned senior diplomats and politicians to push for equal rights for Aboriginal Australians.[23] Activists at home were able to use the language of civil rights to promote their own agendas.[24] International censure was answered by 'prudential diplomacy',[25] a new idealism and Aboriginal activism. In regard to migration, the gradual relaxation of the White Australia policy was driven by a mix of humanitarian concern for the millions of post-war refugees, fears of international reprisals against the racist policy, and economic self-interest in developing a mass labour force for post-war economic development.

Refugees and migrants taking advantage of new opportunities

to settle in Australia were inevitably changing the nation's demographic and cultural landscape. Meanwhile Australians were seeking to improve their economic status while otherwise endeavouring to maintain the status quo. What emerges is a complex picture of changes that were remoulding the vision of Australian nationhood. A mix of key players was operating in various national and international arenas, sometimes promoting conflicting agendas. The Australian government was responding to the erosion of old global networks based on racism and colonial power and was seeking to capitalise on new opportunities and alliances that were vital to national development and defence while also striving to meet new international standards of democratic nationhood. This included building alliances with the new decolonised states in the Asia Pacific region. The government's critics at home and abroad drew on new human rights conventions like the 1948 Universal Declaration on Human Rights to push for Indigenous equality within the nation and recognition of Indigenous rights.

Guiding Australia through these anxious times was the paternal figure of Prime Minister Sir Robert Menzies who held office from 1949 to his retirement in 1966. During his twenty-three years of conservative political ascendancy, Menzies manoeuvred the nation through the labyrinth of change, guided by his own passionate allegiance to Empire, Queen and the British race and a pragmatism that looked to building new networks of commerce and defence that inevitably drew Australia ever closer to the United States.

Cold War paranoia

Fears of global war and invasion continued to haunt the Australian nation in peace time. The editor of the popular women's magazine *Woman's Day* wrote in 1950 of 'a war haunted world … In the morning and the evening that terrible spectre is with us — always.'[26] Like panic about global terrorism today, public fears then were fanned by the spectre of communism and the tensions of the Cold War, real and imagined. As American writer James Carroll observes in his history of Red scare-mongering in the Pentagon, 'the perception of the danger and the danger itself have a way of becoming the same thing. Shadows take on weight.'[27]

Australia sought national security in defence alliances with the United States. The nation joined the war in Korea in 1950 with a zeal that surprised some older commentators and threatened the diplomatic ties being built within the region.[28] Seventy-one per cent of Australians endorsed the war in Korea as a defence against communist aggression.[29] The editor of the *Woman's Day* forecast optimistically that it would prevent 'the complete destruction of our civilisation and 'ensure that tomorrow's world will be free of war'.[30] Unintended outcomes were the demonstration of Australia's inadequate armed force capabilities and the move in 1951 to rearmament and national service schemes, accompanied by an intensive anti-communist propaganda campaign.[31] In 1954 the anti-colonial war in Vietnam raised fears of the 'Red Tide lapping our northern shores'.[32] and revived fearful memories of the threat of Japanese invasion. As ties were renegotiated with Britain, Menzies made the momentous decision, without consulting his Cabinet, to volunteer Australian territory for twelve British nuclear bomb tests at Maralinga and the Montebello Islands between 1952 and 1956 and further minor trials at Maralinga until 1963.[33] Here the frontiers of science and invasion met as Aboriginal people were forced off their lands to make way for the nuclear tests and for uranium mining and processing plants at Radium Hill in South Australia in 1952 and the Rum Jungle in the Northern Territory in 1954. Uranium was supplied to the United States and Britain for defence programs in the war against communism with little financial gain for the nation.[34]

The extent of public obsession with the atomic age was evident in its myriad representations in popular culture. This reached extreme levels in the United States and there was fallout for Australian audiences now enjoying American culture and commodities. Atomic symbols were embraced as a 'Madison Avenue marketing tool, as an emblem of progress, entrepreneurship, hope' with breakfast cereals promising a morning burst of 'atomic energy.' This mingled with a sense of dread eloquently expressed in the Doomsday Clock that was started at seven minutes to midnight in 1947 by the journal *Bulletin of the Atomic Scientists*.[35] The mutagenic potential of radioactive rays was highlighted in science fiction movies such as *Attack of the Crab Monsters* (1951), and the threat of invasion and global warfare (by aliens from outer space) was repeated in films like *Invaders from Mars* (1953) and *When Worlds Collide* (1951). Closer to home in Melbourne movie extras lined the streets posing as doomed citizens awaiting the final deadly radioactive cloud with Hollywood stars Ava Gardner, Gregory Peck, Fred Astaire and Anthony Perkins in Stanley Kramer's *On the Beach* (1960), based on Australian author Nevil Shute's best-selling novel.[36]

The popular Australian *Pix* magazine featured articles on the bomb with graphic photographs and headlines. The cover of the June 1957 edition showed an atomic explosion with the headline 'THE BOMB AND YOU: Facts you should know on those nuclear tests: Cancer and leukaemia the legacy.' There was also a cartoon by Eric Jolliffe whose idiosyncratic 'Witchetty's Tribe' series created humour by depicting Aboriginal people as primitive desert dwellers who made surprisingly modern comments about topical events. This showed the mushroom cloud of an atomic bomb exploding on the horizon while an Aboriginal man holding spears commented to his companions, 'I told that Warramunga mob not to tinker around with uranium.'[37] It is chastening then to realise that Aboriginal families not picked up by government patrols experienced the full impact of the atomic clouds that spread out across the continent from the British tests. Matatjara woman Jessie Lennon and her family were camped near Coober Pedy when they were caught in nuclear fallout from the Emu tests. Jessie recalled, 'I siphoned water out of the drum and I saw this shadow go past and I looked up. What was that shadow? … And it started to look hazy … Bluish smoke rolled over … Came in — filled up the hills, the holes — rolled in along the ground — to the tree tops … Right over the top of us.'[38]

Australia was second only to the United States in levels of hostility and political anxiety about communism, although this did not reach the fever pitch of the McCarthy witch-hunts in the United States. The Menzies government narrowly failed to outlaw the Communist Party of Australia (CPA) in 1951 but it continued to represent communism as a 'coordinated international conspiracy directed from Moscow' that threatened the social order of Australia and all other democracies.[39] By promoting Cold War anxieties in this way the government diverted public attention away from pressing issues of inflation and housing shortages at home. Fear of the enemy within, convincingly used in war-time propaganda against German, Italian and Japanese residents, was now used to target suspected communists as aliens whose allegiance was to Moscow and put them under surveillance by the Australian Security Intelligence Organisation (ASIO). 'Communist' became the tag for any critic of the government and strikes and protests were taken as proof of a communist conspiracy to weaken the country. Even the Commonwealth public service was accused by ASIO of harbouring communists within its ranks.[40] In this climate of fear and suspicion the Australian churches joined together to fight the spread of communism and other demoralising influences, calling on citizens in language familiar to us today, to commit themselves to the nation's core values and preaching the power of the family as protection against 'alien and radical influences'.[41]

Communists and Aboriginal issues

In the spirit of paranoia and finger pointing the government claimed that much of the criticism of its Aboriginal policies was the work of a communist plot led by Moscow via the CPA. The party had indeed taken a strong stand on Aboriginal issues since its establishment in Australia in 1920, a reflection of the international communist movement's opposition to colonialism as an integral component of world capitalism. The party also opposed racism on the grounds that encouraging race hatred between white and black workers prevented working-class solidarity and so cleared the way for capitalist exploitation of workers. This argument was also used to attack the White Australia policy as a 'capitalist weapon against the working class'.[42] By 1931 the CPA had formulated an 'emancipatory' Aboriginal platform that advocated full citizenship rights and autonomy through rights to land, access to social services and cultural recognition.[43] During the 1940s the CPA supported the strike by Aboriginal pastoral workers in the Pilbara region and in the 1950s and 1960s took a strong stand against forced assimilation, arguing instead for Aborigines' right to choose to live as members of the general Australian community or in their own autonomously controlled communities.[44] Aboriginal people were encouraged to join and become actively involved in its programs, however they were expected to follow party doctrine, which took precedence over any Indigenous political aspirations.[45] Ray Peckham was an Aboriginal CPA member, dancer, unionist, co-founder of the newspaper *The Aboriginal Worker* (1963) and representative of the Sydney-based Association of Aid for the Progress of Aborigines. He visited Moscow in 1964 where he spoke out on Aboriginal wages, segregation and lack of civil rights.[46]

Senior politicians and bureaucrats sought to trivialise CPA criticisms by claiming that they were politically motivated inventions driven by Soviet ideologues. Sue Taffe argues that during the 1950s the government saw this as an integral part of the 'war of ideology being waged between the Soviet Union and the West'.[47] In a speech in 1962 the federal minister with responsibility for Aboriginal affairs (Sir) Paul Hasluck alleged that the CPA was intent on creating 'a great deal of mischief' by provoking racial conflict and international criticism of Australia.[48] In the following year he claimed that the party was painting Australia as 'one of the Western powers that can be discredited nationally so that the African and Asian nations will get a picture of us as a country full of racial antagonism and racial prejudices, and generally, in the international sphere, to lessen our influence and to besmirch our name'.[49]

This was *precisely* how Soviet communists were representing Australia in the international arena. In the context of Cold War politics and the growing decolonisation movement, the Soviets escalated their attacks on colonialism and argued in the United Nations for freedom for all colonised populations, including Indigenous peoples. From the late 1950s Australia was the target of damaging allegations of racial oppression and discrimination and even genocide by Soviet leader Nikita Khrushchev and the Soviet media. In 1961 Khrushchev spoke out in the General Assembly demanding the 'final liberation of all peoples from colonial oppression'. Describing the devastation wrought by colonisation on Indigenous peoples he claimed that 'the population in a number of colonies … decreased by nearly half. It is common knowledge how the native population was exterminated in Australia. Mr Menzies who spoke here should not forget that.'[50] In an English broadcast to South East Asia commenting on the White Australia policy, Radio Moscow claimed that Australia had 'developed racism to the level of State policy' in its racist immigration legislation and endorsement of South Africa's 'misanthropic apartheid'.[51] In 1959 the Communist press in Peking quoted from a government pamphlet to support the allegation that Aboriginal people were moved from their traditional lands to make way for mining and left to survive 'only on the fringe of hope and often on the fringe of despair.' The newspaper also included Australian Communist author Frank Hardy's comment that the death in 1959 of Arrente artist Albert Namatjira following his detention on a charge of supplying alcohol to another Aboriginal man was 'a mute indictment of capitalist society'. There was also Hardy's claim that the controversial Max Stuart trial in the same year was a 'frame up'. Stuart had been sentenced to death for the rape and murder of an eight-year-old girl but doubts over his alleged confession eventually led to a royal commission and the commuting of his sentence to life imprisonment.[52]

In a confidential letter to its overseas diplomats in 1962 the Department of External Affairs warned that these attacks demonstrated how 'in the sphere of modern international politics Australia's prestige may ultimately depend as much, if not more, on her treatment of aborigines'.[53] The criticisms continued and in 1963 the Soviet press reported on the 'annihilation by racist-colonialists of the native population in several parts of the world … the British colonialists have nearly totally annihilated the native population of Australia'.[54] In the same year in the United Nations Trusteeship Council the Soviet delegate confronted his Australian counterpart with the claim that Section 127 of the Australian Constitution, which stated that in 'reckoning' the Australian population the government should exclude 'Aboriginal natives', was clear proof of official discrimination.[55] Once again senior officers cautioned that these criticisms could 'seriously prejudice the reputation of our country in the eyes of the world and even make difficult some aspects of our participation in world councils'.[56] Such comments can be read as 'prudential diplomacy' as John Chesterman suggests, but Tim Rowse argues that they also indicate 'a certain idealism' amongst diplomats and government officers in External Affairs who 'admired the liberalism of the United Nations'.[57] Sue Taffe also acknowledges that requirements for the department's senior staff to remain up-to-date with international issues gave them 'a clearer overview than most of ideas, attitudes and trends'.[58]

Changing the face of the nation

In 1945, three days before the nuclear attack on Hiroshima, the Curtin Labor government secretly agreed on an ambitious new program of mass immigration that would dramatically change the nation's social and cultural landscape. The urgency to build up the population of seven million was motivated by fears over national security following the threatened invasion of Australian borders by Japan and the need for a labour force sufficient for the government's ambitious program of post-war economic development. In demographic terms the government planned an annual increase of two per cent or 140,000 from combined migrant intake and natural increase. However, this level could not be supplied from the usual source of British migrants alone and the government looked to Europe with its millions of refugees and unemployed citizens to fill the gap.

Like Canada and New Zealand after the war, Australia soon moved from reaffirming its discriminatory immigration polices to a massive migrant intake to meet new labour demands. In Australia's case its shifting geopolitical circumstances, marked by increasing engagement with Asia during the 1950s and 1960s, was a further impetus for change. As discriminatory selection processes were relaxed new populations of immigrant minorities and heterogeneous population profiles developed, although it was not until 1973 that Australia formally discarded its anachronistic White Australia policy.

The proposal to take in large numbers of European migrants represented a significant shift from a policy that had privileged British immigration, and it had to be persuasively explained to a potentially hostile Australian public. In parliament in 1946 the new Minister for Information and Immigration, Arthur Calwell, was at pains to reassure the public that 'for every foreign migrant there will be ten people from the United Kingdom' and that 'our population shall remain predominantly British'. He urged Australians to 'give their maximum assistance to … assimilate more and more people who will come from overseas to link their fate with our destiny'.[59] Mass immigration had strong bipartisan support and in 1949 the new Menzies Liberal government boosted the annual intake, rashly promising that 50 per cent would be from Britain. However, this proved impossible to sustain for long, and as rates of British and then European migration fell during the late 1950s the government was forced to look even further afield to non-European countries for its migrant intake.

Australia's migration program proved a resounding demographic and economic success. Between 1947 and 1961 net migration to Australia reached 1.3 million, and with natural increase the Australian population 'spectacularly' grew to 10.5 million. The birthplaces of net migration for the period were:

Britain and Ireland	407,799 [one third of total]
Southern European (Italy, Greece)	334,112 [one quarter]
Eastern Europe (Poland, Baltic States, Yugoslavia)	248,000 [one fifth]
Northern Europe (German, Netherlands)	226,339 [one fifth]
Others	80,634.[60]

In 1966 one out of every seven Australians was born overseas — the highest proportion of overseas-born in the world outside the state of Israel. Immigration provided 50 per cent of the labour force growth between 1947 and 1973.[61] Despite economic ups and downs after the war and fears of another depression in the early 1950s, the nation entered a sustained boom in the mid 1950s that continued into the early 1970s and raised the living standards of millions of Australian families. This new prosperity was built on mobilisation of capital including private investment from the United States, innovations in technology and management and the massive intake of migrant workers. Their labour drove the unprecedented expansion in heavy industry, manufacturing, resource development and monumental public works schemes like the Snowy Mountains Scheme that brought economic prosperity and boosted national pride and feelings of security.

Economic development also brought the distractions of mass consumerism that were fanned on by an aggressive new advertising industry. From this emerged what historian John Murphy described as a growing sense of 'complacency born of affluence, ruled over by a self-satisfied form of conservatism'[62] that left Australia seriously out of step with international trends. In the arts, for example, the Menzies government promoted outmoded nationalistic paintings in a realistic style at a time when modernism was in vogue. When Australia received its first invitation to the prestigious Venice Biennale in 1958 it filled its pavilion with conventional landscapes by Sir Arthur Streeton and Arthur Boyd while the United States exhibited the latest works of abstract expressionist painter Mark Rothko. Rather than presenting a positive image of Australia this showcased the nation as a cultural backwater. A report by the former Australian ambassador noted, in a reference to the stylised realism of Soviet art, that 'unflattering comparisons were made between Australia and the Soviet pavilions'.[63] The sophisticated outlook of many European migrants and the cultural diversity they brought to Australia only gradually came to influence this cultural parochialism.

The government may have remained parochial about migrants

at home but the nature of its immigration program inevitably drew it into new international arenas of collaboration. Accustomed to a cosy relationship with British migration officials, Australian officers had a quick baptism in the complexities of working in cross-cultural contexts with agencies like the International Refugee Organisation and European officials responsible for the selection, transportation and resettlement of immigrants in their new host countries. Along with the United States, Argentina, Brazil, Venezuela, Canada, New Zealand, South Africa and Israel, Australia was one of the chief receiving countries for the 4.5 million migrants and refugees who left Europe between 1945 and 1952. Displaced persons and refugees from non-English speaking backgrounds, they were survivors of Nazi slave labour and concentration camps, and exiles who refused to return to homes now under communist rule.

Australia was also involved in a new discourse emerging in UN-directed initiatives relating to immigration. In 1951 Australia signed the UN Convention on Refugees. Over the decade bureaucrats and scholars, most of them demographers from the Australian National University, contributed to international research directed by the United Nations Educational, Scientific and Cultural Organisation (UNESCO) intended to ensure economic benefit, social progress, cultural enrichment and mutual understanding for migrants in their new host countries. In 1952 Australia was one of eight countries invited to contribute to a UN study that would formulate recommendations to facilitate migrants' 'final assimilation' into their new homelands. To this end the Assimilation Division of the Department of Immigration documented Australia's commitment to assimilation, its strategy of developing community networks to promote the policy and its insistence that migrants learn to speak English and become naturalised citizens. Research from Australia was included in the first volume of UNESCO's series *Population and Culture*, which examined the ways that immigrants influence the social and economic life of their host countries. Australia also contributed to the UNESCO *Way of Life* series, which provided summary overviews of the national cultures of migrant and host countries in order to facilitate assimilation. The *Australian Way of Life* volume included chapters by prominent Australians on the familiar topics of the Australian character, the family, political and economic institutions, religion, education and external relations. There were no chapters on Aboriginal people or Australian art and culture.

UNESCO initially promoted migrant assimilation but, as research from its international surveys pointed increasingly to the complexities of resettlement processes, it began to move towards a policy of 'cultural integration of migrants'. This was the theme of the 1956 UNESCO Havana Conference, which addressed the orientation, resettlement and integration of immigrants in seventeen migrant countries and the crucial role of the intact family unit in successful integration.[64] In this context 'cultural integration' referred to 'conformity within the framework of cultural pluralism' where difference was acceptable as long as it did not lead to 'domination and disunity'. The successful process of cultural integration reflected the 'predisposition of the immigrant to change'. of the 'receiving society to recognise differences', and 'the degree of stability of the sociocultural structure of the receiving area'.[65] Australia participated in the conference, represented by demographer W. D. Borrie from the Australian National University who published a survey of the conference papers in 1959. However the government maintained its commitment to assimilation.[66]

Universal human rights

These contributions reflected Australia's active role in the early years of the United Nations. In 1945 an Australian delegation led by the Labor Minister for External Affairs, Dr Herbert Vere Evatt, joined fifty other original member states at a meeting in San Francisco to hammer out the text for the Charter of the United Nations, which was signed on 26 June. The Charter built on the ideals of its predecessor, the League of Nations, in promoting peace and social and economic progress and, in the shadow of the war, adopted a sweeping human rights agenda to prevent such global tragedies in the future. Rights ranging from equality and non-discrimination through to self-determination and independence for colonised peoples were enshrined in the Charter and subsequent instruments. Dr Evatt was elected President of the United Nations General Assembly from 1948 to 1949 and in this role presided over the momentous proclamations of the 1948 Declaration of Human Rights, the 1948 Convention on the Prevention and Punishment of the Crime of Genocide and the 1949 Geneva Convention. Dr Evatt saw the United Nations as 'the sole forum for resolving of international disputes', however the Menzies government (which took office in 1949) was less convinced and followed more of a diplomacy agenda in international affairs.[67] Still there was no escaping criticisms from the Soviets and decolonising nations of the yawning gap between the discourse of universal human rights and the racial landscape of 'White Australia'.

The Universal Declaration of Human Rights reflected the fundamental belief in the 'simple fact of the common humanity shared by every man, woman, and child on earth, a fact that … put linguistic, racial, religious and other differences into their proper perspective.'[68] This was symbolised in the United Nations headquarters in New York, completed in 1952. Designed by an international team of architects, the vast General Assembly Hall displayed the United Nations emblem — a map of the world, as seen from above the North Pole, flanked by olive wreaths as a symbol of peace. In the Security Council Chamber the central mural by the Norwegian artist Per Krogh depicted 'a phoenix rising from its ashes' — a vision of a new world after the war — with brightly coloured images representing hopes for a better future and equality represented by 'a group of people weighing out grain for all to share'.[69] However the United Nations membership was made up of a vast cultural mosaic of sovereign member states who, although required to work together in the interests of international peace and equality, quite naturally acted to protect their own domestic concerns on many issues. Its corridors were a hothouse of Cold War polemics, post-colonial turmoil and fallout from armed clashes and threats of conflict between India and Pakistan, the United States, mainland China, Soviet Russia and Korea, and Palestine and Israel in the Middle East.

There were inherent contradictions between the promise of liberation through universal rights and the potential for universalising assimilatory forces to trample on the rights and freedoms of minority groups. As sociologist Alastair Bonnett observes, 'the universalist promise of equality demands the submission, the self-obliteration, of those to whom it is "offered". "We can all be one," it is suggested, "if you become like me."'[70] This was the credo of assimilation — the pay-off for equal rights was cultural conformity. From the mid-1950s this contradiction was central to the growing critique of assimilation as the best model for the incorporation of minority groups into nations. But in 1947 UNESCO's first Director-General, scientist Sir Julian Huxley, had unashamedly preached an extremist message of forced universal assimilation in his booklet *UNESCO: Its Purpose and Its Philosophy*. He wrote that 'the task is to help the emergence of a single world culture with its own philosophy and background of ideas and with its own broad purpose'. This would be achieved by using 'the techniques of persuasion and information and true propaganda that we have learnt to apply nationally in war, and deliberately bend them to the international tasks of peace, if necessary utilising them — as Lenin envisaged — to "overcome the resistance of millions" to desirable change'.[71] Assimilation prevailed at the final meeting of the committee drafting the United Nations Declaration in 1948. After debate stalled — Soviet Russia and Lebanon favouring pluralism on the one hand and the United States and France favouring assimilation on the other — participants finally gave in to the force of the United States argument and agreed to drop the proposed 'article on minorities'. This article asserted the rights of well-defined linguistic, ethnic, or religious groups to establish their own educational, cultural and religious institutions and to use their own languages in the courts.[72]

Australia could thus safely look to assimilation as a compromise of cautious change that would meet international human rights agendas with all their internal contradictions while appeasing national concerns and avoiding a backlash at home. Indeed, in response to a survey in 1952 by the United Nations Economic and Social Council Submission on Discrimination and Minorities, the federal government claimed there were no populations in Australia that fitted the UN definition of a minority group as people who 'possess and wish to preserve stable ethnic, religious or linguistic traditions markedly different from those of the rest of the population, who are of sufficient numbers to develop such characteristics, and who are loyal to the State in which they live'.[73]

Race and racism

A further pressure on Australia was the concerted attack on racism in the United Nations, driven by the terrible lessons of the mass extermination of racial and ethnic minorities in the Nazi Holocaust and the repudiation of biological racism by scientific researchers during the inter-war period.[74]In the 1930s scientists Sir Julian Huxley and A. C. Haddon (who had conducted much of his empirical research in the Torres Strait Islands at the turn of the century) had insisted that 'race as applied to human groups should be dropped from the vocabulary of science'.[75] As Director-General of UNESCO, Huxley was determined to eradicate the very notion of race and with it the social and psychological effects of racism. The central message was that in a democratic and free world all people were equal and all had the right to the same protections and benefits.[76] The implications for governments were clear: advance for racial minorities meant removing the barriers to political, legal, economic and social equality and assimilating them into the nation's dominant cultural heartland. There was a strong assimilatory aspect to this approach, which assumed that 'othered' racial groups freed from the constraints of race would conform to the ways of the dominant group. This new discourse of race positioned Indigenous peoples as racial minorities to be assimilated into the nation.

Race was 'Australia's Achilles heel'.[77] As Indigenous theorist Marcia Langton points out, race was central to the construction of the nation.[78] The designation of Indigenous peoples as racial minorities may have shielded the government from embarrassing questions about sovereignty and colonisation but it put Australia on notice that it was open to accusations of discriminatory treatment of Aboriginal people.[79] Once again assimilation offered a solution by removing the discriminatory policies and laws that attracted international criticism and offering to Aboriginal people a package of equal citizenship rights and equal access to government services. In turn they were required to conform to mainstream Australian values and cultural practices. In the process, issues of sovereignty and colonialism could be swept under the carpet.

UNESCO spearheaded its attack on race on the fronts of education and scientific research, convinced that better understanding of the processes of racism and the harm it brought would help to shift attitudes and behaviours. The UNESCO model influenced government anti-race campaigns around the world over the next two decades. In 1950 UNESCO convened a group of eminent specialists in the fields of psychology, biology, cultural anthropology and ethnology who subsequently issued *The Race Question*, the first of a series of *Statements on Race* (1952, 1964, 1967), which critiqued biological theories of race. It concluded that 'biological differences as exist between members of different ethnic groups have no relevance to problems of social and political organisations, moral life and communication between human beings'.[80] The UN Statement of Race of 1950 described this project as 'one of the most important contributions in the last century to an understanding of race and racialism'.[81] However, already in 1953 a UNESCO paper by Dominican Reverend Father Yves M. J. Congar discussing the position of the Catholic Church on race criticised the focus on science to the detriment of philosophy, theology and history and the political and historical realities of race — all vital elements for the study of race relations.[82] Twenty years later the reviewer of a new edition of UNESCO's *Race and Science* (1973) observed that there was still public confusion between 'race as a biological fact' and 'race as a social phenomenon' and advocated further research into race relations, socioeconomic environments and the symbolic meanings and uses of race.[83]

UNESCO's initiatives introduced a new language of equality to race relations and a drive for change that was groundbreaking at the time. However, what is striking in retrospect, as Marcia Langton points out, is the extraordinary survival power of racialism — a reflection of its central role as a 'pre-eminent organising idea in world affairs'.[84] The 1963 Declaration on the Elimination of All Forms of Racial Discrimination noted that despite some progress, racial discrimination based on race, colour or ethnic origins continued 'none the less to give cause for serious concern'. It expressed alarm that there were governments that continued to impose racial discrimination 'by means of legislative, administrative or other measures, in the form, inter alia, of apartheid, segregation and separation, as well as by the promotion and dissemination of doctrines of racial superiority and expansionism in certain areas'.[85] In its 1967 Statement on Race and Racial Prejudice UNESCO reminded the world that 'racism grossly falsifies the knowledge of human biology' and urged nations to speak out against prejudice and discrimination.[86]

While UNESCO's war of words and ideas failed to dramatically shift resistant community attitudes and behaviours, international political and economic imperatives did have some impact. Racial equality became a new rallying cry for progress and unity for nations like Australia that had previously used racial difference and inequality to unify their citizens against 'outsiders'. The determination to eradicate racism also provided a marker of political legitimacy and allegations of racism could provoke international condemnation of states. (Soviet leaders, as we have already seen, used the race ticket against the United States and its allies, including Australia, as ammunition in its Cold War rivalry and opposition to colonial rule.) International condemnation of South Africa's apartheid system came to a head following the Sharpeville Massacre in 1960 when 300 police officers opened fire on thousands of black demonstrators killing 69 and injuring 186. International repercussions followed rapidly: in 1961 South Africa was forced to withdraw from the British Commonwealth, its apartheid policies were condemned in the United Nations General Assembly in 1962 and in the following year the Security Council established a voluntary arms embargo against South Africa.

The dismantling of race barriers coupled with decolonisation unlocked labour and capital and access to valuable resources, facilitating new economic alliances and development within and across national borders.[87] As networks of empire were eroded they were replaced by new relations of international trade and development between first and third world countries, led by the United States with former colonial powers seeking to maintain their financial interests. For Australia, endeavouring to keep apace with the new opportunities, there was an urgent need to review its race-based policies of immigration. In the short term this involved the relaxing of controls to bring in the European migrants who would provide the muscle power for developing the nation's major industries, capital works and new mining ventures. In the long term the task of cementing economic ties with Australia's near neighbours in Asia meant reviewing and eventually shelving the White Australia policy.

Within Australia assimilation provided a convenient solution for dealing with the new wave of displaced Aboriginal people whose lands and resources were now taken up for mining and resource development and for land schemes for returned servicemen from the early 1950s. The public explanation was that they were being moved to enable them to be trained to become assimilated citizens. The promise of a new mining boom in the mid-1950s prompted the West Australian government to excise 16.2 million hectares from Central Reserve lands for mineral exploration by private companies in addition to lands already taken by the federal government for atomic weapons research and military and weather surveillance. In 1957 West Australian parliamentarian Bill Grayden exposed government plans to remove Ngaanyatjara children from their families at the United Aborigines Mission at Warburton Ranges in the Central Reserves to be educated at Cosmo Newberry 360 miles away and trained to be pastoral workers. He also held public screenings of a devastating film showing injured, diseased and malnourished Aboriginal children and adults at the Warburton Aboriginal Mission.

Meanwhile in Queensland the government leased 348,000 hectares of Aboriginal reserve land to Consolidated Zinc in 1957 to develop what is now the largest bauxite mine in the world. This was the traditional country of eleven landowning groups, most of whom lived at the Presbyterian missions at Weipa and Mapoon that had been operating since the 1880s. They were left with only a couple of hundred hectares to live on. In the early 1960s both communities were forcibly moved to other sites, and those Mapoon residents who refused to leave were trucked out by the government and their homes burned to the ground to prevent their return.[88] The Queensland government's brutal treatment undermined the federal government's efforts to promote an image of humanitarian reform and benign assimilation to the world and epitomised the state's recalcitrant response to these advances generally.

Widespread censure of the West Australian and Queensland governments in the media provided opportunities for Aboriginal activists to reach wider audiences at home and abroad. During his 1958 concert tour the black American singer and activist Paul Robeson saw Bill Grayden's disturbing film footage and his sense of outrage and grief reportedly forged his determination to 'bring attention to the appalling conditions in which the aborigines lived'.[89] The film is also credited with inspiring the establishment of the Aborigines Advancement League in Victoria, which later joined up with the Federal Council for Aboriginal Advancement. From the early 1950s Council leaders targeted United Nations forums calling for human rights for Aboriginal people.[90] Campaigner Jessie Street observed in 1961 after visiting the United Nations General Assembly that 'one of the main criticisms of Australia is based on our discriminatory legislation against our native people. This criticism is increasing as the numbers of our member nations with coloured races increase. It would enhance the reputation of Australia if a beginning was made to eliminate these discriminations. Australia, South Africa and the Southern States of the US seem to be the only countries where the colour bar still operates.'[91]

The new world order

At the end of the war the tide of history began the dramatic shift towards decolonisation for the 750 million people living in eighty colonies around the world. The movement began in triumph and tragedy when Britain granted independence to Pakistan and India in 1947, an event followed by terrible suffering and a massive death rate due to its inept handling of partition. Debate in the United Nations became bogged down when colonial powers insisted on a gradualist approach where power was transferred only after territories were deemed to be 'adequately prepared'. In practice 'preparation' was a piecemeal and uneven process carried out with no great sense of urgency. At the same time the United Nations introduced a trusteeship system that guaranteed eventual self-determination in the colonies and protectorates under its purview,[92] with special reporting mechanisms and periodic tours of inspection to ensure proper treatment of the people and the implementation of steps to self-government. It was not until 1960 that the United Nations General Assembly proclaimed the Declaration on the Granting of Independence to Colonial Countries and Peoples. This reiterated the 'saltwater thesis' — that is, the right to self-determination of peoples living in a territory that was 'geographically separate (typically by sea, hence "saltwater") and distinct ethnically and/or culturally from the country administering it'.[93] The British government responded by rapidly divesting itself of its colonies. However, David Goldsworthy argues that the Australian government did not share this 'commitment to accelerated decolonisation' and remained loyal to the ties of the Empire.[94] Nor did it celebrate the changing relations within the United Nations — seventeen new African nations had been admitted by 1961.[95] This was reflected in Australia's less-than-admirable role in the Suez Crisis in 1956 and its position on apartheid in South Africa.

Indigenous peoples were deliberately excluded from consideration as colonial peoples under the 1960 Declaration. In 1953 in the General Assembly Belgium argued that confining trustee status only to colonies and protectorates was arbitrary and discriminatory and that this should be extended to include Indigenous peoples as well.[96] However, as historian Ravi de Costa points out, settler states like the United States and Australia 'had much to lose' from such a clause and the proposal was successfully blocked.[97] Significantly, the United States argued that Native American populations had been assimilated and were 'an integral part of the nation'. In this way its representatives sought to exclude itself from the second condition laid out in the saltwater thesis, that of ethnic and cultural distinction from the administering country. This provided a further argument for Australia to assimilate its Indigenous populations: once they were fully assimilated they would have no claim to status as colonised people seeking self-determination under the 1960 Declaration.

The consequences of excluding Indigenous peoples from the 1960 declaration become immediately clear when we compare the requirement by the Australian government that Aboriginal people abandon their culture and way of life to assimilate into mainstream Australian society, with the treatment of its trust territory of Papua New Guinea, which was put on a path to independence and its people 'coached through their culture until deemed capable of autonomy'.[98]

For Australia, decolonisation represented one of the major unravelling 'strands in the geopolitical tapestry'[99] of global networks of power and wealth that it now had to negotiate. Australia was on the wrong side in this new world and its race-based policies and old-boy networks of empire now constituted a hindrance rather than a sign of white superiority and solidarity. Discriminatory immigration and Aboriginal policies, together with criticism of its colonial role in relation to the Trust Territory of Papua New Guinea, which was not granted autonomy until 1975, made Australia vulnerable to exclusion from new trade and political networks developing within its geographic region. The break-up of the British Empire and the necessity to negotiate a place in the British Commonwealth of Nations alongside the new African and Asian states were double blows for Australia, but still the Menzies government did not immediately appreciate the extent of change. Leaders clung to the comforting vision of empire and the 'security, stability and preservation of Western influence' they imagined it still bestowed.

By contrast decolonisation presaged 'the replacement of the known and orderly with the unknown, the unreliable, the alien'.[100] Popular media fed off these fears of social chaos in the wake of colonial withdrawal. In 1957 *Pix* magazine reported sensationally on bombings by 'Muslim terrorists' in the war of independence in what was then French Algeria, and depicted independence celebrations in Ghana with the image of semi-naked dancing black men described as having 'known witchcraft'.[101] An image of a woman from the South African black settlement of Sophiatown on the outskirts of Johannesburg protesting low wages was headlined 'Blood flows in African riots'.[102] When Australia refused to condemn South Africa in the forums of the British Commonwealth and the United Nations — on the grounds that the regime's actions were matters of domestic jurisdiction — it seriously underestimated the power of the new African states. This response inevitably directed critical attention to Australia's treatment of Aboriginal people and parallels were drawn by the Soviets and the new states in Africa and Asia with apartheid in South Africa in terms of lack of voting rights, forced segregation, restrictions on personal freedoms, exploitation of labour, inferior facilities and services, and a multitude of informal behaviours and practices.[103]

Accustomed to dominating global networks of power and commerce, Western nations were alarmed by the emerging alliances of decolonising states. The Bandung Conference of twenty-nine non-aligned Asian, African and Middle Eastern nations, including Communist China, was held in Indonesia in 1955. Billed as the 'first intercontinental meeting of colored people in the history of mankind,'[104] the conference brought together people recently liberated or seeking independence from Western colonial and racial domination. Western nations were excluded. The conference coincided with the height of the 1955 Taiwan Strait Crisis when *Newsweek* in the United States was writing of fears of race war between 'the yellow and the white' and warning that 'the gravest crisis in the destiny of the earth's population [was] at hand'.[105] The presence of 'Red China' at the conference fanned paranoia in the United States of escalating communist control in Asia. Belligerent US threats of a nuclear counter-attack should mainland China invade the islands of Matsu and Quemoy in the Taiwan Strait coincided with the dates of the Bandung conference in mid-April.[106] In Australia the Launceston *Examiner* warned that the conference was 'the beginning of an upsurge of racial hatreds against the West' and showed Australians 'where the sympathies of most of their neighbours lie'.[107]

In fact, discussion at the conference was generally peaceful as participants criticised Western threats of nuclear war and pledged themselves to create a peaceful 'community of neutral nations' that would be a more effective instrument of peace than the United Nations. The resulting Bandung Communiqué called for non-aggression and ties of friendly support and economic cooperation between Asian and African powers, renewal of cultures and religions, greater representation in the United Nations and nuclear disarmament. Colonialism and racism were condemned without qualification and the Communiqué demanded the liberation of all people from colonialism and racism.[108]

Indigenous rights

Indigenous peoples were an anomaly in the United Nations' inclusive discourse on human rights. Of course they had all the protections of its Charter, the Universal Declaration of Human Rights and other covenants, which provided a common standard of human rights for all, including traditional, political and civil rights and basic economic, social and cultural rights. Like many minority groups, Indigenous people could track their discriminatory treatment across these various measures; for example, forced removal of children from their families was identified as genocidal in the 1948 Convention on Genocide. However, their special status and rights as Indigenous peoples were not recognised. As a consequence, argues Makere Stewart-Harawira, they were 'invisibilised' in human rights discourse and the cruelties and injustices perpetuated against them were masked.[109] In contrast to colonial peoples they could not look forward to formal recognition of their sovereignty and rights to self-determination. The prevailing assumption was that they would be assimilated as citizens into nation states.[110]

In contrast to the United Nations, the International Labour Organization (ILO) had over two decades of experience in Indigenous rights through its labour programs and association with American Indigenism earlier in the century. In the early 1950s it took on the task of examining ways to facilitate the social integration of the world's Indigenous populations and its recommendations were published in the 1953 report *Indigenous Peoples: living and working conditions of aboriginal populations in independent countries.* Australia's submission was hardly encouraging with its statement that the Aboriginal population in the Northern Territory would require 'for many years to come the benefits and protection of special legislation and who must be regarded as wards of the state standing in need of guardianship and tutelage'.[111] The resulting Convention Concerning the Protection and Integration of Indigenous and other Semi-tribal Populations in Independent Countries, ILO Convention (No. 107) 26 June 1957 was the world's first specific international instrument for Indigenous peoples.

Although this Convention was not dissimilar to Australia's policy of assimilation, the Australian government refused to become a signatory. The Covenant advocated a form of integration of Indigenous people into nation states through the granting of full rights of citizenship to enable them 'to benefit on an equal footing from the rights and opportunities which national laws or regulations grant to other elements of the population'. Interim protective processes were permitted to achieve this goal but prolonged measures and segregation were prohibited and an annual reporting system on progress in implementing the provisions was included. Of concern to the Australian government were provisions allowing for limited recognition of traditional culture, customary law and rights over land and compensation for lands lost, even though these were tempered by other provisions allowing states to resume land for purposes of national security and economic development. And by characterising Indigenous peoples as 'populations', the Convention undermined their claim to unique status and rights.[112]

De Costa describes Convention No. 107 as marking 'the formal beginning of an international law of the human rights of indigenous peoples'.[113] However, Stewart-Harawira condemns it as a mechanism that ultimately promoted assimilation and argues that this was the reason for its replacement in 1989 by the Indigenous and Tribal Peoples Convention (No. 169).[114] This latter Covenant asserts the right to survival of Indigenous and tribal ways of life and the view that these peoples and their traditional organisations should be closely involved in the planning and implementation of development projects that affect them. It contains articles that address consultation and participation, social security and health, human development and the environment. Covenant No. 169 sets out the concept of self-determination, that is, that Indigenous people are to 'decide their own priorities' and retain customary laws and institutions that may be incompatible with fundamental rights defined in national legal systems and international human rights covenants.[115] To date Convention No. 169 has been ratified by only a few countries, and so far by none in the Asian and Pacific Region, including Australia. Indigenous and other commentators have criticised the Convention for not including Indigenous representatives in the drafting process and for allowing states to easily override traditional customs in the name of other laws of the nation.[116]

In 1970 Indigenous representatives meeting as the United Nations Working Group on Indigenous Populations began years of intensive work on a draft International Declaration on the Rights of Indigenous Peoples that was presented to the United Nations Commission on Human Rights in 1994. Article 3 of the Declaration clearly established Indigenous peoples' 'right of self-determination ... to freely determine political status and freely pursue their economic, social and cultural development'. Article 4 addressed their 'right to maintain and strengthen their distinct political, economic, social and cultural characteristics, as well as their legal systems, while retaining their rights to participate fully, if they so choose, in the political, economic, social and cultural life of the State'.[117] The draft Declaration was passed by the newly established United Nations Human Rights Council in 2006 and has been sent on to the General Assembly for adoption.

In September 2007 an amended version of the Declaration that maintained the rights of Indigenous people to land, resources and self-determination was passed in the General Assembly by 143 member states, with the notable support of Latin American and African nations. Australia, the United States, Canada and New Zealand refused to ratify the Declaration. The Global Indigenous Caucus welcomed the general outcome but local Aboriginal organisations described Australia's position as 'disappointing, but not surprising'.[118] In explaining the decision Prime Minister Howard adopted an assimilatory position arguing that the Declaration's support for customary law was an endorsement of 'separate development inside one country' when 'we believe that [the Indigenous] future lies in being part of the mainstream of this country'.[119] By contrast Australia's Human Rights and Equal Opportunity Commissioner Tom Calma pointed to the anomalous situation referred to earlier where, while Indigenous peoples 'are entitled to all human rights recognised in international law without discrimination', it is also the case that 'without recognising the collective rights of Indigenous peoples and ensuring protection of our cultures, Indigenous people can never truly be free and equal'.[120]

Protest at home and abroad

Criticism of Australia's treatment of Aboriginal people continued on at home and abroad into the 1960s. International criticism escalated in tandem with tensions over South Africa and the growing influence of the new states in Africa and Asia in world affairs. There was considerable support for Australian Aboriginal people from the new states, who strongly opposed all forms of European colonialism and oppression as the denial of fundamental human rights and who saw the United Nations as having a fundamental responsibility to emancipate all colonised peoples.[121] Issues of minority rights and race were also highlighted in the build-up to the debates in the General Assembly in 1961 on the draft Covenants on Civil and Political Rights and Economic, Social and Cultural Rights — the principal human rights covenants under the Universal Declaration of Human Rights, ratified in 1966 — and the 1963 United Nations Declaration on the Elimination of All Forms of Racial Discrimination. In 1961, in discussion on the South African crisis, the Ghana mission to the United Nations threatened to raise 'the Aboriginal question' in the General Assembly.[122] At the same time Aboriginal people were invited to visit the newly independent nations. In 1962 Phillip Roberts, Waipuldaanya or Wadjiri-Wadjiri of the Alawa people of the Roper River district (whose life was retold in Douglas Lockwood's *I the Aboriginal*), and Davis Daniels, Secretary of the Northern Territory Council for Aboriginal Rights, were invited to attend independence anniversary celebrations in Kenya and to meet heads of state from

Tanganyika, Uganda, Zanzibar and Ghana.[123]

The press in the new states also reported on discrimination against Aboriginal people and denial of their civil rights, often framing their stories in terms of more infamous racial hot spots in South Africa and the United States. On his return from the Commonwealth Relations Conference in Lagos in 1962, economist Professor W. Prest of Melbourne University warned that many Africans saw Australia as 'another Southern Rhodesia' and that, 'It [was] not generally realised in Australia that every press report of incidents involving Aborigines is reproduced in the African papers.'[124] An article in the Karachi *Morning News* in 1961 claimed that Australia and South Africa were 'both centres of oppressive racial discrimination' and compared the New South Wales town of Coonamble, which had rejected plans to rehouse Aboriginal people in the town, with Little Rock in Arkansas, the scene of a major civil rights confrontation in 1957 over desegregation of schools. The article carried the provocative headline 'The Question Is, Who Owns Australia?' and outlined a proposal by 'a white Australian' Ronald Funnell, President of the Coonamble Aborigines' Welfare Association, to sue the Australian government for 100 million pounds for 'illegal seizure of Australia from the aborigines'.[125]

There was also interest in Aboriginal issues in Europe. These were linked to broader concerns in the Dutch newspaper *Rotterdam Nieuwsblad*, which reported on the visit of Brisbane Aboriginal university student Margaret Valadian to Strasbourg. The newspaper quoted her criticisms of adoption of Aboriginal children, many of them into Dutch families, and her call for support for equal wages for Aboriginal workers and for governments to compensate communities for traditional lands lost to mining. The article went on to criticise the hypocrisy of Australia's continuing racism in its White Australia policy, its handling of Papua New Guinea, its support for internal apartheid in its treatment of Aboriginal people and the imposition of the policy of assimilation. The article concluded that the government could not claim to be promoting equality while at the same time it deprived Aborigines of their land and property rights and that 'such a blunder cannot be made without incurring the odium of apartheid, and that is exactly what the Australian government itself does not want'.[126] Levels of paranoia within government circles in Australia escalated in response to these criticisms, with claims of communist plots and infiltration of Aboriginal organisations. The Department of External Affairs attacked the overseas press for quoting stories with no contextual or broader explanatory material for readers.

Amongst Aboriginal activists and their supporters in Australia there was a growing sense of frustration with the continuing discriminatory treatment of Aboriginal people, ongoing poverty, denial of political and legal rights and the erosion of Aboriginal culture under the auspices of assimilation. From the 1960s Aboriginal leaders began to attract unprecedented attention on the national and international stage with increasingly vocal protests, their demands moving away from the language of civil rights and increasingly framed within the paradigms of self-determination and Indigenous rights. Faced by this mounting criticism, the government was forced to bite the bullet and a period of concerted legislative reform began in the late 1950s to extend equal citizenship to Aboriginal people, with the federal government showing the lead with its major amendments to the Social Security Act in 1959 and the franchise in 1962 and the states following with their own agendas of reform.

Assimilation, however, continued to come under attack. In 1962 prominent Australian bureaucrat and academic Charles Rowley, Principal of the Australian School of Pacific Administration, published an article in the anthropological journal *Oceania* claiming that assimilation policy was potentially destructive and definitely outdated, having been officially abandoned in the United States in 1934. He also attacked the continuing state of racial exclusion and discrimination in Australia and decried the fact that 'no Aboriginal right of possession to any of the continent … was recognised'.[127] In 1965 Radio Australia broadcast a personal critique of assimilation by a visiting Sierra Leone engineering student, Abdul Iscandari. He warned that assimilation was a 'form of sociological and psychological cruelty' that forced people to give up what is theirs and accept 'all that is foreign to them' and that when the process inevitably broke down Aboriginal people were blamed. Speaking from his own experience growing up in a former British colony he recalled how he was taught to be 'an African with a European mind' and how he considered himself civilised and looked down on his own people only to have a rude shock when he found that 'civilised people' did not accept him.[128]

Rowley's article prompted one officer in the Department of External Affairs to express to his colleagues his 'discomfort in trying to act as an apologist for some aspects of current official policies in the field … If the Americans and the Russians were to attack our assimilation policy we would fare rather badly in the UN.'[129] Alarm was also registering elsewhere within the federal bureaucracy. John Chesterman observes that the confidential letter forwarded by the Department of External Affairs to its overseas posts in 1962 warning of Australia's possible loss of 'prestige' because of its treatment of Aboriginal people 'stands as an illuminating barometer of the bureaucratic feeling as to how Australia's reputation was threatened by the existence of racially discriminatory laws'.[130] In 1962 official Hugh Gilchrist warned senior staff that it would be difficult to mount a defence against accusations of indifference to rights of minorities 'when the big overseas attack is launched, as I think will happen in a year or so', and expressed concern at the 'growing number of petitions (mostly communist inspired) by aborigines and aboriginal organisations to the UN later this year'.[131]

While diplomats and politicians watched anxiously over

Australia's international reputation the federal government at home was embarking on the challenging task of persuading settler Australians to accept the new vision of an assimilated nation. Citizens' fears and anxieties aroused during the war and maintained by the dramatic changes in peacetime proved a fertile ground for the government as it juggled the competing demands of meeting overseas human rights standards, avoiding ruffling voters with unpalatable change, and attracting and settling a huge new intake of European immigrants while managing the increasingly unpredictable course of Aboriginal affairs. These certainly were anxious times for the nation.

2. New White Australia

National identity everywhere … is a site of conflicted meanings, and only our nostalgia for a fictive past leads us to imagine an end to the conflict. What brings tears to the eyes of some generations will be a joke to later ones; a symbol which rouses one ethnic group to fury will give pride and comfort to another nation.

Michael Ignatieff[1]

There is no question of saying to people of another race, 'We are superior to you.' The only thing we say is, 'we are a basically different race, and, therefore, for certain reasons we apply this policy.' The real test is assimilability. Let us be quite plain about the matter.

Prime Minister Robert Menzies, 1948[2]

We watch the news and read the paper. We're not stupid people, we're educated. We know what it means to be non-Australians. If that boat comes back, we'll welcome them and give them food and water. You know why? Because we're all one group — non-Australians.

Tiwi elder speaking of asylum seekers
who arrived by boat on Melville Island in 2003.[3]

The task of promoting a new vision of the nation was the perfect challenge for a government in the 1950s when shaping mass opinion was the new dream industry. Australia's first international mega-event, the 1956 Melbourne Olympic Games, provided the opportunity to present the nation to the world. But what look should the Games promote? Old images of the bush, the billabong and the lone stockman no longer prevailed and consensus on the new Australia hovered between Anglo-Celtic tradition, international modernism and American style. Disagreement over the nation's image was just one of several flare-ups in the course of the 'Friendly Games.' Melbourne almost lost the event when union go-slow tactics and a stoush over federal and state funding responsibilities seriously delayed work on the construction of the Olympic Stadium and Village. Seven nations boycotted the Games over international crises in the Middle East, Asia and Eastern Europe.[4] All this discord inspired Australian teenager John Ian Wing's dream of an Olympic Games where 'war, politics and nationalities will be forgotten' and his idea for a new closing ceremony that has become part of Olympic tradition where, instead of marching as national teams, athletes mingle together and wave to the crowds as a symbol of world peace and unity.[5] Like *The Family of Man*, this international performance laid an optimistic finish over a troubled world.

The image finally chosen for the Games was the 'determinedly Anglocentric' nation celebrated two years earlier during the first visit to Australia of the newly crowned Queen Elizabeth.[6] Grand public ceremonies celebrated Australia's links to Britain and the Empire, as in the painting of an imagined Royal welcome in the Herald and Sun News-Pictorial's *Royal Tour to Australia and New Zealand in Pictures* (1954). This showed a crowd of white male officials and soldiers, a schoolgirl, a merino ram, and an Aboriginal man holding boomerangs and a shield, all towered over by the royal monarch as she graciously surveyed what was hers.[7] The opening Games ceremony, intended to be an 'international, ecumenical occasion', was similarly a 'tribute to God, Queen and Country' with the Duke of Edinburgh officiating and the *Halleluiah Chorus* and *God Save the Queen* performed at the beginning and conclusion of formalities.[8] In stark contrast to the extravagant Indigenous and multicultural performances that marked the opening of the Sydney Olympics in 2000 there was little evidence of Australia's non-British heritage. Organisers anxious to impress sophisticated international visitors with a modern Australia had to make do with Melbourne's new cosmopolitan cafes (established by European migrants) and a city skyline suggesting prosperous modernity. This was international modernism in an Australian idiom that prefigured today's 'urban, elite Australianness defined as cosmopolitan — good coffee, fusion cuisine, urbane and trendy or "cool"'.[9]

The federal government presented its vision of an assimilated White Australia in the official souvenir book, *Australia — Your Host: XVIth Olympiad*, which reflected the emerging discourse of a nation where old and new settlers and Aboriginal people could live together as equal citizens. The book began with an introduction to the city of Melbourne, then tracked the progress of the Olympic flame from Darwin down the east coast to the opening of the Games and around to the north coast of Western Australia. The emphasis was on White Australia but there was a brief nod to post-war migrants in a reference to the new continental cuisine in Melbourne's hotels and suburban homes. There were no photographs of traditional Aboriginal life — which certainly would have been found in the country covered — only shots of assimilated Aboriginal people: an immaculately clean young man polishing a Darwin fire engine, an Aboriginal stockman, a smiling farm worker holding out a pineapple and, in the book's final image, an Aboriginal woman and four children with two white men, one a policeman, listening to a radio perched on the bonnet of a Land Rover outside the Birdsville Hotel. No doubt they were tuned in to Olympic events even in this impossibly remote place.[10]

With an eye to impressing overseas audiences, the federal government began during the 1950s to flood the public domain with images of old and new settlers and Aboriginal people living amicably together in a modern new Australia united around a shared common culture and a new commitment to equal citizenship and living standards for all. This vision represented an enormous shift from a White Australia forged from Federation by racial exclusion and discriminatory treatment of non-British migrants and Aboriginal people. To achieve it required a corresponding shift from race to culture as the dominant unifying ideology, and a move from race-based laws and controls to cultural assimilation as the dominant process for managing diversity and change and protecting existing hierarchies and networks of power and privilege. New tools and symbols of persuasion were available to the government to promote its new imagined Australia, and, as we shall see here and in subsequent chapters, the federal government directed its energies more to advancing its unrealistic vision of an assimilated nation than to providing practical instruments to achieve its promises of equality and citizenship and a better life for all.

Forging a white nation (1901–1950)

Australia is a settler nation forged by more than two centuries of immigration into Indigenous lands. Like other settler societies our history is characterised by seemingly irreconcilable conflicts over sovereignty, land and nationhood between Indigenous peoples and old and new immigrant populations. From the Federation of Australia in 1901 through to the early 1950s the dominant unifying vision of a White Australia drew a heavy veil over these differences.[11] The building blocks were racial purity and cultural uniformity buttressed by the racialist theories of Social Darwinism, national anxieties about possible invasion by Asian countries to the north, and pragmatic fears that competition from labourers from China and the Pacific Islands would lower wages and working conditions. There was also the insistence that those permitted entry had to be capable of assimilating into the culture of the nation. Australia had a legacy of assimilation dating back to early colonial times, from reforming convicts into respectable members of the working class to the policies to assimilate Aboriginal people and immigrants in the 1950s. This in turn was related to 'pre-existing philosophies, policies and institutional practices concerning unacceptable, "problem" populations in all the Western European countries and their colonies'.[12]

Of course Australia was never culturally uniform. Aboriginal Australia alone had 250 distinct languages and during the colonial period settler colonists arrived from all parts of the globe. However in the fifty years from Federation settler Australians sought to build a nation what was uniquely homogeneous in terms of race and culture. The pillars of British racial origins and cultural heritage and settler adaptations to the new world shaped this White Australia. The target group for building the nation was British migrants and over the years this created a nation with an Anglo-Celtic core culture and a social hierarchy dominated by Anglo Australians. The *1901 Immigration Restriction Act* set the limits of Australia's migrant intake by establishing the precedent of refusing entry to non-whites — usually Africans, Asians and Pacific Islanders. This was not explicitly stated in the legislation but was achieved by administering the infamous dictation test that required applicants to correctly write out a passage of fifty words dictated to them in any chosen language — a ruse intended to give wider scope for rejecting migrants, as it could simply be one that the applicant did not know. Other legislation allowed the government to deport members of these groups and other undesirables already resident in Australia. The few who escaped deportation survived on the margins of society. Levels of non-British European migration were also regulated through policy directives formulated on the basis of race.

When it came to Aboriginal people, their exclusion from White Australia was achieved through a rigid framework of discriminatory federal and state laws.

As Andrew Markus has observed, White Australia was much more than the infamous *1901 Immigration Act* used to exclude 'unsuitable' immigrants. It was a 'constituent element of the Australian Federation' and was concerned with 'racial purity in the widest sense'.[13] Anthropologist Ghassan Hage defines White Australia as a discourse based on belief in the superiority of British civilisation forged from the attributes of British racial stock and upheld by the British race. All other races and cultures were believed to be inherently inferior and their presence represented a threat to the nation's racial and cultural purity and its civilised standard of living. Indeed, the rising living conditions from Federation were seen as visible proof of the 'racial causal logic that link[ed] White Australian racial identity and high civilised standards of living'.[14]

Australia was a nation made white by the 'crimson thread'[15] of British blood ties that were maintained through immigration policies targeting settlers from 'Home'. This was a nation where whiteness bestowed citizenship, status, power and privilege. Adapted from British models, the nation's core cultural, political and economic institutions and the networks of power and privilege that grew up around them worked to advantage settlers who met the ideal racial and cultural profile. The nation's official history that began with British discovery and settlement stamped white ownership and supremacy across the continent. Settlers of British origin were the principal actors in this historical narrative. The pivotal role of British race and culture in shaping national identity was highlighted by the federal Minister for Immigration Arthur Calwell when he proclaimed in his speech to parliament announcing the *1948 Nationality and Citizenship Act* that 'to say one is an Australian is, of course, to indicate beyond all doubt that one is British'.[16]

White Australia and immigration

As a migrant nation Australia was kept white by privileging the selection and resettlement of British migrants through relaxed entry conditions, assisted passage schemes, generous land grants and special rights as British subjects. These privileges highlight just how crucial 'Britishness' was to immigration practices in Australia.

British migrants were the single largest national group arriving annually from 1788 to 1996 and in most years prior to the 1960s made up at least half the yearly intake.[17] By contrast, under the White Australia policy, prohibitions and restrictions were imposed to limit the intake of non-British migrants. These controls over migrant intake had the desired effect of making Australia demographically whiter in the decades following Federation. Between 1901 and 1947 Anglo-Celtic dominance increased from 87 to 90 per cent while Europeans remained steady at 7 per cent and the total of 5.4 per cent for Asian and Aboriginal populations (1.9 per cent and 3.4 per cent respectively) fell to 1.1 per cent.[18] Still, this was a small return for the government's huge investment in controlling immigration.

Historian David Dutton describes a 'complicated picture' of assessment of European migrants according to their country of origin. European nations were ranked into hierarchies based on 'racial origins, capacity, and desirability and a disorderly mass of characterisations and stereotypes' that determined whether their citizens would be judged to be suitable migrants and future citizens of Australia.[19] Hierarchies shifted in response to broader social trends so that strong public support for European migration before the First World War declined with war-time national hatreds and the racialisation of European enemy nationals into the 1940s. This was evident in the treatment of German migrants who were welcomed as settlers in the nineteenth century but were then subjected to intense racial hatred and discriminatory treatment during the world wars, including internment and deportation. This continued between the wars in heightened pressures to assimilate and restrictions on German migration that only began to be lifted from 1950. Italian migration was similarly dogged by Australia's immigration policies so that only small numbers were taken in before the Second World War and they too found themselves painted as the enemy with the outbreak of war. Many Australians did not count them as 'white' and they were not initially envisaged as part of the post-war migrant intake.[20]

Differential treatment of non-British migrants continued with settlement in Australia. While most British migrants settled into a familiar version of 'Home', migrants from Europe encountered an alien culture that they were expected to adopt in a one-way, linear process of assimilation mapped out for the public imagination by the American sociologist Robert Ezra Park during the 1920s.[21] Governments did little to assist them in this difficult process. Conditions of assisted passage in post-war immigration programs also enabled the government to direct European, but not British, migrants to work as directed for a period of two years.

There were major disparities in rights to citizenship. Prior to the introduction of the status of Australian citizen in the *1948 Nationality and Citizenship Act*, persons born in Australia and new British migrants were all classed as British subjects with the same rights. European migrants could apply to become naturalised British subjects under the *1903 Naturalisation Act,* which excluded Asians, Africans and Pacific Islanders. From 1948 British immigrants could apply to become naturalised citizens after only twelve months residency and they retained their status as British subjects. They also had the vote and from 1958 had full access to all social security benefits. There was little pressure on them to take up Australian citizenship. When asked in that year what benefits British migrants would gain by becoming Australian citizens, the Minister for Immigration Alexander Downer replied that there were none.[22] There was little expectation that they would take part in any "citizenship bargain"— their compliance was assured'.

Labor spokesperson Leslie Haylen told Parliament in 1956, 'I know that it is the aim of the Australian people generally to preserve their national character ... There are no great problems here for British immigrants ... For them assimilation into the Australian way of life is like walking from one room to another. They give us no enduring problems for settling into this country, because they are some of us and because they are the most desirable of immigrants.'[23] By contrast, European migrants were expected to take up citizenship. They were required to register on arrival as 'aliens' under the *1947 Aliens Act* and to remain under government surveillance with the threat that they could be interned, deported or refused citizenship.[24] To qualify for citizenship they had to be resident in Australia for five years and were required to demonstrate competency in English and renounce their national allegiances — requirements added during the anti-German hostilities of the First World War.[25] Prior to 1973 they were designated as 'naturalised citizens' and distinguished from persons born in Australia and British migrants who were classed as 'citizens'.

White Australia and Indigenous people

As a settler society Australia was built on repeated waves of migrant settlement and the ongoing dispossession and removal of Indigenous peoples from their traditional lands. This set Indigenous people on a very different trajectory to either old or new settlers within White Australia. Historian Patrick Wolfe argues that integral to the process of 'settler-colonial invasion' was the 'elimination of the natives' from the new settler landscape, either through 'outright homicide ... [or] more ostensibly benign policies such as assimilation, removal or reservation, which continue long after the frontier'.[26] As Wolfe suggests, assimilation has been a recurring process in the destiny of Indigenous people in all settler colonies. Native American historian Donald Fixico classifies as 'cultural transformations characterised by the word "assimilation"' all the various measures introduced in the United States directed at taking over Indian land and relocating the people to reservations, residential schools or urban areas. He concludes that the government's recurring solution to the 'Indian problem' was to bring the people into mainstream American life, economy, and culture.[27] This mirrors the goals of Indigenous policy in Australia. Following on from the original frontier wars into the present, Aboriginal policies, whether called protection, biological absorption, assimilation, integration or practical reconciliation, all embraced the assimilation of Aboriginal people. The practical intention was to manage Aboriginal populations to meet white interests in land and labour and to remove their perceived threat to white sovereignty and nationhood.

By the time of Federation the Aboriginal population had been reduced from an original estimated population of between five hundred thousand and one million people to between fifty and ninety thousand survivors. The 'doomed race' discourse of Aboriginal extinction seemed set to become a reality. Aboriginal people had no place in imaginings of the new nation and settler claims to sovereignty and possession of the land appeared to be assured. In the meantime, to ensure the invisibility of surviving populations, governments invested significant time and energy in developing discriminatory policies and laws — a trend that intensified from the 1930s with evidence of Aboriginal population survival. In 1938 Aboriginal activists protesting 150 years of white occupation alleged in their Manifesto of the Day of Mourning that the government's ultimate intention was 'to exterminate the Aborigines so completely that not a trace of them or their descendants remains'.[28]

Each state, and the federal government from 1911, had its own separate administration for governing Aboriginal populations and in his comprehensive digest of Aboriginal legislation, published in

1987, John McCorquodale identified 700 separate Aboriginal statutes, most passed after Federation.[29] Historians John Chesterman and Brian Galligan[30] observe that the absence in the Australian Constitution of any defining core features of Australian citizenship made possible this indiscriminate process of law-making and the anomalous situation where Aboriginal people were legally British subjects and then Australian citizens but had none of the rights and benefits associated with the status. They argue that this formulation of citizenship was the product of the deep stain of racism that shaped federation and that it was followed 'precisely to allow the States to perpetuate their various discriminatory regimes of governing Aboriginal people and to enable the new Commonwealth parliament to implement a national regime of discrimination'.[31]

Ann-Mari Jordens states that Aboriginal people and migrant aliens were 'both excluded from the imagined community of Australian citizens'[32] and Alistair Davidson asserts that the lack of rights of Indigenous people and the steps migrant aliens had to make to attain citizenship were 'not greatly different'.[33] In making this claim however, Davidson fails to acknowledge the extraordinary sweep of Aboriginal legislation and its intrusive and disabling impact on Aboriginal communities, which went far beyond the disadvantages experienced by European migrants and set in train generations of 'consequential poverty'[34] and hardship that severely reduced quality of life for Aboriginal families across the nation. At the time many Australians regarded Aborigines' straitened circumstances as proof that the presence of non-white races threatened the nation's high standards of living.

Colonial Australia had adopted an ad hoc process of Christianising and civilising Aboriginal survivors of invasion and dispossession in sites scattered across the landscape — missions and institutions, the work place and colonists' homes. Others were dispersed into the community to fend for themselves. Either way the hope was to create menial labourers and domestic servants, although without the meagre rights of other workers. Children were often the target as governments and employers endeavoured to create lineages of reliable hardworking servants. Following the distinction made by Native American historian Philip Deloria, this process can be described as assimilation for 'similarity' rather than 'sameness'. That is, the quest to perfect 'conquered people into similarity — ghost forms of the white conqueror, coexistent but not equal', rather than the later goals of 1950s assimilation policy that sought to achieve social and political equality for Aboriginal people.[35]

A central strategy for governing Aboriginal populations prior to the 1950s was the seemingly contradictory model of dispersal and centralisation or the 'reserve/dispersal mechanism,' first identified by historian Peter Read[36] in his history of government practice in New South Wales. Expanding on Read's original analysis, these forces can be seen as a recurring model in the agenda of assimilation. For Aboriginal people centralised in missions and institutions the pressures of assimilation were all-encompassing. They were trained to become menial workers accustomed to conventional work routines and a sedentary way of life, to adopt Christian beliefs and values, and to emulate settler models of family life. Missionaries, government officers and employers all looked to the assimilation of Aboriginal children in this way to establish future generations of hardworking servants. Paradoxically, rather than being taught to live as independent workers, these people were being trained to live as inmates of institutions.

Assimilation of Aboriginal families dispersed into the wider community was more piecemeal. They were refused government services and kept segregated from white settlers, yet they inevitably had to find work with them to survive. They became assimilated into the local rural or pastoral economy but could maintain some aspects of traditional life, as in the example of Aboriginal workers in the pastoral industry. Some of the families had been forced off communal settlements by governments seeking to reclaim land for white farmers or to pursue policies of assimilation of Aboriginal children. In Victoria in 1886 the government drove a wedge through the colony's surviving Aboriginal population of less than a thousand people who were living as settled communities in centralised institutions. In that year adults of mixed descent were forced out to fend for themselves in a white world, most of them without their children who were kept back to be trained as workers along with the few surviving 'full-blood' people who were expected to gradually pass away in accordance with the doomed race theory of the time.

From the early 1900s the model of centralisation and dispersal was developed into a strict assimilatory regime enforced by the expanding range of new laws and administrations. Queensland favoured mass segregation in permanent settlements, where children lived separately in dormitories to be trained as workers while their parents were sent out under departmental supervision to work for below award wages. The bulk of their earnings was kept from them and never returned, laying the foundation for today's Stolen Wages campaign. New South Wales moved uneasily between dispersal and centralisation, caught between employers' needs for Aboriginal labour and other residents' demands to expel families from their districts. Multipurpose settlements established in Western Australia were described by officials as 'clearing houses' where young people would learn to live as working families while the older generations gradually passed away. It was calculated that after three generations the settlements would no longer be needed.[37]

During these decades the life trajectory for many Aboriginal people was one that began with forced removal from home and family to the drudgery of institutional life and then out to work until finally, after years of back-breaking labour, they finished up with no family, no savings and nowhere to go. Those who escaped this government intervention in their lives were left to survive in neglectful conditions of abject poverty without access to mainstream government services and relying on casual jobs to survive.

The draconian framework of Aboriginal laws was also a force for assimilating Aboriginal people, along with the mainstream legal system that taught and encouraged conformity to conventional Australian values and behaviours and discouraged Aboriginal cultural practices.[38] Like English philosopher Jeremy Bentham's Panopticon, designed to enclose prisoners in an unseen web of surveillance and control, these laws created an invisible disciplinary grid around people defined as Aboriginal by law.[39] In practical terms this legislation enforced economic, social and spatial segregation, neglectful treatment through denial of access to government services, discrimination in employment and ownership of land and property, destruction of families through forced separation and removal, punitive incarceration in Aboriginal institutions, unprecedented control by police and other state officers, and discriminatory punishments to enforce compliance with these provisions.[40] Legal classifications based on blood quantum, lifestyle and association with Aboriginal people divided Aboriginal communities internally into named racial castes, cut them off from the wider community and forced those considered white enough out into an often hostile white world — a further instance of dispersal in action. This system was often implemented capriciously on the basis of superficial physical markers such as skin colour and backed up by threats of punitive sanctions.[41]

These laws were inherently contradictory. They were segregatory *and* assimilatory: intended to keep the races apart and to force Aboriginal people to conform to standards of public and private behaviour acceptable to white citizens, with harsh punishments for failure to conform. They trapped Aboriginal people in webs of dependency on mission and institutional authorities and employers, undermined individual responsibility and initiative, and blocked their entry to mainstream society. It seemed that Aboriginal people required never-ending training and supervision to guide them towards the unattainable goal of assimilation.

The reward for conforming to these laws was to escape their reach. In a similar process to migrant aliens seeking citizenship, Aboriginal people could apply for exemption from the legislation. They had to demonstrate that they led an assimilated lifestyle and, if successful, were obliged to abandon their Aboriginal identity and cut their ties with Aboriginal communities. Like migrant aliens they had to calculate the benefits of this new status against the sacrifices it entailed. However the similarity ends here since Aboriginal people remained subject to other legal restrictions (for example exclusion from federal social security benefits) and exemptions could be revoked at any time. These arrangements had more in common with the situation of *indigenes* in the French colonies who from 1848 could apply for *naturalisation* to escape the harsh regulations known as the *code de l'indigenat,* which allowed police and administrators to summarily punish them for a host of petty offences with fines, corporal punishment, imprisonment, forced labour or by confiscating property. Successful applicants had to renounce their local customary status, which often meant loss of traditional rights and isolation from traditional communities, a trade-off that few were prepared to make.[42]

The injustice of forcing Aboriginal people to apply for citizenship escaped the authorities. Prior to the 1940s exemption was rarely applied for or granted: the hurdles were kept too high and most officials objected that it was only a ticket to alcohol. Efforts to provide a more equitable form of citizenship for Aboriginal servicemen during the war, as in the West Australian *1944 Natives (Citizenship Rights) Act*, maintained the right to revoke the 'privilege' at any time and imposed restrictions on contact with Aboriginal people. Little wonder that few Aboriginal people applied for exemptions or certificates, sometimes referred to as 'dog tags'.[43]

Versions of Assimilation

Two versions of assimilation emerged in the 1930s, each responding in different ways to new scientific research findings about race and to demographic evidence that refuted the claim that Aboriginal people were a race doomed to extinction. Each sought a solution to growing official concern over the future for an increasing Aboriginal population in an intractably racist society.

From the perspective of biological assimilation, race was an indelible stain that could only be erased through the application of race engineering to gradually 'evolve' Aboriginal people into 'white men'.[44] This theory was driven by new scientific research claiming common origins for the Aboriginal and Caucasian races and explaining race mixing in terms of Mendelian theories of genetic inheritance. The promise was that Aboriginal physical features could be 'bred out' in an ultimate solution to the race problem. In practical terms this meant state control over Aboriginal reproduction through arranged marriages of lighter castes and support for interracial marriages with white Australians, previously prohibited by law. This approach to assimilation was discussed in the press in Western Australia during the early 1930s and was outlined in detail in *Australia's Coloured Minority* by A. O. Neville, Chief Protector of Aborigines in Western Australia (1915–1940). For Neville the goal was the eradication of 'colour' and the assurance of 'a mono-cultural dream of "whiteness"'. However, like the writers of campaign pamphlets in the 1950s, his endeavours to soothe white anxieties over racial difference were overwhelmed by his 'narrative organised around "raced" classification' that relentlessly reproduced Aboriginality as irreducible difference and reinforced the anxiety that Australia could never be white.[45] Nevertheless his eugenic solution was adopted as policy in Western Australia and the Northern Territory in the 1930s and, controversially, as national policy in 1937 but, not unsurprisingly, it fell out of favour across the nation after the war. Still, anthropologist Diane Barwick found that Aboriginal people in Melbourne in the 1960s spoke of government programs of 'breeding out' and 'solving the Aboriginal problem by marrying the dark and white'. She concluded from her archival research that governments also assumed implicitly that the 'eventual assimilation of the Aborigines will come about through marriage with whites'.[46]

Professor A. P. Elkin of the Anthropology Department at the University of Sydney was the driving force behind the policy of social assimilation. Elkin's model, outlined in 1932 in the pamphlet *A Positive Policy for the Aborigines* and in 1945 in the book *Citizenship for the Aborigines; a National Policy,* was a response to scientific research that rejected the rigid divisions and hierarchies of biological race theory in favour of a return to the Enlightenment vision of a universal humanity. Social assimilation rescued Aboriginal people from the stamp of race theories that branded them as inherently inferior and condemned them to eventual extinction. Rather than race, it was the legacies of culture and history that had to be overcome, and their hope for the future lay in Elkin's model of social assimilation, which promised full citizenship, better living conditions and an equal place in Australian society. Social assimilation's promises of full citizenship marked a significant shift from earlier ad hoc practices of training for assimilation. Although Elkin claimed the policy as his own, it had much in common with proposals made by representatives of women's organisations from the 1930s as well as sociological theories of assimilation developed in the United States from the 1920s.

Elkin's stages of change outlined in his influential paper 'Reaction and interaction: a food gathering people and European settlement in Australia'[47] can be read as a roadmap for assimilation. The significant point on the map is a fork in the road at the stage of 'intelligent parasitism' that offers two new directions, redolent of the choice between good and evil offered in Bible-thumping sermons of the past. On one side is the void of pauperism and cultural loss with 'all its attendant evils', on the other is a broad road grounded in Aboriginal culture and community that leads to Aborigines' 'intelligent appreciation' of western ways and whites' acceptance of their right to become responsible citizens, which prefigures the final stage of full assimilation. Elkin's void was inhabited by the 'detribalised' people of southern Australia; the chosen ones on the road forward were the 'authentic' Aborigines in remote central and northern Australia. As Russell McGregor points out,[48] this was 'an inversion of popular wisdom' which held that those with the longest contact were free from the impediments of tradition and the most likely to advance to assimilation. However Elkin had been impressed by the positive way in which Aboriginal people with a strong cultural and community life in northern Australia had adapted to change during the war. He considered that in these conditions there was the potential for the blending of Aboriginal traditions with the 'new' in a process that 'safeguard[ed] for them their ties to the past, to the land, to one another, and to the "eternal dream-time"' and laid 'the foundations for future development'.[49]

By contrast Elkin believed that Aboriginal communities in the south were hindered by a 'false sense of social solidarity based on economic dependence on government and societal rejection' tainted with 'resentment and alienation'. He was horrified at the prospect of ghettoes of Aboriginal families dependent on the welfare of the state. The findings at the time of fieldwork in southern rural and urban areas of Aboriginal community solidarity and rigid race barriers between black and white only confirmed his conviction that families should be driven out into the community once they were self reliant to prevent the growth of large communities dependent on the welfare of the state.[50]

Elkin's views had clout. In addition to his status as Australia's leading anthropologist and a dignitary in the Anglican church, he was a respected adviser to government and renowned expert on

Aboriginal issues. Governments around the nation followed his advice in moving towards a policy of assimilation and the gradual extension of citizenship rights to Aboriginal people. The initiative was shown in the 1939 federal New Deal for Aborigines in the Northern Territory and the *1940 Aborigines Protection Act (Amendment) Act* in New South Wales, with other states following suit. However, when the federal Minister for Territories (Sir) Paul Hasluck took over the reins of Aboriginal policy-making in the 1950s, Elkin found to his chagrin that he was increasingly marginalised from the action. It was Hasluck, not Elkin, who framed the iconic federal definition of assimilation announced in 1961 that 'all aborigines and part aborigines are expected to eventually attain the same manner of living as other Australians and to live as members of a single Australian community enjoying the same rights and privileges, accepting the same responsibilities, observing the same customs and influenced by the same beliefs, hopes and loyalties as other Australians'.[51] Reflecting on his career in an article published in *Quadrant* magazine in 1957 Elkin celebrated his many earlier achievements working with federal and state governments, including his contributions as the longest serving member of the Aborigines Welfare Board in New South Wales; however he made no mention of his few collaborations with Hasluck.[52]

Like the vision of an assimilated Australia, Elkin's model of Aboriginal assimilation held out the promise of a rosy future for Aboriginal people that would maintain the nation's reputation overseas and please the new humanitarianism in Australia. For governments it suggested a convenient way to achieve egalitarianism. Aboriginal families would be relocated to the suburbs and their lands resumed for economic interests and they would eventually disappear into the suburban landscape. Another advantage was that, according to international convention of the time, Indigenous peoples who became assimilated waived their claim to special rights. This solved issues of sovereignty and land ownership and also left governments free to leave Aboriginal affairs behind and to focus their energies on building a new and prosperous White Australia.

Keeping Australia white

We have seen how the race-based model of White Australia became increasingly untenable from the late 1940s. At home the government's mass migration program loomed as a threat to British racial and cultural hegemony and there were new sensitivities about Aboriginal civil rights and the repercussions surrounding Australia's policies on relations with the 'Near North' and the nation's standing generally in world affairs.[53] The problem facing the government was how to respond positively to these developments without directly challenging entrenched racism and thereby prompting a public backlash. What strategies could be devised to manage diversity and still maintain a White Australia?[54]

Dreaming up a new White Australia

The solution was to contain change within the parameters of a *modified* White Australia that would be unified by cultural homogeneity rather than racial exclusivity and that included equal citizenship within the generalised model of the dominant Anglo-Celtic settler culture.[55] The message for settler Australians was that change would not disrupt the status quo but only improve their quality of life and that their fears that 'foreigners' would settle as distinct cultural groups and 'compete with Australian-born labour, or threaten standards of living', were unfounded.[56]

Through the process of assimilation the new cultural diversity brought by mass European immigration would be absorbed into the nation's uniform cultural landscape. Gwenda Tavan writes that White Australia and assimilation were both 'doctrines reinforcing the conception of a core, white British race and culture that had to be protected'.[57] Assimilation of Aboriginal people would proceed through the dismantling of inequalities in citizenship rights, improved living conditions and by refashioning them, along with migrants and the working classes, into middle-class suburban families. By making Aboriginal people invisible in this way, assimilation also shielded the nation from criticism over issues of Aboriginal sovereignty and rights. Assimilation could even be invoked to rationalise Australia's continued opposition to Asian immigration. In his introduction to the published papers of the 19th Summer School of the Australian Institute of Political Science held in Canberra in 1953 the Minister for Immigration Harold Holt argued that given the 'important differences of tradition and culture which would make assimilation of Asian settlers so much more difficult', Australia could afford to overlook the 'weighty impact of events and opinions from other parts of the world'. However, he added that 'the same arguments cannot be advanced with equal force to justify restrictions on settlement by Europeans ... There can be little doubt that the force of world opinion would compel us to open our doors to as many new settlers as our economic circumstances would reasonably enable us to accommodate.'[58]

The vision of a White Australia cut across old and new values and truths. Despite official claims, immigration policies continued to endorse exclusion on the basis of race — at a formal level in the case of Asian immigration and in departmental practice for Europeans. In 1956 the unofficial rule for migrant selection was summarised as '75 per cent or more of European descent, fully European in upbringing, mode of dress and way of living'.[59] An immigration officer explained that 'a person who, whether by cast of features or by colour of his skin or by mode of living, is not readily assimilable here, should not be admitted for permanent residence'.[60] Of course the nation had never been uniform, culturally or racially. Nor was forced cultural assimilation an unfamiliar process. What *was* new was the extraordinary range of diversity in terms of cultures, histories and life experiences now coming together within the nation and the Herculean challenge of assimilating all of this into a core shared culture. In the midst of these changes government assurances that European migrants and Aboriginal people would rapidly merge into the social landscape and that this could be achieved without changing Australia's cultural practices, values or institutions, looked distinctly improbable.

The new vision of an assimilated White Australia was truly a 'white nation fantasy'.[61] Jean Martin describes the government's message that migrant cultural diversity would be assimilated into an unchanging core culture as the 'assimilability thesis' — an ideological position created and maintained to 'legitimate a policy that the state had to sell to the community'.[62] For Emma Greenwood the 'central fallacy' of assimilationist ideology was 'that migration was not mutually transformative and that Australian culture could remain statically Anglocentric and homogeneous'.[63] The truth was that *everyone* had to change. The pressure to assimilate was greatest for migrants and Aboriginal people, but successful assimilation also depended on more enlightened attitudes and behaviours in the wider Australian community. The entry of 1.3 million immigrants between 1947 and 1961, almost two-thirds from Europe, and the government's move to break down Aboriginal segregation inevitably altered the nation's demographic, social and cultural landscapes. At best assimilation became what Gwenda Tavan calls a 'transitional doctrine' that 'allowed (settler) Australians to make sense of, contain and ultimately accept social and cultural change, by gradually, if equivocally, incorporating the reality of an ethnically mixed population into popular conceptions of the Australian nation'.[64] For migrants and Aboriginal people this was a complex and difficult time of adjustment, with new opportunities and openings for change as well as failed government promises and personal disappointments. In the end the vision would fade in the wake of Australia's inevitable transformation into a culturally diverse nation.

In creating an assimilated nation, the Australian government faced three intertwined projects of change.[65] First there was the project of nation building — promoting a national vision of a 'shared history, common spirit, and a unique and exclusive way of life' epitomised in the new White Australia.[66] This was essentially a propaganda exercise that involved publicity campaigns and events to promote support for the government's vision and the acceptance of Aboriginal and migrant families. Then there was the assimilatory project of changing Aboriginal people and immigrants using the carrot of citizenship and a better life and the stick of condemnation for failure to conform. A further task was to dismantle the formal structure of laws and procedures that stood in the way of equality for Aboriginal people. Achieving these tasks promised to relieve national anxieties by building Australia's reputation as a humanitarian nation; confirming Australia's rights of sovereignty by absorbing Aboriginal people into the nation; ensuring a trained migrant labour force for post-war development and alleviating the costs of providing for Aboriginal people as a separate population.

The new official wisdom was that Aboriginal people and European migrants were minority populations within Australian society. However, there was little crossover in policy making or implementing government programs of assimilation; senior officials and their publicists treated them as distinct problem areas. Academics were similarly divided: the embryonic research on immigration in Australia was carried out by social scientists while anthropologists claimed expertise in Aboriginal assimilation. For them, initially at least, assimilation represented a positive intervention and Tim Rowse writes that they considered migrant and Aboriginal assimilation as 'two parallel projects of nation building'.[67]

In practice there were major differences between the projects of Aboriginal and migrant assimilation. Aboriginal people were already Australian citizens yet for their assimilation even to begin required major legislative and administrative reform across federal *and* state jurisdictions. Then there was the legacy of entrenched racism, neglect of the state's duty of care to its Aboriginal citizens, and Aborigines' own oppositional cultures to contend with. Furthermore, the ways in which assimilation was implemented often ran counter to its stated aims and led to further Aboriginal resistance rather than support. Meanwhile the greater cultural and racial whiteness of most European migrants automatically gave them a measure of acceptability that eluded Aboriginal people, although darker Southern Europeans were singled out for some discriminatory treatment and labelled as 'wogs'.

Despite the enormousness of the task of Aboriginal assimilation, the government chose to pour its resources into promoting assimilation of European migrants. The government's substantial commitment to this task, deemed vital to ensuring sufficient labour for post-war development, helped to carve out a place for European immigrants within the nation. Considerably less time and resources were spent promoting Aboriginal assimilation with predictable outcomes for Aboriginal people that fanned the flames of the new Indigenous protest movements of the 1950s and 1960s.

Imagining the nation

The government's efforts to promote a new White Australia mirrored the processes of nation building identified in Benedict Anderson's classic study. Anderson defines nations as imagined communities made up of millions of individuals whose unity is shaped by their allegiance to particular unifying sets of myths and symbols that express national unity and homogeneity and that take precedence over discord and difference.[68] The symbols of this modern new Australia in the 1950s — the Australian way of life, the family and suburban living — were widely used in public campaigns to conjure up the government's vision of an assimilated nation.

Several factors augured well for this new way forward. The ideals of equality for all through assimilation fitted with the public's new spirit of humanitarianism and international outlook following the war. However, historian Frederick Alexander noted that already by 1948 Australians were backsliding. Haunted by feelings of helplessness in the unfolding theatre of world events their attention turned back to Australia where 'the sun continued to shine ... beer supplies were adequate ... and the pervasive racing industry continued to thrive'.[69] There was a strong sense of national unity and interest in Australian identity fostered by nation building during the war, the euphoria of victory, and the impetus for post-war development. The spirit of nationalism was evident in the overwhelming public enthusiasm for the 1954 Royal visit and the 1956 Olympics Games. In 1954, fifty-three years after the design was originally chosen, the 'Australian National Flag' was legally adopted as a major symbol of nationhood. Politically, federal leadership and priorities had been boosted by the decision in 1942 to hand responsibility for collecting and distributing income tax to the federal government. A further development was the new status of 'Australian citizen' that came into existence on Australia Day 1949 that gave Australians a new sense of their identity. From this time citizenship acquired a growing symbolic significance through the new forms of naturalisation ceremonies promoted by the federal government to encourage European migrants to appreciate Australian citizenship as an entitlement and also to mark the final stage in the process of assimilation.[70]

Citizenship is of course more than symbols and national celebrations and the government also sought to instil a public spirit of civic mindedness and to inscribe democratic ideals in the acts and interactions of daily life through various forms of civic education.[71] The media working in tandem with other social institutions was one way of achieving this goal. In 1946 Sir Richard J. F. Boyer, Chairman of the Australian Broadcasting Commission, recommended 'the co-ordination of education by radio with the work of schools, universities, Workers Educational Association, libraries, and most interestingly, with its sister in the modern scientific achievement, the film'.[72] There was also a growing voluntary movement with organisations seeking improvements for their communities through joint action and networks of reciprocity.[73] Setting the example of good citizenship promised to assist the humanitarian aims of assimilating Aboriginal people and migrants into the Australian community. In creating its campaigns for an assimilated nation the government built on these various layers of government and community. Left out of the loop were Aboriginal people and immigrants and their organisations and information networks.

Tools of persuasion

If today is the age of political spin then the 1950s mark its birth. Around the world people's ideas, attitudes, loyalties and behaviours were being 'massaged' in new directions, through exhibitions like *The Family of Man*, UNESCO publications against racism, advertising strategies to cultivate mass consumerism, and political campaigns to ensure allegiance to democracy and capitalism or communism. Even the religious crusades led by American evangelist Billy Graham at the time drew on new techniques of mass manipulation and control. The Australian government's campaign to promote its vision of an assimilated nation was developed in this context of 'beefing up' the nation through optimistic messages of material progress and assurances of citizens' safety and security from threats from within and without. This mix of patriotism and fear is a potent force for creating national unity. It was familiar then from war-time propaganda and remains an integral strategy in today's war on terror.

The PR industry

In 1955 the father of the public relations industry E. L. Bernays wrote that 'the engineering of consent … is the very essence of the democratic process, the freedom to persuade and suggest'.[74] American sociologist Vance Packard was more circumspect however. In his best selling book *The Hidden Persuaders* (1957) Packard attacked the new advertising and public relations industries that he believed were insidiously engineering US society using techniques adapted from mass psychology, psycho-analysis and sociology, including depth psychology and subliminal tactics. He argued that information on public opinion collated from polls, focus workshops and interviews was used to create campaigns that manipulated potent national symbols to persuade the public to accept new opinions and allegiances. Packard's concern was that these techniques could be used to shift the United States from a democratic nation to a totalitarian state.[75] Today these tools of mass persuasion barely raise an eyebrow and are considered regular tools of trade in managing public opinion.

Australia's fledgling market research, mass advertising and public relations industries introduced to Australia from the United States during the war were light years away from Vance Packard's nightmare of totalitarian control. While there may have been public concern and censure locally, generally speaking Australia's communications industry in the 1950s was 'pragmatic and guarded' and supported the status quo while excluding the discordant and marginal. In the late 1950s Australia had its own Public Relations Institute and there was a small but growing network of consultancies staffed mainly by ex-journalists working to ensure positive news coverage in the quality press for corporate and government clients.[76] The work of the PR men and journalists introduced a new level of structuring of news sources and hence of news stories. Their clients included the Prime Minister, the Australian Atomic Energy Commission, large corporations such as Caltex and other oil companies, the banks, churches, army, police and major political parties, with the exception of the Labor Party with its 'very puny budget'.[77]

The government followed war-time and public relations precedents in endeavouring to control information about Aboriginal and migrant issues in the public domain by pumping out carefully constructed 'pre-organised' and 'pre-digested' news stories in releases to the media.[78] Commenting on the government's messages, historian John Murphy notes that the boundaries of propaganda and fact were often blurred and that they reflected the values and beliefs of the dominant middle class: 'They were written to urge political sentiments upon a middle-class readership but also can be read the other way round — as the way the middle class likes to see its own sentiments and values.'[79] The potential to influence perceptions through the press was significant in a nation where a single firm, The Herald and Weekly Times Ltd, controlled 43 per cent of daily newspaper circulation throughout Australia in 1960.[80] The Australian Gallup Poll showed that an average of an hour and ten minutes was spent reading the morning and evening papers each day.[81] However, the strategy of working through the press could continue only as long as the government maintained a firm control over public knowledge about Aboriginal and migrant people, whether through the media or its own publicity campaigns. The federal government had little experience in promoting positive attitudes about either group and its publicity in the past had reflected the entrenched racism of Australian society. There was however the legacy of the federal government's impressive successes using propaganda to forge national unity and compliance during the war.

Government infrastructure

The Department of Information (1939–1950) had coordinated Australia's wartime efforts, adopting, like other allied nations, a combination of strict censorship of public information and the use of propaganda promoting the nation's war effort and the danger of enemies at home and abroad. The didactic materials created for the propaganda effort were often crudely constructed and patronising with little viewer appeal beyond the heightened emotions of war. The example of a propaganda film produced by the independent newsreel company Australia Today in 1941 provides insights into the film genre of propaganda at the time.

Australia's Fifth Column (1941) employed racial and cultural stereotypes to target Australia's German population. In building up an atmosphere of fear and impending disaster the film used the fanatical-sounding voice of Dr Joseph Goebbels and the image of a swastika casting a shadow across a map of Australia amid warnings about Germans in Australia, including missionaries living with Aboriginal people in Central Australia, said to be 'waiting for the downfall of the country that has sheltered them and given them security'. A passage with resonance today called on viewers to combat the 'darkening terrorism that threatens the entire free and civilised world'. Having created a climate of fear the film suddenly shifted gear to reassure viewers that government officers were 'working day and night to stamp out this enemy within. We as loyal citizens must do our part' and reminded them in terms familiar to audiences today that the 'pick of Australian manhood' was 'fighting for the cause of liberty and freedom and to keep us free from the terrorism that threatens the civilised world'.[82] As thousands of German Australians found to their dismay, crude propaganda that portrayed them as cruel barbarians was highly successful in spreading paranoia and it left a legacy of suspicion to be overcome, along with war-time enmities, in welcoming German immigrants to Australia in the 1950s.

Commenting on the legacy of British war-time propaganda,

J. B. Black argues that the many differences in options and actions in peace time reduced its relevance, even in Cold War conditions.[83] However conditions in Australia encouraged continuity of practice. In 1950 the Department of Information was pared down to the Australian National Information Bureau (ANIB 1950–1973) and the Commonwealth Film Unit (1940–1973), both attached to the Department of Interior.[84] In peace time their role was to document aspects of Australian daily life, civic and diplomatic receptions and national economic and cultural development for promotional purposes to attract international trade, immigrants and tourists, to encourage international goodwill and to educate audiences at home and abroad about government policies. Representations of assimilation were required to be positive, reassuring and non-threatening, demonstrating an achievable way forward. That this was carried out is evident in the thousands of photographs of smiling families of immigrants and Aboriginal people in the ANIB archive. There was also a new interest in the capacity of documentaries to convey information about government agencies to new audiences and to promote national pride, so that film became intricately involved in post-war training of citizens.[85]

ANIB and the Film Unit worked collaboratively with the Department of External Affairs in promoting Australia overseas and with the Department of Immigration, which had its own public relations section from 1955. Coordinating the Aboriginal campaign was more complex, constrained by limited resources and the hurdles created by divided state and federal responsibilities and paranoia over international sensitivities. Although the crude propaganda techniques of war were abandoned, elements of their didactic style and drab look survived in the new campaign materials — the legacy of a paternalistic government that assumed it knew what was best for its citizens and that the public would willingly take up whatever materials were put their way.

Symbols of persuasion

The 'effectiveness of propaganda,' wrote Alex Carey, 'depends on the availability of emotionally charged symbols or ideas that can be manipulated by propagandists.'[86] Attitudes and behaviours were not changed through appeal to reason as claimed by UNESCO, or even legislation, but through emotions and the 'non-logical'.[87] The emotion-packed symbols of persuasion for nation building in 1950s Australia were the Australian way of life, the Australian family and the Australian suburbs — imagined ideals of a lifestyle to strive for and codes of behaviours to emulate. They were also brands used to promote the nation, suggest its history, unify the people and sell its resources and products. In the campaigns to sell assimilation, idealised images invited Australians to take their rightful place in the suburban nuclear family home — eating dinner around the kitchen table, relaxing in front of the TV set and entertaining neighbours.

These parochial symbols of Australian nationhood left no room for representing the varied lifestyles, memories and stories of European migrants and Aboriginal people or the significance of their traditionally strong family values. Nor was there a place in the symbols' sunny optimism to incorporate their often tragic experiences, or even the terrible memories of Australia's service personnel during the war. All of this pain and sorrow had to be repressed in silence. Government studies on the incidence of mental illness among migrants during the 1960s reported 'alarming' levels of schizophrenia among eastern Europeans that were attributable to the psychological legacy of the war and the stresses of migration and assimilation, which one politician described as a 'Gethsemane for migrants'.[88]

These symbols were self-consciously Australian in content but they were also the same tools for nation building used around the world at the time. The potent iconography of 'family' was used, as we have seen, to promote international unity in *The Family of*

Man, but more often to represent the *heart* of the nation, with the image of the gendered nuclear family as the norm. In the context of the Cold War the American Way was a powerful symbol of national loyalty and allegiance and for marking difference to communism in terms of conservative values of 'social harmony, freedom, democracy, the family, the church, and patriotism'.[89]

Australian way of life

The concept of a national way of life was not unlike the term assimilation — its lack of clear definition made it a useful tool for suggesting general consensus about whichever meaning was being claimed at the time.[90] Sociologist Robert Van Krieken points out that the term might be better understood as 'a rhetorical device employed to create the very thing it is meant to describe'.[91] There were probably as many perspectives on the 'Australian way of life' as people writing about it, which prompted James Jupp (1966) to question its usefulness at all in providing a model for migrant assimilation: if the Australian way of life was so 'ill-defined' then there were innumerable ways that migrants could respond to it. He observed facetiously that 'if there was any doubt about the features of that society there was always the RSL, the Protestant clergy, the headmasters of public schools and the ABC to inform newcomers'.[92] Jupp advocated instead a model of Australian society that highlighted the many communities that made up the nation.[93]

For Australia in the 1950s the concept was a powerful rallying point for the nation to 'defend and justify an assumed homogeneity',[94] a brand for promoting Australia to potential immigrants, investors and tourists and a shorthand way of explaining local ways of doing things that were familiar to the majority but not always clear to newcomers and people marginal to society. As in the case of the United States the Australian way of life was also used negatively to define what was un-Australian, as in the comment by a federal member of parliament in 1951 that in contrast to Australia, communism was 'a complete way of life' intent on 'dominating every person under its banner, so as to render him a serf to an idea'.[95] In fact the term was so widely used at the time that one columnist complained she was 'sick and tired of hearing people bleating about [it]'.[96]

The official version emphasised lifestyle, family, home ownership, suburban living, mateship and a fair go for all. The government film *The Way We Live* (1959)[97] pitched it to aspiring migrants through images of suburban housing, leisure, work and consumer goods; and depictions of transport, health, education and financial assistance services, cultural institutions and social organisations. Designed to counter images of 'bush and billabongs', the film focused on urban living and Australia's growth potential. Politician and UN dignitary Dr Herbert Vere Evatt focused on political ideals in an article entitled 'The Australian Way of Life' published in the United States between 1942 and 1945. He wrote that 'Australia is a democracy. Political freedom in Australia is basic' and boasted that Australia was one democracy amongst the many UN member states that ensured for its citizens the Four Freedoms defined by Churchill and Roosevelt under the 1941 Atlantic Charter — freedom of speech and expression, freedom of worship, freedom from want, and freedom from fear.[98]

Retired lawyer Frederic W. Eggleston pointed to Australia's unique migrant origins in the book *The Australian Way of Life* edited by George Caiger for the UNESCO *Way of Life Series*.[99] He described Australia as a nation of English, Irish and Scots[100] whose 'common mores of a homogeneous community' underpinned 'her immigration policy … she believes she is entitled to a selective immigration policy designed to determine a population capable of carrying on the way of life and the standards she has adopted. Apart from this Australia is racially tolerant and has no discriminations of any importance against foreigners.'[101] Writing under the name of fictional character Nino

Culotta, John O'Grady presented a highly gendered view of the Australian way of life in *They're a Weird Mob*, a fictional account of the assimilation of an Italian migrant.[102] Life for Australian men was based on hard physical work, a culture of heavy drinking, the never-ending regime of teasing and testing mates and a host of male rituals from shouting a beer to bucks' nights. In this way of life women represented the home, marriage, emotional life and, perhaps, domestic bliss.

But there were other, more critical, views of the Australian way. Expatriate writer George H. Johnston described the dark underbelly of 'race fear', 'economic fear' and 'insularity' that lurked below the image of high standards of living and employment, social equality and a robust democracy. These insecurities created 'a form of xenophobia so stubbornly rooted that an atom bomb would scarcely dislodge it' and aroused the 'deepest suspicions and … resentments' for those who did not assimilate thoroughly.[103]

This xenophobia found expression in numerous public comments at the time about fears of racial violence, race-mixing, mixed race populations, a drop in living standards and of being 'swamped' by Asians. Academic H. L. Harris explained in his study of the White Australia policy in 1947 that 'we do not want anybody who looks, speak or thinks very differently from ourselves … we want people who are almost if not quite indistinguishable from ourselves or will rapidly become so'.[104] A letter to the *Sydney Morning Herald* in 1962 claimed that 'to open the migration gates to subject Australians to the shocking racial disturbances that regularly make the headlines from other parts of the world would be the greatest act of folly, and those responsible for it would warrant the condemnation they would surely receive'.[105] The Returned Soldiers' League energetically pursued its xenophobic concerns over Australia's security in peace time with its insistence that White Australia meant excluding any non-British migrant group.[106] Prominent Brisbane doctor and barrister Sir Ralph Cilento claimed that the White Australia policy had given Australia one of the highest standards of living in the world and prevented 'the whole land from sinking to the coolie level of living of their colored competitors'. He warned Australians to beware of 'the mindless mob ... sentimental do-gooders, sensation hungry beatniks, bottle blondes (of both sexes) and the avant-garde eggheads' who would change the policy and bring 'invasion from foreign germs that would be brought in by indiscriminate Asian migration'.[107] Unionists campaigned in support of White Australia, concerned that 'to flood this country with unskilled Asian labour, would only disrupt our economy, and add to the unemployment that already exists'.[108] A Broome pearling master wrote in an opinion piece for the *Daily News* in 1963: 'Give them [Asian migrants] an inch and they will take a mile. They would infiltrate right throughout the country. There would be no stopping them once they were here.'[109]

Australian family

If the Australian way of life expressed the style of the nation, the family was its heart. In 1950s Australia marriage, family and home were 'the containers of happiness'.[110] For Sir Robert Menzies the middle-class family with its 'home-centred independent individualism' and its values that were 'universally and self-evidently true' was the 'best possible guide'.[111] This was the prototype for the 'petit bourgeois family — frugal, hardworking and home centred' eulogised by Menzies in his famous 1942 radio broadcast *The Forgotten People*,[112] that drew inspiration from his memories of growing up in a small town in the Wimmera district of Victoria. He later recalled how the family spent evenings 'reading to each other, and discussing matters with each other. This produced a very well knit family atmosphere ... we got to learn something about the things that mattered in the world ... we acquired some moral and spiritual standards.'[113] During the 1950s, images of the family were used to sell governments, political parties and a host of consumer products and services. Manipulated to show the family under threat as in a 1949 Liberal Party advertisement warning that 'the family was socialism's no. 1 target', they also targeted broader social anxieties.[114] Photographs in popular magazines like the *Women's Weekly* of celebrity families from the Queen and the Royal children Prince Charles and Princess Anne to Hollywood sex symbol Jayne Mansfield and her baby son provided models for readers to aspire to. There was also a boom in personal family imagery spurred on by advertising campaigns like Kodak's 'Capture family life in colour slides and movies … naturally Kodachrome film.'[115]

Menzies' dream of an ideal Australian family did not match demographer Wilfred Borrie's claim at the time that 'there is no Australian family, but there are many Australian families.'[116] This diversity reflected Australia's history of 'movement and adaptation' on the 'stamp of British origins'. Borrie distinguished families by location (metropolitan/extra-metropolitan), occupation (manual workers/white collar workers) and class (lower/middle/upper), rather than structure. He noted the central place of the family in Australian society that was recognised in a range of government supports — the basic wage established in 1907 to ensure a liveable wage for a married couple and three children; child endowment introduced in 1941; the maternity grant, hospital and medical subsidies, pre and post natal clinics, medical inspection of primary school children and free education.[117] He also noted the many changes impinging on family life at the time — technology, demographic shifts, urbanisation, the emancipation of women, the declining role of religion, the growth of the 'cult of hedonism'[118] and the trend to smaller families of three children in urban areas.[119]

The family was the goal of an assimilated nation and the vehicle to achieve it. The ideal family in the 1950s was suburban, middle-class and nuclear — less British and less home-bound and certainly less frugal than Menzies' ideal family, but just as gendered and self-sufficient. The pictorial promotional pamphlet *An Everyday Australian*,[120] produced as part of the government's assimilation propaganda, showed this new young suburban family in their brick home with its garden setting, modern furnishings and appliances and other consumer goods, including the new family car. It depicted the husband leaving for work in the city, the wife at her housework, and the family enjoying the weekend cleaning the car, picnicking with friends (including the unlikely sight of Asian guests, possibly allowed into Australia under the Colombo Plan) and playing sport. Without distinction for class, race and ethnicity this unit — male breadwinner and dependent spouse and children — represented the focus for domestic life, work, education, security, personal happiness and citizenship around the nation.

Marriage and family were the choices made by settler Australian couples after the war — marriage rates for women aged between 20 and 24 climbed from 31 percent in 1933 to 59 per cent in 1954 and for men aged between 25 and 29 the rate soared from 44 per cent in 1933 to 64 per cent over the same period.[121] Newly arrived single migrants sought to follow their example, and with single men initially outstripping single women, some migrant men were obliged to find spouses through arranged marriages and 'mail-order' brides. 'Marriage madness' gripped the country as more couples took their vows, married at an earlier age and started a baby boom with their average of two or three children. With generous government incentives and support, home ownership was now within the reach of the typical Australian family. For Menzies this was the 'defining trait of the genuinely egalitarian society'.[122] In the midst of a post-war housing crisis federal and state governments joined forces to create an infrastructure of generous financial support that drove the massive push to home ownership amongst settler Australians and new migrants. They provided tax incentives for young families, extensive suburban development and building projects, advice and special loans for returned servicemen, and assistance for low-income homebuyers. Between 1947 and 1961 home ownership increased from 50 to 70 per cent of Australians and 90 per cent of the population owned their own homes at some time between 1946 and 1970.

Of course, government generosity wasn't even-handed. European migrants had to wait five years until they could become naturalised citizens and so benefit from government incentives, and even then the many migrant families with working mothers were ineligible for the tax deductions. And governments did not consider private home ownership for Aboriginal families as an option at the time.

Australian suburbs

The suburb was the site where the national symbols came together — the way of life, the family unit and the suburban home and garden. This was the new urban frontier of Australian settlement. A dominant image of mid-twentieth century Australia is of families carving new homes out of paddocks being converted into suburban housing estates. On the edge of nowhere hundreds of thousands of families came together from older middle-class suburbs, inner-city working-class areas, and much further afield in Britain and Europe. There was even a sprinkling of Aboriginal families from country reserves in state housing areas. Most of these families moved voluntarily, responding to the call of home ownership, but others were pushed there by the bulldozing of their homes in inner-city slums and Aboriginal fringe camps.

As practical models of the way of life Australians were meant to aspire to, the suburbs were the engines of change for assimilating one and all into a homogeneous middle-class culture. They were also central to post-war economic development and its demand for housing for millions of families, and to the individual they offered a 'sense of security, return to order, and a chance to revive plans interrupted by the war'.[123] Similar processes of suburbanisation were taking place around the Western world. France, for example, witnessed the consolidation of a new suburban 'pared-down, and stream-lined French household' as families moved to urban areas from the countryside, encouraged by consumerism, modernisation and new styles and standards in the modern home.[124] Like working-class and European migrant families in Australia, they too left behind extended family and a familiar lifestyle to become the new unit of modern capitalist society — the nuclear family, tied down by mortgages, monotonous regimes of work and schooling and the temptations and demands of consumerism. The uniformity of this lifestyle was reinforced by a shared daily routine, informal codes of behaviour and dress, and a secret mutual surveillance. Tim Winton writes of his childhood in the suburbs: 'the men of our street went to work and left the driveways empty. They came home from the city tired, often silent. They scattered blood and bone on their garden beds and retired to their sheds. All day the women of the street cleaned and cooked and moved sprinklers from the garden to keep things alive. Later in the morning the baker arrived in his van red-cheeked from civilisation, and after him the man with the vegie truck. At the sound of their bells kids spilled out into the dusty street and their mothers emerged in housecoats and pedal pushers with rollers in their hair.'[125]

Suburban homes were a symbol of modern living but dreams of the new home, writes Chris McAuliffe, 'raised the spectre of compromise' as couples struggled to balance finances, budgets and mortgages (despite generous government support) with the need for a new car, furniture and white goods and the costs of raising a family. It was Alastair Grieg's 'suburban imperative' that locked homeowners into a global economy of advertising and consumption.[126] The result was house styles that were simple and practical in design, made with cheap available materials and often self-built from the plan. Uniform exteriors were modified by the minutiae of flower beds, curtain patterns, garage doors and cement pathways. Interior design often looked back to the owner's childhood homes rather than internationalist modern open plan architecture — to the despair of architect Robin Boyd who complained of an 'aesthetic calamity' in the suburbs.[127] There were other cracks in the suburban dream, with frequent delays in infrastructure provision (public transport, roads, sewerage, street lighting), complaints from women weighed down by dreary domesticity, social isolation and suburban neuroses, and concerns over the 'fragility' of community and lack of social life.[128] A new generation of writers and artists were both repelled and mesmerised by the new suburbs. Some were alienated by the 'epitome of uniformity' achieved there and avoided the subject. Others, like Patrick White and John Brack, were drawn to the ambivalence they perceived in this 'existential wasteland': 'distinctions between genuine and artificial culture, mythical and actual identity, historical dreams and everyday life.'[129]

For many families their new suburban home was the symbol of their new prosperity and an important investment for the future. Mark Peel writes that these were times of upheaval and anxiety for working-class families moving to the suburbs from the inner city, building their first home and finding new employment, with women living isolated lives in their homes after the crowded life in the city. But the families were rewarded with new clean homes and a gradual escape from poverty. With full employment available the move marked the 'starting point for family success stories,' with a modest home and their children's education providing a sound investment for the family's financial security.[130] By contrast, for the majority of Aboriginal families home ownership or even a rental home in the suburbs would remain an impossible dream for decades to come. For Aboriginal families accepted for state housing accommodation, daily life became a testing ground of assimilated living with government officers and disapproving neighbours checking the upkeep of the house and gardens, the family's adherence to the rhythm of school, domestic chores and work, and the maintenance of respectable standards of behaviour inside and outside the home.

Systemic inequalities created by a government that proclaimed equality for all were behind these radically different outcomes for Australian families. The truth was that despite the cheerful imagery of government campaigns, the families who ended up sitting comfortably in their own suburban homes supported by full-time employment and the trappings of modern life were mainly white middle and working-class Australians and recent British migrants. These were the intended beneficiaries of government programs to build up the nation, the families that fitted the mould of White Australia.

The power of not knowing

Most settler Australians had no grounds to question the accuracy of the government's claims for a new White Australia or any inclination to challenge its authority. During the 1950s public misinformation and ignorance about conditions for migrant and Aboriginal people and their cultural backgrounds were widespread. There was little personal contact or interaction between them, and the public relied on general knowledge mediated by experts whose interpretations were shaped by Australia's monocultural outlook and the paradigms of their professions and disciplines. Marcia Langton writes of how the paradox 'of the physical proximity but social distance' between black and white Australians has created a situation where few settler Australians actually know or relate to Aboriginal people. Here, the 'densest relationship is not between actual people, but between white Australians and the symbols created by their predecessors. Australians do not know and relate to Aboriginal people. They relate to stories told by former colonists.'[131]

US academics Nancy Tuana and Charles Mills remind us that

this fog of ignorance and misinformation surrounding race and cultural difference is never a benign condition: it does things. It is not a simple lack of knowledge — a gap passively waiting to be filled, something that we will come to know better as we push out the boundaries of research and experience. Rather, it is 'often constructed, maintained, and disseminated and is linked to issues of cognitive authority, doubt, trust, silencing, and uncertainty'.[132] Tuana warns that just as we seek to comprehend the 'variety of features that account for why something is known, we must also understand the practices that account for not knowing, that is, for our lack of knowledge about a phenomena or, in some cases, an account of the practices that resulted in a group unlearning what was once a realm of knowledge. In other words, those who would strive to understand how we know must also develop epistemologies of ignorance.'[133]

Not knowing can actually work to preserve ignorance by bestowing value on misinformation and failing to question its veracity or authority. In a world of separation and suspicion of the other, hearsay and imaginings can take on the appearance of fact. Contradictions abound, untruths multiply and conversations slip unchecked from one unfounded claim to the next. Repeated by government and the media, this kind of misinformation can take on a new aura of authority and authenticity. Ignorance and misinformation can be harnessed to target specific groups who are defined and stereotyped on the basis of some attribute such as race, gender, ethnicity, class or age — even appearance, as in the case of 'Middle Eastern appearance' today. This is then used to rationalise and normalise their discriminatory treatment. Mills argues that matters of race invite an 'active production and preservation of ignorance. This produces negative political, social and economic outcomes for the targeted racial groups. Meanwhile the perpetrators fail to recognise or understand the conditions that their racism has helped to produce.'[134] We can see these processes in operation in historian Judith Brett's account of the opinions of

Prime Minister Menzies, which were representative of the insular attitudes of the time, even amongst the nation's educated political elite. Menzies was often characterised as 'British to his bootstraps' and his Anglophile nature was immortalised in his reverential speech to Queen Elizabeth in 1963 when he quoted a line from the sixteenth-century English poet Barnabe Googe, 'I did but see her passing by, and yet I love her till I die.'

Menzies grew up in Victoria's Wimmera district amongst families of German Lutherans and Aboriginal survivors from the Wotjoballuk people. The Lutherans, whom he recalled as 'hardworking, self-reliant, religious families', epitomised the petit bourgeois virtues that Menzies praised in his radio broadcast *The Forgotten People.* However, this escaped Menzies' attention since they were displayed 'in a foreign idiom, and so were all but invisible to a discourse which located these virtues in the historical experience of the British race.'[135]

Menzies' memories of the Wotjoballuk people were submerged in a welter of stereotypes. He recalled in an interview in the late 1960s that 'they lived in a rather primitive way, they weren't a significant element in the community — er — I don't think there was any prejudice against them. I think it's not always understood that the Aboriginals, like most of us, like to live together and be themselves and by themselves; they didn't have any particular ambitions to be anything else … They were rather an idle community, and at that time of course, it hadn't occurred to do something with them.'[136] This comment completely overlooked the history of the nearby Ebenezer Aboriginal Mission that operated from 1859 to 1903 when the government resumed the land and relocated the residents to Lake Tyers. In a draft encyclopaedia entry Menzies referred briefly to the 'many disastrous conflicts' of the past and concluded that the 'Indigenous racial problem' was 'of no great magnitude, though it does give rise to a good deal of debate and, of course constant demands to improve the status of the native people. But there is no internal race problem either quantitative or qualitative, in the sense that there is in the United States or in South Africa.'[137]

Brett concludes that Menzies' 'dismissive comments … failed to extend any imaginative human sympathy to the Aborigines; he continued to think of them in the Social Darwinist terms of the turn of the century, seeing them as the lowest rung on the ladder of human races and blaming them for the destitution to which the white invasion had reduced them'.[138] Other middle-class Australians followed his example and 'hardened their hearts' against Aboriginal people while at the same time they resented Aborigines' ease on the land and their claims on 'white consciences'.[139] These attitudes continued on over the decades. In 1988 Aboriginal activist and writer Kevin Gilbert wrote, 'still they do not hear. To the contrary, many say: "Aboriginals get too much."'[140] Eight years later Pauline Hanson famously gave these views a very public airing in her maiden speech to parliament:

> I have done research on the benefits available only to Aboriginals and challenge anyone to tell me how Aboriginals are disadvantaged when they can obtain 3 and 5 % housing loans denied to non-Aboriginals. This nation is being divided into black and white and the present system encourages this. I am fed up with being told, 'This is our land.' Well, where the hell do I go? I was born here and so were my parents and children. I will work beside anyone and they will be my equal but I draw the line when told I must pay and continue to pay for something which happened 200 years ago. Like most Australians I worked for my land. No one gave it to me.[141]

Hotly debated at the time, Hanson's views seemed to follow her out of the public limelight when she lost her seat in parliament in 1998. However, today's retro-marketing of assimilation is giving these attitudes a new respectability.

Like other supporters of assimilation, Menzies offered the defence that underpins any rhetoric of assimilation — that a united, culturally homogeneous nation prevents the 'coming into existence of acute divisions in society'.[142] This claim still has a familiar ring. In 1996 historian Geoffrey Partington wrote that 'there can be no doubt ... that only an Australia unified in the essentials of sovereignty and law can provide the conditions in which Aborigines and all others can flourish culturally and materially'.[143] Pauline Hanson also asserted in her maiden speech to federal parliament that 'a truly multiracial country can never be strong or united. The world is full of failed and tragic examples, ranging from Ireland to Bosnia to Africa and closer to home, Papua New Guinea. America and Great Britain are currently paying the price.' At the same time Prime Minister Howard picked up on the mood in a campaign that historian Leigh Dale argues 'mirrored Robert Menzies' call to the "forgotten people"'.[144] He spoke forcefully of his 'desire to focus on things that unite Australians and not things that divide them ... My view is that we are one nation.'[145] Howard's promise to 'mainstream' Australians was that not only would they be at the 'centre of his policy agenda but that they would be his policy agenda.'[146] In 2006 and 2007 Howard continued to labour the point in comments that 'the premium must be upon, the emphasis must be upon, the dominant consideration must be, the integration of people into the Australian family'.[147] He also claimed that 'the core culture of this nation is very clear; we are an outshoot of western civilisation. Because we speak the English language our cultural identity is very heavily Anglo-Saxon. It doesn't mean that it isn't distinctively Australian, but you have to recognise that there is a core set of values in this country.'[148]

The knowledge makers

In the 1950s governments and academics were the principal mediators of official knowledge about migrants and Aboriginal people. They influenced each other in their research and application of findings in policy and projects, and reached out to shape public opinion as well. Most shared a simplistic vision of culture as a 'unitary, fixed category' and a 'relatively closed set regarding its rules and players' that fitted the official vision of assimilation but entirely overlooked the reality of Australian society that was an increasingly 'decentered, fragmentary assemblage of conflicting voices and institutions'.[149] Academic research then was not the socially robust knowledge we strive for today, the outcome of many different actors working jointly in networks to create knowledge that is 'demonstrably valid' across a broad range of contexts.[150] This was a narrow slice that reflected political and academic agendas and paradigms of race, colonialism and paternalism.

Aboriginal and migrant people were largely excluded from the loop of knowledge making. As long as they were not fully participating citizens they were also excluded from the democratic processes that shaped the policies that influenced their lives. It was politicians and bureaucrats, guided by their professional and personal take on Aboriginal issues and sometimes advised by academics, who created the policies — balancing the interests of key stakeholders, the voting majority and the public purse against what they perceived to be the needs of Aboriginal and migrant people.[151] Judith Bessant and Amanda Wilkinson describe the process as follows: '

> … 'white' policy makers create knowledge about indigenous people and the belief that they (as spokespersons) are simply a substitute for indigenous people. In other words, what researchers and policy-makers say becomes what the

indigenous populations are supposed to have said, thought and felt. We refer to popular ideas about claiming to know what is in the 'best interest' of indigenous people without speaking to indigenous people. This has led to policies based on claims that it was 'in their best interest' to be removed from their family and to be raised and educated in the modern and 'superior ways' of others.[152]

Academic research and migrant assimilation

The sociological study of immigration and assimilation was vastly underrepresented in Australia in the 1950s. By contrast the United States had a thriving research agenda dating from the 1920s, shaped by Robert Ezra Park's iconic theory of assimilation as a unilinear, one-way, staged process of change experienced by immigrant populations that moved 'gradually, progressively, and inevitably' from contact, through conflict and accommodation, to assimilation.[153] Park's model became the 'hegemonic theory in the study of ethnic and race relations' into the 1960s and supported a 'cottage industry' devoted to measuring and assessing behavioural and attitudinal changes in the process of assimilation.[154] The very different situation in Australia reflected its reliance on British migration and its monocultural outlook: prior to the post-war European migration schemes, issues of migrant assimilation had seemed largely irrelevant. Sociology was not founded as an academic discipline in Australia until the 1960s and the bulk of early research was undertaken by demographers at the Australian National University. They were inevitably influenced by Park's original model but their own demographic studies and their participation in international debates and research through UNESCO gave them a broader comparative vision of processes of change in action.

These influences were reflected in the mix of convention and critical edge in the work of demographer Wilfred Borrie.[155]

Borrie adopted a conventional view of assimilation as a 'psychological, socioeconomic and cultural process resulting in the progressive attenuation of differences between the behaviour of immigrants and nationals within the social life of a country'.[156] He also followed accepted practice in ignoring the two-way processes of assimilation between immigrants and host societies and constructing the host society as an amorphous homogeneous entity.[157] This model of assimilation directed him (like his colleagues in anthropology) to calculate and compare markers of assimilation and difference in assessing the success of the policy of assimilation that included 'spatial distribution, occupation (dispersion or concentration), intermarriage with Australians, proportion of children born in Australia, language spoken in the home, whether children were bilingual, and "rates" of naturalisation.'[158] As Rowse observes, the view that assimilation was 'primarily something that migrants did … became a working assumption of this field of study, as it did, generally, in the study of Aborigines' assimilation'.[159] This view was evident in Borrie's otherwise groundbreaking studies of the experiences of assimilation in the Scandinavian, German and Italian communities that arrived in Australia from the nineteenth century. It was a reflection of the popular assumption that 'migrant' meant non-British that Borrie, himself a migrant from New Zealand, did not think to trace the history of the sizeable population of New Zealanders of mainly British background then living in Australia.

Australian researchers played a significant role in presenting the nation's position on assimilation in international forums. Borrie was a key player in UNESCO forums and in 1956 represented Australia at the Havana Conference that advocated the new policy of integration. Exposure to international debate released Borrie from the stranglehold of the conventional model of assimilation and from this time he began to advocate a form of managed pluralism. In 1959 he published a report on the Havana Conference which juxtaposed the models: assimilation, he argued, demanded complete conformity to 'the national way of life', often through compulsion and racist selection criteria to exclude 'unassimilable types' while integration required conformity in economic and civil matters but retained cultural differentiation within a united social framework.[160] The mass migration and population displacements of the post-war period had prompted a shift in the United States as well to a more nuanced understanding of the complexities of adjustment in immigration, and US academic Milton Gordon's more rigorous 1964 definition of assimilation distinguished seven aspects of the process — structural, cultural, marital association, identification, attitude reception, behavioural and civic assimilation — and acknowledged the mutual interchange between migrant and host communities in assimilation.[161]

At the 1961 Australian Citizenship Convention delegates proposed a new vision of the Australian way of life that combined settler and migrant cultures with the principles of equality of opportunity, the right to a fair go, social and legal justice, and a standard of living that supported 'decent family life and pursuit of happiness under conditions that guaranteed human dignity for all'.[162] Even Prime Minister Menzies was prepared to admit in 1958 that Australian culture was being enriched 'by the lively minds and experience, and the lively imaginations of thousands of people whose cultural background is remote from our own' and he told the 1963 Convention that 'Australia as a community [was] experiencing a change into something rich and strange'.[163] From the early 1960s there was a growing migrant voice at conventions with 'vigorous debate' over assimilation, naturalisation and Australian norms and values,[164] and from 1965 the federal government began to move away from assimilation to a policy of integration.

Models of Aboriginal assimilation

When it came to Aboriginal issues Australian governments kept a tight control over public information, which was constructed to give the best possible impression of their policies. This was backed up by informal rules of silence down the line. In the early 1950s there was no up-to-date published government information about Aboriginal populations apart from ministerial speeches and government reports. Such was the dearth of material that diplomats in overseas posts were obliged to distribute this dull reading to their international colleagues. Statistics on Aboriginal populations and living conditions were collected in the main by police officers, and with Aboriginal people excluded from the national census there was little reliable data to guide government officers in planning what would now be called 'evidence based' programs of change. This gap in knowledge was often filled by advice from anthropologists that was shaped by the research paradigms and agendas of their discipline base.

In contrast to sociology, anthropology had a long history in Australia dating from the nineteenth century with the first chair established at Sydney University in 1925 and discussion of Aboriginal assimilation dating from the 1930s. In colonial times and in the twentieth century anthropologists presented themselves as experts on the past, present and future of Aboriginal people and their cultures. Their writings and advice shaped and reinforced official policies and administration, influenced popular representations and provided explanations of the past and predictions for the future. In fact a major goal for A. P. Elkin was to make anthropology an integral tool of Aboriginal administration. Significantly, given the emerging public position of Aboriginal activists in the late 1950s, Elkin and his protégés continued to represent Aboriginal people as a minority group rather than as Indigenous people with special rights. In a paper written in 1961 Ronald Berndt classified Aboriginal and migrant people as minority groups; he acknowledged Aborigines' physical and cultural distinctiveness but saw a common assimilated future for both. This put anthropologists accustomed to representing Aboriginal opinion on a collision course with Aboriginal leaders advocating a new agenda of Indigenous rights.

The principal focus of anthropological research was the analysis and documentation of traditional Aboriginal life. A generalised view of Aboriginal culture as a homogeneous model with local variations promoted by social anthropologists like Elkin distracted attention from the great diversity in Aboriginal cultures. Anthropologists' representations of remote Aboriginal communities as culturally genuine in contrast to the cultural no man's land of mixed race communities in 'settled areas' shaped official practice in relation to these populations and reinforced popular stereotypes about Aboriginal primitiveness and cultural breakdown and degradation. For anthropologists the imperative of cultural salvage and rescue took precedence over the study of social change and assimilation in remote Aboriginal communities. This was particularly so for museum-based anthropologists who popularised traditional art and design in publications and exhibitions at the time. The public was entranced by accounts of traditional Aboriginal life derived from popular anthropology and framed by the discredited nineteenth century paradigm of social evolution with its images of Stone Age culture and Aboriginal extinction. For the period 1930–1990, the 54-page index for *Oceania*, Australia's major national anthropological journal, listed only thirty papers dealing specifically with social change in rural and urban areas and only eight were studies of assimilation. This *absence* of knowledge influenced the government's rudimentary approaches to implementing assimilation and encouraged established precedent rather than new ways of working with Aboriginal people.

Elkin was known in government circles for his policy of social assimilation but it was his account of traditional Aboriginal culture in *The Australian Aborigines* (1938) that won him popular acclaim and made him *the* authority on Aboriginal culture at home and abroad. Elkin was the dominant spokesperson on Aboriginal anthropology from 1932 when he took over the Anthropology Department at Sydney University until his retirement in 1956, and his book was the only comprehensive accessible account of Aboriginal culture prior to the 1950s. In the preface to the first edition Elkin explained that the book was 'offered as a contribution to that understanding which will inspire our attitudes to, treatment of, and work for, the Aborigines'.[165] Based on his fieldwork research in the Kimberley, Central Australia and outback New South Wales, the book provided a fresh view of Aboriginal culture as a functional system and a satisfying way of life. However it also reinforced popular misconceptions that living Aboriginal cultures survived only in remote areas and emphasised the imperative for anthropologists to salvage what little culture remained. The book had phenomenal success and by the 1960s was in its fourth edition, selling in Australia, England and the United States with a pirated version circulating in Russia and translations into French and Italian underway.[166]

In his booklet *Citizenship for the Aborigines: a National Policy* (1944),[167] Elkin clarified the model that would shape state government policies of assimilation from the late 1940s. Like Park, Elkin promoted assimilation as a unilinear, one-way path from the traditional past to a modern future. His model of Aboriginal cultural change proposed a series of stages that moved from 'tentative approach' to 'clash', 'intelligent parasitism', 'intelligent appreciation', 'assimilation' and finally 'citizenship'.[168] This model provided a framework for mid-twentieth century studies of the assimilation of 'mixed-race' communities but researchers had to struggle to condense the diversity of situations they encountered into both its rigid parameters and their own preconceptions. Anthropologists working in remote areas, including Elkin, continued to focus on documenting traditional life and envisaged a more gradual path of change that incorporated elements of Aboriginal life, at least in the short term.

In the closed world of Aboriginal affairs, anthropologists' findings played a role in reinforcing assimilation policy. In addition to his fieldwork Elkin was an adviser to governments. He directed all anthropological field-research through the Australian National Research Council over a period of more than twenty years from 1933 and taught most researchers and many field-officers in the discipline into the mid-1950s. His influence was also evident in Perth, where his students Ronald and Catherine Berndt established the foundations of a new anthropology department at the University of Western Australia in the early 1950s. Their students collected a wealth of family and cultural information that measured the progress of local Aboriginal communities towards the goal of assimilated living. Following Elkin's example of practical anthropology, the Berndts encouraged local policy makers and administrators in Aboriginal affairs to draw on this research and to undertake their own anthropological studies. Elkin's work shaped most potted accounts of Aboriginal history until Charles Rowley's historical trilogy broke the mould in the early 1970s.[169] An exception in documenting this history was Diane Barwick whose research with Aboriginal people in Victoria in the 1960s wedded archival study and anthropological fieldwork to produce a new understanding of Aboriginal historical experience.

Academic models of migrant and Aboriginal assimilation began to shift during the 1960s in response to more nuanced research into the complexities of assimilation. Old models lost their hegemonic status with mounting criticism of their ethnocentric perspectives and lack of explanatory power in the face of research showing continuing ethnic diversity despite decades of pressure to assimilate. With recognition of the value of community life for assimilation or integration to work cultural pluralism became the new hegemony. Two new federal policy initiatives were adopted during the 1970s — Indigenous self-determination and multiculturalism — and assimilation was assigned to the proverbial dustbin in public debate. However, in the wake of mass global migration and world terrorism since the 1990s, assimilation has been revived in academic research and government policy-making as nations seek to manage existing cultural diversity and to deal with pressures to take in new migrants from diverse backgrounds while striving to preserve their own original national core cultures.

With the benefit of hindsight we can see how ignorance and misinformation could work to cloud the ability of political leaders and the public to see what assimilation meant for others. The public was sustained in their misconceptions by glowing reports of government protection and care and by their own self-interest. In relation to Aboriginal people they seemed to be blind to the devastating impact of generations of racial segregation and punitive neglect — the world that, as Charles Mills argues, they helped to create. Popular anthropology claimed that Aboriginal people in southern Australia had 'lost their culture' and that they would easily assimilate into the Australian way of life. Official statements claimed that migrants and Aboriginal people would be carefully and wisely guided towards assimilation. Beguiled by claims of a fair go for all, the public failed to see the challenges confronting those burdened with the responsibility to assimilate and blamed them for any shortcomings. In this ignorant world the vision of an assimilated nation could spread out virtually unchallenged. As we have seen, critics from the CPA for example were thoroughly discredited and refused a public hearing. Official images of a white nation of happy suburban families also distracted the public from the many other changes going on around them. As long as they listened only to each other they would never see the flaws in the vision. As Miriam Dixon observes, 'the nation lives ultimately in people's minds'.[170] This would change over the decade with the growing clamour to know more and as Aboriginal people gained a stronger public voice to present their own situation directly to the public.

Clockwise from top left: Government publicity shot (1958) [Courtesy National Archives of Australia: A1200 L25653]; Arthur Calwell, Minister for Immigration, welcoming 100,000th British migrant, Isobel Savery (1949) [Courtesy National Library of Australia: nla.pic-an24717043]; Migrant Publicity Pamphlet (1963) [Courtesy National Archives

Selling Assimilation

Part II

of Australia: C 3939 N1957/75106 part 2]; Government publicity shot (1959) [Courtesy National Archives of Australia: A1200 L31940]; Training for bath time (1958) [Courtesy National Archives of Australia: A1200 L25659]; Haebich family outside the Lutheran manse, Wollongong (1960s) [From author's private collection].

3. Promises

In the days ahead we are going to see many exciting places, talk with many unique people. There will be much discussion and instruction on the Question. The Problem. Let them die out. Assimilate them. Put them on reserves. Forget them. Wait. Keep out the do-gooders. And in all our comings and goings, reeling, all of us, with revelation of wonders, I will be haunted by that daily frieze impasted on banks and tourist agencies and galleries and gem shops and rock shops. Patient. Waiting. Moving, if at all, from one side of the street to the other. The women and girls squatting in ripply black silk circles around groomed trees in a groomed park. Looking on.

Charmian Clift, 1970[1]

During the 1950s and 1960s the federal government flooded Australia with images of Aboriginal and migrant families posed in the nation's suburban heartlands living the Australian way of life. Familiar scenes of Aboriginal desert hunters and overcrowded town camps now jostled with images of modern Aboriginal families showing dad, mum and the kids eating together around the kitchen table, relaxing in the lounge room, greeting white visitors and attending neighbourhood meetings. Migrant families were depicted blending into suburban life accompanied by stories and beaming pictures of those who were 'making it' in their adopted home.

These images were an integral part of the government's campaigns to promote the new White Australia to the nation and appease its critics overseas. They covered the dramatic changes impacting on Australia with a veneer of cultural uniformity and the promise of equality of opportunity and prosperity for all. The campaigns were the first concerted national effort by an Australian government to mould opinion in this area of public life. The messages and images were highly visible in the public domain and were refracted in the media, popular culture and social institutions such as schools. While it is not possible to gauge exactly how the campaigns influenced public ideas at the time, their prevalence in the public domain is certainly testimony to their *potential* to influence opinion significantly — the enduring power of the vision of an assimilated nation is evident in its continuing influence on popular debate to this day. My interest here is to identify the instruments of government that shaped the campaigns, how their messages were constructed and what sets of meaning they conveyed to their various audiences.

The campaigns were separate projects of nation building and there was little crossover between the areas of Aboriginal affairs and immigration, despite their common goals of promoting a White Australia. Federal government priorities were reflected in significant practical differences between the two. While neither campaign was adequate for the task, the Aboriginal campaign was a more limited low-key affair compared to the publicity resources, prestigious national events and high profile advisory committees and community organisations rolled out to promote migrant assimilation. Yet there were far greater challenges in dealing with the legacy of generations of entrenched racism and discrimination against Aboriginal people. The number of stakeholders who had to be consulted — none of them Aboriginal — and the political sensitivities involved bogged down planning and produced dull campaign materials that contrasted with the more appealing messages pumped out through the Department of Immigration's clear line of command.

The discourse of assimilation was carefully constructed around imagined narratives and outcomes designed to sell the vision of White Australia. This mirrored back to settler Australians their own dreams of a prosperous modern life encapsulated in the potent symbols of nationhood and markers of assimilation discussed earlier — the Australian way of life, the Australian family and life in the suburbs. The message was that migrant and Aboriginal people could be slotted into these same dream images with no disruption to the nation. This assumed that Aboriginal and migrant families also shared the dream and that they had the will and the wherewithal to achieve it. In this way they were locked into a new set of public 'expectations' concerning their capabilities, destinies and dreams. These expectations — 'dense economies of meaning, representation, and act'[2] — conjured up ideas of passive conforming individuals from homogeneous Aboriginal and migrant cultures who were all able and willing to become assimilated. Families who met these expectations were promised acceptance as equal citizens in a White Australia; there was no mention of those who might fail to conform.

Representations of Aboriginal people and European migrants participating as equal citizens in a White Australia were an unexpected interruption into Australia's visual landscape, yet they were comfortingly familiar and persuasive. In his study of representations of Native American assimilation in the United States Philip Deloria argues that they focused on the 'idea of assimilation' and overlooked the multitudes of complicating and often contradictory factors that impinge on the actual 'encounter'.[3] Similarly Catriona Moore and Stephen Muecke conclude that 'assimilationist formations' in Aboriginal films of the 1950s ignored the 'multiple contours' of Aboriginal experience and their considerations and concerns. They repeated cinematic forms and practices that reproduced racism in an uncritical way and reflected official discourses rather than the immediate concerns of Aboriginal people.[4] The result, concludes Emma Greenwood in her study of 1950s migrant promotional films, was a 'closed discourse, where hosts encountered a superficial and illusory image of their own society and national characteristics … In getting to know these foreigners the Australian public simply met a beguiling image of themselves.'[5]

Selling migrant assimilation

The idea of a national publicity campaign to promote immigration was first proposed by the Commonwealth Immigration Advisory Council (1947–1970) whose representatives from peak national bodies in industry, business, unions, service organisations and local government advised on matters relating to European immigration. They argued that by presenting a positive spin the government could entice settler Australians away from their isolationist attitudes to 'foreigners' and this in turn would prevent the development of migrant enclaves. The Council stated: 'They should be made welcome, not driven in upon themselves … and then blamed for creating little colonies of their own.'[6]

The campaign to sell assimilation pumped a bewildering array of new images and messages into the public arena as the government sought to reassure settler Australians that the new intake of European migrants would readily assimilate into the Australian way of life. They were encouraged to welcome them and share with them the nation's new prosperity. There would be no competition for jobs and housing, lowering of conditions or growth of migrant enclaves. Immigration was a boon for the nation that would provide urgently needed labour for post-war construction and development of heavy industry, manufacturing and mining. The rapid build-up of population would also assist national defence. The message was that life in Australia would continue to improve but, paradoxically, it would also remain the same.

Infrastructure

The task of promoting migrant assimilation had generous government support, clear policy direction, a single line of command and a target population that could be sold to the public as essential for national development and security. Results from opinion polls showed some popular support for the immigration program — as long as national standards of economic development, employment, and law and order were maintained, and the European migrants became assimilated and were not too visible. It seemed that Australia might indeed remain white and prosperous.

The newly created federal Department of Immigration (1946–1975) provided national leadership for the enterprise, with a strong political direction provided by ministers including Arthur Calwell and later Harold Holt, both prominent statesmen at the time. State and federal governments had previously conducted their own immigration programs, directed at attracting British migrants, and there had been no urgent need to sell the idea of British migration to settler Australians. The new department thus had few precedents to follow and instead had to overcome the legacy of negative war-time propaganda concerning German and Italian migrants. Nevertheless it was well placed and resourced to conduct a comprehensive campaign. From 1955 the Department had its own public relations unit and journalists and it had a good working relationship with government film and promotional staff built up in the late 1940s when Arthur Calwell held the portfolios of Immigration and Information.

The Department of Immigration directed a good deal of its resources to promotional activities, despite its many other practical responsibilities for new migrants. The Department published its own monthly magazine *Good Neighbour* with a distribution of 42,000 and also arranged public events and press photo opportunities, distributed stories promoting assimilation to the media and forwarded advertising and information material to audiences at home and overseas. As we will see the prestigious Australian Citizenship Conventions (1950–70) provided a major forum to demonstrate national support for immigration and assimilation and together with the Good Neighbour movement provided citizens with the opportunity to demonstrate the principles of assimilation through the example of their own good citizenship.

Persuading settler Australians

The campaign discourse constructed the imaginary world of the new White Australia as achievable and desirable and as the only way forward. Settler Australians were given images of what they *wanted* to see — a white, middle-class nation and grateful, hardworking migrant families who blended in and quickly shed their 'kaleidoscope of experiences, defying description'.[7] Migrants saw a hopeful destination to start their lives anew. Recurring themes and tropes appealed to Australian audiences with little critical understanding of the processes of change and all privileged settler values, agency and power and endorsed perceptions of what migrant assimilation entailed. There was the 'disappearing migrant' whose instant assimilation led directly to the 'invisible migrant' who was indistinguishable from other Australians in campaign imagery. Then there was the 'celluloid migrant' a stock figure in promotional films who stood for all imagined newcomers and who, denied any sense of self-determination or individualism, submitted passively to the process of assimilation.[8] Success stories of migrant transformation from alien to citizen were a favourite narrative, along with accounts of migrants enriching Australian society through their labour and their cultures, although this always remained in line with the dominant society's interests.

These devices were replicated in popular culture as Susan Sheridan demonstrates in her analysis of representations of migrants in the *Australian Women's Weekly* during the 1950s — Australia's most widely read women's magazine at the time. Sheridan argues that its migrant stories tell us more about Anglo-Celtic Australian women and domestic culture than the migrant people being written about. The *Weekly's* targeted reader was 'overwhelmingly white, heterosexual, Anglophone, and middle-class' and typically 'the young mother of a family, who does not work outside the home'.[9] For such a reader, representations of migrants and Aboriginal people provided the identifiable difference against which to measure ideals of 'the Australian woman and domestic culture to which the magazine was dedicated to sustain'.[10] In the process they endorsed popular perceptions that 'I am not like that, and I don't want to be'.[11] Sheridan observes that stories of migrant cultural enrichment were suggested by 'stylistic traces in food, design, cultural artefacts' and that what was notable was how Anglo-Celtic interests determined what was valued and taken up.[12] Migrants were also represented as victims, social problems and objects of charity like the deserving poor of Victorian England and from this grew expectations of migrant assimilation and gratitude.[13] Sheridan also points out that while migrant men were well represented in the pages of *Women's Weekly*, sometimes as prospective marriage partners, migrant women were largely invisible. They did not resemble the ideal woman reader and were more likely to be working married women — 32 per cent were in the workforce in 1961 compared to 15 per cent of Australian-born women.[14] This contrasted with campaign materials promoting Aboriginal assimilation where images of Aboriginal women in domestic settings dominated and the men were largely absent. This reflected the government's view of the role of Aboriginal women as the prime agents of assimilation, working in tandem with government to forge conventional Aboriginal homes and families.

Official publicity was a carefully stage-managed process of positive news stories and photo and newsreel opportunities. Advantage was taken of national celebrations such as the Commonwealth Jubilee Year in 1951 when the Jubilee Train criss-crossed Victoria and South Australia distributing 15,000 copies of the pamphlet *Why Migration is Vital to You.* Major national works projects provided visible evidence of migrants enriching the nation through their labour and the Snowy Mountain Scheme (1949–1974) in particular provided a wealth of photo opportunities to showcase the 5000 men from thirty different countries working harmoniously together in a landscape of gargantuan machinery. An example of a major event deliberately constructed to present the public's dream image of immigrants as young, healthy, attractive and British was the celebrated arrival in 1955 of Australia's millionth post-war migrant, an attractive young British housewife, Barbara Porritt, whose busy round of official appearances was avidly reported by *Good Neighbour* and the national media. Such a reassuring symbol of Australian immigration was not a matter of chance however, but had been choreographed from the beginning. The young woman had been carefully chosen by the Chief Migration Officer in London according to criteria drawn up by the department in Australia.[15]

Promotional narratives of migrant transformation and success (as judged by settler Australian standards) had the dual role of convincing the public of migrant commitment to the nation *and* of providing models of assimilation for new migrants. Although assimilation was the Department's core doctrine, its officers were nevertheless tentative about publicly providing a definitive definition when formally requested by the Australian Citizenship Conference, responding that to do so could generate resentment and resistance amongst migrants. This caution contrasted with the federal government's development of a national definition of Aboriginal assimilation that was widely publicised without any sympathy for Aboriginal people. Regarding migrants, officers adopted what they considered to be the less intrusive and 'indirect approach of publishing stories of successful social and economic adjustment'.[16] These stories were regular items in *Good Neighbour* and the popular press and the department's photograph archive contains thousands of images with short titles that encapsulate the move from migrant to assimilated Australian:

> Dutch novelist writes two books with Australian themes
> Greek artist and American wife, a sculptress, in Perth
> Professional singer (British) — she is also a welder
> Norwegian model in popular demand
> Migrant mother visits Baby Clinic
> Migrant helps in dangerous arrest
> Baroness (German) is glamorous beach and sports girl
> Migrant children visit shearing shed
> Dutch society disbands when all naturalised
> Book by migrant (British) 'How to win competitions'[17]

These narratives also appeared regularly in the popular press. Photo-essayist Jeff Carter's stories in popular magazines like *People* included accounts of migrants in rural Australia pitched to readers as Australian 'strugglers and battlers'. 'Million Dollar Valley' told the story of hard-working Italian families in the Ovens Valley who managed to purchase their own properties in the lucrative new industry of tobacco farming after labouring for other farmers for up to ten years.[18] The 1954 Cinesound newsreel, *Beauty Contest for New Aussies* depicted a story of much more rapid transformation. This showed 'beauties from lots of lands' competing for the title and crown of 'Miss Fair' as they changed from their folkloric costumes to bathing suits as if culture was little more than a suit of clothes to peel off. This sentiment was echoed by the male commentator who celebrated the fact that the female contestants were now 'fair dinkum Aussies'.[19]

Government films targeting Australian audiences presented accounts of 'celluloid migrants' in settings that highlighted Australian perspectives on immigration and assimilation.[20] *Mike and Stefani* (1952)[21] was a feature length film made on location in refugee camps in Germany that depicted the sufferings of a Ukrainian couple forced to work in Nazi labour camps during the war and their hopes for a new life in Australia. This film was unique at the time for showing Australian audiences the nightmares that many immigrants had experienced and for its aesthetic qualities that appeal to film buffs to this day. Europe was presented as crippled by the war and the couple as victims of this terror. Documentary footage showing the strict procedure followed in immigration interviews and medical examinations reassured Australian audiences that only suitable migrants could pass the rigid selection process. These realities of the refugee experience however, gradually gave way to the sentimental portrayal of the ideal migrant family in the final scene that showed Mike and Stefani on board the ship to Australia gazing forward to a future that was certain to be 'valuable, satisfying and trouble-free'.[22] Unfortunately, the film was withdrawn shortly after release because its negative depiction of Germany conflicted with Australia's new immigration program, concluded with Germany in 1952.[23] Considered in relation to the war-time propaganda film *Australia's Fifth Column*, the fate of *Mike and Stefani* is a telling lesson in how fickle rankings of European nationalities could be as preference shifted in accordance with broader national priorities.

The films *Double Trouble* (1951)[24] and *No Strangers Here* (1950)[25] resembled more closely the profile of blunt messages and dull visuals of government propaganda films. *Double Trouble* was a comedy that would have raised few laughs outside the culturally isolated world of 1950s Australia. Designed to encourage cultural tolerance, it was based on the clichéd, slapstick narrative of two Aussie innocents getting into trouble in a foreign country where they do not speak the language — learning the hard way that it is not easy being a foreigner in a strange land.

Inspired by the American film *The Cummington Story* (1945),[26] produced there in anticipation of the post-war influx of refugee families from Europe, *No Strangers Here* used actors from the Bonegilla and Bathurst migrant reception centres to depict the experiences of a refugee family in a typical Australian town, as seen through the eyes of the editor of the local newspaper. After receiving a letter from 'A true Australian' complaining about 'foreigners' the editor decided to find out about the New Australian family he had glimpsed in the street outside his office. In contrast to the film *Mike and Stefani*, there was no interest in the family's past. Instead the editor saw only the daily life of a family devoted to becoming assimilated at work, school and play and whose efforts to fit in were accepted by most of the townspeople. Although the film clearly showed where the burden of change lay, the editor's concluding remarks — the heart of the film's official message — attributed the family's success to the townspeople: 'These are ordinary people like ourselves ... you saw how a friendly helping hand helped them settle in all the faster ... the newcomer need never feel a stranger.' The disembodied narration and the absence of any migrant voices fed an impression of passive conformity. In this context the title of the film took on a more sinister meaning of a command to the migrant family: 'We will have no strangers here!'[27]

No Strangers Here was originally intended for commercial release and the producers assured the Department of Immigration that it would be a 'first rate film AND BETTER THAN its American model'. However, the managing director of the Hoyts Theatre chain rejected the option of screening it for paying patrons because it was too long and dull. In his opinion it was 'just a waste of money'.[28] Despite this assessment, the film was shown around the nation over the next three years at official functions and community events organised by the government, Good Neighbour Councils, shire councils, schools and church groups — spreading the impression of immigrants as dull, carbon copies of Australians and deserving of kindly charity.

Reaching migrants

A parallel vision of a young prosperous welcoming nation with sweeping claims of a new Promised Land was used to lure suitable migrants to Australia. In *Selling a Dream: Promoting Australia to Postwar Migrants,* an exhibition at the Australian Archives Gallery in Canberra in 1996, curator Rowena MacDonald shows how the invitation to 'Come to sunny Australia' spread out 'across Britain and Europe in many forms and many languages' with images of family life, the beach and boundless prosperity in posters at railway stations and on billboards, displays in shopfronts, magazines articles and pamphlets describing Australian life from 'the climate to the taxation system'.[29] In seeking to attract migrants Australia was competing with other countries, notably the United States and Canada, that were better known to Europeans and already had thriving ethnic communities and family links. For potential British immigrants Australia offered a wealth of familiar connections and perks but for Europeans it was an unknown destination. Though invitingly distant from the threat of nuclear war and communist invasion it was also far from family and home. Some had been told that Australia was a primitive and dangerous place — a 'wild, faraway country' populated by 'black head-hunters' one woman recalled.[30] These apprehensions were unintentionally reinforced when immigration officials visiting refugee camps screened *The Overlanders* (1946) starring Chips Rafferty, which showed a team of bushmen droving a herd of cattle across northern Australia through inhospitable rugged country and crocodile infested rivers to get the herd beyond the reach of Japanese invaders.[31]

Despite the increasing ratio of European migrants, the campaign materials were primarily in English and pitched largely at British audiences with their depictions of an essentially Anglo-Celtic world.[32] Immigration officers showed the film, *The Way We Live* (1959) at information evenings in Britain, to promote Australia as a 'paradise on earth, a land of beaches, barbecues and big houses — affordable for all'. Audiences were told that 'anyone willing to work and to accept a new — and we believe, better — way of life, can be happy here'.[33] Migrant women might have imagined themselves in the jaunty description of 'Mrs Australia' in *Looking at Australia* as a woman who 'manages the home, controls the family budget, looks after the children, does all her own housework including the washing and ironing, finds time for social and community activities and often plays tennis or golf or some other sport'.[34] Anecdotal evidence however suggests that migrant women found the *Women's Weekly*'s displays of the 'compendium of symbols and preoccupations deemed to be quintessentially Australian' of more practical use in learning about gender roles in Australian society.[35]

The cover of the pamphlet *Australia and Your Future*[36] showed a migrant family nestled inside a map of Australia superimposed over an aerial shot of neat suburban blocks. Inside was the invitation, 'Australia wants you … In this booklet Australia states its case simply and without exaggeration, the good and the not so good, so you can decide for yourself. It's your future.'[37] The pamphlet promised 'jobs for all'[38] with 200,000 workers needed in manufacturing, service industries, commerce, construction, mining, heavy industry and rural work. British readers were reassured by a quote from Arthur Calwell that in Australia 'the sun always shines on the institutions of British democracy',[39] like the Empire on which the sun never sets. The pamphlet continued that the 'first Australians' brought with them 'Anglo-Saxon traditions, ways of life and culture. These their descendants have moulded to their environment and needs. A congenial climate and wide-open spaces have bred a vigorous, out-door, freedom-loving race of people.'[40]

Meanwhile in other pamphlets the true 'first Australians' were mentioned only occasionally as an exotic remnant of the past, the 'oldest living specimen of man — relics of Stone Age people'.[41] In explaining Australian life, possible criticism of the restrictive immigration policies was addressed by the oft-repeated explanation they were not race-based and White Australia was merely a colloquialism. Like any other nation, Australia maintained the right to control who crossed its borders. The pamphlet *The Australian People* gave the impression of a nation of tolerant citizens who were 'notably easy ... to get along with. The usual Australian will treat anyone as an equal, if his own friendliness and frankness are reciprocated.' The impression was of simple childlike people who were 'fond of sunshine and open air life. [They] throng to their beaches and make excursions into the countryside during holidays and weekends.'[42]

These self-congratulatory descriptions reassured European migrants seeking a safe home after the atrocities of the war but for many their reception in Australia was far less welcoming. Historian John Murphy describes a debilitating 'heartless, blank indifference' reflecting Australians' preoccupation with their own commitments rather than 'public-spirited forms of civility', although there were some who welcomed the opportunity provided by the Good Neighbour movement to offer well meant but often patronising assistance to the newcomers. The image of good neighbourliness promoted in campaign materials also contrasts with reports of alarming outbursts of xenophobic hostility with violent attacks — 'street brawls and knife fights' — instigated by gangs of youth in working class suburbs where fears of migrants competing for work were greatest.[43] In William Dick's *A Bunch of Ratbags*, a novel about growing up in post-war working-class Melbourne, the narrator describes how his bodgie gang roamed the streets of Footscray 'looking for some dagoes to do over. Frequently we staged bloodthirsty battles ... doing over eight or so foreigners ... Often we would read about the bodgies in other suburbs fighting with the foreigners, who, my old man said, were trying to take over our bloody country. "We won't have a bloody country if they keep bringing them out. We'll all be a mongrel-bred race," he would say.'[44]

Ethnically motivated youth violence and expressions of xenophobic hostility are still familiar today. This was the lead-up to the Cronulla riots in 2005 when thousands of young people in Sydney — categorised in the often vitriolic media and talk-back radio coverage as 'Australian youth' and 'Middle Eastern outsiders' — clashed at the beach-front Sydney suburb prompting an unprecedented police lock-down of beaches from Wollongong in the south to Newcastle in the north.

Performing good citizenship

In addition to films and pamphlets there were also 'performances' — public staged events where citizens and immigrants could demonstrate support for immigration and assimilation in joint celebrations of Australian citizenship. For the government, citizenship education was an essential step to the final stage of assimilation — naturalisation as an Australian citizen. Citizenship was promoted through publicity shots and newsreel films of naturalisation ceremonies and leaflets promoting its benefits and, for migrants from Europe, informing them of the special qualifying conditions for naturalisation of migrant aliens. The government even overcame its resistance to the public use of non-English languages by advertising in the fledgling migrant press — unselfconsciously called 'the foreign-language press' at the time.[45] Speaking of the government's attitude, a former editor of a Lithuanian community newspaper recalled that in the early 1950s he was obliged by law to print one third of the paper in English. He recalled his opposition to this since 'the paper was not for teaching but for communication — news, things migrants needed to be informed of. If it was in English, nothing could be learnt.'[46] Settler Australians were also drawn into the process of migrant naturalisation and in 1953 the department distributed 50,000 copies of the pamphlet *This is How You Can Help Someone to Become an Australian Citizen.*

Naturalisation ceremonies were built up into significant public performances from the mid-1940s. Under Calwell's ministry the pomp and solemnity of this final rite of assimilation steadily increased, in the manner of similar celebrations in the United States, in order to 'impress upon the new citizen the rights and obligations of Australian citizenship, make the person feel as though he had done something significant for himself and Australia, and inform the community that the person was no longer an alien'.[47] The accoutrements of empire and nation were included with the Australian flag, Union Jack and photograph of the Queen on display. New citizens were obliged to repeat the following oath or affirmation of allegiance: '[I] swear by Almighty God that I will be faithful and bear true allegiance to His Majesty King George the Sixth [Queen Elizabeth from 1954], his [her] heirs and successors according to law and that I will faithfully observe the laws of Australia and fulfil my duties as an Australian citizen.'[48] In the early 1950s the official venue for ceremonies was changed from the local courthouse to council offices with a view to attracting greater media attention. Along with their certificates of citizenship, new citizens were presented with commemorative booklets containing information about Australia's history, national character and political system.

Despite government efforts, the number of migrants taking up citizenship remained low — in 1957 only 35 per cent of eligible migrants had been naturalised.[49] And while a total of 300,000 aliens (non-British migrants) were naturalised between 1946 and 1962 there were still 186,000 eligible adults and 47,000 children who had not been naturalised in 1962.[50] Ann-Mari Jordens points out that it was not ignorance or the want of pomp and ceremony that determined migrants' decisions about citizenship but the careful 'calculation of costs and benefits' of home versus Australia. There was also the differential path to citizenship, which advantaged British immigrants while Europeans had to 'earn' the same rights over a five-year period.[51]

Prominent members of the community were invited to link with government with the intention of making migrant assimilation a truly participatory effort. The Immigration Planning Council (1949–1975) and the Immigration Advisory Council (1945–70) — both made up of representatives from peak national bodies of industry, business, unions, service organisations and local government — together with the prestigious Australian Citizenship Conventions (1950–70) and the Good Neighbour Council (1950–1978), provided the link between government, key stakeholders and community organisations. This arrangement represented an important exercise in participatory democracy and citizenship that also provided citizens with an outlet to lend 'a helping hand.' The Good Neighbour Council was established in 1950 and developed into a national network of organisations promoting the goals of assimilation and demonstrating good citizenship at the local level through celebratory events and programs of assistance to local migrant families.

Established and emerging European migrant organisations like the Italo-Australian Club were largely excluded from these processes. Official wisdom held that they obstructed the goals of assimilation. As Jean Martin points out, to recognise migrant cultural differences in this way ran counter to the government's insistence on rapid change.[52] At official events, migrant organisations were typically represented by the churches (Catholic, Greek Orthodox, Lutheran and so on) or by Anglo-Celtic settler organisations. Following a request from representatives of Greek ex-servicemen to attend the Australian Citizenship conventions, Arthur Calwell advised that he 'did not think it would be wise to send them or any other national group an invitation at this time. They can come into the picture later.' Instead the servicemen would be represented by the President of the Returned Soldiers, Sailors and Airmen's Imperial League of Australia.[53] Left to their own devices the organisations built up community networks through business and social events and maintained their cultures and, where possible, upheld links with their home countries. Meanwhile, with the government and its chosen representatives at the helm, the immigration program inevitably presented a public image of migration and assimilation that fitted the dominant vision of a White Nation.

The annual prestigious Australian Citizenship Conventions (held between 1950 and 1970) were the centre-point of the government's national celebrations of assimilation and citizenship. Up to four hundred key leaders attended the conventions, representing government, business, trade unions, academia, community and voluntary organisations, the churches, armed service organisations and the media. This prestigious gathering was intended to send out a clear message to the public of the level of consensus on immigration, assimilation and Australian citizenship. The conventions also demonstrated democratic citizenship in action by establishing a two-way discussion between government and the community and provided a major site for the government to educate Australians about citizenship issues. They had practical outcomes as well: in 1954 the Minister for Immigration Harold Holt stated that out of the hundreds of Convention resolutions passed, 80 per cent had been acted on by the Department.[54] Migrant organisations were not officially represented in the Conventions until the final meeting in 1970 and migrant attendance at meetings remained low, increasing from 8 per cent in 1953 to 15 per cent in 1965. Not surprisingly then the conventions became a national forum for discussing issues of concern for the interest groups who were represented there. Prime Minister Menzies set the tone at the opening ceremony in Canberra on Australia Day in 1950 when he proclaimed that 'a man, woman or child who comes here to settle is either not accepted and is therefore not admitted, or he or she becomes an Australian — a member of this community, a member of our nationality, a member of our brotherhood, and in the best sense of the word, a member of our family'.[55]

A recurring message delivered by the government was the continuing need for migrant labour to maintain the nation's economic growth and defence capabilities. Migration was represented as a major national investment by Immigration Minister Athol Townley, who told the 1957 Convention that 'people are capital — the most valuable type of capital any country can have' and that the skills and knowledge in each annual migrant intake represented a 'significant monetary saving' of £500,000 in schooling and job training.[56] Geographer Charles A. Price calculated that while it cost the government £100 to bring each migrant to Australia, the expense was more than offset by the trebling of the national income.[57] Early conventions endorsed assimilation as 'core doctrine'[58] and delegates agreed that this meant adopting the Australian way of life, although there was some confusion over exactly what this entailed. The 1953 meeting insisted that migrants show loyalty to the Queen during the much-anticipated royal visit. In 1955 a delegate proclaimed that the nation's origins were 'threefold: British, Christian and democratic' and the convention resolved to draw up a 'charter of Australia citizenship' although this never eventuated.[59] In 1960 an employer claimed that the work place was an important site for assimilation where migrants learned to speak English, socialised with other groups and could freely contribute their ideas.[60]

Once the conventions' ponderous performance of participatory democracy had closed for the day, migrant groups were invited to stage their cultural performances — a clear sign of their peripheral place in proceedings. Over the years these performances shifted from celebrations of Australia's British heritage and individual events of folkloric dancing and displays of ethnic arts and crafts to grand expressions of Australia's national history and identity. 'Pageants of nations' became a popular theme. These were modelled on American Independence Day celebrations of the many cultures that made up the American nation that were introduced earlier in the century to provide new immigrants with meaningful lessons in citizenship, patriotism and civic and community pride.[61] In 1957 migrants in folkloric costume from twenty nations danced before a *tableau vivant* of Old and New Australians who were flanked by flags of the world left over from the 1956 Olympic Games.[62] For the Convention's 1961 tableau *We the People*, immigrants were woven into a narrative of the nation, which progressed by stages from the first settlers to the gold rushes, Federation, the two world wars, pioneers of aviation, sport stars, and finally migrant contributions to Australian development. Aboriginal people were not mentioned at all.[63]

Selling Aboriginal assimilation

Selling the vision of Aboriginal assimilation was a far greater challenge, given the endemic levels of racism against Aboriginal people found in all walks of Australian life. Woven into practices of government, law, administration, services, welfare and employment, racism penetrated into the most intimate areas of Aboriginal family life and was expressed in the minutiae of a multitude of behaviours that segregated black and white. There was also ignorance and the myriad stereotypes that shaped settler Australians' perceptions of Aboriginal people and their capacity to become assimilated. In promoting migrant assimilation the government could appeal to concerns over economic development and anxieties about national security. Also, migrants fleeing Europe for a better life in Australia were presumed to be open to change in adjusting to their new country. However, for most settler Australians the business of assimilating Aboriginal people to meet international human rights standards held little intrinsic value, while Aboriginal people had to be convinced that this new life was achievable and to their benefit. Once again the government turned to the powerful symbols of the Australian way of life, the Australian family and the Australian suburbs to persuade the nation.

Campaign planning

The campaign took shape in 1955 around a proposal by the Department of Territories to publish pamphlets presenting the official view of assimilation for the inaugural National Aborigines Day, approved by the Minister (Sir) Paul Hasluck that year after discussions with the National Missionary Council of Australia.[64] Aboriginal delegate Pastor Doug Nichols had envisaged a day of commemoration to highlight the plight of Aboriginal people and reach the conscience of the Australian public.[65] The department, however, saw the event as an opportunity to celebrate assimilation, focusing on 'the positive being done, not on poor conditions which prompt overseas criticism'.[66] In any event, there was little support for the campaign proposal from senior politicians. Prime Minister Menzies had launched the Australian Citizenship Conventions, but he did not officially endorse this campaign and it would be another six years before the Native Welfare Council of federal and state ministers, alarmed at increasing international criticism, finally gave their formal stamp of approval.

The campaign process was strictly controlled, reflecting extreme government sensitivities over the representation of Aboriginal issues. In 1946, during filming of *Namatjira the Painter* (1947),[67] the Director of the Department of Information, E. G. Bonney, backed by the Native Affairs Branch Director in the Northern Territory, Ernest Chinnery, insisted on his right to delete anything in the script that was not consistent with government policy and to refuse to release funds until the script had been vetted, since 'high national policy is involved … in so delicate a topic as the Australian Aborigines'.[68] In practice this level of control was tempered during the 1950s by the need for interdepartmental diplomacy, while the growing public and commercial interest in the Northern Territory was reflected in increasing requests for permission to film in the area.

In contrast to the migrant publicity campaign there was no well-resourced central federal department to provide a direct line of command, only an office in the Department of Territories and advisors in the new Welfare Branch in Darwin. This absence could be explained as due to the division of federal/state responsibilities for Aboriginal affairs — a convenient excuse frequently used by the federal government to reject requests for state funding. However, this was a different matter, being a campaign directed at national and international audiences, not Aboriginal people. Planning was complicated by an obligation to consult with a range of key federal and state stakeholders — though not Aboriginal leaders. As with the campaign for migrant assimilation, matters remained in the hands of white middle-class men with little informed knowledge or direct experience of the subject, working from preconceived notions and stereotypes. They had no positive precedents to follow, only decades of governments endorsing public demands for ever-greater segregation and control.

A further complication for planners was that the same package of campaign materials was intended for two distinct target audiences: settler Australians who had to be persuaded to accept assimilation and overseas critics who were to be convinced that the process of granting equal rights through assimilation was underway. What was acceptable at home did not always pass muster with audiences overseas who in some cases used the material to bolster their attack on Australia's treatment of Aboriginal people.

In a further contrast to the migrant assimilation campaign the federal government prepared no materials for Aboriginal audiences, except in the case of the Northern Territory. Materials produced by the states such as the magazine *Dawn* (1952–1975) published by the New South Wales Aborigines Welfare Board, provided didactic, patronising information and training materials, with instruction in the practicalities of hygiene, home management and housekeeping. They were a far cry from the materials created to entice migrants to take up the Australian way of life and their clear explanations of the benefits and rights of citizenship.

In Canberra there were three important federal departments to be consulted. The Department of Territories coordinated the process, guided by Hasluck and senior officers in its Northern Territory Welfare Branch. Government reforms there provided the benchmark for representing the goals and achievements of assimilation. The Department of the Interior had a vital role to play in producing materials through ANIB and the Commonwealth Film Unit but their combined experience in representing Aboriginal people consisted of publications that repeated popular stereotypes of Aborigines as 'stone-age men' and a handful of films reflecting conventional views of traditional life.[69] The exception was the assimilation success story in the film *Namatjira the Painter*, which presented the artist's life from his early days growing up at Hermannsburg Lutheran Mission in Central Australia to his acclaim as Australia's leading Aboriginal watercolourist painter. The Department of External Affairs was involved to ensure that materials presented a favourable perspective on Aboriginal issues for the sensitive international arena. At the time it was made up of 'a formidable array of men of high calibre' and held considerable status in the Canberra bureaucracy.[70] Its officers had strong opinions on what they considered appropriate information and their recommendations were usually heeded.

In 1956 Department of External Affairs complaints led to the dumping of manuscripts by two respected commentators, Ernest Chinnery and West Australian author Tom Hungerford. Chinnery's account was rejected because it provided an historical perspective that 'certain foreign powers' could use to 'denigrate' what they saw as Australia's 'neglect of its aboriginal peoples'.[71] The language used by Hungerford was considered inflammatory. This was not so much because of his claim that 'the problem of the Australian government in its dealing with the aborigines is that of integrating in this atomic age a left-over fragment of pre-history', but rather because he raised official hackles with the admission 'that it must at the same time correct the ghastly mistakes and heal the wounds inflicted by earlier administrations … which if left untended would in a short time have brought about the complete annihilation of this ancient, intelligent, gentle, humorous and unique people'.[72]

State governments also had to be included because of their jurisdiction over local Aboriginal populations and the strategic importance of committing them to reform. State representatives attending the Native Welfare Council meetings organised by the federal government in the early 1960s showed a pragmatic interest in using the campaign to combat the 'misrepresentation and misunderstanding' promoted by communists and leaders of new states in Africa and Asia.[73] Their prejudices were further exposed when they opposed the inclusion of journalists from these states in a proposed press tour of Aboriginal camps in 1963 since they could not 'be relied upon to present a proper perspective'. Finally the Minister Sir Paul Hasluck, himself a former journalist, rejected the proposal, calling it a 'junket' and a 'waste of money. All our experience with journalists on such tours is that they drink the grog and write nothing.'[74] A report to the Native Welfare Council in 1961 on public interest in Aboriginal issues demonstrated how prejudiced opinions remained acceptable at the highest levels of government and raised serious questions about its authors' understanding of the policy of assimilation. The report began by slamming journalists for allegedly reporting only stories of 'murders by aborigines, bodily harm inflicted by aborigines on their wives, and larceny'. When they did address other matters, the report claimed, they failed to distinguish the special situation of the 'more primitive aborigine' who 'in his wurlie is far happier and more contented than if he was forced to live in a modern house' — a statement that was totally out of step with assimilation policy. The report went on to claim that the churches could be of 'the greatest benefit to the Government in forwarding the policy of assimilation provided that they [were] not allowed to get out of hand' and rush ahead 'in indecent haste ... it is felt that the slowness of natural evolution is preferable'. On the other hand, members of Aboriginal support organisations were of little use since they offered only extreme solutions that overlooked the complexities of the 'aboriginal question' and 'the aboriginal mind and intelligence'. Aboriginal leaders were not even mentioned.[75]

Community input to the campaign was limited to the National Aborigines Day Observance Committee, which consisted at the time of a small number of white church dignitaries.[76] Requests from Western Australia to build up a broader national network along the lines of the Good Neighbour Council were rejected by the federal government on the grounds that the state should pay since Aboriginal affairs was a state responsibility.[77] The Committee's role in promoting the message of assimilation involved commenting on campaign materials, assisting with their distribution and organising National Aborigines Day events. Its main contribution was to draw up extensive lists of organisations to receive campaign materials. These included government, church, educational, community, business and international interests and their sheer number suggests the wide-ranging influence of the campaign. The Committee also worked with local churches and volunteer groups to organise National Aborigines Day events highlighting assimilation, which included church services, public lectures by politicians and anthropologists, screenings of campaign films, and Aboriginal concerts, art exhibitions and sports days, all covered by the local media.

Campaign materials

The focus of this campaign was a series of pamphlets, some with accompanying films: *Our Aborigines* (1957), *The Assimilation of Our Aborigines* (1958) and the film *End of the Walkabout* (1958); *Fringe Dwellers* (1959) and the film *Fringe Dwellers Parts I and II* (1959); *The Skills of Our Aborigines* (1960), *One People* (1961), *Our Aborigines* (revised edition 1962), *Aborigines and You* (1963), the film *The Aborigines of Australia* (1964) and *Aborigines in the Community* (1965). The pamphlets were considered essential authoritative reading for audiences in Australia and overseas, to be read as a series 'in conjunction', together with recommended anthropological texts such as A. P. Elkin's *The Australian Aborigines* (1938), Charles Mountford's *Brown Men and Red Sand* (1952) and Fred McCarthy's *Australia's Aborigines: Their Life and Culture* (1957). The pamphlets reached around the continent and the world: 80,000 copies of *Our Aborigines* were distributed between 1957 and 1959 and over 150,000 copies of an edited version were printed and sent out between 1961 and 1963.[78] In 1964 some 700,000 copies of a two-page information sheet based on *Our Aborigines* were distributed.[79]

Aimed at a broad readership, the pamphlets presented an optimistic narrative of assimilation that began with an account of traditional Aboriginal life in the past, then moved to the beneficial influence of post-contact government policy and legislation, and concluded with images of Aboriginal suburban citizens and families participating in a modern new Australia. In contrast with migrant campaign materials — where the new arrivals appeared out of nowhere and then disappeared into the images of Australian life — here an official account of the past had to be outlined, especially for overseas audiences, to contextualise official explanations of present-day Aboriginal conditions and to highlight the humanitarian intentions of extending equal rights and conditions to Aboriginal people.

The pamphlets were serious, didactic and dull. Despite

UNESCO claims that new knowledge could change minds and behaviour it is hard to imagine these pamphlets having the power to convert and transform. Still they did present official explanations of Aboriginal conditions and plans for their assimilated future to the public and encouraged their active involvement in achieving this goal. In this way the pamphlets may have contributed to creating opinion favourable to the less controversial goals of Aboriginal activism such as the 1967 Referendum for constitutional change. Compared to the flamboyant representations of Aboriginal 'Stone Age' ceremonies and appalling fringe camps in the popular magazines *Australasian Post* and *Pix* — the black and white layout appeared drab and old-fashioned. These were the extremes of Aboriginal representation at the time — pragmatic government depictions of a problem population and wild imaginings of the primitive and exotic. Still, even these representations could be cumulative in their messages so that images of Aboriginal primitiveness in the pages of *Pix* and of modern Aboriginal families in the government pamphlets, considered together, could reinforce official explanations of the need for special measures for Aboriginal assimilation.

Despite the government's stated objective of eradicating racism through assimilation the pamphlets were replete with the language and classifications of biological race theory. Rather than undermining racism this public exposure in a high-profile government campaign had the effect of giving popular race myths and stereotypes a new authenticity and respectability. Of course, given the central role of race in administering Aboriginal people, it was impossible to explain the past or the present without recourse to its terminology. In the case of the 1961 federal definition of Aboriginal assimilation, as Tim Rowse observes, 'the sense of the whole passage depended on the use of the language of "race" and without the differentiating terms Aborigines and "part-Aborigines", the statement is a tautology'.[80] In a settler society like Australia race was a core defining doctrine and organising principle and it inevitably shaped representations of Aboriginal people. Chris Barker points out, that 'representation is constitutive of race as cultural identity and is not a mirror or a distortion of it'.[81] In calling for a 'politics of representation' Stuart Hall argues that it is not enough to replace the old with new positive images as this campaign set out to do; what is required is a new imagery that 'promotes representations which themselves explore power relations and deconstruct the black-white binary'.[82] Such a shift required the injection of Aboriginal perspectives, which can be seen in the range of imagery constructed by contemporary Indigenous urban artists from the 1970s to the present.

As anthropologists and government were the experts on Aboriginal culture and assimilation it is not surprising to find their approaches reflected in the pamphlets. Anthropological paradigms, some long abandoned by the discipline, shaped the narrative of assimilation. The nineteenth century theory of social evolution framed the narrative of a path from primitive to civilised, the frequent references to Stone-Age man and the account of inevitable Aboriginal population decline into the early twentieth century. The dramatic demographic changes were described in *Our Aborigines* in Social Darwinian terms as the fate of Indigenous populations 'from the dawn of history' when 'invaded by people stronger and more numerous' than they. The 'inevitable clashes' that occurred were due not to ill will on either side or to the practices of land-taking and land-defending, but to 'ignorance', suggesting just how dangerous ignorance can be.[83] More recent agendas of cultural salvage and rescue were also represented, along with the inevitable focus on male Aboriginal traditional life from the writings of a male-dominated profession. Anthropological explanations of Aboriginal people as an earlier wave of migrants and of Aboriginal culture as 'pre-civilisation' sent out a message of Australia's right to sovereignty and nationhood: 'these then were the aborigines in their natural state:

few in numbers; racially apart from the rest of the world; nomads; naked hunters and food-gathers; houseless; artists in primitive forms; mystical; enclosed within firm and intricate social patterns; in a measure stone-age men who had nevertheless fitted themselves to survive where only the wild animals of the Australian bush and desert could survive besides themselves'.[84]

The historical section 'Where are they now?' in *Our Aborigines* was influenced by Elkin's model of cultural change that dominated explanations of the Aboriginal past at the time. In this narrative Aborigines' fate was shaped by their inability to adjust to the rapid changes occurring around them and their 'irresistible attraction' to white material culture. The pamphlet *One People* concluded that 'their philosophy of resignation served them well and they survived by moving to remoter parts or adapting themselves to a sort of parasitic survival on the fringes of settlements'.[85] In the context of these explanations readers could well imagine that replacing Aboriginal cultures with an assimilated Australia was a humanitarian act, however they could not be blamed for questioning whether Aboriginal people were capable of achieving this outcome.

The pamphlets were also structured by the language and organising principles of government report writing. Phrases like 'smooth the dying pillow' and 'promoting the welfare of the aborigines' reinforced the view of Aboriginal people as a social problem requiring government intervention. *Our Aborigines* was divided into conventional administrative sections on populations, policy, services and areas of need. In a concluding section, 'Some problems of administration', the new range of Aboriginal problems was reviewed — citizenship, the franchise, social service benefits, health, housing, education, employment and the future of government settlements and mission stations. Only passing reference was made to Aboriginal employment and only then to explain that present inequalities were because Aboriginal people lacked the necessary skills and that to force the matter would go against their best interests. This contrasted with the migrant pamphlets that welcomed the new labour force and their contribution to national development. Reflecting stereotyped views of Aboriginal people still repeated today, *One People* claimed that they could not be 'left entirely to their own resources' nor would a 'superfluity' of welfare benefit them. The objective was to help them to 'take their place in the modern world; and this is a world of effort, ambition and endeavour — a technological, material world very different from the aboriginal cultural background'.[86]

The images and layout presented a more direct visual account of the road to assimilation. As photographs they carried their own authority — what Anne McClintock refers to as the 'optics of truth'.[87] Arranged chronologically from Stone Age life to modern Aboriginal suburban family they provided a shorthand visual account of the more detailed story of assimilation embedded in the text. In a tribute to the narrative power of imagery, *Assimilation of our Aborigines* (1958) was simply a pouch of photographs with captions to be ordered according to the assimilation narrative. The images could be read as a modern version of an earlier pictorial transformation narrative, seen in the 'before and after' photographs of child rescue through conversion and redemption found in nineteenth-century missionary tracts.[88] For example, the inside cover of *Our Aborigines* (1962) depicted the past as a traditional elder, his eyes downcast and resigned to the approaching end, followed by images of the transformed present and future — Aboriginal children at school, an Aboriginal nurse and field officer and finally a smartly dressed Aboriginal man teaching a classroom of white pupils.

With few identifying details of names or places to distinguish them, the photographs constituted 'a discursive terra nullius' onto which the editors mapped their own messages of assimilation.[89] An original photograph showing Aboriginal people at the remote Hooker Creek government settlement (now Lajamanu), southwest of Katherine in the Northern Territory,[90] was deliberately cropped to transform the scene into the menacing cover of *Fringe Dwellers*, where three vulnerable girls appeared alone in an empty, threatening space. In other instances photographs taken by ANIB staff in institutions in the Northern Territory were used dishonestly to depict images of happy family life. For example, the photograph used in *Fringe Dwellers* of a young woman bathing a child was taken at Retta Dixon Home in Darwin. The effect was to suggest that families were already well on the way to making the transition to assimilation, when because of government delays many remained trapped in fringe camps. This left families open to public censure for appearing to have failed to assimilate.

There was little that Aboriginal people could have done to prevent their photographs being taken and used in this way, and the relaxed images from Retta Dixon Home suggest a willingness on the part of some to sit for the photographs, but they may not have been aware of the ultimate use of the images and the implications to be drawn from their involvement. Writing on the presence of Native Americans in similarly compromised images, Philip Deloria warns against the 'general expectation' that sitters were 'fearful of cameras, duped or coerced' and that they 'failed to understand or think critically about the uses of their images'. In explaining why they may have agreed to be represented he writes, 'some motives, of course, are unknowable. Others cluster together in identifiable clumps: escape; adventure; economic need; cultural celebration; educational outreach.'[91]

Spreading the message

The pamphlets and their explanations of Aboriginal conditions were widely used to promote assimilation through good citizenship and understanding and in this way to discourage racism in the community. Distributed annually to coincide with National Aborigines Day celebrations and dispatched on request throughout the year, they were studied in school history and social studies courses, quoted in sermons and Sunday School lessons and even handed out as in-flight reading on the former Trans-Australian Airlines. They were also displayed for public use in the University of Queensland library collection, in the 'aborigine room' at Glenray Technical College in Victoria, and at Bingara in New South Wales the local newsagent put twenty-five copies in his shop window. The NSW Department of Railways bus tour to Taree distributed copies to passengers who later attended an Aboriginal corroboree. In Sydney the Kogarah Presbyterian Church used the pamphlets as part of a special studies course for teenagers to explore the churches' role in Aboriginal assimilation, along with an ambitious display of photos, leaflets, art works, artefacts and school books from Ernabella Mission and screenings of slides and films including *Men of the Mulgas*, *Children of the Musgraves*, *Namatjira the Painter* and *End of the Walkabout*.[92]

Essays written by senior students at Ulverstone High School in Tasmania in 1959 based on their study of the pamphlets confirmed concerns expressed by the Department of External Affairs about spreading the wrong impression. The message of assimilation was overlooked in favour of recording the new facts they had gleaned from the pamphlets: that there were no Aboriginal people in Tasmania, that Aboriginal people were the original owners of the continent, that they were primitive, that white settlement had driven them into remote arid lands or town fringe camps, that they lived in terrible conditions, suffered from poor health and died early and that their situation was worse than that of black people in the United States, Britain and Africa, despite Australia being a rich country and signatory to the United Nations Declaration of Human Rights.[93]

Mixed messages

The pamphlets beamed back to settler Australians a 'beguiling' image of themselves living harmoniously with Aboriginal people in an assimilated White Australia. Expressed in the familiar language and paradigms of race and stripped of the 'multiple contours' of Aboriginal encounters with assimilation, this represented a reassuring and comforting vision of the future. However, at the same time stereotyped views of Aboriginal people as primitive and incapable of change challenged this optimistic view of Aboriginal assimilation and set up a tension that found expression in mixed messages about what could be achieved.

The pamphlets were a clear statement of commitment to a white Anglo-Celtic Australia — a statement of Australian nationhood and sovereignty expressed through images of Aboriginal people enfolded within the state as fully participating citizens. They also suggested just how far Australia had progressed in its short history from primitive world to modern nation. Even the accompanying maps showing Aboriginal reserves dotted across the continent sent out a message of the nation's claim to greater rights of ownership of the land. Posed images of Aboriginal families in suburban settings emphasised the superiority of settler culture and triggered the feelings of security and stability deliberately evoked in political campaigns through images of the family to 'make those challenged by social change feel relaxed and comfortable'.[94] The message was that Aboriginal people would join the working class and adopt the gendered divisions of women's domestic duties and men's paid work that structured the suburban nuclear family.

Assimilation was presented as a seamless and inevitable process of cultural and social absorption of Aboriginal people into the nation. Like the immigration campaign this conveniently glossed over the many changes needed to develop an assimilated Australia. The pamphlet *The Assimilation of Our Aborigines* explained that 'in its simplest terms assimilation means that, to survive and prosper, the aborigines must live and work and think as white Australians do so that they can take their place in social, economic, and political equality with the rest of the Australian community'.[95] Aboriginal culture was depicted as a primitive relic and a spent force and Aboriginal people as clean slates ready to be assimilated. Hence the numerous images of Aboriginal people being taught by white people — a further contrast with migrants who apparently needed no such period of tuition despite their foreign origins.

As in the film *No Stranger Here*, assimilation's challenge for settler Australians was reduced to the simple gesture of offering a kindly 'helping hand'. This reinforced feelings of benevolent superiority and, as with the immigration campaign, suggested an outlet for readers' often-misguided humanitarianism. On the cover of the pamphlet *Aborigines and You* an Aboriginal man looked up to the reader for help and the text provided a list of 'What you can do': offer friendship and a helping hand; provide guidance in personal and social problems; assist with the children's education; help with employment and managing money; encourage a pride in their aboriginal ancestry; and encourage other Australians to make them feel welcome.[96] There was also a summary list of voluntary organisations working with Aboriginal people suggesting a high level of voluntarism but without the coordination and funding support provided by the government to the Good Neighbour Council. These bodies included international organisations (Lions International, Apex, Rotary, the Boy Scouts, The Save the Children Fund); national bodies (National Aborigines Day Observance Committee, Country Women's Association, YMCA, YWCA, National Missionary Council of Australia); state bodies (One People Australia League, Abschol, Aboriginal–Australian Fellowship); and finally the numerous groups who provided 'on the spot care' as required.[97] Steve Mickler has argued that drawing settler Australians and Aboriginal people into the domain of Aboriginal affairs in this way was a factor in the loss of state control over public information about Aboriginal issues that began during the 1960s. A consequence was that media representation became increasingly critical of the government and the policy of assimilation.[98]

Paradoxically the discourse of Aboriginal assimilation inevitably drew public attention to the seemingly indelible markers of Aboriginal cultural and physical difference and raised the possibility that Aboriginal people might never be assimilated and would always remain racially and culturally distinct from other Australians. Philip Deloria raises the question in relation to representations of assimilated Native Americans: 'were "civilized" Indians really civilized or just playing the part? Were they truly modern? In other words, could you trust that Indian people were truly malleable — and thus, ripe, for assimilation — when deep down you suspected that they would always remain racially different?'[99] A section in the pamphlet *One People* titled 'Some successful Aborigines', possibly inspired by the migrant success stories in the newspaper *Good Neighbour*, demonstrated this paradox.[100]

In the rest of the series Aboriginal people were unnamed and represented 'generic' stages on the path of assimilation, while here the individuality of these people was acknowledged. They were named and represented as active successful leaders and included Harry Penrith, sportsman and public servant; singers Jimmy Little and Harold Blair; Harry Huddleston who represented his fellow workers at the opening of the Warragamba Dam in New South Wales in 1960; Captain Reg Saunders and Timothy Hughes, both soldiers who saw active overseas service during the war; Phillip Prosser, a serving army officer, and his wife, a trained nurse and missionary; and Charles Perkins, outstanding soccer player. Yet despite their success in assimilating they remained indelibly Aboriginal — the essential message of the story was that they had been able to succeed in spite of this impediment.

In contrast to the narratives of migrant assimilation these pamphlets contained frequent references to racially defined disabilities that necessitated continued government intervention in the lives of Aboriginal people and the need for ongoing training and supervision. Aboriginal people were designated as a problem population disadvantaged by race, culture and social circumstance, whose advance to successful assimilation was obstructed by problems of 'health, housing and education (vocational, cultural and moral)', as well as lack of hygiene, their nomadic existence, regressive culture and general apathetic and lax behaviour. In short 'Aboriginality' was a problem and welfare agencies and intervention were essential for their advancement.[101] Yet the pamphlets also claimed, quoting from the 1961 federal definition of assimilation and reflecting the intent of ILO Convention No. 107, that government interventions were only 'temporary measures not based on colour but intended to meet Aborigines' need for special care and assistance'.[102] Aboriginal people generally were represented as passive objects rather than subjects of history; they were anonymous problems, victims who did not initiate activity or endeavour to control their destiny. Even a recent increase in the Aboriginal population was attributed in *Aborigines and You* to 'the application of enlightened policies, scientific approaches, and increasing goodwill on the part of other Australians'.[103]

There were also mixed messages about family life. In *Aborigines and You* fringe-dwellers were described as people who 'float between two worlds — one which is gone and irrevocable and one which, for many, seems beyond their reach'.[104] The pamphlets showed Aboriginal people living as suburban nuclear families yet there were also hints of a different Aboriginal future. What was the future for Aboriginal men? They predominated in traditional settings depicting the past but were often absent from scenes of assimilation as if they were somehow peripheral. When they did appear they were often posed in subservient roles with white authority figures rather than as the head of the family. Women and children were the way forward: their images dominated the pamphlets, reflecting their perceived central role in the process of assimilation. The women were represented as young wives and mothers responding enthusiastically to training in domestic duties and as single girls employed in women's work such as nursing. Historian Anna Cole observes that this imagery reflected a more general interest at the time in reforming and monitoring young women to become 'standard bearers' for modernist innovations in the home.[105] However, as estimates of Aboriginal child removals demonstrate, the targeting of young women as the bearers of assimilation had a long history in Aboriginal affairs.[106]

The proliferation of images of children and white authority figures suggested ongoing commitment to Aboriginal assimilation through the removal of children from their families, despite official promises to maintain intact nuclear families. In *Fringe Dwellers* two-thirds of the images were of children, with captions that underscored their significance to the goals of assimilation: 'The programme of assimilation throughout Australia concentrates particularly on children. For many of them, and in due course their children, hopes of assimilation are high.'[107] The pamphlet finished with two images of Aboriginal girls — one in a dug-out hole in the ground holding a rabbit, with all the stereotyped associations of dirt and disorder and of the rabbit and girl as vermin to be removed from the rural landscape, and the other a happy, clean girl who is taking a shower. This, the pamphlet suggested, was the choice that Aboriginal parents had to make for their children.

Continuing criticisms overseas

The campaign pamphlets may have been useful in informing settler Australians, but they failed to meet standards for overseas audiences. Officers from the Department of External Affairs objected that *One People* was 'thoroughly unsuitable for overseas readers', being riddled with inaccuracies, contradictions, stereotypes, negative impressions and poor editing and failing to answer questions raised overseas concerning Aboriginal legal and political rights.[108] They also expressed their frustrations in representing assimilation positively and defending it against growing accusations of indifference to minority rights.[109]

In 1961, following a recommendation from the Native

Welfare Council, work began on a revised edition of *Our Aborigines*, considered by many government officers to be the most comprehensive and useful of the pamphlets. Despite the many inadequacies identified by External Affairs and the escalating international race tensions at the time, the editors seemed to be oblivious to the pamphlet's intrinsic racism and their revisions were largely cosmetic: reports on the states and territories were updated, the map of reserve lands was corrected, population estimates were increased from 74,214 in 1957 to 100,000 in 1962, and terminology was standardised to replace 'full blood', 'half blood' and 'whites' with 'Aborigines', 'part Aborigines' and 'other Australians'. The section on Aboriginal citizenship, much criticised for its lack of clarity, added the woolly and misleading explanation that 'Australian Aborigines are Australian citizens by virtue of the Nationality and Citizenship Act 1948–1960' and that the special legislation under which they lived 'in no sense' derogated from their 'citizenship in the sense of their status as Australian citizens'.[110] The pamphlet failed to explain that the legal status of Australian citizen had no specific rights attached to it; nor did it explain the link with discriminatory laws controlling Aboriginal people. Images of suburban families and assimilation in action replaced those of traditional life and, in response to the controversy surrounding the death of famous Arrernte watercolour artist Albert Namatjira in 1959, the original final image showing him sitting with a little white girl was removed and replaced with the image of a young white teacher directing a classroom of Aboriginal students. The text was also edited to remove senseless content such as the caption 'On the way to assimilation, Aboriginal mission worker whose missing tooth is a sign that he is a fully initiated member of his tribe.'[111] Demand for *Our Aborigines* continued with over 500 copies distributed each week and before the year was out a second printing of 15,000 was ordered. Complaints from External Affairs also continued, and included comments from the Australian Ambassador to Mexico that the pamphlet produced 'unfortunate impressions' of race relations in Australia and that given current international sensitivities it did not do well to expose the depth of racism in this way.[112]

These concerns prompted the Department of External Affairs to branch out on its own in promoting Aboriginal advancement overseas. In 1964 it published the pamphlet, *The Australian Aborigines*, which concluded that 'even assuming that resources, goodwill and enthusiasm were unlimited, [assimilation] would inevitably be slow and difficult'. Responding to criticisms that assimilation was a form of 'cultural liquidation' the pamphlet claimed that minorities everywhere were disadvantaged in this way and added that assimilation did not necessarily mean the loss of Aboriginal identity, pride and culture.[113] The department was also considering a program of Aboriginal art exhibitions overseas to promote a positive image of Australia, inspired by the success of curator Dorothy Bennett's Aboriginal art exhibition in Tokyo in 1965,[114] and the success of two Qantas art documentaries directed and scripted by Geoffrey and Dahl Collings. *The Dreaming* (1964),[115] which examined Arnhem Land rock paintings and their links to the Dreaming, received an award at the 1964 Venice Biennale Festival for Films on Art. *Pattern of Life* (1964)[116] showed Aboriginal bark paintings with music performed by Murngin men from North Eastern Arnhem Land and Tiwi men from Melville Island.

Conflicting visions

This closed discourse of a new White Australia had a tenuous hold in a rapidly changing nation, its survival dependent in part on the government's capacity to control public imaginings and representations of Aboriginal and migrant diversity and to maintain its ascendant role in mediating knowledge about them. Excluding Aboriginal and migrant voices and strictly controlling their contacts with its critics were central to the government's success. But public discussion at the Australian Citizenship Conventions was already showing signs of a shift away from assimilation and towards integration in the late 1950s.

That the more rigid controls over Aboriginal assimilation were beginning to crack was evident in two very different documentary films about Aboriginal people released in 1964 and reviewer response to them. *The Aborigines of Australia*, directed by Ian Dunlop, was produced by the Commonwealth Film Unit for the assimilation campaign and won the Australian Film Award silver award (shared) for documentary in 1964. Critic Sylvia Lawson described how the film endeavoured to cover in the space of forty-four minutes the 'whole, many-faceted, inwardly tangled subject' of Aboriginal 'tribal life, mission and Government reserves, fringe dwelling, stock work, the situations in country towns and inner suburbs, the lot'.[117] This led to the 'inevitable general point … that under Our Policy, things are getting better all the time'. Lawson found the film 'defensive to the point of timidity', demonstrating 'hyper-sensitivity on the part of the sponsors to outside scrutiny' and a determination to 'make the present stage of assimilation look more successful than it is'. She noted the numerous 'evasions' and the bland turning away from vital issues of living conditions, work on pastoral stations, reserve living and Australia's 'grim' history.

The other documentary, also reviewed by Lawson, was *A Changing Race* made by BBC producer Therese Denny for the Australian Broadcasting Commission. This film showed how the combination of an outsider perspective, a more independent funding source and, significantly, Aboriginal voices could produce very different perspectives. For Lawson the film was the 'straightest possible brand of film reportage' and had the effect of 'cramming the viewer's head with aboriginal faces, feelings and words'. It 'pull[ed] no punches' and constituted 'propaganda of almost incendiary energy'. Denny began with the historical context and then introduced viewers to conditions on reserves today through interviews with Aboriginal speakers — a major breakthrough in film making in Australia that greatly impressed Lawson: 'all the film's words were spoken by aborigines, who speak for themselves; and they add up, not to complaint … or accusation … but to a plea … that they take more of their own destinies on their shoulders.' The result was a film that contained 'wretchedness and pathos, but also pride and realism … [and] some astoundingly clear judgements'. In contrast to *The Australian Aborigines* the fate of this documentary was to languish in obscurity. Lawson noted that the ABC appeared reluctant to circulate the film and provided no publicity, that there was only one Sydney television screening and no copies were available in any film library.

These contrastive outcomes for the films suggest emerging tensions over how Aboriginal people were to be represented to the public. On the one hand there was the federal government with its account of Aborigines as primitive people rescued by colonisation and now being prepared for citizenship in an assimilated nation. On the other, new public narratives were emerging from Aborigines' accounts of a violent and oppressive colonial past and their visions of a future society that would acknowledge the special rights of Indigenous Australians. These conflicting visions of the nation have continued down the decades into the present with their own distinct historical trajectories and their own champions and detractors.

4. Practices

No more woomera, no more boomerang,
No more playabout, no more the old ways.
Children of nature we were then,
No clocks hurrying crowds to toil.
Now I am civilized and work in the white way,
Now I have dress, now I have shoes:
'Isn't she lucky to have a good job!'
Better when I had only a dillybag.
Better when I had nothing but happiness.

Noonuccal, 1981[1]

Let us leave aside the question that they may not want to [assimilate], and the possibility — I would myself put it at higher than a possibility — that very determined forces of opposition will appear. Suppose they do not know how to cease to be themselves.

W. E. H. Stanner, 1979[2]

To rely on 'education' to bridge the gap between the old way of life and a new way independent of it, was our policy from 1954 onward. The Aboriginal future was to be one of 'development through individualism.' The new Aboriginal was to be made into an 'independent unit' in a life-system like ours. It did not matter if Aboriginal society and culture fell to pieces. We could fit them together again in a better way. Yes, there would be inevitable human costs but we would have to brace ourselves to be equal to the burdens carried on Aboriginal shoulders.

W. E. H. Stanner, 1979[3]

I grew up in Wollongong in a community of post-war European migrants torn from their homes during the war and then spun out to the other side of the world to end up as labourers in the Port Kembla steelworks. My father was the local Lutheran pastor and he ran our family home and the church next door as a one-stop welfare shop, advice bureau and spiritual home for migrants. Appropriately, our church home later became the headquarters of the Illawarra Ethnic Communities Council. As a child I had no inkling of how our little household was being shaped by an official policy that gave minimal government assistance to European migrants and urged community organisations and the churches to take up the slack. Our whole family was caught up in what we saw as the task of helping these families settle in to their new home. This meant assisting them to make the adjustment from hostel life to work in the steelworks and a home in the suburbs — a local manifestation of the policy of assimilation, although we didn't see it that way at the time. Although our family had arrived from Germany a century earlier, we now lived in a world of diverse European cultures, languages and identities, surrounded by new styles of cuisine, clothing, and homes. We saw how some German families were treated as the enemy by Australians still hurting from the war, so that many adopted the motto of being 'Australian in the street, and German at home' — assimilating outwardly but maintaining their cultures in the home. Little was said openly about the horrors many had lived through but sometimes we'd hear raised voices and sobbing coming from meetings in Dad's office and the shadows of this pain seeped out into our hearts.

In a straight line across to the other side of the continent, my partner Darryl Kickett was growing up in a very different world. Darryl's extended Nyungar family lived in the Narrogin district of the Great Southern wheat belt. This was their 'run': a loosely defined area encompassing bushland, farms and local towns that was inscribed with Nyungar knowledge and connections. Survival here depended on knowledge of family, country, bush skills and rural work. Here Darryl's family could pitch their tents, get access to bush tucker and fresh water, find paid seasonal farm work and meet up with other families. The sounds and smells of the bush dominated his childhood. But the new imperative to assimilate was squeezing in around his family, although they may not have seen it that way. His parents responded to the new opportunities that arose: they took up a small block of land in Cuballing but were unable to get finance even to build a basic shelter; his father found work with the local shire but was suddenly dismissed; and Darryl and his brothers went to school — the first generation of Nyungar children allowed to do so — but this meant moving away from home, first to study in Narrogin and then to start apprenticeships in Perth. Their parents followed them in the late 1960s and set up home in a state housing commission house near Fremantle where Darryl's father found work on the wharves. The family seemed to be living out the assimilation dream, but this too was illusory. They did not see themselves blending into a new White Australia but identified strongly with the expanding network of Nyungar families coming to live in Perth and they maintained strong ties with home. Other families who may have wished to blend in found that this goal was blocked by entrenched racism and government actions that cut across the official policy of assimilation for Nyungar families. This contradictory situation is discussed in detail in the next chapter.

These two brief examples indicate how the official discourse of assimilation fragments into a multitude of stories when we transfer our attention from the *idea* of assimilation to actual *encounters* with assimilation in time and place and when we begin to insert the multiplicity of voices, agendas and ideological, political and economic frameworks of key players. What emerges is the diversity of people with their differing views on race, culture and assimilation that change over time; their varied experiences as they negotiate public expectations and institutions of assimilation that seek to dominate and transform them; and their own contributions as initiators of actions and ideas that attract and influence mainstream society. The process of unravelling and problematising the discourse of assimilation began with Aboriginal and migrant protests in the 1960s and has continued on in the wealth of personal reminiscences and academic historical studies published since then. Yet the nostalgic narrative of the success of assimilation in mid-twentieth century Australia still holds currency today.

In the previous chapter we analysed the federal government's campaigns to sell its vision of an assimilated Australian nation; here we examine federal leadership in the task of assimilating European migrants and Aboriginal people and, in so doing, expose the complex processes shaped by the idea of assimilation and how they were progressively eroded by the intricacies of encounters with assimilation. As with the promotional campaigns, migrant and Aboriginal assimilation were separate undertakings but in this case they were diverging rather than parallel projects. The divergence reflected differences in federal and state powers for these domains: immigration was largely a federal responsibility while, with the exception of the Northern Territory, the states controlled Aboriginal affairs. The consequences for positive advances in Aboriginal assimilation were disastrous: state control meant ongoing tunnel vision and pinched budgets when the situation called for the injection of generous funding and visionary planning. While federal government models for migrant and Aboriginal assimilation drew on shared imaginings of the familiar unilinear, one-way path, there were also significant contrasts in planning for how both groups would move along this path — reflecting the different government expectations of migrant and Aboriginal competency to respond to the call of assimilation. For them, 'New Australians' were positioned as modern and adaptable and, as we saw in the publicity photographs, capable of immediate assimilation; by contrast the oldest Australians would require far more intensive training, possibly over several generations, to catch on.

Assimilating European migrants

The project of assimilating the massive intake of European migrants involved two major tasks. The first was to ensure an intake of migrants most likely to readily assimilate into the mould of White Australia. The next was to assimilate newcomers through a process that would appease settler Australians and enable the government to meet its objectives of national development and security. Federal leadership, coordination and funding were essential to ensure the success of these tasks.

The post-war migration program was the first major break with the tradition of British migration upheld since Federation. Department officers had limited experience in organising a program of this scope and few relevant precedents to follow. Before the war governments had busied themselves with the task of restricting the entry of 'aliens' to Australia and encouraging and organising British migration — a relatively streamlined affair given the 'crimson thread of kinship' linking the two nations. The new program, argues James Jupp, was 'innovatory in bringing in large numbers of non-British aliens' but was also 'conservative in terms of adhering strictly to the White Australia Policy'.[4] With little comprehension of the difficulties confronting European migrants, officers planned a project of minimal assistance involving limited government expenditure that would promote rapid assimilation while avoiding any public backlash. The result was a model that Brian Murphy argues, 'relied primarily on the absence of direct measures to achieve it'.[5] The presumption was that 'the less done to distinguish newcomers from 'old' Australians, the better … as a result intervention at the official level was slight and limited to what would easily translate into a community benefit.' This view was encouraged, according to James Jupp,[6] by the apparent success of the government's equally minimal provision for assimilating displaced persons arriving in Australia between 1947 and 1952.

The Department of Immigration led the charge, supported by an expanding army of government officers who coordinated migrant selection, transportation, reception and initial employment.[7] Key national leaders and community volunteers were also involved through government committees and the Good Neighbour Council. The federal government took financial responsibility for the overall program but with the expectation, as decided at the 1949 Premiers' Conference, that the states would assist with access to existing services such as schools, hospitals and welfare. As pressures on state services increased in tandem with migrant intakes this arrangement became a point of conflict in the ever-volatile relations between state and federal governments over funding arrangements.

'Populate or perish'

'Populate or perish' was the government's catch-cry for an immigration program that irrevocably changed Australia's demographic profile. Capitalising on the large-scale out-migration from Britain and Europe following the war and into the 1960s, Australia entered into agreements with the International Refugee Organisation, the United Kingdom, and governments in Europe for free, assisted and paid passage for refugees and new migrants to Australia. Between 1947 and 1961 immigration and natural increase catapulted the nation's population to 10.5 million.[8] The proportion of overseas-born in the Australian population increased dramatically from 9.8 per cent in 1947 — the lowest point of the century — to settle at around 20 per cent by 1970 — the original level at the time of Federation.[9] Although the government sought to keep its promise of an annual 50 per cent intake of British immigrants, levels averaged only 37 per cent between 1945 and 1961.[10]

The first phase of the immigration program was the arrival between 1947 and 1952 of 170,700 sponsored refugees and displaced persons from camps across Europe. In 1951 Australia signed the United Nations Convention on Refugees and took in a further 90,000 refugees between 1952 and 1970. The war had left eleven million people homeless and unwilling or unable to return to their home countries, amongst them survivors of Nazi slave and concentration camps, those escaping Soviet occupation and persecution, and ethnic Germans fleeing or expelled by vengeful governments in Eastern Europe. In 1947, in a gesture to international humanitarian concern and addressing the need to flesh out its new mass immigration program, Australia agreed to an annual minimum intake of 12,000 people from the one million refugees being resettled by the International Refugee Organization (IRO) — the greatest intake proportionally by any country except the United States. Ethnic Germans were excluded from the IRO project. This intake of refugees and displaced persons was an attractive proposition for the Australian government: many were young and single and virulently anti-communist. The IRO paid the bulk of their transportation costs and Australia was required to pay only £10 per adult and to provide for their reception and resettlement. In return they were required to enter into a form of indentured service by taking up two-year labour contracts to work as directed. This provided a hardworking and tractable mobile workforce that the government could direct to specific areas of employment as required.

To ensure the assimilability of new migrants the Department of Immigration instituted a strict system of screening and selection — depicted in part in the film *Mike and Stefani* — for medical fitness and compatibility with the physical and cultural profile of White Australia. These culturally diverse European migrants were a contrast to the familiar Anglo-Celtic intakes. They came principally from the Baltic states of Estonia, Latvia and Lithuania, the Ukraine and Croatia. Later refugees came from Hungary (1956) and Czechoslovakia (1968). With their memories of traumatic war-time experiences and with no prospect of returning to their homelands they were seeking a permanent new home and had little choice but to accept the deprivations of their early years in Australia.

This phase was a testing ground that paved the way for the dramatic increase in European migration to Australia during the 1950s. It demonstrated to the government that there would be no public backlash as long as settler Australians remained convinced that migration was essential for national development, did not constitute a threat to living standards and employment and that the new migrants would assimilate into mainstream Australia.

The immigration program shifted a gear in the early 1950s. The IRO was dismantled in 1952 and with it went the valuable source of refugee migrant workers. In the same year falling prices in overseas exports caused an unemployment crisis that led to a temporary reduction in the annual migrant intake. British migration also dropped dramatically as economic conditions improved at home and government sponsorship offers like 'Bring-out a Briton' and ever more enthusiastic advertising failed to maintain numbers. Better conditions at home also drove increasing departure rates, estimated by demographer C. A. Price at between 6 and 14 per cent between 1947 and 1961 for British migrants and half that for Europeans.[11] The government accordingly restructured its immigration program by forging agreements for assisted passage with European countries — the Netherlands, Italy, Austria, West Germany, Greece, Spain, Belgium and Yugoslavia. These agreements specified intake levels of identified categories of skilled workers and so brought a new range of skills to Australia, at the same time maintaining a supply of directable workers who could be placed with specific industries after being processed through the government's reception and training system. All assisted British migrants were exempt from this requirement. For the first time migrants were selected from amongst the millions of displaced ethnic Germans — the 'Volkdeutsche' — but only after ex-servicemen's organisations had been reassured that they would be carefully screened to exclude former Nazis. Still, as Mark Aarons has demonstrated, many still managed to migrate and settle in Australia.[12]

There was a further shift in the late 1950s when European migration also began a steady decline in the wake of improved economic conditions following the formation of the new European Economic Community (1957), and the new focus on the movement of guest workers within Europe. Between 1961 and 1967 the Italian government stopped assisted migration to Australia due to discriminatory treatment of Italian migrants. Prime Minister Menzies remained opposed to non-European immigration, responding in 1963 to the criticism that racial discrimination was the heart of Australia's immigration policy with the comment, 'Good thing too — right sort of discrimination.'[13] However to meet Australia's continuing need for migrant labour and with an eye to international dissatisfaction with its restrictive immigration policy, the government announced plans in 1964 to begin recruiting skilled workers from Turkey and Lebanon. This marked the first substantial intake of Muslim populations into Australia and the first major official transgression of the White Australia policy in the post-war immigration program. Moves to dismantle the White Australia policy had begun in 1956 when the *Immigration Act* was amended to allow non-white residents of at least fifteen years the opportunity to apply to become Australian citizens. Then in 1958 the dictation test was abolished. Further revisions in 1966 allowed non-white residents to apply for citizenship under the same conditions as European residents. Finally in 1973 the Whitlam government removed all remaining vestiges of racial criteria from Australian immigration policy. Historian Matthew Jordan concludes that this eventual outcome was not so much the result of 'a moral "awakening" whereby Australians and policy makers in particular suddenly renounced the wickedness of their past ways … [and] underwent a profound conversion to the cause of anti-racism'. Rather it was the result of a process of gradual reform that was 'justified consistently and solely on the grounds of diplomatic expediency … [The] over riding concern was the perceived geopolitical repercussions of perpetuating a discriminatory immigration policy.'[14]

Models of assimilation

The government's model for assimilating European migrants during the 1950s and 1960s grew out of the initial refugee phase. James Jupp notes that from the government's perspective the refugee settlement policy provided valuable unskilled labour, accommodated dependent women and children at a minimum cost, provided basic education and medical services, prevented ethnic community formation and generally kept workers and their families away from settler Australians. However from the perspective of the refugees it represented an encroachment on their civil liberties through controls over employment and movement and the forced separation of families. At the same time, it categorised them as deficient in language and work skills and imposed Australian culture on them while their own cultures were devalued; and it failed to acknowledge their many psychological and emotional needs, focusing instead on 'crude materialistic terms of housing, food, and jobs'.[15]

Jean Martin's study of the assimilation of a cohort of displaced persons points to the special need for understanding migrants coming to Australia from war-ravaged Europe. Her brief outline of their experiences reflects the lives of many other migrants who came to Australia during the 1950s: 'most of them had lost close relatives during the war; they had left their own homes unwillingly, suffered privation and humiliation, and, after the end of hostilities, experienced years of empty, idle uncertainty before their future was finally decided by resettlement overseas'.[16] They all suffered the pain of leaving family, friends and homeland; the disparity between their old and new homes in terms of culture, social institutions, technology, language, lifestyle and the minutiae of daily life; and the loss of identity and status. From her 1953 study Martin analysed four sub-processes in her subjects' path to assimilation: 'learning new behaviour patterns and adopting new values and norms; assuming new roles within the social structure of the host society; coming to feel a sense of belonging in the new society with all that this implies in terms of self-perceptions, allegiances and responsibilities; and finding satisfaction in these new activities and loyalties'.[17]

A survey of settler Australian 'orientations' to assimilation by sociologist Ronald Taft in 1960 showed a mix of responses. There was a snug fit between a sizeable proportion of settler Australian respondents' views and the message of the federal government's promotional campaign with roughly a third convinced that immigrants should assimilate as quickly as possible. However the majority favoured a situation of mutual tolerance and gradual change through social interaction and none opted for a system of pluralism where differences were preserved. Most believed that little or no change was required to settle into Australia, significantly underestimating the challenges involved. Over 60 per cent were opposed to migrants speaking their own language in public or creating ethnic communities and they favoured compulsory naturalisation of aliens as soon as they were eligible.[18] These attitudes were expressed jokingly in John O'Grady's novel *They're a Weird Mob,* but there is a sting in the conclusion where Nino Culotta reflects on those migrants who have not yet become assimilated Australians:

> There are far too many New Australians in this country who are still mentally living in their homelands, who mix with their own nationality, and try to retain their own language and customs ... Cut it out. There is no better way of life in the world than that of the Australian ... I've heard parents in shops talking to kids in their homeland languages, and the kids translating into English, and making the purchases. This is disgraceful. Those parents should be bloody ashamed of themselves. They came to this country because their own is impossible and by their own laziness make this one impossible for themselves also. It makes me very irritable.[19]

Many migrant families experienced the verbal and even physical abuse of such 'irritable' Australians who interrupted private conversations in trams, restaurants and on sidewalks with the directive that if they did not want to speak English then they should go back to where they came from. Similar accounts of name calling and exclusion appeared in letters to the editor in the *Women's Weekly,* prompting responses of sympathy from some Australian writers but also blame for not developing their skills in English, or patronising advice such as 'do not segregate yourselves as so many Italians seem to do'. There was also evidence of resentment and ridiculing when Australian respondents used invented broken English and foreign accents to express their opinions.[20]

The federal government provided only minimal support for migrants during reception and resettlement. I have analysed four overlapping phases that directed them towards the goal of assimilation: Australianisation; joining the workforce; living in the community; and becoming a naturalised Australian citizen. This approach was intended to prevent the growth of ethnic enclaves, keep government expenditure to a minimum, calm public anxieties, and utilise migrant workers for national projects.[21]

Australianisation

Australianisation involved basic training for adults in 'survival' English language and cultural skills that would prepare them to settle into work and Australian life, while impressing on them the need for rapid assimilation. From 1951 the process was managed through a tripartite system where the Department of Immigration coordinated policy and funding, the Commonwealth Office of Education was responsible for providing materials, teacher training and advisory teachers, and state Education Departments selected and appointed staff.

The first stage of the process began with English lessons in the camps before departure and on the ship to Australia and continued for several weeks after arrival in special reception centres for European migrants. The largest, longest serving and most notorious was the Bonegilla Immigration Reception and Training Centre established by the Department of Immigration in 1947 near Albury in a former prisoner-of-war camp. Conditions there were unwelcoming and inferior to those provided for new British migrants. Newcomers were accommodated in unheated army Nissen huts converted into single sex dormitories of up to twenty-six residents. The forced separation of married couples was a source of constant complaint from residents, along with the canteen food, which was distinctly Australian in style — a clear expression of the message of assimilation. Residents received twenty-five shillings a week from which they paid twenty shillings for their keep leaving five shillings for 'pocket money', and they provided roughly a third of the labour for maintaining the centre. Children attended special classes to familiarise them with the state school system and there were English lessons for adults but still for most residents it was a monotonous life.

Frustrations could spill out into conflict with camp authorities and between residents. In 1952 two thousand disillusioned Italian residents rioted when the national unemployment crisis kept workers stranded at Bonegilla for periods of up to six months. Military personnel and squadron vehicles from the nearby Bandiana army base were sent to help to restore the peace.[22] In a subsequent article in the *Australian Medical Journal* Sydney psychiatrist Dr I. A. Listwan claimed that migrant camps like Bonegilla were 'breeding grounds for hatred and violence' and should be abolished. He pointed to the enmities aroused by accommodating together antagonistic groups like Germans and Eastern Europeans and the negative effect of living conditions that reminded residents of war-time experiences and the 'hopeless atmosphere' of refugee camps in Europe. He also warned that the authoritarian treatment and inferior living conditions in the camps worked directly against the goals of assimilation and suggested that the residents should be scattered in small holding units in cities and rural towns.[23] However Bonegilla remained open for business. In 1961 another full-blown riot broke out, also motivated by frustrations over lack of employment.[24] Staff and police helped to restore the peace and the Criminal Investigation Bureau was brought in, a curfew was imposed, several migrants were charged with assault and vandalism, and allegations of communist infiltration were levelled against the rioters. This heightened level of protest and reprisal was exceptional in the history of Bonegilla but nevertheless was suggestive of the simmering underlying tensions of life there.

The next stage of Australianisation was outreach teaching for migrants joining the workforce and families living in the community. English lessons which included citizenship information were offered in evening classes after work, and there were special ABC radio programs like the series *For New Australians.* There were also the Department of Immigration's publications and other booklets in simple English advising about migrants' rights and responsibilities and offering useful information, such as *Rules of the Road, Safety in the Bush* and *Birds and Flowers of Australia.* English classes were regarded as essential for workers, to ensure occupational health and safety.

Joining the workforce

From the migrant centres a steady supply of workers left to take up jobs in heavy industry in Port Kembla and Newcastle, factories in Melbourne, large public works projects, on farms and in government institutions. As far as the government was concerned, joining the workforce was a vital stage in the process of assimilation where workers learned about Australian values and developed skills while they also built up financial security for themselves and their families.[25] By contrast, governments paid little attention to the task of placing Aboriginal people in secure employment. For migrants with few other supports available to them work was vital to survival and remaining in employment was essential, regardless of the conditions.

Placements were arranged by officers from the Commonwealth Employment Service according to available work. There was no attempt to match migrant work experience and trade and professional qualifications, which were generally not recognised in Australia or overlooked because of language differences. Most workers were classed as labourers or domestic workers and were often sent to work at sites unpopular with Australians such as the all-male construction sites of the Tasmanian and Snowy Mountains hydroelectric schemes. During construction of the Snowy Mountains Scheme between 1949 and 1974 two-thirds of its 100,000 employees were European migrants. Employment choices relegated most European workers to the working classes although those whose English was significantly more fluent than the 'survival' level taught to adults migrants were able to move out of their menial labouring occupations and some eventually retrained and resumed the professions they had practised at home.

Workers and their families lived in hostels until they found their own accommodation — not an easy task given the high demand and cost of rental properties and the difficulties migrants faced in getting finance to build their own homes. Families were frequently separated, with wives and children left behind until working fathers, sons or daughters were able to arrange housing. Conditions in the hostels were spartan and in 1950 mothers at the Cowra Holding Centre went on strike and flew a black flag as a sign of mutiny over the quality of food provided for their children.[26] Unrest at centres in 1952 saw residents staging hunger strikes at Maribyrnong in Victoria and demonstrating at Amberley in Queensland and at Matraville and Villawood in Sydney.[27] These events have been largely forgotten, but at the time they contradicted the government's promotion of Australia as an ideal destination for migrants. Nor did they fit the cherished image of Australia as a non-violent society. Now fifty years later Maribyrnong and Villawood are immigration detention centres riven by allegations of breaches of human rights and reports of riots, hunger strikes, escapes and self-harm incidents.

Living in the community

To assist with migrants' early adjustment the Department of Immigration's Assimilation Division appointed thirty-nine trained social workers in 1949 from a profession dominated by Anglo-Celtic Australian women. Paradoxically their numbers dropped steadily as the numbers of immigrants increased, falling to twenty-four in the early 1950s and then to fifteen in 1959. In addition to doing casework they were expected to keep the government informed about migrant conditions and needs, and to spread the message of assimilation. They also worked with the Good Neighbour Council network of community volunteers and church migration committees.

While there were no formal restrictions on migrants forming their own national groups, the government's clear message was that migrants should join community groups like the Good Neighbour Council, the Country Women's Association, returned services organisations or scout and guide troops. Still, as James Jupp observes, most ethnic minority groups, like migrants everywhere, did develop their own organisations and newspapers over time. Most started from scratch with cultural and language activities, entertainment, mutual assistance, and a language newspaper. Jupp emphasises that the structure of ethnic organisations was well developed before the advent of official multiculturalism, when the government co-opted them into consultation and service delivery from the 1970s. In 1977 the Department of Social Security listed almost two thousand ethnic community organisations in the states and territories.[28]

Migrants were directed to seek assistance with schooling for their children, and medical care and welfare needs from the relevant state government departments. Within these agencies staff had no prior expertise in dealing with non-English migrants and either endeavoured to treat them as any other client, leading to confusion and neglectful treatment, or were aggressively assimilatory in demanding client conformity. Government assistance to meet the need for specialist expertise and increased services was not provided; meanwhile federal and state governments battled over who should pay. While social workers in different states reported variations in how migrants were treated it became clear that at this important level assimilation was not progressing as expected.

Some serious gaps in meeting client needs reflected government policy. Since the desire was for migrants to learn English, the government did not provide interpreter services and they were only introduced in the early 1970s after sustained lobbying from migrant organisations. For many years migrants had to rely on the assistance of ethnic churches and the Commonwealth Bank, which distributed booklets to mothers with phrases to use in hospital and made its interpreters available for contact during urgent medical cases and birthing.[29] Other services such as mental health were in a hopeless state after years of government neglect and its officers were chronically unprepared for the growing call on its services by migrant communities.[30]

A serious area of neglect was in the provision of special education facilities for migrant children in state schools. Governments considered that primary age children in particular were ideal fodder for assimilation and they were placed directly into the general classroom to be immersed in the English language, school routines and the nation's civic and moral values. They were expected to learn a sense of national pride and patriotism by participating in celebrations of events like Anzac Day. The pivotal role of language was emphasised in an article by a primary headmaster in 1951 who wrote that English was vital to 'the success of the whole immigration project … English must be spoken to the pupils and by them, all day and every day, in every activity, in school and out of it.'[31] Special English classes were recommended in the 1956 Haines Report in South Australia but the idea was dropped by the Director of Education.[32] A suggestion from the floor by a migrant father at the South Coast Regional Conference of the New South Wales Good Neighbour Council in Wollongong in 1960 asserting that monolingual teachers could benefit from the assistance of migrant teachers drew the response that they were welcome but needed to have sufficient education, be fluent in English and have no accent.[33] The rapid increase in numbers of migrant children and the effects of the baby boom put increasing pressure on buildings and teaching resources during the 1950s and brought relations between state and federal governments to a head as the states struggled to keep up with demand and the federal government refused to provide necessary funding for improvements.[34]

Clearly the assimilation service model was not able to adequately meet migrant needs and cater for their language and cultural differences. This situation began to reach crisis point as pressure on mainstream facilities and services mounted with each annual migrant intake and the baby boom in settler Australian families. There was a groundswell of complaint, as Brian Murphy points out,[35] from teachers, health and welfare workers, as well as union and employer organisations concerned that the gap between policy and achievement was not only undermining the goal of assimilated citizens but was maintaining difference and laying the basis of a 'sizeable underclass' of European migrants. At the same time R. F. Henderson's 1966 *Poverty Report* (published in 1969) identified for the first time certain groups of European migrants as seriously economically disadvantaged, a shock for a public accustomed to reading stories of migrant success and prosperity.[36]

In these conditions the government could hardly maintain its expectation that migrant families would simply disappear into the community. Ethnic community networks and organisations inevitably developed to fill the gaps in government service provision and lobby government to improve services. Ethnic churches and others like the Lutheran Church with its ethnic associations and connections also entered the fray — hence our family involvement with assimilation referred to earlier. The government's political opponents and the popular press picked up on migrant disadvantage that the government refused to see. In 1960 federal Labor politician Leslie Haylen attacked the government claiming that 'poor housing, horribly insanitary conditions and exploitation by landlords and sometimes by employers are not the ways to encourage assimilation. These are not the ways to encourage migrants to become part of the nation, to cast away forever their European background and become Australians in the strongest sense of the word.'[37] Articles in the popular press addressed migrant housing shortages and praised the ingenuity of their makeshift accommodation, drawing attention to the very real difficulties they faced in making a home. The 'casualties' of assimilation were also addressed: an article in *Pix* magazine in 1957 described the tragic plight of 'vagrant migrants … a lost race of despondent, neurotic misfits' who had 'gambled their lives in a new world and lost. Maladjusted, beset by language problems, burdened by horrible memories they just can't forget.'[38]

Taking up citizenship

For the government the proportion of migrants taking up citizenship remained disappointingly low. Naturalisation or 'neutralisation' as it was referred to by some migrants was considered the final stage in the process of becoming an Australian citizen and visible proof of assimilation into Australian life. The low rate for non-British migrants was raised by delegates at the Australian Citizenship Conventions during the 1950s. Along with the media they blamed migrant ignorance and apathy and claimed that migrants wanted the privileges but not the responsibilities of citizenship and they warned that large numbers of non-citizens represented a threat to national security. Similar accusations were made against Aborigines who did not show sufficient enthusiasm for the goals of assimilation. But for many migrants the decision of whether to take up citizenship was a very emotional issue that required a careful balancing of the costs and benefits of taking the irrevocable step of cutting formal ties with their country of birth.

The rise and fall of the Good Neighbour Council

The fate of the Good Neighbour Council[39] — one of the federal government's major initiatives to promote migrant assimilation — provides telling insights into changing federal trends. Its original significance for federal policy was driven home by senior Department of Immigration officer J. T. Massey at a Good Neighbour Council gathering in 1951 when he claimed that 'we are pioneering a rather complex honorary service of superlatively great value and in personal goodwill and helpfulness ... There is a colossal job ahead if Australia is to properly assimilate thousands of British and other New Australians.'[40] Built on the nation's existing network of voluntary organisations it quickly expanded into a national system with 300 local branches and 10,000 volunteer members. Federal funding reached one million dollars in 1965 and staff levels grew from three to seventy-eight between 1950 and 1975. However, during the 1970s it was increasingly viewed as a 'relic of the assimilation era,'[41] and, as Jupp points out,[42] its slow demise followed the collapse of the conservative political hegemony in 1973 until it was finally closed in 1979 on the recommendation of the 1978 Galbally Report, the cornerstone of the federal government's new policy of multiculturalism.

In creating the Good Neighbour Council the government tapped into the wealth of good will and social capital built up by voluntary organisations and positioned itself to make a considerable saving in expenditure by using voluntary workers to further its assimilation goals at the local level. With a core membership of middle-class conservative settler Australians, it could also be relied on to commit energetically to the task of promoting conformity to the values and identity of White Australia. Their middle-class attitudes and notions of kindly charity inevitably shaped their expectations of migrants and affected how they represented them to the wider community. In practice the Good Neighbour Councils offered an 'openhearted, if not naive, attempt to extend a hand of welcome'.[43] Their work was carried out through deed and example, as they assisted families in resettlement, promoted community acceptance through various events from naturalisation ceremonies to ethnic performances, and provided the example of good citizenship in an assimilated society. Member prejudices and loyalties were artlessly expressed at the South Coast Regional Conference in Wollongong in 1960. All speakers were settler Australians committed to the assimilation of European migrants and bound to British immigrants by ties of 'blood': 'we have a common heritage, and they have no language problems, so that they are more easily assimilated'. A Wollongong representative praised how migrant culture was enriching Australia through music, theatre, films, art and sport. Even Australian men, the speaker claimed, were turning to the fashions inspired by migrant men's 'love of colour, their preference for suede shoes, desert boots, the draped line in tailoring and their delight in the more casual and colourful sports wear' while for house-proud Australian woman there were the delights of Swedish furniture and glass and German cutlery and porcelain.[44]

The Council's 1963 promotional film *The Helping Hand*,[45] which focused on the work of volunteer staff rather than migrants' needs, sounded alarm bells for a government already concerned that despite glowing annual reports to the Citizenship Conventions the Council had become a self-serving organisation that met the interests of its staff, volunteers and some British migrants first, but was increasingly out of touch with its European migrant clientele and had lost its edge in creatively representing them to the community. While the Department of Immigration moved towards a policy of migrant integration in 1962 the Council remained staunchly assimilationist. A particular frustration for the Department was that since the Council reported directly to the Australian Citizenship Conventions, there was no way of controlling its activities apart from the drastic action of terminating its funding and closing it down.

The Good Neighbour Council was increasingly out of step with new pluralist directions in federal policy. The Department of Immigration was beginning to work directly with migrant organisations in resettlement and delivery of welfare services and in the late 1960s prepared to transfer to them many of these responsibilities. At the same time the government began to dismantle its apparatus of assimilation: the Australia Citizenship Conventions ceased in 1970 and, under the Whitlam government, the Department was amalgamated with other departments in 1974 and the immigration intake was reduced significantly. It was only a matter of time before the Council would go. The organisation itself was teetering on the brink due to declining levels of voluntarism.[46] The death blow came in 1978 when the Galbally report advised that it was 'no longer possible to envisage a suitable role' and 'we could therefore find no reason to justify continued funding of Good Neighbour Councils by the Commonwealth government'.[47]

The Galbally Report recommended multiculturalism as the key for developing new policies for migrant services and programs and the Liberal Coalition government under Prime Minister Malcolm Fraser adopted multiculturalism as the new vision of nationhood to replace the tarnished image of White Australia. In his speech on multiculturalism in 1981, Fraser mapped out the new vision of a nation that celebrated its diverse ethnic and cultural origins and embraced diversity as a unifying force rather than a cause for division. In a reference to the by now discredited assimilation policy, Fraser acknowledged that enforcing conformity cost people their 'identity and self-esteem', drove a wedge between generations and groups, and posed 'a real threat of alienation and division' within the nation. By contrast, diversity was a 'source of wealth and dynamism' that encouraged integration and openness between citizens. Fraser appealed to the image of a 'cohesive nation that draws strength and unique character from its diversity'. This was certainly a dramatic shift from the past; however, there was also continuity with White Australia. At the core of Fraser's speech and, as he claimed, at the core of multiculturalism was a 'framework of shared fundamental values' that provided the minimum conditions for securing well-being and equality of opportunity for all Australians. These 'fundamental values' would be shaped by the nation's core Anglo-Celtic derived institutions.[48]

Aboriginal assimilation

The 1950s offered a rare window of opportunity for the government to deliver the rights of citizenship and improvements in living conditions that assimilation promised to Aboriginal people. The Aboriginal population in 1950 was estimated at only 80,000. Making up less than 1 per cent of the Australian population this was a mere fraction compared to the 14 per cent of immigrants who arrived between 1947 and 1961. Former government patrol officer Jeremy Long observed in 1964 that this made the Aboriginal problem a 'relatively manageable one' compared to New Zealand where Maoris were 6.65 per cent of the total population.[49] According to Long the majority of Aboriginal people lived in remote and rural Australia, one third of them under direct government control in settlements and missions.[50] Public attitudes had been softened by the race atrocities of the war and a new feeling of humanitarian interest in the 'Aboriginal problem' warmed to the idea of Aboriginal people living as responsible citizens rather than, as many imagined, draining the government purse on welfare. Aborigines' experiences during the war had reinforced their determination to push for citizenship rights and a better quality of life, goals which could only be achieved by engaging more directly with the nation. Their contributions to the defence of Australia, a 'core value' in citizenship at the time, brought a new pressure to respond to their demands.[51] State governments had assimilation on the agenda, although institutionalised racism and entrenched discrimination threatened to throw a spanner in the works at every turn.

Given the scale of government programs of post-war

development and the advantages extended to other citizens and immigrants, it should have been a routine matter to extend the same opportunities to Aboriginal people. Such a view was expressed in an Australia Day address in 1956 by Reverend Gordon Rowe, Secretary of the Aborigines' Friends' Association in Adelaide and member of the South Australian Aborigines Protection Board. 'I know that the cases are not exactly parallel, but if this country can assimilate a million migrants in ten years — and we all ought to be glad that it has done it — surely it could absorb the comparatively few thousands of its own aboriginal people who have already reached or are approaching the civilised state of living.'[52]

However, the opportunity was missed. This was a situation that demanded vision, strong leadership, national cooperation, a generous budget and a new way to work with Aboriginal people. Without these requirements it was impossible to extend full citizenship rights and equality to Aboriginal people or to fulfil the promise to settler Australians that Aboriginal people would be assimilated into a White Australia. The process was weighed down by a tangle of baggage — special legislation and administrations, separate and inferior services, entrenched ways of addressing Aboriginal problems, doubts about Aborigines' capacity to become fully modern, racial prejudice and segregation, miserly funding — which made Aboriginal assimilation a far more complex and daunting challenge than the task of assimilating immigrant populations.

Wrangling between the states and the federal government held up the essential task of dismantling the entire scaffolding of discriminatory legislation and administration that made equal citizenship and better living conditions for all Aboriginal people an impossibility. Governments failed to grasp the opportunity to negotiate a common ground with Aboriginal people. The result was a series of frustrating delays in essential reforms and long stand-offs over vital funding for resources so that change took place at a snail's pace over a twenty-year period. Meanwhile Aboriginal people were left to negotiate their way through a maze of broken promises and in the end *they* were blamed for the slow pace of assimilation. As tensions escalated over the decade Aboriginal organisations developed into a powerful oppositional force to government.

Federal and state: divided responsibilities

Built into the Australian Constitution was the logic that Aboriginal people were somehow outside the nation and the purview of federal government. Over the years a range of players contested this assumption — Aboriginal people, government officials, missionaries, women activists and academics. They saw Commonwealth intervention as the solution to a range of issues, from Aboriginal citizenship rights to uniform Aboriginal legislation, and these demands were raised in several federal forums before the issue was finally resolved in the aftermath of the 1967 Referendum. The Commonwealth played the issue for its own advantage; this meant avoiding additional expenses or responsibilities while creating an impression of humane leadership when Aboriginal issues attracted criticism, especially from overseas.

The federal government was initially unwilling to take on the responsibility and expense of control over Aboriginal affairs. The matter was not put to the vote at the inaugural Conference of the Commonwealth and State Aboriginal Authorities held in Canberra in 1937 but delegates still managed to pass a resolution seeking financial assistance for the states to address Aboriginal conditions that brought 'discredit upon the whole of Australia'. The meeting also passed a 'destiny of the race' resolution calling for Aborigines' 'ultimate absorption by the people of the Commonwealth'.[53] In preparation for the massive developmental challenges following the war, the federal government included the right to legislate for Aboriginal people in the 1944 referendum on post-war reconstruction powers but the public rejected the package. In 1950 Elkin proposed a meeting to devise a 'convergent system of national policy' as recommended in his 1944 booklet *Citizenship for the Aborigines.* He pointed out that it was in the Commonwealth's interest to provide direction and funding to the states, as it would bear the brunt of any international criticism.[54] While the Menzies government responded by making overtures towards national leadership, this was mainly to promote the policy of assimilation; the government continued to support state control while resolutely resisting any major change to the status quo, especially in the area of funding.

A stalemate developed as states called on the federal government to assist them through special grant funding under section 96 of the Constitution and the federal government refused to issue funds unless the states agreed to conditions on their use of the money. The pattern of state requests for funding and federal knock-backs persisted into the early 1970s when the federal government finally took control of Aboriginal affairs nationally with the major responsibility for funding Aboriginal programs. Recent developments suggest another fork in the road with the federal government back pedalling on special Aboriginal funding in favour of mainstreaming services, while at the same time pointing the finger of blame at the states for the unacceptable levels of substance addiction, domestic violence and child abuse in many Aboriginal communities.

The losers in the stand-off in the 1950s were Aboriginal people. The truth was that no government was prepared to shoulder the costs involved in making real improvements to their living conditions. A 1958 West Australian government report estimated that it would cost £2.4 million to improve Aboriginal conditions across the state and requested the funds from the Prime Minister as a special purpose grant over three years.[55] The approach was roundly rejected on the grounds that this was a state responsibility. The *West Australian* newspaper reported that the

Prime Minister showed 'contemptuous rejection of moral responsibility' in not responding to state requests for urgently needed top-up funding.[56] However the state government made no move to increase its own levels of Aboriginal funding to achieve better conditions. The onus was put back on Aboriginal people in the cruel Catch 22 argument outlined in the 1958 report and repeated around the nation: 'if he is to be acceptable to white society — and without this there can be no future for him — his mode of living and his whole outlook on life must undergo a complete transformation. He must live as we live and generally conform to the requirements of white civilisation.'[57] But how could 'he' achieve this without the basic materials to do so? This was the tragic fallacy of Aboriginal assimilation.

The war years: a taste of freedom

In the 1950s many Aboriginal people were more than ready for positive change. For decades they had been calling for equal citizenship rights through formal deputations to politicians, as witnesses to government inquiries and in statements to the press. They had also demanded better living conditions, equal pay for equal work, the return of Aboriginal children to their families and for the government to hand back Aboriginal land. Yet their voices were rarely heard or listened to. Even Aboriginal leaders, performers, sportspeople and employees leading modern lives that crossed race barriers were seemingly invisible. This began to shift during the war years as Aboriginal people proved that they were as capable as anyone else of adjusting to the dramatic new changes and opportunities. Elkin was one observer who took note of how Aboriginal people in the army camps in the Northern Territory adapted to their changed circumstances and this convinced him of their capacity to become assimilated. He wrote in 1949 that 'the younger aborigines are on the march to become part of, or to play an intelligent part in, the new way of life. This is the turning point for which some of us have been seeking. It is the tide in the affairs of men which must be taken at the flood.'[58]

Robert Hall estimates that 4000 Aboriginal and Torres Strait Islander people enlisted in the services and that several thousand more worked in army-controlled camps in the Northern Territory.[59] Barriers dividing black and white were challenged in the armed forces and the camps and the mass movements of troop arrivals and civilian evacuations in northern Australia threw people of all kinds together. Still, some officers viewed Aboriginal people as potential enemies, like non-British Australians and colonised people to the north who could become 'subversive in the event of invasion by means of bribery or propaganda'.[60] Even with the imminent threat of Japanese invasion in the Kimberley the army did not consider arming Aboriginal people.[61] Everywhere there were new freedoms as government resources and staff were redirected to the war effort. Evacuation of white missionaries left the Aboriginal community at Forrest River Mission in the Kimberley in charge of their own affairs for the first time. Aboriginal teacher Connie Nungulla McDonald recalled this as a 'happy time. Observing my people taught me that we were capable of running our own lives. It gave me a glimpse of what life must have been before the gudiyars [white people] … [This experience] enabled me to see more clearly what the government system was doing to us and to realise that some of the missionaries treated us like animals or convicts.'[62] Aboriginal women and children in missions around Darwin were evacuated and sent south to Adelaide and across to Sydney for their first taste of city life. In 1943 in the remote Pilbara region of Western Australia, Aboriginal pastoral workers began their long strike for equal wages and conditions — branded a communist-inspired plot by the government.

In the south there was a new demand for Aboriginal labour. Settlements and missions were emptied as workers were commandeered for war-time labour on the home front. For some there were opportunities to work in factories in the city. There was a new level of prosperity, with domestic and rural workers in full-time employment and often on full pay with cash to spare to spend on popular fashions and entertainments — films, music, magazines, pulp novels, gambling, drinking and the round of agricultural shows. Anthropologists from the University of Sydney in the late 1940s and the 1950s studying local mixed-race communities suggested a new openness amongst the families to the promise of better living conditions and full citizenship that assimilation seemed to offer. However, their research also identified obstacles facing the communities including entrenched small town racism, a strong loyalty to their own cultural ways and extended family groupings, and deep resentment at their treatment by the government and white people generally.[63]

The end of the war brought a frustrating return to discriminatory conditions that jarred with war-time sentiments of a united nation fighting for the freedom of all. This was a frustration for colonised people around the world who fought alongside their colonial masters during the war and then found themselves back at square one when hostilities ceased. The situation for Aboriginal people was aggravated by the knowledge of the Aboriginal dead and wounded forgotten in national celebrations and of Aboriginal service personnel who were refused government entitlements that were provided for other returned soldiers — including housing loans, land grants, educational rehabilitation and training opportunities.[64] People were forced out of jobs to make way for non-Aboriginal returned servicemen, and new migrants seeking work were given precedence. Promises made in government campaign materials of a better life and the all-pervading advertising for suburban life and commodities failed to materialise for Aboriginal people. Barriers of race were reasserted, and controlling administrators and local police were back in earnest. Restrictions on Aboriginal access to alcohol took on a new meaning as a symbol of oppression in protests by Aboriginal and white ex-servicemen demanding the right to have a sociable drink together in the pub. The Returned Sailors, Soldiers and Airmen's Imperial League of

Australia (later the Returned Services League of Australia) joined Aboriginal servicemen to lobby for a limited form of citizenship rights and in 1949 the federal government granted the vote to Aboriginal people who were serving in or who had served in the defence forces.

There were protests at the slow patronising grind of bureaucratic change, the government's failure to deliver on its promises and the pressures to abandon their way of life for the values and goals of white Australia. Now there was also the example of other oppressed people around the world, expressed in the movement for colonial independence and in the United States in the renewed demands by Native Americans and Afro-Americans for political rights with their war veterans often leading the struggle.[65] Reflecting on these developments in 1965, anthropologist W. E. H. Stanner observed that history shows over and over again how Aboriginal people were required to 'give up something as the price of good relations with us' and to do this in advance with no 'promissory note of good to come in return … The application of the policy of assimilation is one more in a long line of approaches with a remembered history. Wherever aboriginal life now touches that of Europeans, which is virtually everywhere, old injuries still rankle. They predispose people, who usually have no clear idea of what our intentions really are, to suspect that the old, old story is being told again … The acid test of assimilation is whether it can create an increasing motive to believe in it. One must remember that it is somewhat incredible to many Europeans.'[66]

Extending a helping hand

The support of all Australians was essential for Aboriginal assimilation to succeed and there was evidence of fertile ground for this cause. Rather than a 'great Australian silence'[67] there was actually a great clamour of interest in Aboriginal people and culture in the fifties. Some settler Australians were anxious to see reflected in

Australian society the ideals of freedom and democracy that had accompanied the nation's involvement in the war. There was also a growing fascination with representations of Aboriginal culture and ponderings about the Aboriginal experiences of assimilation, inspired in part by the government's campaign.

John Murphy cites a 1954 opinion poll where three-quarters of respondents had no prior contact with Aboriginal people, yet the overwhelming majority — 84 per cent — claimed to have given some thought to the 'aborigine question' and 75 per cent supported granting the vote to Aboriginal people in federal elections. There was less clarity on other issues and 35 per cent were unable to decide whether 'half-castes' should be grouped with whites or 'full-blooded aborigines'. Murphy concludes from the survey that a significant majority of Australians appeared to endorse the idea of Aboriginal equality, but that there was less support for 'the practicalities of assimilationalist policy, with its closure of reserves, promises of integration into white society, and the idea that mixed-descent people were to be treated as "white people"'.[68] The South Australian Minister of Works Hon G. G. Pearson expressed a similar view when he told the 1961 Native Welfare Council that 'assimilation was a policy which the community required governments to subscribe to but itself refused to have any part in'.[69]

It is true that there were frequent angry protests from settler Australians objecting to Aboriginal families moving into their neighbourhoods. But there was also the expanding movement of Aboriginal and settler activists working together to promote Aboriginal rights. These are well documented in Aboriginal autobiographies and histories. Less well known are efforts at the community level to lend a helping hand to Aboriginal families. While the public may have objected to having Aboriginal people living in their neighbourhoods, it was quite a different matter when it came to acts of kindly charity. With the federal government refusing to fund a national network to promote Aboriginal assimilation, groups of well-meaning but untrained and unsupervised volunteers set off to do good to local Aboriginal families. Some states supported an embryonic community process; the Native Welfare Council in Western Australia worked through a central committee in Perth and a sprinkling of local citizen groups — there were ten across the state in 1961. Made up of mainly middle-class white volunteers — typically local professional men and church leaders — their efforts to promote assimilation often served an element of civic pride as they sought to clean up unsightly town camps and impose their sense of order on local Aboriginal families.

For women there were new opportunities to help through charitable community work, employment in the helping professions and by adopting or fostering Aboriginal children. Anthropologist Diane Barwick observed of volunteerism in Melbourne in the 1960s that 'every [Aboriginal] city household ... had the experience with white do-gooders, whether kindly, neurotic, dishonest, religious or political reformers'.[70] A former member of the Armidale Association for the Assimilation of Aborigines, which included wives of academics at the newly established University of New England, commented that 'to ignore the situation, to close our eyes to the way people were living — that would have been wrong'.[71]

The 1950s also saw non-denominational men's business groups doing voluntary work with local Aboriginal communities. In 1955 the Apex National Convention endorsed a plan for its 120 member clubs to assist Aboriginal communities to better their living conditions and to work to reduce racial prejudice and promote trust between black and white. In practice this meant making improvements to huts on reserves and encouraging local women's organisations to give lessons in 'nutrition; how to sew; how to treat children and elderly people who were sick; how to take advantage of medical services and medicines; how to allow children to attend school and the need for them to go regularly and do homework and to study'.[72] Commenting on the often-patronising assistance offered, non-Aboriginal activist Jack Horner noted that it was 'well-meaning and popular, full of whitefella notions that by changing the environment you change the human being'.[73] Still, with little other support some families were grateful for even this help. A women assisted by the Armidale group observed in retrospect that, 'You wouldn't knock anyone that was tryin' to help yer. I know they done a lot, the people of Armidale, the assimilation people, it was all voluntary, they gave a lot of their time.'[74]

For those who preferred to read about Aboriginal people there was a kaleidoscope of writing in popular magazines, from the frivolous to the offensively racist. Stories familiarised the public with the jumble of stereotypes of Aborigines as primitive, exotic, romantic and assimilated and occasionally raised important issues for discussion. They highlighted the gap between the primitive past and Australia's modern present. At one level this disjunct seemed to contradict the possibility of Aboriginal assimilation, but when considered in the context of the official narrative, it provided further ammunition for the urgency of forcing change on Aboriginal people. Pictorial magazines like *Walkabout* (1934–1972) catered to public fascination with traditional Aboriginal culture with romanticised accounts of an homogenised cultural past often symbolised in iconic images of lone Aboriginal hunters silhouetted against an empty landscape.[75] The more populist *Pix* magazine and *Australasian Post* added Aboriginal stories to their usual fare of 'sex, crime, sport and curiosities' and tales of 'individual human courage' told through sensational photographs and bizarre headlines.[76]

A short article from *Pix* presenting an unusual take on assimilation in remote Australia typified this inventive style of reporting. Headlined 'Native nomads cling to wilds: Despised aborigine goes walkabout to get away from the white man', its layout suggested a stereotypical story of Aboriginal cultural degeneration and collapse. However the text told a different story of cultural revival with Aboriginal people fleeing 'the deadly monotony of missions and compounds' for a 'life of nomadic wandering'. Tacked on to this was an attack on 'the white man' for 'relegating the aborigines to the position of outcast, derelict, someone hardly worthy of consideration', followed by a generalised account of desert survival knowledge that enabled the 'black man [to] live and fatten where the white man would starve', and a quote from botanist H. H. Finlayson's book *The Red Centre*, which was popular reading at the time.[77] There was even a petulant account of assimilation by Elkin in *Pix* magazine in 1963, headlined 'From the Stone Age to Today: the Aborigine' in which he explained that 'as the person who suggested the term I can say that it was meant simply to indicate that aborigines should have the same opportunities, privileges and responsibilities as ourselves, citizens of Australia. It was not meant to suggest that the aborigines as a race, or even the part-aborigines, should be lost in the general community or absorbed by the white race.'[78]

Susan Sheridan has documented a cross-section of views from racist stereotypes to patronising humanitarianism published in the *Women's Weekly* letters to the editor and regular columns. The narrative of successful assimilation was represented in the fascination with Harold Blair's career from his early trip to the United States to study singing to his appointment at the Melbourne Conservatorium, his marriage, and his sponsorship of the Harold Blair Holiday Scheme, which brought Aboriginal children from rural areas to holiday with families in Melbourne.[79] By the 1970s there were overt criticisms of assimilation in the *Weekly* including an interview with a young Dutch photographer who stated that 'I see assimilation as being something really nasty. To me it means the loss of the Aboriginal language, the art, the culture … Rate them as citizens of the country, but as citizens of a unique culture that should be preserved.'[80]

Hasluck and a new national leadership

Assimilation had a champion in federal government in the 1950s — Paul Hasluck, Minister for Territories (1951–1963) with responsibility for Aboriginal affairs in the Northern Territory and for the mandated territory of Papua New Guinea. Hasluck was the first federal minister to take an active national position on Aboriginal affairs. In this role he negotiated Australia's iconic 1961 national policy of Aboriginal assimilation — no mean feat given the frustrations of extracting agreement from obstinate state governments. (No such national policy was considered appropriate for migrant assimilation.) He also oversaw new ordinances introduced in the Northern Territory from 1953 intended to remove race from the legislation and usher in a new period of assimilation. Hasluck considered his greatest achievement to have been his role in driving legislative reform federally and in the states, a long and cumbersome process that accelerated from the early 1960s and was only completed in the straggling state of Western Australia in 1972. Historian Raymond Evans explains that the Queensland government claimed that legislation passed in 1965 and 1971 liberated Aboriginal people from control but in practice this meant that residents could be forced off the settlements permanently, leaving the land free for development by mining and tourism interests.[81]

Hasluck was a politician seeking pragmatic outcomes. Like his state colleagues he was influenced by Elkin's vision of assimilation, but there was also his own background in Western Australia as a journalist and trained historian — he wrote the first history of the state's administration of Aboriginal affairs in 1938. As a reporter travelling with the Moseley Royal Commission in 1934 he viewed first-hand the range of Aboriginal conditions across the state and, as an active member of the Australian Aborigines Amelioration Association in Perth in the 1930s, he wrote a series of articles in the *West Australian* newspaper calling for 'a new public opinion'.[82] Hasluck also brought a fresh new international perspective to the portfolio, having served as a senior public servant with the Australian delegation to the momentous San Francisco Conference that framed the United Nations Charter, where US President Truman proclaimed that 'with this Charter the world can begin to look forward to the time when all worthy human beings may be permitted to live decently as free people'.[83] Impressed by the power of international opinion, Hasluck raised the possibility of criticism of Australia's treatment of Aboriginal people in his first address to the House of Representatives in 1950 when he called on Australians to 'cleanse this stain from our forehead or we shall run the risk that ill-intentioned people will point to it with scorn'.[84]

Hasluck embraced the UN doctrine on race and human rights and UNESCO's educational programs to combat racial prejudice: extending equal rights and citizenship to all and the prohibition of discrimination on the basis of 'race, colour, creed or sex' — a cocktail that dovetailed with the agenda of assimilation. As Marilyn Lake explains, in Hasluck's view the cost for the cocktail was the 'denial and disappearance' of difference, for Hasluck 'universal rights meant citizenship enjoyed uniformly ... non-discrimination meant a refusal to acknowledge difference as a condition to which special rights might be attached — rights that could not be enjoyed uniformly by all citizens'.[85] This position later brought him into conflict with Aboriginal leaders, anthropologists, feminists and other activists in a growing critique of his rigid model of assimilation.

In keeping with his liberal outlook, Hasluck regarded race not Indigenous rights as the central issue; Tim Rowse argues that Hasluck saw assimilation as 'an attack on the "social problem" of "race"'.[86] The task was to improve the situation for all Aboriginal people to the extent that Aboriginal physical features would 'no longer signify any difference of behaviour and outlook'.[87] Hasluck later wrote 'we rejected the idea that race ... made any difference between human beings. We tried to think of the Aborigines as we thought of ourselves, not as another race but as fellow Australians.'[88] Given the post-war climate of humanitarian concern this seemed an achievable goal. Assimilation was the mechanism to achieve it and welfare provided according to need not race would be the way out of the morass of Aboriginal poverty. However, far from being erased, race continued on in practice in the Northern Territory and in the enunciation of national policy. Race remained a persistent and pervasive influence at all levels of government.

Hasluck wanted pragmatic solutions for the various 'local assimilation scenarios' he observed. In contrast to Elkin he believed that only a remnant Aboriginal culture survived around the continent, with 'crumbling groups ... living under a fading discipline' linked by 'tattered threads of kinship'.[89] In his opinion there was no future for 'Aboriginal cohesiveness, community or culture'.[90] This view of a decaying society rationalised a program of social engineering to shape a new assimilated Aboriginal population. For Hasluck assimilation was an individual matter. His liberal view of society was 'as an aggregation of freely thinking and freely acting individuals' and, as Russell McGregor points out, advancement for Hasluck was 'individualist in process' and 'individualist in outcome'.[91] He later wrote that 'the behaviour of the individual, the response of the individual, the aspiration or the effort of the individual, the heart and mind of the individual person are at the core of our problem'.[92] In this he seriously underestimated the continuing hold of Aboriginal cultures and the forces binding individuals to family, community and country. These were forces he considered to be an impediment to change rather than, as Elkin argued, a supportive bridge to gradual assimilation.[93]

A national forum

Hasluck began his drive for a national coordinated approach to Aboriginal affairs in 1951 when he put a proposal to Cabinet to establish an Australian Council of Native Welfare, made up of ministers and permanent heads of departments, to meet annually and make recommendations to federal and state governments. This was not a step towards Commonwealth control, he emphasised, but reflected the government's obligation to attend to 'the welfare of the people of Australia as a whole, its concern for the reputation of Australia internationally and its implied obligations as a member of the United Nations'. With an eye to official sensitivities he explained that while 'international obligations may only be implicit, they nevertheless constitute an undertaking which should be honourably observed and failure to observe them will expose Australia to criticism overseas'. Hasluck also argued strongly that only with additional federal funding could the states advance the policy of assimilation.[94] Cabinet agreed to the proposal for a meeting but made no reference to the vital matter of funding.[95]

Mindful of the power of publicity Hasluck actively sought media coverage in the lead up to the meeting in Canberra in 1951. Although Elkin was not invited to the meeting Hasluck asked him to write a comprehensive article for the *Australian Quarterly* to challenge what Hasluck described as the 'brief and garbled' media coverage of Aboriginal issues, and Elkin duly obliged.[96] Australian correspondent for the *Times* Roy Curthoys was invited to write with an eye to overseas opinion, especially in Russia since 'the Soviet bloc has been very busy discrediting us, and we ought to answer them by letting the world know of our positive and forward-looking measures in the interests of the natives'.[97] Parliamentarians were contacted in a similar vein and John Cain Senior, Labor leader of the opposition in Victoria, was told 'we can not hold up our heads in international company or talk realistically about communist oppression, until we act positively to redeem a race that is slowly moving to extinction through our own neglect and abuse'.[98] Hasluck could express these ideas in a confidential letter but he was outraged when

Soviet Leader Khrushchev made similar observations soon after in the United Nations.

The meeting must have been a keen disappointment for Hasluck. He was the only minister in attendance and only three of the states were represented. This reluctance to participate meant that it would be another ten years before the first full meeting would take place. State authorities who considered themselves experts in the area no doubt resented outside interference and, anyway, most were already on their own path to assimilation. New South Wales, Western Australia and South Australia had adopted the policy, Victoria and Tasmania had few formal barriers to assimilation and only Queensland was resisting change. Rather than national concerns, it was local variables that determined how the states channelled Aboriginal people towards assimilation through variations of the earlier mentioned models of dispersal and centralisation or the 'reserve/dispersal mechanism'. New South Wales had adopted assimilation as early as 1940, encouraged by Elkin's vision of streaming its estimated population of 10,000 Aborigines out of the reserves and camps and into houses in town. This also promised a way for the government to free itself of its Aboriginal problem as families were directed to mainstream government services.

By contrast Queensland resisted assimilation until the early 1960s and maintained discriminatory laws and practices into the 1980s. This reflected the state's long history of ruthless repression of Aboriginal people, epitomised in its colonial Native Police force.[99] It also favoured strict racial segregation and vigorously opposed the policy of absorption adopted at the 1937 national conference in Canberra, and it dragged its feet over assimilation, supporting an extensive network of segregated community institutions (nine missions and five government settlements) that held over 40 per cent of the state's estimated Aboriginal population of 19,500. The Director of Native Affairs Office invested heavily in this gulag — two-thirds of its annual revenue of £1.6 million in

1960 alone. Despite this expenditure, historian Ros Kidd has demonstrated that conditions there were generally appalling and contributed to endemic levels of Aboriginal ill-health.[100] This vast sum of money (compared to expenditure in the other states) was drawn largely from forced deductions of Aboriginal wages. The Queensland government acted as an employment broker, hiring out workers for low wages and paying workers on its own settlements minimal amounts, and was not keen to give up this revenue-raising venture. Finally in 1963 it formulated a two-pronged approach to assimilation through the existing institutional apparatus and an expanding social welfare program in the community; legislation to implement the policy was introduced in 1965.[101]

Despite this disappointing beginning, Hasluck reported enthusiastically to parliament on the outcomes of the 1951 meeting. The determination to develop a uniform definition of assimilation — something avoided by the Department of Immigration — had led to agreement that assimilation meant that 'all persons of aboriginal blood or mixed blood in Australia will live like white Australians do' and he predicted that this would have a beneficial effect on state and federal planning for services, citizenship, missions and settlements. Keen to avoid any parochial opposition to the policy Hasluck pitched assimilation as 'distinctively Australian', being based on equality of opportunity and equality of life, which he described as the 'two characteristic principles of Australian democracy'. This was a nation where men could 'stand on their own worth' and 'coloured people' could become part of the general community 'as soon as their advancement in civilisation permits'. Nor was the appeal to human rights inherent in assimilation something foreign to Australia to be addressed, as Hasluck put it, 'in a strange accent' since the fundamental principles were contained in its national institutions and heritage of English law. Hasluck stressed the need for a gradual approach to assimilation since many Aboriginal people remained 'primitive' and 'stone age' and 'by reason of ignorance and primitive habit (not race) were not ready to enter the general community'. Concluding his speech he proclaimed that the Council was embarked on 'a humane task; we have founded our resolve on a faith in the capacity of human beings; we have shaped our plan on the best traditions of democratic life in Australia. We want all those who are trying to build a better Australia to join us in this effort. We want to make sure that every one living in our country will be able to have a happy and a useful life — a life worthy of a human being.'[102]

A 'long, slow job'

Hasluck's reference to the retarding influence of Aboriginal primitiveness reflected a common misconception at the time, and one that worked against the goals of assimilation as it antagonised many Aboriginal people by forcing them to earn and learn rights and benefits that were their due. The assumption was that Aboriginal assimilation was a long haul — a matter of generations for some. This reflected entrenched assumptions about Aborigines' limited capacity to change and become modern citizens and the continuing need for guidance and tutelage. This also mirrored the 'gradualist' approach to change advocated by colonial powers in the United Nations who, reluctant to abdicate their political power and economic interests, insisted that colonised peoples should be granted independence only after a long period of training.[103] The fallacy in this approach, which stifled the very changes it promised, had been highlighted a century earlier by the abolitionist Lord Thomas Babington Macaulay when he observed that, 'the maxim is worthy of the old fool in the old story who resolved not to go into the water till he had learned to swim. If men are to wait for liberty until they become wise and good in slavery, they may indeed wait forever.'[104] Yet administrators continued to follow the principle. Magistrate H. D. Moseley who led the 1934 Royal Commission in Western Australia claimed that Aboriginal people were like 'apprentices who must be taught, as much as a child is taught about their new status'. A West Australian politician argued in parliament in 1951 that the 'Aboriginal adult' has 'the mentality of a wayward child' and unless he 'for two to three generations is disciplined and controlled' the 'problem' can never be solved.[105] Political historian Charles Rowley wrote in 1964 that these views were symptomatic of colonialism generally and assimilation in particular:

> Colonial policies amounted for a long time to deferment of rights, and periods of tuition in the meantime; tuition before rights. This attitude to other racial groups is deeply in-built into western culture; people must be specially taught (by us) to be saved. It has become the automatic overt reason for deferment of change, which we really want to defer for other reasons ... The last in a long series of rationalisations ... was the 'assimilation policy', which as officially propounded was notable for putting tuition before rights, and was used to justify the restraint of Aborigines in multi-purpose institutions. The new purpose of these was declared to be 'tuition'; or 'training' leading to 'assimilation'.[106]

Aboriginal leader Bill Ferguson articulated his frustrations when he told a 1937 Select Committee inquiry into Aboriginal administration in New South Wales that the government should abolish the Aborigines Protection Board and 'listen to the voices of the Aborigines themselves.' He demanded the immediate granting of full citizenship rights and equal education since 'we are not an inferior race, we have merely been refused the chance of education that whites receive'. Ferguson argued for the development of a secure land base created by transferring all reserve land and housing stock managed by the Board to

Aboriginal control and in the case of houses built in town, to 'give the people the deeds of ownership — a straight out gift'.[107] Such a proposal was anathema to Elkin, who proposed 'a slow phasing out' of the Board with himself as chief advisor and supervisor of the process. He assured his colleagues that 'as a result of our efforts, the Board will no longer be necessary in a generation or less'.[108] Elkin maintained a distinctly managerialist position on Aboriginal assimilation and remained convinced that guidance was always essential — a conviction that ensured a continued role for anthropologists in policy-making, administration and research and underpinned his claim to be the longest serving member of the Board.[109]

Many politicians and authorities followed Elkin's lead during the 1950s and stalled on the issue of extending full citizenship rights to Aboriginal people. Instead they advocated a qualified form of 'contingent rights' like Western Australia's Certificates of Citizenship, which required Aboriginal applicants to demonstrate their suitability and then imposed a form of apprenticeship where retaining the new 'privileges' was conditional on fulfilling new responsibilities under the watchful eyes of the police and department officers. Hasluck, in keeping with his commitment to human rights, advocated the granting of full citizenship rights. In 1952 he told the *West Australian* that Aboriginal people found present forms of citizenship 'hedged by conditions … irksome and even offensive' and that race-based laws should be repealed so that it would no longer be 'colour or a fraction of colour or any other racial or genealogical reason but [only] the test of whether he or she stands in need of special care and assistance'.[110] However, his intention to write race out of Northern Territory ordinances was blocked by a deft sleight of hand. All explicit references to Aboriginal status were removed from the *1953 Welfare Ordinance* and the supposedly non-racial term 'ward' was inserted to refer to people requiring the 'special care and assistance' of its protective welfare measures. However, ward referred mainly to people who were ineligible to vote and in the Territory this meant Aboriginal people. The result was that the majority of Aboriginal people of full descent were classified as wards under the *Ordinance* and 'half-castes' were exempted.

Models of phased assimilation

Governments around Australia adopted variations of an assimilation package of overlapping phases that reflected Elkin's original model.[111] The goal was to extend to Aboriginal people the full range of citizenship rights and responsibilities encapsulated in the three categories of T. H. Marshall's classic definition of democratic citizenship — civil, political and social — and to bring their standard of living to equal working-class suburban conditions. This one-way, unilinear process mirrored the goals for assimilating migrant families but the process was inevitably far more complex.

Migrants entered the path to assimilation from designated arrival points in Australia, then followed a set program organised and controlled by the government that took them from reception centre to work to the suburbs; they had little opportunity to vary their way as they worked to create financial security for their families. They came with varying assets and skills and incentives and were given minimal assistance. As long as they appeared to assimilate rapidly and brought economic benefit to the nation they were tolerated. Most Aboriginal people, on the other hand, started from a position of no rights, general poverty, limited education, poor health and racial exclusion. They came from various points around the nation, largely in remote and rural Australia — institutions (settlements, missions, New South Wales reserves, children's homes) on or near their traditional lands, pastoral stations, camping reserves, fringe camps and conventional town dwellings — and had been subjected to varying degrees of oppression and control. To achieve Aboriginal assimilation governments had to remove restrictions preventing Aboriginal people from accessing mainstream services and benefits, create better working conditions, combat white racism and train Aboriginal people to live as assimilated people. The major vehicles for change were the large-scale Aboriginal institution and the nuclear family; the destination was the suburban Aboriginal nuclear household.

Such a major undertaking required vision and human and financial resources to achieve. Instead reforms took over twenty years to implement and institutionalised racism and Aboriginal poverty continued. At the end of the assimilation period in the early 1970s, governments could rightly showcase their momentous legislative reforms; however, outside of the statute books the equal playing field — a prerequisite for the achievement of assimilation — remained an elusive dream.

Assimilation in the Northern Territory

For Hasluck federal initiatives in the Northern Territory provided a model of assimilation for state governments to follow, one that would appease critics at home and abroad. The *1953 Welfare Ordinance* enacted a process of assimilation through family welfare that held out the eventual goal of full citizenship for all Aboriginal people there. The ordinance sought to deal with them on the basis of need not race and to deliver welfare rather than administer people through punitive controls. However, it proved to be yet another variation of the assimilatory model of dispersal and centralisation and, despite best intentions, it remained wedded to race categories. All 'part-Aboriginal' people were automatically exempt — a move welcomed by the Darwin Half-Caste Progressive Association led by Joe McGinness — and were directed to apply to mainstream service agencies for assistance. Some applicants were able to obtain rental housing through state housing authorities but they were strictly monitored to ensure that they conformed to imposed standards of suburban life.

The majority of Aboriginal people of full descent were gazetted as wards in a special Register of Wards compiled by the Territory Welfare Branch. Their future was to be assimilated into conventional domestic family life, 'steady work', 'financial responsibility', hygiene, schooling and training for work through the familiar processes of institutional life followed from colonial times. Subsequent ordinances emphasised the importance of employment in this program and the goal of developing in wards 'a sense of responsibility, and not idleness and profligacy'.[112] Echoing the general notion of Aboriginal change, Hasluck told parliament that this would be a slow and gradual process that meant waiting for 'generations before the old tie of the bush, the tie of tribal law, the tie of tribal kinship, is loosed sufficiently for them to come our way. We have to be patient, in those cases, for generations.'[113]

The conventional approach of institutionalising Aboriginal people to achieve these goals was adopted and people were removed from their homelands around the Territory and concentrated in settlements, missions and pastoral stations, the new transit points for the path to assimilation. The bulk of the dramatic increase in funding for Aboriginal affairs in the Northern Territory from £166,000 in 1954–55 to £1.2 million in 1962–63 was used to develop the necessary network of institutions and to build facilities that would attract white staff.[114] A 1961 report by the Welfare Branch on the remote Beswick settlement southwest of Katherine described a 'planned programme of social development ... so that he/she and/or his/her children will be able to participate in everyday Australian life'; the starting point for this process of change was 'upsetting the Australian aborigine's entire social tradition'.[115]

Tim Rowse provides a searing analysis of the goals, instruments for change and impacts of these settlements and how they failed to prepare Aboriginal people for assimilated living in mainstream Australia.[116] The central core, also found in migrant centres like

Bonegilla, consisted of communal dining rooms, shared ablution blocks and separate houses for white staff. Various forms of accommodation — mainly transitional huts and makeshift camps — surrounded this central compound. For migrants the reception centres were just that — sites where they were processed and prepared before they were sent out to jobs organised by the Commonwealth Employment Service. By contrast, while the Aboriginal settlements were claimed to be preparing their residents to be streamed off into an assimilated way of life, it was also assumed that they would develop into permanent rural communities. This seeming contradiction was rationalised by the claim that it could take three generations before Aboriginal people would be ready to enter the community — and conditions there seemed set to make this into a reality. This was yet another example of the Macaulay maxim of enslaved people having to wait forever for their liberty.

Rowse demonstrates how the treatment of Aboriginal people in the settlements undermined their rights as human beings and citizens and how 'training' frequently contradicted the goals of assimilation. A system of food rationing was manipulated to enforce citizenship training and the combination of artificially low wages, payment in rations for work, and the denial of unemployment benefits plunged these new communities deeper into poverty. White staff disrupted traditional family practices *and* the learning of new forms of family life by taking over most mothering duties: washing, dressing, playing, providing meals and the education of the children. In doing so they seriously disrupted mother-child bonding, whose significance for positive child development was then beginning to be widely recognised. Aboriginal people were excluded from decision-making and it is hardly surprising then that many developed little interest in the 'rewards' assimilation offered them, or indeed that many were turned into opponents of the program.

At the same time authorities continued to remove children of mixed descent from their families motivated by the ideals of assimilation and the perceived need to rescue the children from life in the camps. Hasluck explained to the Australian Association for the United Nations in 1961 that 'half-caste children found living in camps of full-blood natives ... should, if possible, be removed to better care so that they have a better opportunity for education' in order to prevent them from growing up with 'neither full satisfaction' of tribal life or 'opportunity to advance in status'.[117] During the 1950s Aboriginal child welfare was gradually mainstreamed and new options were created for placing children in cottage homes in Darwin; with adoptive parents; in foster homes; and to be educated in boarding schools and children's homes in the southern states. In the 1970s the Aboriginal children's homes in the Northern Territory were closed and by 1974 four hundred Aboriginal children were living there with white foster families or in child welfare institutions.

Reforming federal legislation

Legislative reform was an essential stage in the model of assimilation. With governments in control of the reform process, change should have proceeded with relative ease. Instead the opposition and resistance demonstrated by politicians and administrators made this into yet another frustrating and drawn out process in the federal and state arenas. Hasluck's proposed federal meetings could have provided the leadership to pressure recalcitrant states to speed up their reform agendas but as it turned out, the federal government itself was slow in coming to the party. It was only from the late 1950s that the Attorney General's Department progressively reviewed all federal and state legislation and pushed for the repeal of race-based provisions in the lead up to debate in the early 1960s on the United Nations International Convention on Racial Discrimination (1965) and the International Covenants on Civil and Political Rights and Economic, Social and Cultural Rights (1966). It was in the context of mounting international pressures in the late 1950s and early 1960s that the federal government introduced major reforms and it was protests by Aboriginal organisations and their supporters that led to the granting of equal wages for Aboriginal people in 1966, and the 1967 referendum.

The least problematic initiative for the federal government was to extend the federal franchise to all Aborigines. This was a potent symbolic act that was guaranteed to appease critics, but its force was lost in the rhetoric of the 1967 referendum so that it is widely assumed that it was the referendum that led to the granting of the vote. In 1962, on the recommendations of its Select Committee on voting rights for Aboriginals, the federal parliament introduced a bill to extend the franchise to all Aborigines. In South Australia, Victoria, Tasmania and New South Wales, Aboriginal people already had the right to vote in state elections. Western Australia and Queensland followed suit in 1963 and 1965 respectively. In introducing the bill in federal parliament, Hasluck reiterated his firm position on Aboriginal assimilation that 'it has been our ideal that we should not be a nation with divisions of race or class, or a nation of different selves, but that we should be one people, with one destiny, working together to serve one national good'.[118]

However the federal government's most significant reform for Aboriginal families was to remove the discriminatory exclusions that withheld from them the Australian welfare state and federal benefits for widows, mothers, the aged, sick and the unemployed. For decades Aboriginal families in need had been seriously disadvantaged by the inferior support provided by state authorities. Issued by local police or in centralised institutions — native hospitals, government settlements, missions and children's homes (all subsidised at levels far below other government institutions and where Aboriginal people could be detained indefinitely) — support was cheap and nasty and detrimental to Aboriginal wellbeing and quality of life.

The process of reform had begun in the 1940s when child endowment was made payable for all Aboriginal children except those classed as 'nomadic' and amendments were passed to allow exempted Aboriginal people access to pensions and other benefit payments. Finally, between 1959 and 1966 all exclusions were repealed and Aboriginal people now had 'in a statutory sense at least' equal rights in the social security system. The states had pushed for these changes despite their own miserly support for Aboriginal people. As John Altman and Will Sanders argue, they did so in anticipation of the sizeable financial benefits they stood to gain as authorities appointed to receive social security payments on behalf of recipients, the greater proportion of which they would be allowed to retain for expenditure on the recipients' welfare, leaving only pocket money to be passed on. This arrangement would continue until they judged the recipients capable of handling their own financial affairs and receiving direct payments. Welfare payments also enabled state authorities to cut expenditure on rations.[119] By the 1960s benefits were mainly paid directly to recipients, resulting in a huge injection of cash income into the pockets of Aboriginal families around Australia. This newfound financial independence enabled recipients to seek better living conditions off the reserves and to escape from the exploitative arrangements on pastoral stations as documented by Mary Anne Jebb for Aboriginal workers in the West Kimberley.[120]

A national definition of assimilation

Finally in 1961, in the context of mounting world tensions about race and with specific attention to the situation in Australia, a full house of ministers and senior bureaucrats responded to Hasluck's call for a national meeting of the Native Welfare Council. This was a crowning moment for Hasluck when delegates reached agreement on a national policy of assimilation.

> The policy of assimilation means that all aborigines and part aborigines are expected to eventually attain the same manner of living as other Australians and to live as members of a single Australian community enjoying the same rights and privileges, accepting the same responsibilities, observing the same customs and influenced by the same beliefs, hopes and loyalties as other Australians. Thus, any special measures taken for aborigines and part aborigines are regarded as temporary measures not based on colour but intended to meet their need for special care and to assist them to make the transition from one stage to another in such a way as will be favourable to their future social, economical and political advancement.[121]

However, despite the passage of ten years since Hasluck's first attempt, and the high level expertise gathered around the table, the discussions and reports only highlighted how slowly the states were moving and how unenlightened the thinking had remained. Progress on legislative reform was disappointing and demonstrated continuing support for the 'liberal approach' to removing barriers to citizenship in accord with 'the capacity and advancement' of the individual rather than wholesale removal of discriminatory laws. Discussion on methods to advance assimilation still stressed the 'long, slow job' and reports from the states showed little advance in health, education, child and family welfare services, housing, vocational training and employment. It would still be some years before the repeal of all discriminatory legal restrictions for Aboriginal people. Victoria had taken decisive legal action in 1957, New South Wales and South Australia followed in 1963 and Western Australia in 1964 and 1972. In 1966 most Aboriginal people in Western Australia were still designated as 'natives' under law and less than 17 per cent of the estimated state population of 21,900 had been granted citizenship. Although Queensland had protested at the 1951 meeting that the move to citizenship rights already existed, the process only began there in earnest in 1965.

Delegates agreed to an ambitious ongoing program of meetings and research but as the decade proceeded it became clear that they were swimming against the tide as pressure for federal control gained momentum and their conservative assimilatory approaches became increasingly out of step with strident voices of protest in the community. When the next meeting was held in 1963 Hasluck was Minister for External Affairs and in 1965 delegates shifted the intent of his definition of assimilation towards one of integration by changing the clause 'are expected eventually' to 'will choose to live'. The 1967 referendum and subsequent political events spelled a major shift away from state control of Aboriginal affairs and ushered in a significant new federal leadership role, from which perspective Hasluck's initiatives for assimilation looked very old fashioned and paternalistic. In 1972 the new Whitlam Labor government began to replace assimilation with the policy of self-determination, which was more in line with developments in international debates on Indigenous rights. In the same year the federal government also introduced a new legal definition of Aboriginality, subsequently adopted around Australia, that moved away from imposed racial categories to criteria of self-identity, descent and confirmation by the Aboriginal community.

Clockwise from top left: Coolbaroo Club *film promotional photo [Courtesy David Dare Parker, Photographer]; My wife and I want to vote cartoon [Originally published in* Citizens *(1964) by the Department of Native Welfares and reproduced courtesy of the Department of Indigenous Affairs; Family with Holden (1960s) [Courtesy Darryl Kickett's private collection]; I bring home my wages cartoon [Originally published in* Citizens *(1964) by the Department of*

Assimilation in Nyungar Country

Part III

Native Welfares and reproduced courtesy of the Department of Indigenous Affairs]; Responsible drinking cartoon [Originally published in Citizens *(1964) by the Department of Native Welfares and reproduced courtesy of the Department of Indigenous Affairs]; Three Nyungar men enjoying their first beer in a Narrogin hotel (1964) [Courtesy* West Australian *Newspaper]; Family with hunting dogs (late 1940s) [Courtesy Darryl Kickett's private collection].*

5. Good Citizens

You can give a man the right to drink, but if he has no right to work on equal terms with other men, no right to the legal wage of his country, no real right to education, no property rights, no social equality, then his one right becomes a mockery.

Dorothy Lilley, 1964[1]

If we do not address the economic place of Aborigines in this nation, we will all continue to pay for an unemployment rate of four times the national average; our health budget will be drained caring for a people whose rate of kidney disease, diabetes and infant mortality far outstrips the non-indigenous population; and years of costly litigation will continue …

The only way forward is through co-existence — and that means mutual respect and recognition of indigenous rights and historical realities.

None of us, least of all Aboriginal people, wants to be having this debate in another five years. We have to get it right this time.

Darryl Kickett, 1997[2]

In 1964 the West Australian government published a curious comic book called *Citizens* to inform Aboriginal people and the general public of its assimilation goals.[3] The depictions of assimilated family life and good citizenship were familiar from federal campaigns promoting the Australian way of life and commercial advertising images of happy families. The Aboriginal family in this booklet had achieved a new level of prosperity with their immaculate suburban home filled with all the 'mod cons' — a car, television, electrical appliances and furnishings. Family members showed a new confidence based on the assimilation of middle-class aspirations and values. Dad was a white-collar worker who wore a suit, hat and tie; mum kept house dressed in fashionable slim-waisted frocks and spiky high heels; and two sons went to school wearing long socks and overcoats. The parents were shown exercising their new voting rights and discussing current affairs with friends and visitors. This husband told readers, 'I bring home my wages to pay for food, clothes and house rent … my wife and I care for the health, teeth and eyes of ourselves and our children' and 'as good citizens we are interested in the government of our state and country'. Several hotel scenes showed respectable Aboriginal men having a drink at the front bar and couples enjoying an evening together in the hotel lounge — unexpected images given how barriers of race and gender had preserved Australian hotels as the domain of white masculinity, but these illustrated the changes following the proposed introduction of Aboriginal 'drinking rights'.

This imagery was familiar enough at the time, but what was curious was that it had been sixteen years since Western Australia first adopted the policy of assimilation and these fundamental elements of the package were only now being advertised. The images were *aspirational* — the vote and other legislative reforms were still to be passed by parliament — and the Minister for Native Welfare, E. M. H. Lewis, admitted to the *Bulletin* that living conditions for Aboriginal people in no way matched those shown in the cartoons. Instead they depicted 'copybook families at a more advanced stage than they are now' that he hoped would 'play on [Aborigines'] pride in their race, and urge them to prove they can behave as well as the white man'.[4]

Case study: Western Australia

Using Western Australia as a case study we now turn our attention to how state governments met the obligations that lay at the heart of assimilation. These included the classic rights of citizenship, described by John Chesterman as 'the political, legal and social rights that are integral to a person's membership of a political community'.[5] The aspirational images accompanying the promise of assimilation also suggested a further level of equality, encapsulated in Amartya Sen's more ephemeral vision that goes beyond conventional indices of income, wealth, health and education to embrace qualitative dimensions of personal happiness, self-respect, the respect of others, the right to participate in community life, and the freedom to choose what to do and what to value.[6] These all seemed to be present in the imagery of assimilation with one exception — the element of choice. Here lies one of the paradoxes of assimilation — this vehicle for creating free and independent Aboriginal citizens started from the premise that *they had no choice but to become assimilated.* Here too lies the basis for a fundamental difference in opinion between governments and most Aboriginal people, who insisted — explicitly and often implicitly — on the right to choose whether to retain their Aboriginal identity or not and to have all the rights and benefits enjoyed by all other Australians, *regardless* of which choice they made. This is true equality.

The fact is of course that the West Australian government failed to fulfil most of its obligations or only did so over an unacceptably long period of time. What we find there is an outdated machinery of government with limited goals and resources cranking along in a sea of opposition and resistance to change. We see blustering between vested interest groups, government officers' dreams of reform and their disheartened returns to the drawing board, and politicians and the public trotting out old solutions in new guises. At the time governments held Aboriginal people to ransom for delaying assimilation; what this case study clearly shows is that governments failed to deliver on their promises to Aboriginal people.

Conflicting visions

Western Australian made its first tentative moves towards a policy of Aboriginal assimilation in 1948 when the newly elected conservative government set out to reform the jumble of Aboriginal policies and programs left by fourteen years of Labor government. Reform was in the air and the minister for the new portfolio of Native Affairs and leader of the National Party Ross McDonald explained that the government was also responding to the 'current outlook of the natives as the result of the war, the growing number of half-castes [and] public sentiment'.[7] In 1948 the government made two significant appointments that would shape its way forward: Magistrate F. E. A. Bateman was invited to survey Aboriginal conditions around the state and to recommend a program of reforms, and a new Commissioner for Native Affairs, Stanley Middleton, a former senior bureaucrat in native administration in Papua New Guinea who had trained at the Australian School of Pacific Administration in Sydney, was appointed to implement the government's program. These men brought very different approaches to the task.

Bateman's narrow, practical approach was rooted in attitudes and practices of the past. Yet his opening comments resonate with today's rhetoric of practical reconciliation: 'there is a danger of becoming too idealistic. While admitting that the aborigines have been badly treated in the past and that our treatment of them today leaves much to be desired, I believe that it is important to realise their limitations and to approach the problem in a practical way.' His major proposals for positive change in the south of the state consisted of a selective housing scheme and education 'to fit these people into our economic and social structure'. His other recommendations repeated stereotypes and worn-out solutions that had exacerbated Aboriginal poverty and marginalisation in the past. He described families living on reserves as 'idle, unreliable, fond of drinking and gambling and generally useless' and, like the authors of every prior major government report, recommended their removal to segregated settlements. He did not elaborate on their fate there but he was well aware of the appalling conditions at existing institutions and commented in his report that 'sanitation and hygiene are merely words without meaning at Moore River [Settlement]'. When it came to schooling he advocated the segregation of children in 'colleges' in good agricultural areas to change them from a 'nomadic, idle and discontented race to a settled, industrious, contented section of the community'.[8] Bateman followed earlier recommendations dating from the 1905 Roth Royal Commission in suggesting a new field system for managing Aboriginal populations that would be independent of the police, and in this instance the government agreed to his proposals.

By contrast Stanley Middleton brought a fresh proactive perspective to the job that often set him in opposition to his political masters, fellow bureaucrats and the public — as well as Aboriginal people. Middleton's deep shock at the situation of Aboriginal affairs in the state and his outspoken criticisms also set him apart from his more complacent colleagues. In his annual reports he described the draconian legal powers that he had inherited as 'unparalleled in the legislative treatment of any other people in the Commonwealth or Pacific territories ... repugnant to basic humanitarian and welfare principles, devoid of any common ground with the people we are trying to help and creative of more misunderstanding, dissatisfaction and abuse than any other piece of similar legislation known in the free world today'.[9] The Department of Native Affairs was a 'rundown, unorganised administrative shambles' and a 'morass of apathy, neglect and prejudice'.[10] He was shocked by the extent to which race-based practice pervaded departmental practice and expressed his dismay at the use of personal dossiers and 'caste' cards that 'obsessively mapped and meticulously recorded' fractions of Aboriginal descent — as far as '21/23rds' — in working with departmental clients.[11] He suggested to his minister that the 'accidental destruction' of the cabinet of these cards would be of 'untold benefit' to Aboriginal people.[12] On Middleton's first visit to Moore River Settlement north of Perth he was struck by the contrast between the 'smiling laughing chattering' of the villagers who greeted his patrols in Papua New Guinea and the Aboriginal 'inmates' who 'just sat there absolutely silent and just stared and it was almost unreal. There were no greetings ... not a word. They simply stared at you with a fixed gaze.'[13] This description brings to mind images that would have been circulating at the time of inmates of concentration camps in Nazi Germany

Middleton saw his mandate as being to extend full citizenship rights to Aboriginal people and to 'lift' them to 'equality with what we consider the normal standard'.[14] His catch-cry became 'assimilation into the general community on the basis of reasonable equality in all facets of community life'.[15] At the 1951 meeting of the Native Welfare Council in Canberra he called for national action to repeal all discriminatory laws and introduce 'special welfare acts' along the lines of Hasluck's original model for the Northern Territory.[16] He was determined to professionalise and modernise the department. This meant phasing out the use of police officers as agents for the department at the local level, and creating a system of field officers along the lines of the British colonial model implemented in Papua New Guinea. The department's many controlling and punitive tasks would be cut back to reflect a purely welfare role. All existing inferior services for Aboriginal families — mostly provided in run-down multi-purpose institutions — would be terminated and they would be directed to professional mainstream agencies instead.

By denying Aboriginal people access to mainstream services of health, housing, education, and child and family welfare over the generations the government had helped to create the endemic levels of Aboriginal poverty, ill-health and institutionalisation that Middleton observed around the state. Middleton actively sought the advice and cooperation of a select group of Aboriginal people in planning the changes he sought. However, many Nyungar people were reportedly 'very bitter in their attitude to the department ... [they] never fail to argue that all this talk of a fair spin for the native ... is eye wash when a coloured man is not even free to walk in the main street'. Many stubbornly maintained that they would never 'apply for citizenship rights, that they don't want assistance from the Department and will pay their own way'.[17]

Middleton's reforming zeal was inevitably obstructed by a tangle of oppositional forces that caused frustrating delays and forced him into compromises that went against his own goals of assimilation. The heart of the issue was that there was no match between the state's limited intentions and Middleton's grand vision. Nor could his force of determination break through the entrenched racism that he encountered everywhere without full government support, and that was not forthcoming. There was also a fundamental difference of opinion between Middleton and his political masters over the best way forward. He advocated rapid legislative reform so Aboriginal people could respond proactively to assimilation, while they insisted on a gradual process using existing legislation to control and guide change. The result was a road to assimilation that was long and bumpy where the destination always seemed to be just beyond the horizon. Little wonder that Aboriginal people felt frustrated by the shamefully slow pace of change and treatment that contradicted assimilation's promises of equality and better living conditions.

The bumpy road to assimilation

Planning for assimilation was in some respects an act of the imagination in the 1950s. There was no national census data on Aboriginal populations and state information only gradually improved as welfare officers took over from the police in collecting local statistics. The government could feel generous with funding allocations that increased almost fourfold between 1948 and 1959 when the annual grant topped £848,792, although they only represented an average of 0.6 per cent of total annual expenditure from the Consolidated Revenue Fund. In 1958 the Select Committee Inquiry announced that it would take £2.4 million to improve Aboriginal conditions across the state — a staggering figure then, especially as there was no hope of federal assistance.

Endemic institutionalised racism at all levels of government bogged down Middleton's goals and he wrote of its 'chilling effect' on his work.[18] As he pushed for legislative reform, politicians repeated the same old arguments that Aboriginal people were not ready and that change had to be gradual and closely controlled. The member for the southwest province H. L. Roche claimed in parliament in 1950 that an Aboriginal adult had 'the mentality of a wayward child' and that unless the population was 'for two to three generations ... disciplined and controlled' the 'problem' could never be solved.[19] Middleton later recalled that he encountered 'the same antagonistic attitudes wherever I went because of the changes I was talking about' and that he was treated in a 'very nasty and critical way'.[20]

Middleton was in the unenviable position of pushing for citizenship and equality from within an administrative culture that was directly opposed to these reforms. Tim Rowse writes of the 'bureaucratic inertia' that comes from the effort of having to pursue new policy objectives using the tools of outmoded institutions and social arrangements that 'have their own dynamics which may counter the intentions the reformer has of them'.[21]

Slavoj Zizek similarly comments on how 'remnants' of a 'prior regime that remain imbricated after the shift … can govern the form and function of the regime that takes its place'.[22] Little wonder that Middleton's administration often reverted to earlier aggressive forms of forced change such as the removal and institutionalisation of Aboriginal children as optimum strategies for assimilation. On the one hand Middleton was committed to the assimilatory goal of creating and supporting intact nuclear family units carved out of the networks of extended Aboriginal families. He advised his field officers to create relations with these families as 'friend, philosopher and guide'[23] and in his final annual report in 1961 he congratulated Aboriginal parents — 'To these people I would like to say, in officially parting: Good work! Keep it up!'[24] Yet like his predecessors and colleagues he was also trapped by the belief that removing Aboriginal children from their parents was in many cases the only way to secure a better future, and there was a dramatic expansion of children's institutions under his administration.

Middleton's efforts to make all mainstream government services accessible to Aboriginal people required a strong mandate from government. This was initially forthcoming and in 1948 the Education Department was instructed to stop excluding Aboriginal children from state schools and to enforce compulsory attendance instead. Despite complaints from teachers and white parents the government was resolute on this new principle. In the following year the Department of Public Health was instructed to accept Aboriginal clients, despite an outcry from staff and other patients.[25] The Department of Child Welfare however, had to negotiate over a twenty-year period from 1951 before it took full control of Aboriginal child welfare. This resulted in a period of parallel and sometimes competing services. With greater surveillance of Aboriginal families and the facilities of *two* departments now available for child placements, removals began to escalate. The State Housing Commission was similarly tardy in taking control of Aboriginal housing needs, which it only finally managed to do in 1972. This contributed to the continuing chronic state of sub-standard accommodation for Aboriginal families when the success of the assimilation agenda rested on moving them into conventional housing.

These mainstream departments were geared to meet the needs of settler Australians, and in dealing with migrant and Aboriginal clients they could be aggressively assimilatory. Without the checks and protocols that we have today, discriminatory practice inevitably continued on down the chain of command. Teachers maintained segregation in classrooms and playgrounds and local medical officers devised separate arrangements for treating Aboriginal patients. The Department of Child Welfare initially refused to accommodate Aboriginal juvenile offenders swept up in the expanding net of punitive youth surveillance, prompting Middleton to object in a letter to his minister in 1952, that 'since such treatment postulates SEGREGATION, how can we convince an already sceptical public and outside World that we have seriously endorsed the policy of assimilation?'[26] Conflicts over rights to control local Aboriginal communities erupted as police officers were replaced in their role as agents for the department with a network of field officers. In frustration Middleton told his staff: 'I am afraid that we must be prepared to suffer indignities at the hands of subordinate officers of other Departments, local authorities, officials and others whose views towards the natives are reflected in their attitudes towards officers of this Department.'[27] In fact Middleton's own field officers, some with years of experience in colonial administrations, were not immune to local prejudices. The District Officer for the Southern district had observed sympathetically on his appointment in 1949 that in thirteen years of service in India he had seen 'no parallel to the wretched living conditions of the Natives of the District in my charge'. However, in a subsequent report on the 'character and characteristics' of Nyungar people he provided a long list of 'defects' with the only positive attributes identified as 'love of children', 'generosity' and 'sticking together'.[28]

The Department of Native Welfare (formerly the Department of Native Affairs, renamed in 1954) was itself an expanding bureaucracy with professional staff in head office and a network of dedicated welfare officers spread across the state, and by 1967 it employed 112 staff. It also managed an expanding range of institutions and their staff — thirty-four new places including children's homes, missions, hostels and grandiosely named 'boarding schools' were established between 1948 and 1971. The department had a significant public profile and recognised expertise in Aboriginal matters. There were no performance indicators or benchmarks built into the process of assimilation to assess its work and signal a cut-off point, and it was widely believed that its Aboriginal clients would always need special assistance. It was in no hurry to phase itself out of the action. In 1968 academic Henry Schapper attacked the department for hanging on rather than completing the task of assimilation. In his opinion its abolition 'would be conducive to Aboriginal integration whereas a separately organised administration is conducive to Aboriginal separatism'.[29] The Department of Native Welfare continued to operate however until 1972 when it was finally dismantled and its staff, clients and facilities were transferred to the Department of Community Welfare, and the State Housing Commission took over responsibility for Aboriginal housing.[30]

Assimilation's targets: a test case

For its initial target the government decided on the Aboriginal population of approximately 3500 people living in the southwest region who in 1951 made up around 17 per cent of the total estimated state Aboriginal population of 21,092.[31] Officials assumed that they would willingly take up the offer of assimilation. Anthropological research and popular hearsay agreed that they lived in a cultural limbo, dispossessed of their traditional lands and culture and excluded from the society of their white neighbours. They were described as 'gypsy like groups'[32] whose 'old ways [had been] destroyed [and] replaced with half-caste children, strong liquor and vice'.[33] In fact Aboriginal people in the southwest had forged ways of life and identities that blended Aboriginal traditions and settler culture. At the end of the Second World War they were culturally, economically and politically diverse. This reflected differences between rural and urban communities, loyalties to family, community and country, divisions between 'nor'westers' and 'sou'westers' living in Perth, and in personal experiences of legislative controls and institutionalisation.

In 2006 continuing misunderstandings about Aboriginal identity in the region and whether their 'old ways' had been 'destroyed' were put to rest when the Nyungar people proved their right to Native Title over the Perth Metropolitan Area in the Federal Court of Australia under the stringent legal 'test' for Native Title that requires Aboriginal people to demonstrate a continued link to traditional country, culture, and practices.

In focusing attention on Aborigines' need to assimilate, the government failed to appreciate the extent of racism that would have to be overcome. This region was no pushover for reform. Racism was a normalised way of life here. Carolyne Dean describes in her study of continuing racism in post-war Germany how society had 'assimilated it, learned it, performed it, believed it, and then came to conceive it and live it as normal'.[34] These words apply equally to the nature of racism in the southwest of Western Australia in the 1950s. The relatively small Nyungar population should have been easily absorbed into the vast farming landscape. Instead the people loomed large as an imagined threat to moral and social order in the minds of white residents who vigilantly policed and enforced barriers of race. Daily life was sharply segregated along the lines of race, either by legal sanctions, government rulings or informal social barriers. Aboriginal children were kept out of the schools; people in urgent need of medical care were turned away by doctors and hospitals; curfews were imposed to drive families out of town before nightfall; and whole communities were forced to live in rough bush shelters on scraps of unwanted land next to town sanitary and rubbish depots without water or sanitation services. They sat cordoned off at the back of the town cinemas, were refused entry to concerts and dances, could be imprisoned merely for entering a hotel and were not welcome in most country churches. Even war veterans were routinely excluded. The exceptions to the rule were employers of Nyungar workers and businesses who accepted their trade. Middleton stated that this level of racism had made Nyungar people 'very bitter' and 'turned them into a Fifth Column'.[35]

This level of segregation helped to shape Nyungar communities with their own loyalties and values that included a strong distrust of outsiders and authority and a readiness to stand up for their rights. They relied for their survival on knowledge of country, work with local farmers and the support of large family networks. Like any Australians they wanted the best for their families and protested against the denial of their rights and unfair treatment — epitomised in the actions of the Native Union and its leader William Harris who lobbied the government during the 1920s for the vote, railed against the injustices of the *1905 Aborigines Act* and called for the right to 'live up to the white man's standard' but 'in our own way'.[36] Bonds of national identity and loyalty may not have been strong amongst these people who were largely excluded from the nation, but their men had enlisted in both world wars and their families had contributed significantly to the local war effort through their labour.

Nyungar families were pushed along the road to assimilation by a shrinking rural job market, pressures to maintain large dependent family networks, government interventions to force conformity, and the expectations of settler Australians. But there was little access to the things that they deemed the bottom line for a good life — stable family life, adequate housing, regular work and income, and rights to property to establish a secure economic base. Rights that other citizens took for granted were deemed 'privileges' for Nyungar people that they had to earn and repeatedly prove themselves worthy of. The step of seeking acceptance as an assimilated individual demanded the greatest price: to abandon the old, accept the superiority of the new, and remain permanently on trial in a world where the goalposts for acceptance were continually being shifted.[37] Little wonder then that most Nyungar people continued to rely on ties of family, community and place as a base from which to negotiate their way through the changes and opportunities of assimilation.

Native Welfare Committees

Exactly how did white residents in the southwest respond to the call to break down the barriers of race and welcome Nyungar families as equal citizens in their towns? Middleton took the challenge to them using 'every conceivable medium and technique' to explain the policy.[38] He met with a brick wall of resistance. Locals claimed that extreme levels of race 'hatred' made the goal of assimilation in the region an impossible dream and they demanded that the government continue to support segregation. Some demanded more 'rural training centres' where Nyungar families would learn over the generations to 'take their places, working and living among the white communities'.[39] Like Bateman they ignored the dismal failure of the existing native settlement scheme in achieving these goals. A yet more extreme proposal was to remove the entire population to be resettled in 'the vast areas of our rich northern lands'.[40] The *Narrogin Observer* claimed that nothing could be done to turn Nyungar people into 'respectable members of the community. They appear to lack all sense of responsibility and decency.'[41]

Middleton responded in 1952 by initiating a network of Native Welfare Committees grouped together under a state Native Welfare Council (the Aboriginal Advancement Council of WA from 1964), based loosely on the Good Neighbour Council but without its prestige or generous financial support provided by the federal government. Within a couple of years the network had grown to eight committees in country towns mainly in the south dedicated to promoting assimilation through 'good neighbourliness' free from the constraints of racism. The duties of the Native Welfare Council, which was made up of affiliated youth, service, business and church organisations, were to advise the minister, organise public conferences, publish a monthly newsletter, engage in fundraising, promote National Aborigines Day events locally, and distribute federal assimilation campaign materials. The Council also acted as a lobby group and voice for Middleton in the community. In 1953 it supported his bill to extend citizenship rights to Aboriginal people across the state and lobbied the federal government (without success) to provide urgently needed funding for assimilation programs and to build up a national body on the lines of the Good Neighbour Council.[42] In 1959 the topics for the Council's annual conference were 'electoral enrolment of natives' and 'Parliamentarians' views on advancing natives towards the responsibilities and privileges of taking part in Parliamentary elections'.[43] In 1964 the Council developed an ambitious program for housing homeless families, educating adults and promoting 'good neighbourliness' that all stalled when federal funding was not forthcoming.

The history of the Narrogin committee provides some insight into action at the local level. Its perceived standing was evident in the official guest list at its inaugural meeting, which included the Minister for Native Affairs and the Commissioner. The committee of representatives from the town's churches and businesses agreed to 'promote the welfare and assimilation of natives', improve their 'spiritual well-being' and assist them with housing and training and to become industrious workers. Like volunteers in the Good Neighbour movement they saw their tasks as providing practical assistance to families and organising activities — film and lecture evenings, sports days, and special prayer meetings — to inform Nyungar families about assimilation and to bring them together with local townspeople. Early in the piece they explained that 'we find it difficult to know just what to do for our native folk in order that we can help them without spoiling them'. However this would prove to be the least of their problems. Nyungar families and town residents ignored their invitations and events were often attended only by 'the kind folk who arranged [them]'. On the town reserve where Nyungar families lived in humpies and tents the committee erected a couple of huts to rent to selected families to train them for their new responsibilities as householders. However the exercise was abandoned when the committee learned that it had no power to evict families who failed to pay rent and refused to move out when ordered to do so. Then the department refused permission for the committee to build a meeting hall on the reserve because this would encourage 'little Harlems'. They also found that Nyungar families were not as passive and naive as they had assumed and reportedly 'laughed to see white men working for them' and played on local town rivalries by shifting their allegiances between the committee and the town's Native Welfare Association.[44]

Good citizens

Aboriginal people were in the peculiar situation of being citizens whose status, David Mercer suggests, was best described as 'citizens minus' — a reference to the catchcry 'citizens plus' used by Canadian Aboriginal peoples in the 1970s to express their political aspirations.[45] In 1948, along with all other Australian-born residents, they were granted Australian citizenship. Yet a multitude of discriminatory acts and regulations straightaway stripped them of the rights and benefits enjoyed by other citizens and subjected them to draconian controls that applied only to Aboriginal people. In Western Australia the government had passed more than thirty-seven such statutes since the first act in 1844 that constituted Rottnest Island off the Perth coast as an Aboriginal prison. Over the years these laws had operated to promote settler interests at the expense of Aboriginal rights and had maintained White Australia in the southwest. Despite its commitment to assimilation it was not likely that the state would readily see them swept away. For Middleton and his supporters the immediate repeal of these laws was a fundamental step in the move to assimilation. These were the battle lines in the struggle for legislative reform in Western Australia that lurched on for twenty-four years before the statute books were finally cleared in 1972.

'Not slaves, not citizens'

Middleton was impatient for reform. Influenced by Hasluck's more enlightened national vision, he wanted to take the radical step, for the times, of erasing all legal racial classifications of Aboriginal people. Frustrated by government delays Middleton turned to the press to promote his ideas. In 1952 two critical and emotive articles under the title 'Not Slaves, Not Citizens' written by Middleton but published under the name of Des Stuart, the wife of writer Donald Stuart, appeared in the *West Australian* newspaper. The second article began 'Not Pagans, not Christians; not white, not black; not half-castes, but outcastes. Such are we, who are the descendants of the original half-castes,' and it continued in a paraphrase of the famous speech by Shylock in Shakespeare's *Merchant of Venice:* 'Hath not (a native) eyes? Hath not (a native) hands, organs, dimensions, senses, affections, passions? Fed with the same food, hurt with the same weapons, subject to the same diseases, healed by the same means? If you prick us, do we not bleed, if you tickle us, do we not laugh? If you poison us, do we not die? … Have we not been turned away from your places of worship?'[46]

The gloves were now on. Middleton narrowly avoided government censure over the articles following an inquiry by the Public Service Commissioner,[47] but there was also support for his views. In January 1953 a deputation to the Minister for Native Affairs of leaders from the churches, the Native Welfare Council and the Women's Service Guild insisted that all Australian-born people regardless of race should automatically have all the rights and obligations of citizenship. Middleton was now a member of the Australian Labor Party and in the lead up to the 1953 state elections he advised on its new eight-point platform that included full citizenship rights for all Aboriginal people as well as 'adequate housing and education, encouragement of aboriginal land settlement, and a "fair" wage for aboriginal workers'.[48] Shortly after taking office the Labor government presented a bill to parliament proposing full citizenship for people of mixed descent, the repeal of the bulk of the *1936 Native Administration Act* and the creation of a purely welfare role for the department. However, hostile conservatives in the Legislative Council defeated the bill arguing that citizenship and freedom from departmental control were 'not in the best interests of the native population' and that access to alcohol would lead to 'riots and drunken orgies, and … it [would] not be safe for [white] women to walk out after dark'.[49] Taking revenge on Middleton they attacked him for being 'foolishly intemperate in his statements. One might almost say he has been foolishly impertinent.'[50] A watered-down version of the bill that made no mention of citizenship rights for Aboriginal people was passed in the following year. The *1954 Native Welfare Act* was a tentative, piecemeal step towards change. Nevertheless it was significant in confirming the welfare and assimilation roles of the renamed Department of Native Welfare and in removing discriminatory controls over Aboriginal employment as well as the powers to forcibly remove Aboriginal people to reserves and otherwise restrict their movements. A consequence was the emptying of adult inmates from the Moore River and Carrolup settlements. Most were given a one-way train ticket to Perth, where some remained while others returned to the homes they had left many years before to try to pick up the threads of their lives. From this time the settlements were developed as rural 'boarding schools' for Aboriginal children.[51] To encourage continued public interest, Middleton introduced in 1954 an occasional information broadsheet *The Helping Hand*, described as 'a bulletin of information on the current work of the Department, its officers and matters of interest affecting the welfare of natives in Western Australia'.[52]

Biding time

Middleton responded to this Pyrrhic victory by promoting the other avenue open to Aboriginal citizenship, the system of certificates of citizenship introduced in Western Australia in 1944 — despite his misgivings. He encouraged Aboriginal people to apply and advocated a more liberal attitude in granting certificates, although he had no direct control over the process, which was presided over by local magistrates. A consequence was that annual applications increased from 83 in 1952 to 2202 in 1961, with 1652 certificates granted in that year.[53] Flooding the market in this way sparked complaints from police officers frustrated in their efforts to ensure that the growing number of certificate holders did not supply alcohol to 'natives in law'. Some police introduced crack-downs to the extent that in 1952 officers threatened a Fremantle resident that he would lose his certificate of citizenship if he failed to clean up his yard as instructed by the Fremantle City Council — an injustice averted by Middleton.[54] A magistrate in the goldfields township of Cue claimed that

Aboriginal people did not 'appreciate the full meaning of citizenship' and should be instructed in its 'privileges and obligations' before applying. Middleton's deputy responded that there were many Australians who did not understand citizenship so why should Aboriginal people be expected to be 'experts' and, echoing the words of Lord Macaulay cited earlier, he advised that 'it is only in practising that we improve as citizens'. He added that many Aboriginal people resented the whole process and refused to even apply.[55]

Middleton had been a lone voice in 1953 when he complained to his minister about 'the treatment of citizenship rights as a cloak to be put on and taken off at the wishes and whims of officialdom … relegating it to something more consistent with the procedure of a department store than a dignified, basic birthright'.[56] Five years later the report of the state's *Select Committee on Native Matters* (appointed in the wake of the public controversy over Aboriginal conditions at Warburton in the Central Reserves, the vast area encompassing the Gibson and Great Victoria Deserts now referred to as the Ngaanyatjarra Lands) concluded that 'anything more calculated to destroy the self-respect and self-confidence of such people would be difficult to imagine. Indeed, it provides any native so inclined with a ready-made excuse, satisfactory to himself, for his evasion of responsibility and for the squalor of his life.'[57] Reverend Dowding, father of the future premier of Western Australia Peter Dowding, presented evidence to the select committee. He proclaimed that 'citizenship is a right and not a gift', and, drawing on the Declaration of Human Rights, asserted the right of all people regardless of race to participate in the democratic government of their country. He added that the test of a society was how it cared for its 'weaker members' and that citizenship was 'the beginning and not the end of the matter' since is was 'our bounden duty to enable them to live as members of an Australian community'.[58] Another witness to the Committee quoted from the ILO Convention No. 107, which stated that Indigenous people should 'benefit on equal footing from the rights and opportunities which national laws or regulations grant to the other elements of the population'.[59] The Select Committee Report soundly denounced arguments for more gradual legislative reform and rejected as unfounded public fears about increasing alcohol consumption and violence and concluded that not to grant immediate full citizenship to Aboriginal people would be 'un-Christian, un-democratic and un-Australian'.[60]

Citizenship and drinking rights

Despite these passionate and expert calls for change, another five years elapsed before major reforms were approved, by which time Middleton had retired in poor health. The new Commissioner Frank Gare carried legislative reform forward in a climate of growing pressure from the revived federal Native Welfare Council meetings, the federal lead in legislative reform, growing international scrutiny, and strengthening Aboriginal activism.

The *1964 Native Welfare Act* was a major turning point in the history of Aboriginal legislation in Western Australia that pointed the way to full citizenship rights for Aboriginal people. Significantly its stated aim was to 'promote the integration of natives into the general community and to provide special welfare measures during the transitional period', wording that heralded major changes in the administration that were only gradually realised. The remaining discriminatory powers in the *Native Welfare Act Amendment Act 1905–1960* were repealed including the Commissioner's guardianship of children and controls over property, wages and deceased estates, and prohibitions on cohabitation, sexual contact and alcohol. The definition of 'native' was retained to enable people of Aboriginal descent to continue to draw on services still provided by the department. All discriminatory clauses in other statutes (including the caning of Aboriginal juveniles under the *Criminal Code*) were also repealed, with the exception of the *1944 Natives (Citizenship Rights) Act* and the prohibition on alcohol in the *Licensing Act*.[61] The reasons for this will soon become clear.

To prevent a public backlash against the changes Commissioner Gare instigated an 'educational campaign' that was the 'most intensive of its kind ever undertaken in Western Australia'.[62] There were press interviews and meetings with key stakeholders, including Nyungar people, and 2000 copies of the cartoon booklet *Citizens* with its message of Aboriginal assimilation and citizenship were distributed. The *Daily News* dubbed the images of Aboriginal suburban life as 'pie in the sky' and added that the pamphlets showed 'how easy it will be for natives to have a drink in a pub … But it is really very necessary for [Aboriginal people] to feel it is easy for them to have a family in a house ahead of, or at least parallel with, the right to drink in a pub.'[63] In fact the real focus of departmental activity was on convincing the public to accept Aboriginal drinking rights. An unintended consequence was that in the mainstream press much of the debate addressed this issue at the expense of other rights.

Today the symbols of Aboriginal rights in the 1960s are the vote and the 1967 Referendum. The fact that drinking rights were also held up as a sign of Aboriginal advancement has faded from public memory, hurried along by present-day alarm about substance abuse in Aboriginal communities and debates over the reintroduction of prohibitions to curb alcohol consumption. The campaign was led by Aboriginal servicemen and their mates, protesting against Aboriginal exclusion from hotels, and this was taken up as a citizenship rights issue by service organisations, on the grounds that men who fought for their country had demonstrated the highest level of good citizenship. In 1946 the Returned Sailors, Soldiers and Airmen's Imperial League of Australia lobbied the prime minister to this end and continued after the war to argue for citizenship with drinking rights for Aboriginal ex-service men.[64] In 1952 the Narrogin delegate to the League's

West Australian Congress, H. L. Willis, warned that Australia could be criticised in the United Nations for its treatment of Aboriginal people and posed the question that 'if these people don't measure up to our standards who is to blame?' The Congress then passed a resolution that 'native returned servicemen with honourable discharge' who applied for certificates of citizenship should be granted the right automatically.[65] Then as now, Aboriginal drinking rights was a hot public issue, with beliefs and stereotypes about alcohol and Aboriginal people shaped by sensationalised theories of 'racial' intolerance to alcohol that linger in today's unfounded genetic explanations. Not surprisingly the government's handling of the issue was a case study in defensive campaigning. As Commissioner Gare explained, the booklet *Citizens* was designed to drive home the point that 'there [was] more to citizenship than the right to drink'.[66]

For a start these rights were to be conditional and confined to the southwest region. The 1963 reforms proposed drinking rights on a trial basis in the South-West Land Division where the people 'had already reached an advanced stage of assimilation, lived in or close to towns and could easily be contacted [about] how to regard and handle their new privileges'. Contingent on their appropriate behaviour was the continuation of drinking rights within the region and their gradual extension throughout the state.[67] Achieving this took a quirky legislative manoeuvre. With the only remaining prohibition on alcohol contained in the *Licensing Act* this statute was amended to prohibit the sale of alcohol to 'natives' in designated areas of the state as proclaimed by the Governor. So on the first of July 1964 the whole of the state outside the South-West Land Division was proclaimed a prohibition area for 'natives' under the *Licensing Act.* For Aboriginal people in these areas the only access to alcohol was to apply for a certificate of citizenship. Sanctions for persons, Aboriginal and non-Aboriginal, who supplied alcohol to Aborigines without these certificates remained in force. This arrangement of giving rights to some Aboriginal people while excluding others provided a relatively simple way for the government to subsequently remove the right should it be deemed necessary. Of course this conditional granting of rights also fitted existing practices, from exemptions to citizenship certificates, that worked to keep Aboriginal people under direct surveillance and so reassure settler Australians that Aboriginal behaviour would be controlled, with the threat of revocation of rights for failure to conform.

There was a flurry of promotional activities in the lead up to 'D (for drinking) Day' — the day that hotels would open their doors to Aboriginal patrons. Officers from the Department of Native Welfare conducted public information campaigns, lectured local councils, policemen and publicans and sent field officers out to instruct Aboriginal people about 'socially accepted methods of drinking' and their new civic responsibilities. The Minister E. M. H. Lewis repeated patronising stereotypes of Aboriginal men when he entreated the local shires to 'give natives a go' since 'they will be in strange surroundings and to many of them it will be a feeling like a schoolboy during his first day at school. Like the schoolboys, some will settle down quickly while some will take more time.'[68] Field officers were instructed to emphasise to Aboriginal people that 'you must prove yourself worthy of the new deal by your behaviour and attitudes in hotels. Avoid any arrogant or "cocky" attitude — try and behave as though you had always enjoyed the right. Be clean and tidy and in this way don't give anybody the opportunity to criticise you on these grounds.'[69]

It soon became clear to the department that its pitch was out of touch with Aboriginal opinion. For them alcohol access was a serious issue along with electoral rights through automatic citizenship. Alcohol restrictions were a huge social barrier that limited access and participation in most of the recreational activities available to the wider community. Field officers reported that Nyungar people were not interested in being lectured about drinking rights. One officer expressed surprise at 'the seeming casualness with which the natives of this Division are taking the program. It seems that the long-awaited privileges are no more than the minimum rights anticipated by them and only a small minority will abuse the rights when finally granted.'[70] Many said they were non-drinkers, some already had drinking rights through citizenship certificates,[71] and others were not 'interested in liquor as such so much as they [were] in knowing they have the right of access if they wish'.[72] They also resented the conditional 'trial situation' and the 'prophecy' that they 'would cause trouble'.[73] Aboriginal spokesperson Ernie Papertalk told a meeting of one hundred Aborigines at Mullewa that there were 'much more important matters associated with the new rights such as higher education of children, better housing and stabilisation and responsibility for holding down jobs and fostering mutual respect in the community'.[74]

The department did however correctly judge the heat of white reaction to the granting of Aboriginal drinking rights, which threatened one of the bastions of segregation in the south and a jealously guarded site of white masculinity — the public bar of the country hotel. From the turn of the century metropolitan and country hotels ran a system of prohibition and segregation. Nyungar people were barred by law from hotel precincts and police officers prevented the supply and consumption of alcohol outside hotels as well. Not surprisingly alcohol-related offences routinely topped statistics on Aboriginal convictions. A distinctive drinking culture existed in Aboriginal camps that was characterised by irregular binge drinking of illicit fortified wines and spirits that encouraged rapid drunkenness and aggressive behaviour. This fed into the continuing cycle of police detection, arrest, conviction and imprisonment.[75] The granting of drinking rights raised fears amongst town residents that this behaviour would be transferred to local hotels. More sympathetic observers expressed the hope that the new rights would undermine the drinking culture altogether by encouraging more 'acceptable drinking habits by removing the necessity to drink secretly and fast'[76] and by breaking the nexus of Aboriginal drinking and police.

Neither of these eventualities happened. The Nyungar response to 'D-Day' was subdued as most kept away from the hotels where they knew they were not welcome. Twelve months later the department reported favourably on Aboriginal responses to their new rights, and prohibitions were lifted throughout the state between mid-1966 and 1968. In his 1965 study of drinking rights and Aboriginal assimilation in Narrogin, anthropology student John Hall found few changes in Nyungar drinking culture, while white hostility had continued, expressed in comments to him that the town's efforts to assimilate Nyungar people had been 'heart-breaking' and that they were 'different and must be treated differently'.[77] A few hotels set up dingy 'black bars' for Aboriginal drinkers.[78] In some towns publicans — who risked fines of up to £50 for refusing to serve a client without just reason — only sold Aboriginal people bottles to take home. It was a gross injustice then that Aboriginal people still living on town reserves could be fined £5 or imprisoned for twenty-one days by local justices of the peace for being drunk or merely having alcohol in their possession within reserve boundaries. In 1966 a Justice of the Peace in the Pilbara town of Onslow sentenced a group of Aboriginal men to six months jail for this offence, prompting departmental intervention and the men's release but not before the Law Society had called for reform of the system of local justices and an editorial in the *Daily News* demanded the abolition of this 'rough justice' that 'result[ed] from a limited knowledge of the law'.[79]

A consequence of these continuing inequalities was that patterns of secretive binge drinking, police patrols and high levels of alcohol-related convictions continued.[80] Sociologists Dennis

Gray and Sherry Saggers argue that present excessive consumption and resultant imprisonment, harm and ill-health are due in part to these earlier colonial relations that encouraged patterns of substance addiction and dependency.[81] Present opinion about the causes is divided but there is general consensus that an alcohol crisis is threatening Aboriginal communities across Australia. For some critics, prohibition appears to be the only solution and grog bans have been introduced in many areas.

Altogether these were significant advances in citizenship rights in Western Australia, though they were an unconscionably long time in coming and were enacted in ways that were demeaning to Aboriginal people and that maintained discriminatory practice. Aboriginal people were largely excluded from the entire process of reform and a whole generation grew up before the agenda was completed. In 1972 the 65-year regime of punitive legislation came to an end, but the culture of discriminatory and punitive treatment of Aboriginal people continued on in their dealings with mainstream departments and services.

6. Happy Families

> *The civil rights era officially ended inequality of opportunity, officially ended* de jure *legal inequality. At the same time those civil rights triumphs did nothing to address the underlying economic and social inequalities that had already been in place. It doesn't recognise the fact that the rewards, the house, the Lexus, big bank account, those are not only the rewards, you know of the pot of gold at the end of the game, they're also the starting position for the next generation.*
>
> Dalton Conley, 2003[1]

Five years after the issue of the booklet *Citizens*, at a time when the assimilation period was drawing to a close, the Western Australian government was *still* introducing Aboriginal families to the ways of suburban life. One of a series of initiatives at the time was the film *A House in Town* (1969).[2] When I saw this film recently I was surprised to see in one scene my partner Darryl's parents, Fraser and Rhoda Kickett. Dressed up to the nines they were depicted visiting Nyungar friends in a comfortable suburban home in a scene that looked more like the visit of a welfare officer than the noise and tumble of families catching up. As Fraser drew back on his cigarette, the narrator's voice commented that visits could be 'pleasant without costing much' and, when Fraser looked at his watch, the voice added on cue that 'friends who have not spent the evening drinking will be more inclined to leave at a reasonable hour'. I was immediately struck by the contrast between this scene and its intimation of hopes for a better life and the angry man I met in the 1980s and the desperate condition of the family home overflowing with grandchildren and needy visitors. The film was made shortly after Nan and Pop moved to Perth from Cuballing after Pop was dumped without notice from his job on the local shire road gang. Their two youngest sons, one of them Darryl, had just moved to Perth to start their apprenticeships. With a small housing commission house near Fremantle and Pop working on the Fremantle wharves life was looking good for them. Posing for the film they might well have imagined themselves moving into a similarly comfortable well-furnished home that would become a 'home away from home' for their extended family. The story of Nan and Pop's disillusionment with such government promises is the subject of this chapter.

We have seen how this official imagery of assimilation promised Aboriginal families a new life as modern citizens living in comfortable suburban homes. The invitation to a better life, represented in images of white suburban families, was seen everywhere in advertisements and newspaper and magazine stories. Then there was the federal government's commitment to family life and home ownership as 'a defining trait of the genuinely egalitarian society' and a sign of 'full participation as citizens'.[3] However, it saw the commitment to creating a secure future for Australian families as separate to promises of assimilated living for Aboriginal families.

Australian governments had pledged themselves to ensuring a secure future for other Australians. In the midst of the post-war housing crisis federal and state governments worked together to create the necessary infrastructure to put home ownership within the reach of the average Australian family — through extensive suburban development and building projects, advice and special loans for returned servicemen, tax incentives and cash allowances for young families, and assistance for low income home buyers. As noted in chapter two, between 1947 and 1961 home ownership increased from 50 to 70 per cent of Australians and 90 per cent of the population owned their own homes at some time between 1946 and 1970. During the 1950s and 1960s there was almost uninterrupted full employment for male workers and a new expectation of women working full-time as homemakers and mothers, supported by a whole new world of domestic appliances and other consumer goods as well as an army of professionally trained experts to provide modern scientific advice on infant care, child rearing, coping with teenagers and pleasing hardworking husbands. These initiatives changed the destinies of many middle and working-class families. Home ownership proved to be a major asset and investment for the future, boosted by tax privileges and the rapid appreciation of land and house prices in the 1970s, making it 'the dominant source of privately acquired wealth in Australia'.[4]

Aboriginal families were not included in the national imaginary of a nation of homeowners. By failing to even offer them the chance to be a part of this leap forward, Australian governments missed a golden opportunity for their advancement, the effects of which are still being felt today as we again debate the issue of housing for Aboriginal families. Given the Commonwealth government's generosity to other families it seems cruel and short-sighted to have overlooked the desperate needs of a tiny percentage of the population living in the worst conditions of all. Aboriginal people could well have expected *extra* assistance to help them over the hurdles of poverty left by decades of government control of their lives and neglectful treatment. Instead they were left out of the dramatic move to cheap and affordable home ownership and, in a time of full employment, were left to slip into escalating poverty and welfare dependency. At the same time the government continued to break up families by removing their children. A consequence, as Carolyn Allport points out in the New South Wales context but with relevance for Western Australia as well, was that 'by the end of the 1950s, residential segregation, low wages and poor living conditions continued to be the lot for many Aboriginal people. Along with continuing constant monitoring and harassment by police, welfare officers and station staff, this ensured that Aboriginal people remained second-class citizens.'[5]

The sorry road to nowhere

In Western Australia it was left to the Department of Native Affairs to lead Nyungar families along the road to suburban living. We have seen its track record in delivering citizenship rights to Aboriginal people. How did it fare with this much more costly and complicated task? How did it measure up in meeting its three basic promises of a better life for Nyungar families — a secure intact family; a home in the suburbs with the basic comforts of modern life; and employment and a secure income to support this new way of life?

The bottom line for the department in delivering on these promises was to provide the *infrastructure* to enable Aboriginal families to build a safe and secure future based on adequate housing and services, regular work and income, and property to create their own economic base. This infrastructure was there for settler Australian families. However, its delivery went far beyond the department's resources and funding and, indeed, its expectations of what Aboriginal people could achieve. What then could the department do? Instead of providing Nyungar families with the basic resources for independent living, the department created a family welfare service that enmeshed them in a web of dependency as they negotiated their way through the new pressures of assimilation and suburban life.

The department had a new mandate to assist with Aboriginal

welfare and to promote Aboriginal assimilation. Punitive legal controls over Aboriginal people were being pared back and the new field system of welfare officers was replacing the disciplinary role of the police. Operations were better resourced than ever before with funding increasing from £224,666 in 1948 to £512,642 in 1954 and this trend continued into the 1960s. Other government departments were also beginning to take responsibility for service delivery to Aboriginal people. However, change was slow in coming, funding remained far below what was needed and old patterns of discriminatory treatment of Aboriginal people continued. Government officers fell back on the maxim that 'good enough' was sufficient for Aboriginal families. Despite official images of Aboriginal families living in conventional suburban housing, many remained in makeshift shelters in town camps well into the 1960s. When they finally moved into the suburbs they lost access to their remaining reserve land bases.

In the meantime the department deployed its field officers to train families for a future time when housing and other benefits would become available, building in this way on the assumption identified by Rowley that Aboriginal people 'must be specially taught by us to be saved'. The families' ongoing inferior living conditions left them open to accusations of not living up to new standards of assimilated living by providing proper home conditions for children attending school. This exposed them to the threat of having their children removed, which became the experience of many families. Once again the department deferred change by looking to the children's future rather than taking immediate action to guarantee jobs for Aboriginal adults. It negotiated with the federal government to make social security benefits available to all Aboriginal people, laying the basis for the era of welfare dependency that continues today. Politicians in the United States referred to similar moves at the time to clear Native Americans off reservations and terminate all federal trust responsibilities as 'egalitarianism in action'. However their critics saw it as evidence of the federal government's determination to 'get out of the Indian business once and for all'.[6]

Nyungar families were expected to make major changes and sacrifices in their lives for few tangible rewards. The adjustment from bush to suburbia was difficult enough, let alone having to achieve the transition without the essential infrastructure. There were many other new tensions too — greater government intervention in their lives, the pressures of direct daily contact with white racism, and a raft of new living expenses and significant cultural differences. On top of this the Nyungar population was experiencing its own baby boom and this placed a heavy burden on shrinking family resources. Between 1951 and 1961 the population increased from 3500 to 5500,[7] and the proportion of children in the population grew from 44 per cent in 1950 to 57 per cent in 1955.[8] These figures also reflect better counting methods as field officers took over from police in collecting population data.

For families in rural areas who were expected to make the move to town, their way of life contrasted in virtually every way with the middle-class model. Extended family networks were the heart and soul of Nyungar life. People were highly mobile within their 'runs' — loosely defined areas that encompassed bushland, farms and local towns and that were inscribed with traditional, historical and social knowledge and connections. Here families were assured of the basic necessities of life — a place to camp, bush tucker, fresh water, paid farm or domestic work and meetings with other families for a yarn, a game of cards or a sociable drink. Here too they were safe from prying eyes and the threat of police harassment. Knowledge of family, country and rural work was what mattered. Family dwellings were tents and rough bush shelters on farmers' land or in the bush while doing rural work. In-between jobs they were obliged to camp in town reserves, often situated next to rubbish depots and without water or sanitation services. Waiting there between jobs they were perceived by townspeople as lazy and unwilling to work, fitting existing stereotypes of Aboriginal people. As seasonal rural workers they stayed in family groups — men, women and children — and moved around their runs following jobs with farmers they knew. They negotiated proper wages and paid taxes, but were excluded from union membership and denied other protections of the national wage, arbitration, and workers compensation systems. In the early 1950s seasonal farm labourers could earn up to thirty shillings a day and were employed for six to nine months of the year. In 1957–58 shearers were paid £5 per hundred sheep — often a day's work — making £30–40 a week, shed hands £18–22 a week.[9] With few overheads they could make a fair living but families could accumulate little in the way of savings or possessions, so this was a precarious life in times of hardship.

Denied the same opportunities as other Australian families to improve their conditions in the post-war period Nyungar families were forced instead into the paradigm of 'welfare problem' and eventually into a system of welfare dependency. The fallacy was that the basic requirements for the new life promised in the imagery of assimilation — an intact family, housing and regular employment — remained out of the reach of most Nyungar families into the 1970s. The irony was that they were blamed for this outcome — after struggling to survive under the burden of a system that would have tried the patience of Job. The tragedy was that unlike white families they had no economic base on which to build a secure future for their families.

Promise One: A secure family unit of father, mother and children

A central building block for assimilation was the intact nuclear family with the mother as home maker, father as waged worker, and children as students, all fitting in to the structured spaces and regimented routines of suburban living. In this model children were pivotal for taking assimilation on down the generations, mothers were the vital agents of assimilation within the home, and fathers provided the income to support the process. This new focus on the nuclear family fitted with post-war research by adviser to the World Health Organisation, psychologist Dr John Bowlby, that addressed effects of the widespread child separations of the war years. Bowlby's research highlighted the integral role of the nuclear family as the natural and fundamental unit of society and the deleterious effects of maternal deprivation.

It is surprising then to find that Aboriginal child removals *increased* during the 1950s, despite the official commitment to support families (but not extended family groupings) together. The department's legacy of child removal was rationalised by constructing Aboriginal parenting as dangerous to children's physical and moral safety and an impediment to their advance and assimilation, in contrast to the presumed kindly and beneficial parenting provided by the state and its agents. Middleton was to break with this tradition but had to contend with the department's continuing culture of removal. The contradictions of his position were apparent in his statements that parents and children should remain together and his threats that where children were 'living under unsatisfactory circumstances, not receiving regular and proper education' then as their legal guardian he would order them to be removed.[10] In 1961 he reiterated the 'changeover from institutionalised welfare to family welfare as a matter of firm policy' adding that the 'need to split families no longer exists when better living accommodation and conditions have been provided or obtained. The retention of the family unit ... by modern yard-sticks was considered to be preferable in many ways to the "artificiality" of the best institutions available.'[11] Yet he knew the difficulties parents faced in meeting their new circumstances with their limited resources, which for most included inferior housing and living conditions.

He was also aware of the history of their anguished opposition to losing their children, supported during the 1950s by protesters using the language of human rights. It seemed that officers could not break with the strong culture of child removal or from the view that the success of assimilation rested on the fragile shoulders of Aboriginal children.

Schooling

Schooling for Aboriginal children was made compulsory after the war. For the department however it was not enough to leave this responsibility with Aboriginal parents — although most were keen for their children to be educated — and once again it looked to institutions to ensure positive outcomes. The existing network of settlement and mission schools was expanded and developed into a system of agricultural colleges, boarding schools, cottage homes and children's hostels. This was made possible in part by subsidising children's living expenses with child endowment payments that otherwise would have gone to their families. The children targeted were those prevented from attending school due to distance, lifestyle or parental neglect (as judged by field officers) and parents were also pressured to send their children in voluntarily. Middleton wrote in his 1950 Annual Report that parents who resisted sending their children were 'advised to give [them] the opportunity they have not had themselves. In nearly every case they have put aside their sorrow for the sake of the children and sent them away.'[12]

These initiatives helped to turn around Western Australia's appalling record in Aboriginal education, and in 1964 there were 5300 Aboriginal children enrolled in schools around the state. However, this significant achievement was undermined by the alarming fact that 25 per cent of school children in the south were living in institutions. Such was the legacy of decades of Aboriginal child removal that field officers had to be reminded regularly that their task was not to take children out of their homes but to create better home environments to keep families together.[13]

Secondary and vocational education was a new priority and here too family separation was the basis of advance. The department opened youth hostels in Perth to accommodate selected secondary students and apprentices from the country who were strictly assessed before admission in regards to their schooling, behaviour and personal hygiene.[14] Once there their behaviour was monitored and controlled by hostel managers reporting to the department. In fact, rather than creating assimilated young citizens keen to move out into white society, the young people thrown together in this way developed enduring personal relationships that reinforced their Aboriginal identity.

Mainstreaming child welfare

The transfer of control over Aboriginal children to the Department of Child Welfare promised release from the discriminatory and arbitrary system of forced removals and protection, but it stretched out over more than twenty years, despite all the pressing reasons for rapid change.[15] The slow pace reflected the entrenched culture of removal in the department and the reluctance of child welfare authorities to take responsibility. The *1947 Child Welfare Act* set out an orderly protocol for child separations, with procedures for reporting of cases, notification and liaison with families, Court hearings and parental rights of appeal.[16] However, as reports following the beginning of the transfer of controls in 1954 indicated, this did not resolve the problem of separation of Aboriginal children from their families.

Middleton was a strong advocate for the transfer. He welcomed a proposal in 1950 for close cooperation as 'a forward step in the right direction'[17] and he wrote optimistically in his 1951 Annual Report that this would remove parents' 'bitterness' and foster their 'co-operation and participation' with the department. Middleton's interest also reflected his alarm at the existing ad hoc system of child removal under his predecessors. Police officers removed children as advised by the Commissioner, and sometimes on their own initiative, and then sent them off to a departmental institution, often in such haste and neglect of their duty of care that they forwarded no records, not even of the children's names. Middleton was convinced that many removals ran the gauntlet of the law.[18] In 1950 he wrote to his minister of his concerns about the 'illegal and unsatisfactory procedures of the past' and that 'seldom, if ever, were applications made to the Hon. Minister for Native Affairs for a warrant of committal to an institution in the case of children, which means, of course, that the parents or guardians, could hardly have failed in any application to a Court for a writ of *habeas corpus*'.[19] Fifty years later researchers Rene Powell and Bernadette Kennedy were shocked to read Middleton's notes in an archive file as they searched for information about Rene's removal from Warburton Mission in 1952 without her mother's permission. They concluded that Rene's case was one more example of 'the "not so legal" removal of unknown numbers of Indigenous children in Western Australia in the name of benevolence'.[20]

A consequence of the slow pace of reform was the development of two parallel agencies, each with the powers to remove and place Nyungar children in institutions or with foster or adoptive parents, although some Child Welfare officers were opposed to mixing their charges with Aboriginal children. The Department of Native Affairs established its own adoption and fostering programs in 1951, and in 1962 placed eighty-one children in foster homes and arranged adoptions for a further twenty-nine children.[21] This new focus on placing Aboriginal children with white families attracted interest in the local press, which printed appealing photographs of beautiful Aboriginal babies safe with their new white mothers, often juxtaposed with stories of Aboriginal parental neglect. It was inevitable that child removals would increase. Both departments were operating from models of conventional middle-class family life that predisposed them to condemn Nyungar home conditions and child-rearing practices. Native Welfare reports showed that removals more than doubled from 151 in 1957 to 379 in 1960.[22] Meanwhile the number of 'coloured' children committed to the care of the Child Welfare Department increased from nine in 1955 to 161 in 1963, making up 6 per cent of state children in its care.[23]

In 1972 the new Department of Community Welfare took over full responsibility for Aboriginal child and family welfare and assumed control of all departmental youth and children's facilities. While this brought Nyungar families fully under the umbrella of the protocols and protections of family welfare law, intervention in family life and practices of removal and institutionalisation did not let up. Separation of Aboriginal children continued at rates far higher than for the white community and in 1972 they made up over 20 per cent of departmental charges. Yet the department told the Furnell Royal Commission into Aboriginal Affairs in Western Australia in 1974 that it had 'enough experience to be familiar with the results of parental deprivation on young children and [was] consequently extremely reluctant to remove any child from its parents'.[24] National research across the 1970s was reporting disproportionate numbers of Aboriginal juvenile offenders in welfare institutions.[25] Aboriginal children and adolescents were being separated from their families and placed in assimilatory environments at a time when policy had already moved on from assimilation and integration towards the new policy of self-determination. The paradox can be explained in part by the ongoing assimilatory nature of child and family welfare services that negatively judged Aboriginal child rearing and family processes according to dominant settler Australian models and the families' ongoing economic difficulties.

Promise Two: A home in the suburbs with the basic comforts of modern life

During the 1950s the destitution and poverty in Aboriginal camps around the country had suddenly become visible in the public landscape. This reflected a mix of concern over the dramatic contrast between conditions in the camps and the public dream of home ownership, and worry over possible overseas criticism. For governments, housing was a vital element of the assimilation process. In 1946 the New South Wales Aborigines Welfare Board claimed that 'it is only when living standards are satisfactory that pride and self-respect assert themselves. While aborigines live under primitive, unhygienic conditions they manifest very little desire to change their mode of life and to progress to a stage where they will be received into the community and be able to take their place with success and satisfaction'.[26] In Western Australia an officer from the Department of Native Affairs claimed in 1951 that 'unless an enlightened and progressive policy for the housing of natives is adopted and financed by the government we may well ask ourselves where we are going'.[27]

Like the classroom, the home in the suburbs was a potent instrument of social engineering by a government intent on recreating the values and ideologies of the ideal nuclear family. The structural design of the home, the broader influences of its suburban environment and the interventions by government officers operating together could push Aboriginal families to assimilate gender and generational divisions, domestic duties and hygiene practices, the use of space and patterns of occupancy. The suburban home was a 'contact zone' as defined by Mary Louise Pratt: 'social spaces where disparate cultures meet, clash and grapple with each other, often in highly asymmetrical relations of domination and subordination'.[28] The home was also a tangible sign of the progress of assimilation and a useful photo opportunity for politicians and bureaucrats. However, the irony was most Aboriginal families could not get conventional housing.

The promise to house Nyungar families stretched out over a period of twenty-two years until the State Housing Commission took over responsibility in 1972. Like the mainstreaming of child welfare this transfer provided the semblance of equal treatment for Nyungar families but it did not solve their housing problems, which continue to the present day. Nor did its earlier cooperation with the Department of Native Welfare in building separate dwellings for Aboriginal families do much to relieve the situation during the 1950s and 1960s. The fact was that housing Nyungar families required levels of funding that state and federal governments were unwilling to provide. Nor were state housing authorities willing to allocate homes from their conventional housing stock to Aboriginal families. There was also a heated 'not in my backyard' reaction from local authorities and residents. Opposition was such that some municipalities demanded to be registered as 'prohibited areas' under the *1936 Native Administration Act*, where Aboriginal people not legally employed could be arrested and removed at the discretion of the Commissioner for Native Affairs (prohibited areas were all cancelled in 1954). Middleton was forced to initially confine his building plans to existing Aboriginal reserves.[29] After white residents objected to the prospect of Aboriginal clients in State Housing Commission homes in 1954 the Labor Minister for Housing Mr Graham declared that he was 'determined, irrespective of prejudice … to allocate houses to people of aborigine descent whose applications qualify in the ordinary way … Instead of people being hostile they should be proud of the fact that a native, despite natural obstacles, could raise himself to such a high standard. This is a terrific example of man's inhumanity to man. I am disappointed and disgusted at the attitude of people who display bias against our coloured cousins.'[30] His rhetoric failed to change the situation even within his own department.

What housing choices did Nyungar families have? They could not buy their own homes and the rental market was beyond their limited means even in the unlikely event that they were accepted. The shortage of rental properties had caused the average weekly rent to double between 1947 and 1954 from nineteen shillings and eleven pence to forty shillings and nine pence.[31] The hurdles for getting state housing were high and for many families rent and other costs were crippling. In 1960 the State Housing Commission had 220 applications pending from Aboriginal families around the state. Of its total conventional housing stock, Aboriginal clients occupied only seventy-seven homes, and families had been evicted from or had abandoned forty-seven others.[32] These figures indicate the discriminatory treatment of Aboriginal families by the State Housing Commission. A recent study of Aboriginal access to public housing in New South Wales in this period by George Morgan showed a mix of race, class and gender prejudices operating in assessing Aboriginal people for accommodation: people interviewed in humpies on reserves were ruled incapable of ever assimilating to suburban standards and Aboriginal mothers failed to meet the ideal of the 'capable suburban mother who manages home and family effortlessly'.[33] As a consequence few passed the test; those who did remained permanently on trial under the prying eyes of neighbours and housing officers.

Many Nyungar families continued to live in town camps and reserves — in 1957 around 85 per cent still lived on reserves for most of the year — where their substandard living conditions left them open to threats that their children would be removed because they could not meet the newly imposed standards. Of the twenty-two reserves in the Great Southern district, only five had full facilities of water, lavatories, ablution block and laundry; eleven had water connected, eight had toilets and the remainder had no facilities at all. Government reports didn't even mention electricity.[34] Requests for improvements seemed hopeless given the allocation of only £7019 that year to upgrade 132 reserves across the state.[35] The department intended in the long run to clear the families off the reserves and was not keen to build up an expensive infrastructure. Meanwhile, around the nation a culture of blame permeated discussion about deteriorating conditions on reserves. In New South Wales high levels of infant mortality were blamed on families' unsanitary living conditions and mothers' ignorance concerning infant welfare and 'failure or refusal' to follow instructions from field staff in this regard.[36]

Planners in most states adopted local variations of the Transitional Housing Scheme as their solution to the growing crisis.[37] This curious program epitomised the practices of accepting inferior conditions as 'good enough' for Aboriginal families and of continually forcing them to 'earn and learn' their rights. The official word on the scheme was that it would improve living conditions on Aboriginal reserves in the short term and in the long term prepare families for life in conventional suburban homes. In fact it created a veneer of positive action while it provided sub-standard dwellings that became permanent homes for many families and made the prospect of ever getting conventional housing an impossibility.

The concept as implemented in Western Australia involved families gradually moving through three stages of rental accommodation, with appropriate training at each level: Stage 1 — small huts on gazetted reserves with communal sanitation, ablution and laundry facilities; Stage 2 — self-contained dwellings of up to five rooms on reserves or town blocks; and Stage 3 — conventional homes in suburban state housing estates. By 1964 this had been expanded into five levels and rent varied from six shillings to fifty shillings, according to the type of housing.[38] Adopted jointly in 1953 by the Department of Native Welfare and the State Housing Commission, the scheme had housed 476 families around the state by 1960 — 70 per cent in

Stage 1 huts, 2 per cent in Stage 2 dwellings and one per cent in Stage 3 homes. More than seven hundred new dwellings were completed in 1967, however 63 per cent were sub-standard Stage I huts and only thirty-five were conventional houses.[39] With the state's Aboriginal population counted at 20,990 in 1964 the government still had a long way to go in housing the families — at a time when Australia was experiencing a housing boom. On top of this inferior housing stock were the interventions by field officers and local community groups who assisted, inspected, imposed rules and guidelines for living, and devised patronising systems of rewards and punishments for families. Families who finally managed to move through the various stages were expected to then seek housing from the State Housing Commission with its discriminatory practices in dealing with Aboriginal clients. There was little expectation that Aboriginal families would then move on to the next level of the Australian dream — owning their own home.

Allawah Grove — a transitional housing community

The Allawah Grove Aboriginal Settlement, located in the outer Perth suburb of South Guildford, was established in 1958 by the Department of Native Welfare to provide urgently needed housing in the metropolitan area, but more importantly to operate as a model site for assimilation training along the lines of the Transitional Housing Scheme. In 2005 an exhibition commemorating Allawah Grove held at the University of Western Australia's Cullity Gallery celebrated the community's many positive achievements — strong ties of family and community, the will to survive against overwhelming odds, civic development, and working cooperatively with *wadjelas* (white people).[40] An anthropology thesis written in 1963 by Rosemary Oxer entitled 'Allawah Grove: an experimentation in assimilation'[41] studied the settlement's success in assimilating resident families. It described the difficult living conditions there with overcrowding (a population of 150 adults and children), unemployment (44 per cent of men were out of work), and most families surviving on social security benefits. Oxer also documented an environment of chronic conflict between residents, the department and the administration. This conflict reflected a clash of goals and cultures as well as problems of limited finance, personal differences, and families' resistance to being told what to do by *wadjelas*.

Oxer's research identified the same tension we saw in settlements set up to assimilate Aboriginal communities in the Northern Territory, where residents were expected to become a community while living in what was only a temporary stage leading to an assimilated life outside.[42] Here too facilities provided for short-term use became permanent amenities with obvious consequences for families living there. Oxer found that residents regarded Allawah Grove as their home and most had little interest in the government's assimilatory goals, which included moving 'successful' families off to Perth's state housing estates to be spread out amongst white residents according to a 'salt'n'pepper' settlement principle. Instead Oxer found 'a strengthening of the resolve to maintain a society which, one might suggest, is becoming a stable sub-culture. If this is so, the people are no longer oriented towards assimilation (if they ever were) and the scheme cannot be a success.'[43] Tensions were evident in the succession of administrators — in 1963 the community was into its fourth administration in six years — and the expanding net of rules to manage residents and visitors. Some rules conflicted with Nyungar values and behaviours of hospitality and tolerance. Rule Two, for example, required visitors to sign the Visitors' Book kept by the Superintendent and to leave 'without the use of force' after a stay of two days. Rule Three took a 'three strikes and you're out' approach by threatening 'automatic eviction' of residents who were 'Troublemakers, Drunks, Nuisances' after their third warning.[44]

Oxer's conclusion was that although the government had established Allawah Grove 'solely as a means of hastening assimilation of Aboriginal people into the Australian society, it has resulted in a tight sub-group being formed, the members of which have no desire to move out of the group. The only people to move from Allawah Grove are tenants evicted for breaking their tenancy agreement.'[45]

In 1969, against the wishes of the residents, the government closed the settlement to make way for extensions to the runway at Perth Airport.[46] In his book *Fringedwellers* (1980) Robert Bropho recalls how the people were 'bulldoze[d]' out and 'sent in every direction and put in houses in different suburbs'.[47] With his family he began a journey that took them from state housing and private rental accommodation in Perth, to farming at Mogumber (formerly the Moore River Native Settlement, then run as a farm training school) and reserve living at York where three of the children were taken by Community Welfare before the family decided to return to their former lifestyle: 'that was it, rolled their swags and went back to the fringe-dwelling way of life ... We have given up hope of being accepted for what we are, and my children are scarred for life ... Their home now, as fringe-dwellers, is living under canvas.'[48]

Forever in training

Various historians have pointed to the way that governments from colonial times to the present have constructed Aboriginal women as central to the process of assimilation.[49] In the 1950s they were considered assimilation's 'Trojan horse' introducing mainstream culture and lifestyle into the very heart of the Aboriginal family and community.[50] The training to equip them for this role presented ideals of Australian motherhood and domestic life as natural and normal, and rejected or ignored Aboriginal women's cultural roles such as the shared responsibility for 'growing up' Aboriginal children which contrasted with the clearly defined task of child rearing within the confines of the nuclear family.[51]

In Western Australia in the 1950s training to prepare Aboriginal women for modern domestic living became a fetishlike activity that distracted the attention of everyone — government officers, Aboriginal residents, politicians and the public — from the fact that most families were living in unacceptable conditions that in no way matched the promises of assimilation. Training created the impression of change when the project to provide proper housing for families was stalled. Training could go on indefinitely — shifting from housekeeping and cooking to work skills, civic duties, personal grooming, and a myriad other disciplines of body and mind — and it kept everyone occupied. Politicians spoke of the importance of preparing Aboriginal people for conventional housing; government officers busied themselves with regimes of training and inspections; and town welfare organisations prided themselves for lending a helping hand. Training spread out from the camps to ever more sites — infant clinics, Aboriginal kindergartens, shire halls, local schools and welfare offices. White women's professional expertise was on show everywhere in the form of social workers, child clinic nurses, welfare officers and teachers, and volunteers in church and women's organisations. Between 1954 and 1963 *wadjela* women worked with the local Native Welfare Committee in Narrogin to prepare families in four training cottages for conventional housing, providing lessons in cooking, sewing, handcrafts, hygiene, infant and child care and personal grooming.[52] As adoptive and foster mothers, white women took over the role of mothering from Aboriginal women altogether. In 1968 the department's new Homemaker Service was introduced to assist the growing number of families moving directly into conventional housing. This service employed Aboriginal and non-Aboriginal homemakers to assist families with the transition to town living. Transferred to the new

Department of Community Welfare in 1972, it was developed through careful selection and training in community development into a useful service for Aboriginal families and continued to operate into the 1990s. In these various scenarios Aboriginal women were instructed in the myriad skills they already used daily in caring for large family groupings and making ends meet on pinched budgets, or doing domestic work for *wadjela* families. They knew that their living conditions severely restricted what they could achieve, but they were mindful that failure to appear to try could lead to punishments such as the removal of their children.

The department also produced instructional training films for mothers — *Baby's Bath* (n.d.), *Lilly Feeds Her Baby* (n.d.) and *Good Food Good Health* (1969) — and films like *A House in Town* (1969) and *Welcome to Town* (n.d.) providing advice for families moving into conventional housing.[53] Like the pedagogical films produced for African audiences by the British Colonial Film Unit these films underestimated viewers' capacity to read films and to retain their messages. The British film *Mr Wise and Mr Foolish Go to Town* (1945) presented a simplistic narrative about cures for venereal disease using stereotyped characters and long sequences of dull slow-paced scenes that, research at the time showed, predisposed target audiences of African soldiers to reject its messages.[54] The department's films in Perth had a similar effect on Nyungar audiences who, by the 1960s, were well and truly accustomed to watching television and commercial feature films.

The films *Good Food Good Health* and *A House in Town,* produced in 1969 for the Homemaker Service, instructed viewers in the routines of suburban nuclear family domestic life. Narrated by a Nyungar homemaker, *Good Food Good Health* showed an Aboriginal mother how to make her budget go further by buying and preparing cheap food, failing to acknowledge the extensive practical experience of Nyungar women in making meals for large households on shoestring budgets, often using bush tucker like kangaroo with tasty fillers of damper. The film concluded with the image of the Aboriginal family eating their dinner around the table while the homemaker's voice continued, 'With good cooked food you will build a healthy and happy family.' *A House in Town*, the film in which Darryl's parents made their cameo appearance, moved effortlessly from a scene of overcrowded huts at Allawah Grove to a brick suburban home while a well-to-do male voice claimed that many families had already successfully made the move. Viewers were instructed in the practices of suburban living — mum, dad and the kids eating dinner together, gardening, meeting neighbours, entertaining visitors. The couple visit a furniture shop where friendly sales staff greet them, advise them on economical purchases and arrange for them to put their goods on hire purchase. The film finishes with an Aboriginal homemaker advising a younger woman while the narrator reassures viewers that 'every help will be given to help you make a life in your new home'. In *Welcome to Town* stick figures in a cartoon segment tumble out of cars carrying flagons of wine into a suburban house that suddenly explodes while a prim voice warns, 'Loud parties will cause trouble.'[55]

Nyungar responses

The presence in these films of Nyungar people promoting the messages of assimilation directs our attention to the question of Nyungar responses to the domestic goals of assimilation. Their presence suggests compliance but the matter is complex. Families were surrounded by images and ideas of assimilated suburban living and a public spirit of progressive modernism evident in government promotional campaigns and popular culture. New housing had an appeal for those families seeking an alternative to the rigours of living in camps and keen to exercise their rights and responsibilities as citizens. But this could be a frustrating journey, as Darryl's parents found out. They had to battle Child Welfare authorities to keep the extended circle of grandchildren together. Their Homeswest house was in a dilapidated condition due to the department's failure to carry out necessary repairs. In ill-health, Nan and Pop struggled to stretch their pension cheques to accommodate all the children living with them, as well as visiting relatives. The couple's reward was that they kept their extended family together despite the odds, but the strain took its toll and they both died in thier early sixties.[56] For families there was always the threat that coming to the attention of the department could backfire in punitive consequences such as the removal of children for failing to meet imposed standards in the home. Events at Allawah Grove show another response, also found in town camps, of Nyungar families bound by ties of family and shared experience determined to maintain a communal lifestyle in the face of the pressures to assimilate. Bob Bropho's story suggests that the sheer difficulty of surviving on the outside was also a motivating factor for staying together. Corinne Manning concludes in her study of two similar transitional housing settlements in rural Victoria — Rumbulara and Manatunga — that some of the families resisted the 'assimilationist edge' and continued their fringe-dwelling activities, often causing conflict with the non-Aboriginal settlement managers.[57]

George Morgan's research on Kurri families and the New South Wales state housing program indicates that applicants, the majority of them women, were often ambivalent about the move.[58] While they wanted the better conditions promised by suburban housing, most were unwilling to comply unreservedly with new behavioural demands and refused to abandon their own community life and culture. Of the few families who passed the rigorous assessment process, most took their culture with them. They 'sought to unpack their cultural baggage in a new location' and the behaviour that prompted complaints from neighbours often had 'a hidden cultural logic which was not apparent to outsiders'. Commenting on Kurri families and the Aborigines Welfare Board (AWB), Carolyn Allport observes that the families directed considerable opposition and resentment at the Board on the grounds that it delivered 'too little too late'. Allport makes the connection between housing issues and political activism in New South Wales, observing that 'housing also became enmeshed with wider political struggles around civil rights, so it is not coincidental that the Freedom Rides to break down rural residential segregation began soon after the failure of the AWB [Aborigines Welfare Board] to honour its commitment to improving housing for Aboriginal people'.[59]

Promise Three: Secure employment and a regular income

Economic security was absolutely essential if Nyungar families were to 'attain the same standard of living as other Australians' as promised in the federal government's 1961 definition of assimilation. An assimilated lifestyle brought many new expenses which required regular payments such as rent and utility and service charges and the many other costs for children's schooling, medical bills, home furnishings and so on. Like the home, the work place was also a site for social engineering and, in the 1950s, the focus was usually on male workers. There they could learn the routines, values and social and psychological attitudes and behaviours of working within the modern capitalist system. This contrasted in many ways with the work experience of most Nyungar men before the war years. A typical work profile involved seasonal skilled or unskilled rural employment, working in mobile family groups and moving between farms across the season, award payments paid in lump sums, and long periods of unemployment between seasonal jobs. This was not compatible with assimilated living. It was also precarious work that was not conducive to prudent saving for the future and was especially susceptible to the vagaries of economic change.

In the 1950s — a time of full employment, bountiful

government spending on public works, rapid expansion of industrial and manufacturing industries and guaranteed work for new migrants — Nyungar families were engulfed in an unemployment crisis. Their niche in the rural sector became increasingly uncertain due to a combination of factors: mechanisation of farming, the drop in clearing work with less new land being opened up for development, and falling export commodity prices such as wool that left farmers with limited funds to employ workers.[60] There was also competition from migrant and other workers moving into rural areas, many assisted in their quest for work by the Commonwealth Employment Service, a right denied to most Aboriginal people prior to the 1960s, along with access to other federal government services and benefits. In the Native Welfare Department's 1955 Annual Report the District Officer for the Southern district explained that many farmers who had employed Nyungar labour for years were taking on white workers instead. In 1956 the *Westralian Aborigine*, a newspaper published by the Coolbaroo League in Perth, warned that Nyungar children would suffer due to the 'flooding of New Australian labour' and advised the government to 'heavily cut the intake of migrants and improve the type being brought into the country'.[61] For Nyungar workers who had been excluded from state schools as children and who faced employer prejudice it was virtually impossible to move to new types of employment without government support. Established ways of working and cultural factors such as mobile seasonal work patterns, attachment to working in family groups, and living off the land in their runs, made the change to conventional work and sedentary living a difficult challenge.

The department was well aware of the problems facing Nyungar families. In 1958 an officer from the Great Southern district observed that 'lack of permanent employment is the biggest single factor which militates against the native population of my District attaining to a stable economic position … To this can be directly attributed the partial failure of the scheme to house natives. Those who were evicted from or voluntarily left their State Housing Commission Homes failed only because of their inability to earn enough to meet the financial obligation involved.'[62] All of these factors added to the 'Herculean efforts' families had to make to keep ahead.[63] A sympathetic field officer explained that 'it is a fallacy to think, as some people do, that natives generally are not fond of work and are not concerned at being out of employment. With nine years experience as a Field Officer in the South of this State, I can say that with very few exceptions … native breadwinners are most anxious to be in regular employment and are perturbed at the lack of such employment. Most of them want their own home, no matter how small, and a more stable existence and would welcome any move that would provide these conditions.'[64]

But what could the Native Welfare Department do to relieve the problem? Its track record was unimpressive. For decades it had contributed to an escalating culture of poverty in the south. Departmental controls over access to workers and their working conditions and fees for employment permits and agreements had turned some farmers in the south away from employing them. In many cases it was better for Nyungar families to negotiate their own work contracts and wages away from its interference. Over the years the department had removed Nyungar children to institutions and trained them to become rural labourers and domestic servants and sent them out to work. The intention was that they should never return to their families. In this way the support of the rising generations was denied to aging Aboriginal parents. To attract employers the trainees' wages were kept to a minimum. (Wages were then paid into trust accounts operated by the department, along the lines of the Queensland system. Most workers were paid a little pocket money by their employers and had to contact the Commissioner for Native Affairs for permission to use their savings to purchase personal items. Most claimed they never received the balance of their wages.[65]) Before

1960 most Aboriginal workers were not eligible for unemployment benefits and had to request government rations in times of difficulty. Rations were begrudgingly handed over by the local police and families were often reluctant to seek them out as any calls for assistance could lead to removal to a government settlement. This inequitable system operated equally for the many Nyungar workers who were taxpayers. It is now the subject of scrutiny by the Stolen Wages campaign, established to force governments to return money owed to Aboriginal workers around Australia.

Clearly the department had little experience in generating work and incomes for families. Still, it had managed to pull out all the stops during the war years to organise Aboriginal labour for the war effort. Police officers were instructed to ensure that all adults were in employment and to send any who refused to cooperate to the native settlements to be disciplined. As a result the number of Aboriginal people in employment doubled during the war, not counting an estimated four hundred who enlisted in the armed services.[66] Early in the war William Cooper of the Australian Aborigines League attacked the West Australian government for 'Out Hitlering Hitler' in its treatment of Aboriginal people. Now Commissioner H. I. Bray claimed proudly that 'except in Germany I doubt whether methods such as these have been adopted in dealing with the forced labour of natives'.[67]

Despite this impressive war record in placing Aboriginal workers in employment, field officers in the 1950s worried over their 'inescapable moral obligation to provide a solution' but felt powerless to help. As one officer explained in 1958, 'with the best will in the world this Department cannot solve this particular and pressing problem of unemployment. We cannot create work for natives.'[68] Innovative proposals were made at the 1961 national conference on 'Aborigines in the Economy' (held under the auspices of the Centre for Research into Aboriginal Affairs at Monash University). Allan Duncan from Sydney University's

Department of Adult Education proposed 'incentive schemes' along the lines of the Commonwealth government rehabilitation programs for ex-servicemen where employers were subsidised and shown preference in government contract grants for providing skilled jobs and apprenticeships. Duncan recommended that the Commonwealth Employment Service should appoint staff to work with Aboriginal community leaders to devise employment opportunities.[69] Working through the community development model advocated by Duncan to build on the ambitions and skills of Aboriginal workers and backed by government funding, this approach could have greatly improved Aborigines' capacity to compete successfully in the job market.[70] At the same conference, the representative for the West Australian Education Department E. P. Miller warned that growing unemployment was 'generating a socially explosive atmosphere' and advocated economic assimilation to develop conventional work behaviours and values as the 'first and earliest' step to assimilation. He considered adult education 'fundamentally important' but like his parochial colleagues back home he fell back on the solution of centralised, 'multi-purpose training schools' for Aboriginal boys and domestic training in the home for girls.[71]

The education and training of children and youth for future employment and assimilated life took precedence over assisting Aboriginal adults into the workforce. In 1958 the District Officer for the Southern district recommended that the since the unskilled labour situation would remain 'precarious' his officers should endeavour 'to encourage and insist on the education of native children to well beyond the primary stage, so that in a few years the nucleus of a new stamp of young natives, ready and trained for career employment, will have been established'. He warned that 'unless the provision of Government finances keeps pace with the needs of the native community and the plans for their advancement, this will remain a pipe dream'.[72] Despite the evidence of declining rural employment the department advocated the development of rural training in boarding schools and agricultural colleges that included the run-down premises of Moore River and Carrolup settlements, run by the Methodist and Baptist churches respectively from the early 1950s. Efforts to arrange apprenticeships were delayed because the youth did not meet required education levels, opportunities were mainly in the city and white employers were reluctant to take them on.

Social security

In contrast to its feeble efforts to fulfil assimilation's promises of work, the West Australian government lobbied hard for the extension of federal social security benefits to Aboriginal families in the state. This was not so much an issue of equal rights for Aboriginal people as a financial safety net to relieve the state of the growing financial burden incurred by its albeit limited assimilation program. It could also provide a stop-gap measure until the new generation of workers came along.

Various historians have demonstrated how in Western Australia, and in other states at the time, government initially dipped into child endowment payments available (from 1941) to Aboriginal mothers, to subsidise children kept in its increasing number of children's institutions. With five shillings paid for the first child and ten for subsequent children this would have been a lifesaver for large families, especially with children at school whose needs put an extra burden on budgets already stretched to the limit. For the Department of Native Welfare this represented new funding and a considerable saving and freed up money for other departmental responsibilities. When federal social security benefits became generally available to Aboriginal people from 1959, the state government naturally encouraged Aboriginal families to apply for benefits due to them as their right. This meant a major cash boost for communities and families, with members receiving aged, widow and invalid pensions, unemployment and sickness benefits, child endowment and the maternity allowance. In 1957 only eighteen Aboriginal people in the entire state were receiving unemployment benefits; by 1960, in the southwest alone, 316 people were registered.[73]

Social security benefits provided immediate financial relief in a growing unemployment crisis. However they also relieved the pressure on the Native Welfare Department to take decisive action to improve the job situation. An unintended outcome from the department's perspective was that the injection of benefits propped up the appearance of assimilation by providing the minimum cash required for families pooling their resources to get by. There was some improvement in living conditions and this made it less likely that Nyungar homes would be condemned as 'bad environments' for children. However the long-term effect was that there was no resolution of the Nyungar unemployment crisis, which continued on over the decades while family dependency on social security benefits escalated. Government inaction on Nyungar unemployment was a major root cause of the cycle of welfare dependency that developed in the region. Rather than escaping poverty, families were thrown into a cycle that they could not escape. They could never accumulate enough capital to break the pattern by, for example, purchasing a home that would become a financial asset and investment for the family. Denied the opportunity of home ownership and full-time employment provided for other Australians, they were left to continue on in conditions of poverty and welfare dependency for which they were then blamed.

The point was made earlier that governments had a rare opportunity at this time to address the needs of the nation's small Aboriginal population. This would be the expected response given their promises to extend to Aboriginal people rights and conditions equal to other Australian citizens and the example of massive expenditure on improving the prosperity of settler Australians. The funding required to meet Aboriginal needs was significant but still well within the budgets of the federal and state governments, yet all demurred: the federal authorities claimed that it was not their responsibility, while the states cried poor. The opportunity to make a difference was missed and, as the century advanced and new policies came and went, conditions for many Aboriginal families actually worsened, providing a stark contrast with the rest of Australia. This is the background to the present heavy-handed initiatives to clean up Aboriginal communities.

Australia was not alone in excluding Aboriginal people from the benefits of post-war prosperity. Research in the United States shows how similar discriminatory treatment of African-American families left them disadvantaged economically in the long term, despite the legal and political wins of the civil rights movement. Post-war housing policies, infrastructure and finance advantaged white families, and this, together with racialised real estate practices over the years, laid the basis for their financial success into the present. The inevitable conclusion, reached by sociologist Melvin Oliver, was that 'these were public policy decisions in which, on the one hand people were given access to property, given title and subsequently wealth, and on another hand, where people were not given access to property, did not generate wealth and did not generate the kind of opportunity for the next generation ... all of this is made available to you [or not] as a consequence of racist policies and practices'.[73] In Australia there was a further disabling factor for Aboriginal families. Governments promoted their promises of assimilation to the nation as achievable goals and real outcomes when in fact they were not prepared to put in the necessary capital to fulfil their obligations. Their promises remained just that — promises — and Aboriginal people were left to survive in conditions of abject poverty. In an ironic (if familiar) twist they were blamed for this outcome by the Australian public who, beguiled by the government's assimilation spin, believed that Aboriginal families had failed to act responsibly and proactively in taking up the nation's offer of a better life. Little wonder then that my father-in-law became so angry.

7. Living the Dream

Lauren Marsh and Anna Haebich

> *The dances attracted people from all over Perth, from the 'town blacks' in East Perth to the 'campies' at Bassendean or Lockridge, and even as far out as nearby country towns like Northam. Regardless of divisions within the community, whether you were a 'campie' or a 'townie', a Noongar or a Nor'wester, poor or well off, old or young, the Coolbaroo League dances united the small and dispersed population of the time.*
>
> Stephen Kinnane, 2003[1]

There is still another history of assimilation to be told here. That is, the various ways that Aboriginal people in the southwest responded to the rhetoric of assimilation, and to some of the tangible changes they saw taking place around them. This is a complex and vibrant history that has yet to be fully recounted. Of course the concept of assimilation for Aboriginal people meant different things to different people. For some there was an active resistance; assimilation was seen as yet another attack on the values and identity of a distinctly separate Aboriginal identity. For a small number of others, assimilation rhetoric was internalised, and in an attempt to live outside the jurisdiction of the department, those individuals and families sought to deny their Aboriginal ancestry, laying claims to other ethnic identities, or 'passing' for white. Given the severity of the legislation Aboriginal people were forced to comply with, it is not surprising that some readily grasped at opportunities to be free of its controls. However, in this chapter what will be considered is the response by the majority, which was to actively engage at some level in the process of assimilation and advocate for the promised benefits of assimilation, without surrendering their Aboriginal identity. Central to this response was a more flexible interpretation of Aboriginal identity, and a strategy of harnessing assimilation rhetoric as a way of achieving Aboriginal aspirations for improved health, education, employment, and to secure the same democratic rights as the wider population.

As it would be impossible to address the full range in depth, we focus here on considering Aboriginal responses through the prism of those people living in Perth, and the Perth-based Aboriginal organisation known as the Coolbaroo League. Similar organisations, like the Boatshed in Brisbane and the Sunshine Club in Darwin, operated in most capital cities around Australia in the 1950s and 1960s, seeking to provide social as well as political benefits for their communities through a collective and organised response to the pressures of the time. When considered within an assimilation context these organisations offered significant bulwarks for Aboriginal people to retain their own cultural identities. The Coolbaroo League played an active role in pursuing and securing the benefits of assimilation, while resisting assimilationist attempts to erode Aboriginal cultural identity.

Aboriginal people in Perth

The Aboriginal population living in Perth was distinctive in many ways from Nyungar communities in the rural south. They were exposed to different opportunities for employment, living conditions and social interactions with whites and Aboriginal people from around the state.

City employment opportunities for men included labouring jobs in factories and on the government railways and in-between work like cutting and selling wooden props for backyard washing lines. There was full-time domestic service, and kitchen and laundry work in hospitals and cafeterias for single girls and women, while married women supplemented family incomes by washing for white families. In the 1950s some Aboriginal people worked in lower level clerical positions in the Native Welfare Department, others were engaged under trade apprenticeship schemes, as nursing assistants, and one man worked at Perth Zoo. Employment was one of the main sites of exchange between Aboriginal and white communities.

Granny Bropho, whose large family worked the seasonal grape pick, recalls being approached in the street to do washing. A time would be agreed for her to come to the house, 'and then all of the clothes were chucked out ready for you to wash'.[2] From Granny's point of view as a mother of ten children, white women were essentially lazy, needing help when they had only small numbers of children to raise. Similar views were not uncommon amongst Aboriginal women who worked as domestic servants in white homes. Such assessments of the white family and the white mother strike an ironical note given the administration's assumption that Aboriginal women exposed to the workings of a nuclear white family would 'naturally' want to emulate this model.

Experiences of living conditions were also diverse. Young Aboriginal women working in domestic service lived in white homes, or boarded at the East Perth Girls Home. School-aged Aboriginal boys and girls lived at institutions such as Sister Kate's, or the hostels Alvan House and MacDonald House in suburban Perth. Aboriginal families rented houses in the cheaper inner city suburbs such as East Perth, North Perth, and along the railway line in West Perth. Campsites were set up in bushland near places of employment such as Cresco's, at the fertiliser factory, or in outlying suburbs within easy access of the railway line. Families constructed dwellings of flattened kerosene tins and hessian, and struggled without the basics of electricity, sewerage, or running water. Granny Bropho recalled living in a bush camp without even the basic construction of a tin hut, and her distress at trying to keep her children dry under layers of bushes during the winter rains.[3]

The influx of American servicemen and personnel during the war brought the opportunity for home-front interactions between Aboriginal people and African-American servicemen. Eileen Shang was a young woman in domestic service in Perth at the time and she later recalled the outrage with which local practices and laws governing Aboriginal people were viewed by some of those from overseas. One night out with friends at a wine saloon she was required to show her 'dog tag' — Aborigines' name for the identity cards issued to holders of certificates of citizenship — to prove that she had the right to be on licensed premises. Exemption was a formal process by which the department granted Aboriginal people exemption from the restrictions of the *Aborigines Act.* It had a temporary status and could be revoked at any time. There was a group of African-American servicemen present, and one of them asked her, 'Hey baby, what's this for?'[4] When Eileen explained, the men were 'furious', and tore up the offending papers. According to Eileen, the servicemen thought the conditions for Aboriginal people were far worse than what they experienced back home.

The American military was sensitive to 'inter-racial' mixing between Aboriginal women and African-American servicemen. Early in 1945 the American Shore Patrol joined forces with the Native Welfare Department and the police to patrol inner city areas looking for clandestine liaisons.[5] While extensive searches were made in the creek beds around the East Perth Gasworks, and many houses were visited in East Perth, the patrol was 'without results'. The Acting Commissioner for Native Affairs C. L. McBeath concluded that an 'informant' had thwarted the raids, warning 'natives, who in turn advised the servicemen to keep clear of the Reserve'.[6]

For Aboriginal people coping with the massive impact of forced separation from homelands and resettlement into unfamiliar country in Perth, and indeed for those responding to new arrivals into their country, new strategies of cultural identity helped them to cope. For the generation of Aboriginal people growing up in the southwest after the First World War, and who experienced life in the Moore River and Carrolup Native Settlements, a new system of identification developed, where people were nor'westers or sou'westers, depending on their traditional links to country. A broad division between north and south also set cultural identity boundaries for Aboriginal people living in Perth, who similarly identified as nor'westers or sou'westers, depending on their traditional links. North was delineated as country from the goldfields up, with south being country below the goldfields and across to the southeast border.

Most nor'westers had been sent south to Moore River Settlement as children, where together with Nyungar children they were trained to be rural labourers and domestic servants. There, beyond the scrutiny of the white staff, compound children were taught some northern lingo and southern lingo by Aboriginal adults living in segregated camps. This was the experience of poet, playwright and activist Jack Davis who acknowledged this childhood learning as an inspiration for his later creative writing.[7] This framework of identity was of more intrinsic relevance to Aboriginal people at the time than any identification through notions of caste or degrees of 'whiteness'. As a countryman or woman of the north or south, you had place, kinship, and community expectations, regardless of notions or degrees of skin colour. This system of broader identification existed and operated alongside more specific systems of kinship and ties to traditional country.

Identification within this system was also linked to the commonality of experience under the departmental administrative regime. For nor'westers, differences of language and culture were bridged by the commonality of what it meant emotionally as well as culturally to be removed from family and country. There was an identification with feelings of (mis)placement in country that belonged to other groups, as well as associated imaginings of 'home' and family networks, and coping with different belief systems, languages, and history. There were shared experiences, and aspirations, of one day being able to return home: many contemporary oral histories of adults recounting their experiences of removal as children speak of long-held desires or quests to return and reclaim home.

While the division between north and south fostered and promoted cohesion and a sense of community within each group, it was also the basis for conflict. As a young girl interned in the Moore River Native Settlement, Alice Bassett recalled a state of almost constant conflict between the two groups of children and young adults living in the dormitories. From Alice's perspective the two groups would 'rather fight than have a feed — just like the Irish and the English'.[8] While there is little doubt that the deprivations and overcrowding of the settlements exacerbated conflict, there was also a tendency for the two groups to view one another with some suspicion. The bridging of the two into a more socially and politically cohesive whole was one of the early aims of the Coolbaroo League.

Personal experience of legislative controls also differed markedly according to geographical regions within the state. Broadly speaking, the further you were from the epicentre of departmental control in Perth and the network of police to enforce compliance with the legislation, the less likely you were to experience surveillance and overt control. Some Aboriginal people from northern outpost towns such as Broome or Port Hedland brought with them very different political experiences and aspirations. While many people of these generations had some experience of mission educations, for those who had not been subjected to the conditions and deprivations of the government settlement schemes there appeared to be a greater sense of personal self-esteem. For George Harwood, a young Aboriginal man from Broome with a limited education through the Christian Brothers College, the reality of exclusion and prohibition for Aboriginal people in the city of Perth came as a great shock. From 1921 to 1954 a legal curfew operated in Perth that required Aboriginal people to be out of the central business district by six o'clock at night. Permission to remain beyond this time required a pass issued at the discretion of the Native Welfare Department. The alcohol prohibition for Aboriginal people meant that exclusion from licensed clubs, pubs, and dances was strictly enforced.

George Harwood claimed to have experienced greater inclusion in his hometown of Broome and decided to test the situation. Entering the public bar of a hotel he noticed that 'they were taking a long time to serve me'.[9] It registered on him that the publican was ringing the police, and before long a plain-clothes policeman arrived and stood next to him at the bar, openly studying him. Eventually the policeman said to the publican, 'Oh give him a drink.' George drank a glass of beer, then quietly left the hotel.

The example of George's story can be read in multiple ways. Primarily it was one man's experience of crossing a legal and social boundary and the effects of his blatant disregard of this boundary on both the publican and the police officer involved. George himself attributes the outcome to the way he was dressed, and how he conducted himself. However, regardless of how he was dressed this did not alter the laws that barred him from the premises. George in his suit and tie had exactly the same lack of legal rights as any Aboriginal person subject to the Act in the state. What was different in this case was that George's appearance, and his demeanour, stood outside of the assumptions of the white publican and officer of what was identifiably 'Aboriginal'. In the fixed binary of assimilation rhetoric, George was behaving more 'white' than 'black'. Yet his history, family, kinship connections, personal identification, and the way he operated in his community all remained intrinsic to his Aboriginal identity. It is only if Aboriginal identity is limited to one fixed, static, cultural position that notions of 'loss of culture' or plotted points of progression along an assimilationist spectrum can be claimed. In the example of George Harwood it is not the man who was out of step with his identity, but assimilationist rhetoric, and popular notions of Aboriginal identity, that were out of step with the man.

A state of segregation

Images of segregated seating on public transport, of 'blacks only' train carriages, of laws preventing sexual relations between blacks and whites, of racially segregated schools and milk bars refusing to serve 'black' customers, of night time curfews and men and women forced to carry permits to pass through the city streets after six o'clock — such images resonate more readily in the popular imagination with South Africa during the Apartheid era, or the deep south of the United States during the 1950s. However, this was the social landscape of Perth and the outlying wheat belt areas in the years immediately following the Second World War. For recently returned white serviceman Geoff Harcus, Perth was a deeply racially divided society. 'On the buses, Nyungars sit up the back sort of thing. At the pictures they had to sit up the front.'[10] While these weren't official laws, they were customs and practices the white community had normalised and now expected. For Geoff, this was not the 'freedom' he had in mind to protect when he enlisted to fight for Australia during the war.

In a modern democracy, Aboriginal people in Western Australia were denied basic civil and human rights. Years of constantly amended, revised, and expanded legislative controls resulted in a situation where all aspects of an Aboriginal person's life were subject to legislation, enforced by the Native Affairs Department operating through police officers and its own system of field officers. Oral history accounts reveal the level of personalised policing that Aboriginal individuals were subjected to on a daily basis, especially at the epicentre of control in Perth. As a young woman, newly arrived in Perth in 1942 from the northwest town of Port Hedland, Helena Clarke recalled attending the Esplanade on a Sunday afternoon, a venue similar to the Domain in Sydney, that was popular with left-wing speakers, trade unionists and members of the local branch of the Communist Party of Australia. Helena recalled being regularly trailed by plainclothes detectives suspicious of her attendance at these rallies. In one instance a detective followed her onto the tram, but she managed to shake him off by getting off early and ducking and weaving a different route home. Speaking with the distance of time, Helena recalled her surveillance with humour, saying it happened so regularly she used to wave and say hello to the detectives she passed in the street.

Frank Alberts, a young man with a sight impairment who lived at the Braille Institute in the Perth suburb of Maylands had a similar experience. Walking to a city tram one evening he was stopped by a police officer and questioned for being in the city after curfew.[11] Frank explained that he was on his way home, and even the tram driver intervened in his defence, however the officer followed him back to the Braille Institute. When the matron there realised what had happened she 'made a blue' and the officer was forced to apologise. Young Frank was fortunate he had not been arrested for being in the city after six o'clock at night. He described his encounter as 'my taste of restriction'.[12]

George Harwood was stopped when he first arrived in Perth from Mullewa in 1953 under the pretext that he was not known to police, indicating the level of police surveillance of Aboriginal movement in the city precincts.[13] The intent of the message was clear: the police who patrolled the city of Perth 'knew' the Aboriginal community and monitored their access to the streets; in a segregation framework those targeted for exclusion had to be 'known' and controlled.

The police also monitored and controlled interactions between Aborigines and whites in the city. Under the guise of alcohol restrictions, and the curfew, the police regularly intervened in personal friendships. Geoff Harcus was arrested on two occasions under the rubbery charge of 'cohabitation'. A returned army serviceman, he sought to keep in contact with Aboriginal men he had befriended during the war. He recalled how on one occasion police interrupted his conversation with an ex-army mate, Sporty Jones, in a park in the city and instructed him to move on as it was illegal for him to associate with Aboriginal men. Their concern was to prevent the supply of alcohol to Aboriginal people. Geoff chose to ignore the warning and when the police returned half an hour later he was arrested and spent the night in the lock-up. The charge of cohabitation was dismissed the following day.[14]

In this climate of repressive legislation, tight policing and segregation the Coolbaroo League was formed. Its organisers recognised that the deep division between the black and white community, and the way this division operated, on social, economic and cultural levels, negatively influenced every aspect of Aboriginal life. It is also worth contemplating how such official and unofficial controls shaped and limited the social and cultural choices of the white community as well.

The history of the Coolbaroo League

Anthropologists and administrators looking at Aboriginal disadvantage in the late 1940s saw assimilation as the best possible solution; however, a number of Aboriginal people, also assessing the position of their people, were coming up with a different solution. The Coolbaroo League was a conscious attempt to address the lack of political and civil rights, and to improve the state of health, education and welfare for Aboriginal people. The idea for the League was suggested by Helena Clarke and was modelled on the Euralian Club, founded in Port Hedland in the 1930s by her father, Lawrence Clarke, to promote the rights of people of mixed Aboriginal ancestry, considered to represent a distinct cultural group of their own. Originally from Broome, Helena's family moved to Port Hedland when she was a young girl. Her father, educated at Beagle Bay Mission, was keen for his children to have a wide understanding of political events taking place in the world, and this shaped Helena's interest in political activism. Lawrence Clarke was a respected man in Port Hedland, and Helena recalled nightly visits of Aboriginal people seeking her father's advice. While her family was fortunate in escaping the scrutiny of the department in the south, and the children were not removed from the family home, the Clarkes still experienced the absurdities of legislative controls.

Helena travelled to Perth as a young adult with several members of her family in 1942, 'the year the Japanese bombed Darwin'.[15] It had been her intention to keep travelling, but when her brother-in-law enlisted in the army she decided to stay and live with her sister. For Helena the local Aboriginal people appeared 'down trodden' and without hope. Her initial contact with them was through visiting people in their homes around the inner city area. Card games held in houses was the main point of social contact for the Aboriginal community before the Coolbaroo League dances. The idea for an organisation that would help to bridge the gap between the advantages of the white community and the disadvantages of the Aboriginal community grew in momentum after an initial meeting between herself, Geoff Harcus, returned Yamatji servicemen George and Jack Poland, and two elderly white women active in left-wing politics, the McEntyre sisters. George Poland suggested the name Coolbaroo, a Yamatji word for the small piebald magpie, but whose symbolism was open to other interpretations. For Helena it spoke of a personal identity of people of mixed ancestry, being both black and white; an interpretation of cultural identity that challenged assimilationist rhetoric of identities as 'part Aboriginal' or 'caught between two worlds'. For others the term suggested the political aims of the League — that Aboriginal and white people should work together through a cooperative relationship with law makers and the Native Affairs Department. For others, especially those who attended the dances, the term Coolbaroo referred more to an aspiration, of Aboriginal and white people putting aside differences and joining together in the spirit of equality.

The Coolbaroo League held its first dances in 1946 without the permission, or knowledge, of the Native Affairs Department. Helena had attended a couple of meetings at the Modern Women's Club, a small left-wing lobby group started by communist Katharine Susannah Prichard, and she used these contacts to organise a dance in the basement of their clubrooms in the centre of the city. Few Aboriginal people attended, however as, unbeknown to Helena, the venue was located inside the prohibited area and they would have had to break the curfew. More importantly, Helena realised that for the Coolbaroo League to succeed it required the support and involvement of the Nyungar eldership in Perth. With this in mind League members approached Thomas Bropho and Bill Bodney who had grown up together as inmates of the Swan Native and Half Caste Mission in Middle Swan, Perth, and were now married men with large extended families. Helena's ambitions for the League, its potential to represent the needs of Aboriginal people, and her desire to strengthen the community through community dances, resonated with their political aspirations. Their involvement attracted others to join, and any potential division between nor'wester and sou'wester politics was bridged. Geoff Harcus was one of the few white people who was active and committed to the League for its entire history.

Following the failure of the first dance, the League rented a hall in East Perth where several Aboriginal families lived in cheap rental houses, and from this time onwards, the dances were a huge success. They were for the entertainment of the Aboriginal population, and white people were only permitted to attend by invitation. The 'undesirable' elements of white society seeking to supply alcohol or looking for sexual liaisons with young women were deliberately screened out.

The League also had a committed political agenda and a membership that operated separately from attendance at the dances. Regular meetings were held in houses around the city and Helena recalled that members had 'big dreams' right from the start, one being unconditional voting rights for all Aboriginal people.[16] There were also plans to scrap the prohibited area laws, and for practical measures such as a housing project. 'We wanted a little place where we could prove we could handle our own affairs.' They rejected the assimilationist model of staged citizenship rights with certificates of citizenship — they considered themselves already citizens in their own country. Aboriginal control of the organisation was another key principle and early in the League's inception a constitution was drafted with Helena Clarke ensuring a clause was inserted whereby only Aboriginal people could hold executive positions and make key decisions. The only exception to this rule during the League's history was the decision in the late 1950s to admit Geoff Harcus as a full member as a gesture of appreciation for his dedicated service to the League.

While the Coolbaroo League had big dreams, 'there was no

finance', so raising funds for activities relied on community support. The League operated from 1946 to 1960, apart from a brief period in 1948 when it ceased to operate after Helena Clark returned to Port Hedland for health reasons, and a large fight outside the East Perth hall led police to close down the dances. Then in 1950 many of the original members joined together to reform the 'New' Coolbaroo League. At its height it held weekly dances in the city and an annual ball; it also travelled to outlying country towns to hold dances, published its own newspaper, organised deputations to ministers, ran a youth group, and set up the Coolbaroo Aboriginal Shop — an art and souvenir shop in the city, the first Aboriginal business in Perth. With the assistance of the trade union movement the League rented two small rooms, converted stables, at the back of Trades Hall in Beaufort Street, where they held weekly meetings. Arguably its most significant achievement was that it resisted sustained pressures to transform itself politically or structurally into an organisation befitting an assimilation model. While it advocated for the right of Aboriginal people to have the same rights and benefits as the wider community, these gains were not to be achieved through the trading off of Aboriginal personal identity or community identification with family and country.

The Coolbaroo League and the Department of Native Affairs

During its early years the League met with opposition from the Native Affairs Department and the police. In 1947 the Acting Commissioner of Native Affairs C. L. McBeath wrote in a memo to the police that the Coolbaroo dances were 'not encouraged by the Department'.[17] His stated objection was that the location of the dance hall encouraged an element of 'disruptive natives' in the East Perth area and he expressed his concerns for local white residents. The dances also threatened strategies set in place by the *1905 Aborigines Act* to prevent

Aboriginal people from congregating together in large numbers.

Despite this initial lack of support McBeath subsequently told the local press that he had 'a keen interest in the League' and had 'given it every assistance'.[18] This turnabout may have reflected the growing public interest in the League's activities as reported in the local press, and the generally favourable police reports on the conduct of the dances. Nevertheless, while there were only few arrests for alcohol offences or disturbances, the dances remained subject to police surveillance and clandestine reporting, and the Coolbaroo League dance hall became a regular spot on the weekend nightly patrol. In 1947 the newly appointed Minister for Native Affairs Ross McDonald advised the Commissioner of Police that he would be reluctant to see any 'ban' on the dances, and furthermore thought the dances 'might be guided into satisfactory channels'.

This notion of guiding League activities into 'satisfactory channels' would dominate the way the Native Affairs Department understood its role. When Middleton was appointed in 1948 the Coolbaroo dances had been closed down, and the youth group was barely operating. He was initially cautious and advised against supporting the youth group since any 'development along the lines of the Coolbaroo club could conceivably become a source of embarrassment to the Minister and the Department'.[19] Assimilation policy advocated that 'better class' Aboriginal children should be 'co-opted' into existing white youth organisations such as the YMCA, YWCA, Police Boys Clubs or church youth groups. Groups catering primarily for Aboriginal people were considered a step in the wrong direction. However, this goal was blocked both by objections from white organisations resistant to Aboriginal members and by the Aboriginal community's drive to form their own organisations and provide their own recreational and youth activities.

Early in 1950, however, Middleton had a change of heart, and Geoff Harcus recalled how he approached Bill Bodney about getting the League up and running again. Middleton had a personal vision of how the organisation could fit within the framework of assimilation. The dances, the youth group, and indeed the political membership could be useful training grounds for 'uplifting' Aboriginal individuals and families to the standard considered suitable for the white community. In this way Coolbaroo could fit snugly into the department's maxim of staged training and earning of rights. Middleton's perception should not be confused, or conflated, with how the League viewed its role, or its ongoing autonomy.

Significantly, it is at this point that there is a kind of split in historical memory and representation, regarding how Aboriginal organisations like the Coolbaroo League operated during the assimilation period. What emerged were two distinct separate but parallel narratives. The narrative told by advocates of assimilation presents the organisations as instruments of training and uplift. The other narrative records how Aboriginal members of these organisations used the assimilation rhetoric to improve Aboriginal access to the benefits and entitlements enjoyed by the wider community.

For Aboriginal people involved in the Coolbaroo League, and the majority attending the dances, assimilation meant something quite different to the official reading of the concept. For the government, assimilation — the rhetoric of access to education, raising health standards, repealing government controls over personal lives, granting of electoral rights and so on — meant extending equality to Aboriginal people, but an equality based on the erasure of racial distinctions and discrimination, where Aboriginal people would become assimilated as equals into Australian society. This stood in stark contrast to the League's view and expectation that their access to rights and benefits would be based on them *as* Aboriginal people, not 'coloured' imitations of white Australians. This was a defining point of difference between League members and Middleton who, despite holding a more enlightened view of assimilation than his colleagues in government, failed to grasp this essential difference.

Helena's claims that the League sought to 'raise' standards can easily be confused with assimilation ideals. However, in this instance Coolbaroo was predominantly addressing poverty issues, not notions of conforming to white ideals. Early League organisers wanted young people to take 'pride in themselves' *as* Aboriginal people rather than set them on a path to assimilated whiteness. They did not advocate nuclear families, or breaking ties with country and homelands, or spiritual and cultural beliefs. And they certainly did not advocate systems of monitoring and control such as staged housing, or removal of 'privileges' if people did not conform to white notions of what 'raising standards' meant. Members of the League resisted notions that dressing in particular ways, or engaging with popular culture, was reserved exclusively for the white community — to them, Aboriginal identity incorporated a greater range of possibilities than the binary allowed. Helena believed people had a right to be part of the political system of the state, not through 'earning it' but because it was firstly their country, and because Aboriginal 'freedom' and interests were constantly legislated against. Middleton was initially sympathetic to this view, but his position inevitably shifted as he became enmeshed in the reactionary forces of government that insisted on the gradual extending of citizenship rights.

In Aboriginal conceptions of equality, assimilation rhetoric offered real and accelerated potential for the improvement of living standards. In the non-Aboriginal press much of the scope of debate was reduced to the granting of drinking rights. For members of the Coolbaroo League, access to alcohol was a central concern, but so was the issue of electoral rights through automatic citizenship. As a one-time President of the Coolbaroo League, and a Native Affairs officer appointed under Middleton, George Harwood was often asked by the Rotary Association to speak on

Aboriginal issues at their meetings. George's personal politics held that institutional change could be effected from inside, and he welcomed the chance to have access to such groups. Rotary meetings were often held at the Savoy Hotel in the centre of the city, and George relished the opportunity to shock his audience by telling them that they were breaking the law by having him on the premises. George refused to apply for citizenship as he was morally and ethically opposed to the assumption that he was 'foreign' within his own country. And while he enjoyed revealing the absurdity of alcohol laws to his all-white audiences, he fully understood the implications of those laws. Restriction of alcohol, as with the granting of staged voting rights, held Aboriginal adults in a state of perpetual childhood.

Given these differing aspirations for social and political gains, members of the Coolbaroo League had to walk a careful line with the Native Affairs Department. Under the original Coolbaroo League, Acting Commissioner McBeath had been given 'honorary' member status, as a strategy to allay fears within the department that the League was a communist or revolutionary threat. Such notions might sound fanciful now, but in the context of the Cold War, fears of communist infiltrations were considered legitimate threats at the time. It was also a strategy of 'respect', a recognition of McBeath's status within the all-powerful department that controlled Aboriginal people's lives — though he was not invited to attend meetings and held no political influence within the League.

Middleton's position was more complex. Although he was never granted 'honorary' member status, he actively sought to influence ideology within the League through his relationship with some members. Early in the League's revitalisation Middleton drafted several public speeches for League President Bill Bodney to deliver. However, this was only a short-term practice; most League members insisted on complete autonomy from the department in all aspects of running the organisation.

Middleton had his own vision of assimilation and where his ideas for improved social and economic conditions coincided with those held by League members, he was met with enthusiasm and goodwill. League members welcomed his position on the granting of citizenship rights, and applauded his actions in closing down the Moore River Native Settlement. However, where ideas conflicted, such as in the speed of reform, there was quiet dissent. Aboriginal people were not in a political position to take Middleton on directly: he was Commissioner of the department that oversaw almost every aspect of their lives, and which provided them legal representation and assistance if they were charged with an offence. League members managed his influence in much the way that Aboriginal people generally managed white authority figures such as Native Welfare officers, police, or employers. They did not openly oppose or challenge him, thereby avoiding any repercussions to themselves as individuals, or the League as an organisation. Criticism of the speed of reform was discussed in private at meetings. The League was not active in organising street demonstrations, or public rallies, preferring less confrontational means of conveying its interest in legislative reform. When Bills to amend legislation were presented and debated in parliament, members attended the public gallery, 'to make ourselves seen so they'd know that we knew what was going on'.[20] As a political strategy it is best understood as a form of passive resistance, a strategy that marginalised people globally have tended to use in situations of political inequality.

The Coolbaroo dances

An early aim of the Coolbaroo League was for the weekly dances to break down segregation between the Aboriginal and non-Aboriginal communities. However, aside from the regular attendance of a small handful of white friends who were also involved in other aspects of the League, very few non-Aboriginal people attended. Those that came through invitation, such as officers of the Native Affairs Department, or visiting anthropologists, tended to view the dances as something 'other' to themselves.

From the outset the Aboriginal community claimed the weekly dance as a place of their own. The dances were extremely popular amongst individuals and families living around the city, with attendances often reaching three hundred. Early conflict incited by family feuds, north/south tensions, and alcohol and violence amongst young men, were dealt with primarily by community strategies. Helena Clarke recalled solving the problem of two feuding families by appointing representatives from each family as 'DPs' — door police. The young men wore armbands stamped with the initials DP and their role diverted their energies from arguing with each other to ensuring no one caused disturbances within the dance. Alcohol was strictly forbidden within the hall, and inebriated patrons were turned away at the door. By and large though, the majority of people came along to enjoy themselves. Most happily complied with the alcohol restrictions, and disruptions tended to be isolated to a small number of repeat offenders who congregated outside.

The dances drew on the experiences of older Aboriginal people who had attended dances in missions and government settlements. A small orchestra replaced the tea chest and violin players of the settlement bands, and many of the old time dances were popular at the Coolbaroo dances. Unlike the supper clubs and nightclubs that the wider community attended at the time, the Coolbaroo dances were family oriented, and there was a mixed program of events throughout the evening. Along with formal dances, Aboriginal singers were encouraged to perform with the band, and anyone was welcome to get up on stage and present an item of poetry, recount a story, or perform with a musical instrument. Performers also drew on popular culture of the day. Gladys Bropho, daughter of dance MC Thomas Bropho, was renowned for her rendition of 'Some Enchanted Evening' from the musical *South Pacific* which first toured Perth in 1954.

At the early dances Hazel Wattling regularly performed her version of 'Always', to enthusiastic applause. Aboriginal musicians, such as drummer Ron Kickett, were able to hone their performance skills in front of audiences. Another well-remembered performer was Willis Ellis, who did Al Jolson impersonations — an Aboriginal man impersonating a white man impersonating a Black man. In this way, experiments of popular culture taking place in the wider community were claimed and reshaped to comply with Aboriginal sensibilities.

The dances offered a safe, creative and fun environment for Aboriginal people to experiment with popular culture. Young Aboriginal people passed on the dances they learned from American servicemen, such as the jitterbug, and taught others to jive. The [mis]reading of the dances as imitations of white behaviour assumes that Aboriginal people lived in a cultural vacuum unaffected by the mass popular culture of films, magazines, print media and radio, and completely overlooks the sense of play that underpinned much of the experimentation, including sending up elements of white identity and culture. Aside from the opportunity to exchange amusing stories about white employers, police officers and newsworthy items, the dances often kicked off with Thomas Bropho performing the cake walk — a satirical dance that originated in slave communities in the southern states of America and lampoons the officiousness and self importance of the white boss. Tom's version of the dance followed the traditions of the lampoon, and was intended to inject some light-hearted humour into the opening proceedings, and encourage people who weren't proficient dancers to get up on the floor. Ron Kickett put together a band called Kickett's Kustard Kreek Killers, the name a satirical counter-reference to the white supremicist Ku Klux Klan operating in America.

From the outset the dances held a Miss Coolbaroo event, and in the 1950s ran bathing beauty competitions popular in the wider community at the time. However these events had little of the seriousness or competitiveness of their white counterparts. Joan Penny, a young Nyungar woman living in East Perth, remembered her first time in the competition. After passing inspection by her family at home, to make sure 'there wasn't anything hanging out that shouldn't', she was waiting with the other girls when it suddenly struck her there were going to be 'people gawking at me'. As the line of waiting girls became increasingly nervous, Lizzy Nelly, a Nyungar woman in her late fifties, came to their aid by jumping into a pair of bathers and leading them all out into the hall. The formality of the situation was shattered and it became just a bit of fun. Nor was the judging based on idealised notions of 'beauty' as in white competitions. While there was the occasional invitation of a white dignitary to judge the competitions, for the most part winners were judged by League members. First prize was shared around between families from week to week, and was most often awarded to a girl who 'needed it', that is, whose self esteem could do with a bit of a lift. Young men lampooned the concept of idealised femininity that informed white competitions and it was a favourite part of the evening when groups of them paraded in a mock beauty competition, in dresses, bathers, make-up and wigs. The audiences would hoot with laugher and thunder their applause for an alternative 'Miss Coolbaroo'.

In the mid 1950s the Coolbaroo dances attracted the attention of Aboriginal celebrities and visiting African-American performers. Albert Namatjira and Harold Blair were special guests at Coolbaroo League dances. The Norma Miller dancers and the Harlem Blackbirds took time out after their performances at His Majesty's Theatre and the Capitol Theatre to attend Coolbaroo dances. While the American dance troupes were in town, the League stayed open till the early hours so the visiting artists could come after their shows.[21] The Harlem Globetrotters also attended a Coolbaroo League dance when they were in town. When Nat King Cole toured Perth he was invited to a dance, but was unable to attend. League members went to see him backstage at Subiaco Oval and presented him with a boomerang as a gift. In return Bill Bodney and Ron Kickett were invited to have dinner with Cole at the exclusive Adelphi Hotel. Geoff Harcus recalled how this exposure to the visiting performers directly influenced the League's venture in opening a small nightclub.[22] While the Coolbaroo dances were family oriented, the new Magpie Club sought to cater to adults with an alcohol-free club on the top floor of the old Sunday Times Building. (The four-storey building was marked for demolition, and the League was able to rent rooms cheaply.) The Magpie Club was very popular, and the Harlem Blackbirds performed there impromptu after their shows, but it was short lived as a venue. When the building was demolished the League was unable to find a suitable alternative venue.

At the same time that Middleton was setting up the network of Native Welfare Councils in various country towns, the Coolbaroo League began extending their dances into the wheat belt area. By 1954 monthly dances were being held in Narrogin and York, and irregular dances at Katanning, Pinjarra and Geraldton. Geoff Harcus recalled how, in moving out into the country towns, the League was often faced with racism by local businesses. In one incident League Secretary Nora Shea had booked accommodation by telephone at a Katanning hotel for dance organisers who were staying overnight. Upon arriving at the hotel they were turned away by the owner on the grounds that they were Aboriginal. Geoff recalled the ensuing argument in which the proprietor verbally abused the group, then turned on him shouting, 'And you, you white boong lover, get out of my hotel.'[23] On other occasions League members were refused table service at country milk bars.[24] The League continued to push on with holding country dances, publishing incidents of racism they experienced in their own newspaper, and taking any opportunity they could to get stories in the mainstream press.

Using the media — the Westralian Aborigine

In December 1953 the Coolbaroo League published the first edition of its bi-monthly newspaper, the *Westralian Aborigine*, with the aim of providing an Aboriginal readership with an alternative source of news items to mainstream press. The mass culture of newspapers informed most white people on Aboriginal issues, and the racism and segregation of the period was reflected in the articles and cartoons published in mainstream papers. Despite its history of being a hostile forum, a number of Aboriginal people recognised the influence of the print media and wrote letters to the editors in an attempt to defend themselves against misinformed notions. George Harwood described himself as 'a bit of a letter writer', successfully getting some of his letters published in the *Sunday Times* under the editorship of Victor Courtney. His letters sought to highlight 'the status of Aborigines and how I was a man without a country'.[25] However, overwhelmingly, Aboriginal people were not considered by the editors and proprietors of mainstream newspapers to be part of their reading audience. The Coolbaroo League membership identified a need for alternative news sources for both Aboriginal readers and a wider community interested in broadening their knowledge.

Prior to setting up its own newspaper, the League had published several pages of copy under the banner of 'Coolbaroo News' in the *Progress of WA*, a newsletter published by the National Fitness Council of Western Australia. The new venture was a significant step forward for the League in providing news and information for the Aboriginal community. Middleton was a keen supporter and contributor to the *Westralian Aborigine*, and saw it as a forum for promoting assimilation projects, as well as providing tangible evidence to the white community that Aboriginal 'advancement' was forging ahead under his administration.

The League set up an Aboriginal-controlled editorial

committee that vetted and approved articles for publication. Printing and block mounting were provided at a reduced cost by a local Perth printing company in return for advertising. Ron Kickett, the popular drummer at the dances, and League treasurer, worked full time as a metal polisher, but managed to find the time to drum up advertising support for the paper. Geoff Harcus was actively involved in the general production of the paper, and often used his cousin, journalist Ron Davies to source copy. When each new edition came off the press, the Coolbaroo League committee would gather to roll the papers and distribute them to their subscription list of approximately six hundred.

Articles and items for the newspaper were gathered from a variety of sources. Whilst George Harwood regularly contributed articles, not all items were written by Aboriginal people. Items were also sourced from Native Welfare reports, contributing white writers, such as Middleton, and items of overseas stories sourced from mainstream papers. Whilst the editorials were written by League members, and can therefore be considered to represent League views, in general articles should be read as coinciding with Coolbaroo League sensibilities, rather than as the 'voice' of the League, or of Aboriginal people at the time.

Whilst not all items were written by Aboriginal people, they were subject to League evaluation and approval. What remains significant about the newspaper is its Aboriginal editorial control, its items that were of obvious interest to community members, its photographs of Aboriginal people and family members, and its reportage of deputations and political campaigns undertaken by the League. The newspaper also created a significant archive for posterity and future research. In December 1954 the *Westralian Aborigine* was the only paper to carry a front-page story on the death in custody of Aboriginal man Jimmy Gwiethoona in the goldfields town of Merredin. Gwiethoona had died in police custody in July of that year, and by November charges against the police officer allegedly responsible for his death had been dropped by the Crown Law Department. The League organised a deputation to Justice Minister Nulsen to request further investigation into the death, but had been unable to secure a hearing. The story in the *Westralian Aborigine* promised that the League would continue to exert pressure on the Justice Minister and follow it up in their next edition. The January 1955 edition reported on the League's unsatisfactory meeting with Minister Nulsen, who had refused to order a revision of the case. In a scathing editorial the League accused the Minister of giving the 'natives' of Western Australian 'as little protection as he would give a dog'.[26]

The League's Aboriginal-controlled newspaper was one of the first in Australia, and set the precedent for similar newspapers to follow. Its value for Aboriginal people lay in its role of providing yet another mechanism for strengthening a sense of cultural identity and community survival in response to the oppressive climate of assimilation.

Some academics have attempted to reduce the complexity and importance of organisations like the Coolbaroo League to being little more than vehicles of assimilation.[27] Their political aspirations and campaigns are rendered down to assimilation goals, and community events such as dances are interpreted as 'imitations' of white behaviour, or internalisations of assimilationist ideals. Key members of political groups are analysed and categorised as 'cultural brokers' with claims that more 'sophisticated' individuals — who were by implication less 'authentically' Aboriginal — used their leadership roles to promote government policies of assimilation and further their own personal careers. Such an analysis assesses identity within a limited range of options and fosters and reinforces notions of 'authentic' and 'inauthentic' Aboriginal culture. This analysis fits with a dominant historical narrative that defines the assimilation period as a time of Aboriginal loss — identity and culture loss, in a kind of cultural space pocket, until it was regenerated or reconstructed during 'aboriginalisation' in the 1970s. This scholarship was seduced by Elkin's assimilationist theories and the popular stereotyped narratives of people 'caught between two cultures' that have influenced the [mis]reading of Aboriginal identities and diversity into the present. The success of the Nyungar claim to Native Title over the Perth metropolitan area in the Federal Court of Australia in 2006 should lay to rest any lingering fantasies about the loss of Aboriginal identity during the assimilation period.

Clockwise from top left: Promotional lobby card for They're a Weird Mob *(1966) [Courtesy Fauna Productions Pty Ltd. and the National Film and Sound Archives]; Mrs Frank Clune, Dr. H.V. Evatt, Albert Namatjira, Dame Mary Gilmore and V.M. Leonard (seated at a table having a meal) [nla.pic-an24039750. Courtesy of the National Library of Australia]; Dutch migrant Mrs W. M. Duyker and her Aboriginal clay figures (1958)*

Cracks in the Mirror

Part IV

[Courtesy National Archives of Australia: A12111 1/1958/6/4; Beth Dean on the Cover of Pix *(1950) [Courtesy* Pix*/ACP Magazines Ltd]; Promotional material for* Jedda *(1955); [By arrangement with the licensor The Estate of Charles Chauvel c/- Curtis Brown (Aust) Pty Ltd. Image courtesy National Film and Sound Archives].*

NATIONAL FILM & SOUND ARCHIVE
AUSTRALIAN FILM COMMISSION

8. Paradox

By some strange paradox, as the Aborigine becomes less a primitive man and his way of life recedes into the past, his culture becomes more and more a part of the Australian heritage.

Dennis Dugan, *Herald* (Melbourne), 20 January 1968

It seems a strange paradox that while the vision of a new assimilated White Australia was in its ascendancy there was a parallel burst of interest in Aboriginal culture in Australia and overseas. Across the nation in government promotion, corporate branding, commercial advertising and contemporary fashion and design the look of a new modern Australia was being forged from a sophisticated mix of semi-abstract Aboriginal motifs, designs, patterns and earthy colours wedded to contemporary design principles. There was also a revitalisation of museum research and exhibitions representing Aboriginal cultures and a growing interest amongst visual and performing artists and art curators and galleries.

After visiting Australia in the early 1960s British artist and gallery owner Roman Black enthused over the 'thousands of shop windows' filled with 'pottery, wooden boxes and trays, table-mats, textiles and various knick-knacks and souvenirs decorated with aboriginal designs'.[1] He claimed that this 'new aboriginal art' would take over in modern Australia just as surely as the modern placemats decorated with Aboriginal designs used on Qantas Empire Airways flights had replaced Aborigines' 'wooden dishes'.[2] The sheer variety and volume of commercially produced hybrid objects — evident in the Glenn Cooke Collection of a thousand articles now held at the Queensland Museum — bear testimony to the enormous popularity of these products and to the indiscriminate ransacking of Aboriginal motifs by the cultural elite, skilled craftspeople — many of them European migrants — and amateurs producing for the commercial souvenir market.[3] As a loyal Britisher, Black claimed that the use of Aboriginal emblems during Royal visits had popularised the designs. In fact they were in part a rejection of old-fashioned British tastes in favour of modern international and American styles to better represent the nation.

Once seen as primitive decoration, these designs now symbolised what was unique about the new modern Australia. The 'contemporary' style for Australian homes was based on informality, open spaces, flexible furniture arrangements, form and function over decoration and colours appropriate to local light and climate. Objects decorated with Aboriginal designs and earthy colours fitted in perfectly. At the 1956 Olympic Games the wire Mimi figures from Western Arnhem Land rock art strung above some of Melbourne's major thoroughfares were lauded as ultra modern symbols of Australia. Australian designer Douglas Annand, commissioned to create the central mural for the English ocean liner the *Orcades,* represented the destination of Australia through a mix of decorative elements including x-ray drawings and Mimi figures and symbols from southern, northern and central Australia rendered in ochre and orange. Publications such as Oswald Ziegler's *This is Australia* (1946), Colin Simpson's *Adam in Ochre* (1951) and the edited collection of chapters by expatriate Australians *Sunburnt Country Profile of Australia* (1953) used line drawings based on Aboriginal designs to illustrate chapters and as cover art. To stimulate trade interest in the United States, the Australian Trade Commission mounted the *Australian Aboriginal Art* exhibition in the Rockefeller Building in New York in 1952, with bark paintings and Aboriginal artefacts creating a backdrop to new hybrid creations in textiles, ceramics, monotypes and dance performances.

The boomerang was a popular motif in government and corporate imagery. It dominated the diagonal composition of the poster *Australia* by designer Gert Sellheim — an Estonian-born immigrant who had trained as an architect in Germany. The poster was commissioned by the Australian National Travel Association in 1957 as part of its marketing campaigns to attract tourists to Australia and it received international recognition when it was published in the 1957 edition of *Modern Publicity*, the advertising industry's prestigious annual art magazine.[4] During the 1959 national tour by US evangelist Billy Graham, the preacher's rostrum was decorated with a large boomerang covered with Aboriginal designs and symbols set below the national coat of arms to brand the scene as Australian for international media coverage.[5]

At the same time, a renewed international scientific and academic interest in Aboriginal culture captured the local public imagination. The government capitalised on this fascination in the United States by promoting Aboriginal culture to consolidate political and economic relations established during the war. In such a gesture the Australian government appointed ethnologist Charles P. Mountford to undertake a lecture tour in 1946. Mountford's presentations attracted audiences of up to four thousand people and prompted the appointment of the 1948 American–Australian Scientific Expedition to Arnhem Land, which was co-sponsored by the Smithsonian Institution of Washington, the National Geographical Society (publisher of the

National Geographic magazine) and the Commonwealth of Australia (through the Department of Information). Led by Mountford the team was made up of fifteen researchers from archaeology, anthropology, psychology and the natural sciences, and journalist, photographer and government liaison officer, Bill Harney. At the time this was the largest and best-equipped enterprise of its kind ever seen in Australia. The expedition sparked a popular four-page spread in *Pix* magazine of cartoon caricatures by Eric Jolliffe who camped for a fortnight with the expedition on the beach at Yirrkala.[6] Colin Simpson, then a writer and producer for ABC radio, joined the expedition at Oenpelli and recorded ceremonial songs for radio broadcasts and wrote up his impressions in his best-selling book *Adam in Ochre,* which sold 23,000 copies in hard cover between 1951 and 1967 in Australia, the United States, Yugoslavia, France and Japan. Three hundred bark paintings collected by Mountford during the expedition formed the core of the South Australian Museum's Aboriginal art collection and were distributed to all state art galleries in 1956, becoming, for most, the first Aboriginal art works in their collections.

UNESCO also contributed to the revitalisation of museum-led research and exhibitions of Aboriginal culture. As part of its 'pedagogy of peace' UNESCO encouraged member states to develop and exchange museum exhibitions of local cultures, to enable 'one country to speak directly to the people of another and to reveal its essential quality in a way otherwise impossible.'[7] Australia was the first nation to produce an exhibition under this exchange program. The 1953 *Australian Aboriginal Culture* exhibition, developed with federal government funding and support under the auspices of the Australian UNESCO Co-ordinating Committee on Museums, toured galleries and museums in the United States for two years and hundreds of thousands of catalogues were distributed to visitors. Back in Australia the exhibition toured only briefly but the catalogue was distributed around the nation and the new Aboriginal Gallery opened at the Australian Museum in 1958 was influenced by its conceptual structure and design principles.

UNESCO also encouraged interest in Aboriginal art through its *World Art Series,* jointly funded by UNESCO and the New York Graphic Society to pay tribute to ancient art cultures and to salvage and preserve them as part of world cultural heritage. In 1957 UNESCO endorsed the proposal to include Aboriginal art as the third in the series, following volumes on the Ajanta Buddhist cave temples, monasteries and wall paintings in India and the ancient Egyptian capital of Thebes. Mountford was invited to work on the project with a committee of leaders from Australia's art world, including Hal Missingham, the Director of the Sydney National Gallery; artist Margaret Preston, well-known for her application of Aboriginal design; Desiderius Orban, Hungarian-born artist and chair of the Australian UNESCO Committee for the Visual Arts; and Sydney art critic Wallace Thornton. The resulting volume, *Australian Aboriginal Paintings — Arnhem Land,* with thirty-two pages of full-colour photographs of rock art and bark paintings, brought Aboriginal art to a new international audience and heralded new directions in the field, with the growing involvement of art dealers, curators, gallery directors and private collectors and researchers from Australia and overseas. Aboriginal art gradually became the preserve of state art galleries, and with increasing interest from university-based anthropologists as well there were new collaborations as well as tensions between researchers vying to lead the field.

A paradox?

While Aboriginal people were being directed to assimilate into the Australian way of life, elements of their cultures were being incorporated into the national visual landscape. This was a multifaceted process of cultural assimilation that enmeshed settler Australians and new European immigrants in aspects of Aboriginal culture as they sought from it commercial profits, ways to represent national identity, creative inspiration, a sense of belonging and knowledge and understanding. Acknowledging this process considerably complicates the accepted view of these decades as a time of one-way assimilation. Book-ended by an earlier period of neglectful attitudes and a subsequent period of prohibitions on the appropriation of Aboriginal art, the 1950s and 1960s were unique in the unfettered exploitation of Aboriginal cultures in pursuit of research, nationalism and economic interests. This laid the basis for today's multi-million dollar art and tourism businesses and international brands to express Australian national identity evidenced most recently in the prominent place of Aboriginal and Torres Strait Islander cultures in the opening ceremony of the Sydney 2000 Olympics. What is different today of course is that Indigenous Australians now play an integral role in interpreting and performing their own cultures for non-Indigenous audiences. In the 1950s and 1960s they were largely left out of the loop.

The imperatives of assimilation and appropriation may have been paradoxical but they were not antithetical. Ann Maree Willis[8] argues that they were of 'the same coin': Aboriginal people were denied the right to practise their cultures while powerful governments and the public selected elements that they valued and admired to exploit as commodities for their own benefit and profit. In this way Aboriginal cultures became 'part of the nation's cultural capital, part of its heritage, a past living on in the present, a resource located somewhere between the nation's natural features and cultural landmarks'.[9] Nicholas Thomas argues that the continuing uneasy dynamic found in the 'interplay of dispossession and repossession that defines the history of settler societies' bestows on acts of cultural appropriation a character of dual instability that combines in some proportion, 'taking and acknowledgement, appropriation and homage, a critique of colonial exclusions, and collusion in an imbalanced exchange'.[10] Thomas's model allows us to critically explore the complex ambivalent responses of creative artists who sought to seriously engage with Aboriginal cultures in mid-twentieth century Australia. He writes that they 'were captivated by indigenous objects and performances, and sought to communicate their visual drama, even if they lacked understanding of their ritual significance. Encounters were marked by moments of awe, respect and partial understanding as well as misrecognition and hostility. It is this uncertain combination of acknowledgement and denial that has characterised the settler–indigenous relation in general.'[11]

In this chapter the uneasy encounters of settlers and immigrants with Aboriginal cultures in the 1950s and 1960s provide the context for an analysis of the creation and performance of the 1954 modern ballet *Corroboree.* When the Queen visited Australia in 1954 she attended two public corroboree performances. The first, in the Queensland town of Toowoomba, was a scene familiar to the monarch, of black colonial subjects performing for her entertainment — in this case Aboriginal dancers and musicians brought over from the Northern Territory. The enormous gap between Queen and Aboriginal subject was emphasised in the headline in *Pix*, which described the event as 'STONE AGE CULTURE FOR ROYAL VISITORS — WEIRD RITUAL DANCE OF NT TRIBESMEN HAS CLIMAX IN SAVAGE KILLING'.[12] At the Royal Gala evening in Sydney the Queen watched the modern ballet *Corroboree,* choreographed and performed by American migrant Beth Dean who was applauded by local critics for her 'world-class production' that found in the raw material of a 'primitive' culture the idiom to express the quintessentially modern Australia.[13] Yet there was something about the ballet's combination of Aboriginal culture and Australian nationalism that left a sense of uneasiness and discomfort. Once the ballet's initial novelty had worn off it was largely forgotten, like the clutter of hybrid domestic objects from the 1950s that languished in obscurity until they were rediscovered and restored to public memory by collectors of kitsch, cultural historians and museum curators.

Modern, primitive, kitsch

The story of the creation of the ballet *Corroboree* begins in the uneasy relationship between modernism and primitivism that formed part of its broader context of creation in the mid-twentieth century. At the time, artists uncritically accepted the modernist practice of finding creative inspiration in 'primitive art'. Marianna Torgovnick explains that for Western audiences 'the general idea of the primitive becomes a place to project feelings about the present and to draw blueprints of the future … The West seems to need the primitive as a precondition and a supplement to its sense of self: it always creates heightened versions of the primitive as nightmare or pleasant dream.'[14] Modernist critic Clement Greenberg has argued that the 'precondition for kitsch' is the borrowing and taking advantage of a cultural tradition 'for its own ends. It borrows from it devices, tricks, stratagems, rules of thumb, themes, converts them into a system, and discards the rest. It draws its life blood, so to speak, from this reservoir of accumulated experience.'[15] Philosopher Roger Scruton observes that kitsch is the scourge brought by modernism to 'pre-modern people … their immune systems seem helpless in the face of this new contagion; today the mere contact of a traditional culture with Western civilisation is sufficient to transmit the disease, rather as tribes were once rescued from their darkness by colonial adventurers and missionaries, only to die at once from smallpox or TB. A century ago, no African art was kitsch. Now kitsch is on sale in every African airport — antelopes, elephants, witch doctors, and hobgoblin deities, skilfully carved in ivory or tropical hardwood, imitating the enchanted figures that inspired Picasso but, in this or that barely perceptible detail, betraying their nature as fakes.'[16] This was the fate of Aboriginal cultural elements swept up in the appropriations of the 1950s and 1960s. The consequence of this process of cultural colonisation, Andrew Lattas argues, was that they became imbued with 'meanings [they] never had' and were made to speak the 'cultural truths' of others.[17]

From the African masks that inspired Picasso in the early 1900s to the Native American sand paintings that stimulated Jackson Pollock in the 1950s modern artists have sought and found in tribal art and culture new forms, languages, energies and even personal transformation. For some artists the abstract decorative elements were paramount. During the 1920s French artist Fernand Leger created spectacles that incorporated primitive forms muted and stripped of their 'rawness' to please popular tastes and his 'stereotypical reduction' of African designs spread through to contemporary design and fashion and the vogue for 'African' masks, rugs, fabrics, jewellery, silverwork and furniture.[18] For Picasso, primitive art provided a radical new language of forms that broke with tired modes of Western artistic expression. For abstract impressionist artists like Pollock, 'primitive expression' was a compelling revelation of 'powerful forces [and] the immediate presence of terror and fear'.[19] Caught up in Western imaginings of raw untameable emotions inherent in the primitive but lost to modern life, they sought out transformation through what they saw as its savagery and excess and surrender to shamanic rituals.

The quite different response of Australian modernism to 'primitive' Aboriginal culture reflected the nation's settler society origins. The appropriation of Aboriginal culture was another manifestation of the ongoing exploitative relationship between settlers and Indigenous people that had begun with colonisation and the taking of Aboriginal land, resources, labour, women and children. Typically, Australian modernism was conservative, neither seeking to challenge art forms nor promote internationalism, but to appropriate from Aboriginal cultures the means to express national identity and affirm settler supremacy.[20] The Australian nation was created from 'assemblages of people, economic activity and cultural forms from elsewhere' but with a national identity moulded from its central Anglo-Celtic core.[21] Aboriginal culture provided 'a sign of the nation's distinctiveness'[22] and a potent 'mark of identification'[23] to symbolise Australia's unique heritage and distinctive landscape and flora and fauna. It also provided a long history of an imagined ancient mythological past to mirror the pasts claimed by European nations. In this narrative Aboriginal culture represented the first stage in the nation's development where the new assimilated White Australia represented the final stage, in which Aboriginal people and their cultures were disappearing and settler colonists owned the land and the nation's resources. The 1954 UNESCO exhibition and the Australian Museum's Aboriginal Gallery (1958) presented this narrative to the public with all the authority bestowed by major cultural institutions with their brief to convey habits of collective and national consciousness.[24] There were also glimpses in popular magazines like *Walkabout,* with its iconic images of Aboriginal men as noble savages looking out into the distance in 'the crude nationalistic trope of gazing into the future while being rooted in the past', an image also used in the government's pamphlets to promote assimilation.[25]

There was a whiff of the 'unsettling irony of imperialist nostalgia'[26] in hybrid products like Dean's *Corroboree.* This seemingly 'innocent yearning' for Indigenous cultures concealed settler 'complicity' in their brutal oppression and destruction by settler colonialism,[27] and mingled a sense of guilt with relief that the battles were over and that settler curiosity about diabolical or quaint customs could now be freely indulged. Aboriginal curator and writer Djon Mundine summarises this process: 'so you don't see Aboriginal people in these places anymore, or you make sure you don't see them in those towns so you make facsimiles … people often talk about the dead heart, the spirit of Australia, the great loneliness etc — all these things that relate to the supposedly vanishing person.'[28] Both of the corroborees for the Royal visit can be seen as remnants of once savage performances now safely contained within the spaces and forms of 'civilisation' for the enjoyment of settler Australians and their monarch. Similarly the museum expeditions committed to salvaging and documenting Aboriginal culture helped to distract attention from settler guilt and responsibility for the original acts of cultural destruction.

These displacements only served to reinforce and maintain underlying paradigms and practices of race and power. Julie Marcus[29] notes that while producers and consumers may not have intended these popular hybrid commodities to be racist, yet they were just that and they were far from innocuous. Decorating Australia's suburban lounge rooms they visibly sustained paradigms of race and white superiority in the practices of daily life. Marcia Langton, citing New York artist and critic Coco Fusco, observes how interrogations of these stereotypes today by Aboriginal artist Destiny Deacon remain significant since what has 'grown ingrained over time cannot be easily dismissed as ridiculous and then simply cast off … [They are a reminder of] a painful history of bigotry and disempowerment' and thus 'enable us to understand that past.'[30]

Modernism in Australia

There is no 'simple formula' for mapping the 'transmission of modernism' to Australia.[31] The Menzies government may have been hostile to abstract modernist painting but it happily commissioned promotional materials based on the latest in modern graphic design. Ann Stephen, Andrew McNamara and Philip Goad argue that 'ideas about the modern' filtered into mass and popular cultural forms far more readily than they did into traditional high art forms of culture. New information was transmitted through networks built up through overseas travel and commissions, access to trends and debates reported in trade magazines, mass reproduction of images, and the training and skills brought to Australia by European migrants connected to modernist movements such as the Bauhaus in Germany. There was an immediate practical and economic application for modern design principles, generated by the growth in the manufacturing industries, the housing boom, the new advertising industry, and the expanding tourist market. There was already an interest in Aboriginal design dating from the 1920s with Margaret Preston, and in the 1930s the Jindyworobaks advocated the use of Aboriginal motifs as designs for a new national imagery. From the early 1940s museum anthropologists Charles Mountford and Fred McCarthy provided a 'bank' of Aboriginal motifs for designers to draw on, material that was not subject to expensive copyright fees demanded by overseas design companies.[32] Art workshops were established in some Aboriginal communities to produce commercial objects for the market and a few Aboriginal-run souvenir shops were opened like the Coolbaroo League's outlet in Perth. The only independent Aboriginal designer and entrepreneur at the time was Bill Onus whose studio in Melbourne was famous for its souvenir boomerangs and boomerang tables. European migrants with the skills to create the new range of commodities grabbed the opportunity to escape from unskilled labouring jobs. As Richard White observed, this set up a 'tension between the sophistication and skills of craftspeople, their numbers boosted by migrants from Europe, and the amateurism and commercialism of the souvenir trade. Both ransacked Aboriginal cultures for motifs.'[33] Post-war embargoes on cheap Japanese ceramics proved a boon to the local ceramics industry, and numerous small studios like the Martin Boyd Pottery and Studio Anna Pottery in Sydney were set up to create decorative works to meet the new fashion for exotic design and images.[34] Many of these studios employed migrant potters from Greece and Germany.

The response to modernism in the visual and performing arts was more muted. As Stephens, McNamara and Goad observe, many local artists were aware of the latest developments in modernism but were blocked by 'institutional resistance' in their efforts to practise and sell modernism to 'a not-always-unreceptive Australian public'.[35] The arrival of cosmopolitan refugee and migrant artists played a role in promoting modernism to Australian audiences and eroding this resistance. In this context Aboriginal art was initially regarded as largely decorative and of little interest to serious artists. Some painters were attracted to creating powerful realistic images of Aboriginal people: Jewish painter Yosl Bergner's scenes of Aboriginal oppression witnessed in Melbourne during the 1940s; Arthur Boyd's *Bride Series* painted in the mid 1950s after a trip to Alice Springs; and Russell Drysdale's images of Aboriginal alienation inspired by a visit to the Coen races in North Queensland in 1953. This view shifted as some artists began to seek a more embodied connection with the natural environment and Aboriginal people. Terry Smith writes of a significant development in Margaret Preston's work from the 1940s when, immersed in Aboriginal bark, body and rock art painting and living in the Australian bush, she was inspired to create her most profound modernist works.[36] Colin Symes and Bob Lindgard[37] noted a growing connection between Aboriginal art and abstract expressionism. Artist Tony Tuckson, who later became Deputy Director of the New South Wales Art Gallery, took up abstract expressionism in 1956 and this drew him to consider 'processual' aspects of Aboriginal art such as the degree to which it drew on intuitive forces and the imagery of the unconscious. In 1958 Tuckson travelled to Arnhem Land with Sydney physician and collector Dr Stuart Scougall and went on to curate *Australian Aboriginal Art* (1960–1961) — the first major travelling exhibition of its kind to tour state art galleries in

Australia. Artist and anthropologist Karel Kupka, who made two trips to Arnhem Land for the Swiss Basel Ethnographical Museum, also acknowledged the symbolic dimensions of Aboriginal art, in his publication *Un Art à l'État Brut* (*Dawn of Art*) published in French in 1962 and English in 1965 although, as the title of his book indicates, he continued to classify it from an evolutionary perspective as Stone Age art.[38]

The cultural middlemen

Today we are accustomed to seeing Aboriginal artists and art curators presenting and interpreting Aboriginal art in the public domain and we are attuned to the debates and prohibitions on the unauthorised use of Aboriginal art work. However, this was not always the case and this position was only gradually reached after decades of often-bitter negotiation, debate and legal challenges that carved out an authoritative position for Aboriginal custodians and artists, backed up by legal precedent and protections. Initially, museum anthropologists were the dominant cultural middlemen, reflecting the convention dating from the nineteenth century that museums were responsible for the collection, analysis and exhibition of Aboriginal material culture in their pursuit of 'scientific' theories of human and cultural evolution. In this milieu Aboriginal art was considered as a primarily decorative element, used to embellish Aboriginal artefacts and important cultural sites and in painting bodies for ceremonies. The UNESCO *Australian Aboriginal Culture* exhibition included sections headed 'Decorative art', 'Bark paintings', 'Rock engravings' and 'Cave paintings' as aspects of material culture. Today we would be more likely to see the works classified as art and displayed in galleries rather than museums. As the cultural middlemen, museum curators interpreted Aboriginal culture and art for the public, through exhibitions, lectures and publications, popularising the commercial use of Aboriginal design motifs, and in a host of ways helping to shape public imaginings about Aboriginal culture and people.

Australian museums have always played a major role as sites where white audiences can explore in an 'organised way … the worlds and things of the [Aboriginal] "other"'.[39] Into the vacuum created by the separation of white and black in 1950s Australia, the authoritative voice of the museum injected textual and visual narratives of Aboriginal culture and society, shaped by the frameworks, codes, conventions and values of science, anthropology and museology and broader sociopolitical imperatives.[40] Aboriginal people were not part of these processes of research, interpretation and display. As with the production of campaign materials to promote Aboriginal assimilation, it was white middle-class males who were interpreting Aboriginal cultures through the paradigms and methodologies of their professional background. These concerns determined which artefacts were collected and how they were classified, interpreted, and displayed for public exhibitions. Salvage work to preserve Aboriginal cultures had become a major focus of museum anthropologists responding to the discourse of 'cultural extinction' that pointed to the destructive influence of 'civilisation' and the new threat of assimilation in remote Australia.

Museum anthropologists also extracted symbols and motifs from Aboriginal ceremonies, artefacts and rock art sites and gathered them together in publications and exhibitions for the use of students, designers and artists. Here the original meanings of the designs in Aboriginal cultural life were of little significance. When Roman Black began his Australian tour the South Australian Museum was one of his first ports of call. The Museum's Curator of Anthropology Norman Tindale told him that field research was the 'most urgent and important duty, as in a comparatively few years there might be no aborigines as we know them left'.[41] At the Australian Museum in Sydney he met Curator of Anthropology Fred McCarthy, whom he praised for inspiring most of the painters and craft workers interested in the subject.

Fred McCarthy was the first university-trained museum anthropologist. For much of his career funding constraints left him office-bound, cataloguing and systematising the collection to make it accessible to the public and for scientific study. By contrast, the South Australian Museum had a strong tradition of fieldwork, initially with Aboriginal groups in Central Australia and later in Arnhem Land. McCarthy's research was limited to documenting rock art sites near the Hawkesbury River to the north of Sydney. This drew the criticism of anthropologists at Sydney University who undertook long periods of fieldwork in Aboriginal communities, endeavouring to study the totality of their way of life. Not surprisingly, given the grounding of museums in scientific evolutionary theory, McCarthy saw Aboriginal art as an early stage in human cultural development that was not equal in 'abstract and imaginative qualities, or the richness of design' to other primitive art or the 'magnificence' of western traditions.[42]

McCarthy promoted Aboriginal art as an 'unexploited storehouse of inspiration for our designers' in his publication *Australian Aboriginal Decorative Art* (1938) and the exhibition *Australian Aboriginal Art and its Applications* (1941).[43] For many years *Australian Aboriginal Decorative Art* was a principal source for artists and craft workers, introducing them to a wide range of artefacts with explanatory text identifying their use, region and mode of manufacture and the distinctive Aboriginal art regions in Australia. McCarthy's 1941 exhibition, held at David Jones' Sydney auditorium, attracted three thousand visitors and was an eclectic mix that juxtaposed authentic traditional Aboriginal objects with the new hybrid works mixing modern and Aboriginal design. On display were artefacts from various museum collections, bark paintings from Arnhem Land, reproductions of rock and ground art, and Aboriginal crayon and finger drawings on paper. The hybrid works included photographs of murals and designs on buildings, ceramics decorated with Aboriginal designs, glassware, jewellery, fabrics printed with motifs based on Gulmari shields from North Queensland, bark paintings and rock art, Gert Sellheim's *Arunta* design fabrics and his iconic poster *Corroboree*, and works submitted by local art students. Significantly, reviewers responding to the exhibition praised the Aboriginal works but were ambivalent about the hybrid applications. In this they foreshadowed the eventual triumph by the 1970s, in contradiction to Roman Black's predictions, of authentic Aboriginal art over these modernist works.[44]

McCarthy's career expanded during the 1950s, due in part to his growing involvement in fieldwork with Aboriginal communities after his participation in the 1948 Arnhem Land expedition. Another break was his appointment as co-curator with Norman Tindale of the 1953 *Australian Aboriginal Culture* exhibition. The exhibition carried considerable 'cultural authority' in a broad institutional sense with its backing by UNESCO, the International Council of Museums and the Australian government. Billed as 'the most comprehensive display of Australian aboriginal culture that has ever been assembled' the exhibition sought to 'pay tribute to the ancient culture of this minority group, to express the hope that it will receive the recognition it deserves, and to emphasise the importance of preserving a permanent record of a culture which is inevitably being modified through contact with Western civilisation'.[45] This statement carried major assumptions that were mirrored in the exhibition — that the imperatives for Aboriginal culture were salvage, preservation and international recognition.

The exhibition presented a generalised view of Aboriginal culture and consisted of a series of themed panels that introduced the Aboriginal population and provided 'snapshots' of traditional Aboriginal life. The panel titles reflected a mix of museum research areas and topics to attract public interest and imposed a universal grid over the diversity of Aboriginal life: 'Who are the Aborigines? Where did the Aborigines come from? Tribal territories. The Aborigines' world. The women's way of life. The men's way of life. Habitations. Economic life. Fire without matches. Games and music. Dress and adornment. Trade and exchange. Religion and ceremonies. Ceremonial life. Magic and medicine. Decorative art. Bark paintings. Rock engravings. Cave paintings. The boomerang. Combat and conflict. Old age and death. The Aborigines' new world.'[46]

Aboriginal groups mentioned in the exhibition were principally from northern and central Australia, reinforcing the museum's view on the authenticity of remote Aboriginal cultures and the invisibility of traditional Aboriginal life in southern Australia. The history of British colonisation and its devastating impact on Aboriginal cultures was not mentioned at all. Reproductions of early photographs showing healthy Aboriginal people in traditional contexts suddenly gave way in the final panel to images of Aboriginal people living an assimilated way of life within the Australian nation. These views were reflected in the Australian Museum's Aboriginal Gallery, curated by McCarthy, which opened in 1958. The gallery remained *in situ* into the 1990s and for the hundreds of thousands of school children and other local, national and international visitors it was formative in shaping their understanding of Aboriginal cultures.

Charles Mountford was a very different kind of anthropologist from McCarthy. He was self-trained, worked as a Commonwealth public servant, had only an honorary position with the South Australian Museum, and had experience in the field rather than with museum collections.[47] He was a keen film-maker, photographer and writer and his works provided popular introductions to traditional Aboriginal life.[48] Like McCarthy, he also initially encouraged the use of Aboriginal designs in hybrid works. However, following the 1948 expedition to Arnhem Land, Mountford pursued a more serious interest in Aboriginal art and from his research there produced a book, *Art, Myth and Symbolism,* and three ethnographic films, with Aboriginal-inspired music by his composer friends Mirrie and Alfred Hill. During the 1950s and 1960s he continued to conduct fieldwork research in the north and also travelled overseas to do research and to promote Aboriginal art in international exhibitions in London and Germany. In 1965 he published to popular acclaim *The Dreamtime: Australian Aboriginal Myths* with paintings by Ainslie Roberts.[49]

In 1976 Mountford became the subject of legal action that showed significant shifts in relations between anthropologists and Aboriginal custodians. In that year the Pitjantjara Land Council lodged a breach of confidence claim over his publication of secret sacred information placed in his trust by Pitjantjara elders during the 1940s. The court upheld the claim and acknowledged the deep religious and cultural significance of the material and the possible serious damage that could follow its revelation to uninitiated men and women and children and the book was withdrawn from sale.[50] In recent years museums have undertaken repatriation programs to return Aboriginal cultural heritage, tangible and intangible, to Indigenous communities. In 2007 the Australian Broadcasting Commission program Radio Eye reported on a repatriation project initiated by historian Martin Thomas to return to Aboriginal custodians sound recordings made by Colin Simpson for the Commission during his stay at Oenpelli with the 1948 Arnhem Land Expedition.[51]

Corroboree 1954

These various trends and movements provided the broader contexts for the creation of the 1954 modern ballet *Corroboree.* This hybrid creation celebrated the modern Australian nation using dance forms and mythology from Aboriginal performance combined with Western conventions to express Australia's unique identity. The ballet was conceived in the crosscurrents of 'awe, respect, partial understanding as well as misrecognition' of

Aboriginal culture that Nicholas Thomas wrote about.[52] In the rest of the chapter we trace its creation by the choreographer/dancer Beth Dean and its place in the paradoxical relationship between the policy of Aboriginal assimilation and the appropriation of Aboriginal culture.

In 1953 Dean was invited by Dorothy Helmrich of the Arts Council of Australia to choreograph a ballet for the Royal Gala Performance based on Australian composer John Antill's orchestral score *Corroboree.* This was a singular honour for a woman who had only migrated to Australia from America in the late 1940s and an expression of faith in her ability to create a ballet that would sensitively express the qualities of Aboriginal culture and the Australian nation.

The desire to learn more about Aboriginal performance was a motivating factor in Dean's original decision to migrate to Australia with her Italian-Australian husband, singer and producer Victor Carell. The couple later recalled that they were inspired by a meeting with Charles Mountford on his lecture tour in the United States in 1946 and the vision that he painted for them of the 'centre of a continent where, surrounded by empty silence, an old man, with bearded face and jutting eyebrows, sat chanting. The shadows about him were peopled with leaping, virile young men, their dark glistening bodies ochre-daubed and decorated in fantastic designs of feather down.'[53] Dean may have also heard of the power of Aboriginal performance through descriptions by iconic American modern dance pioneer Ted Shawn, who toured in Australia in 1947. Shawn described Aboriginal performances he saw in the Northern Territory as 'so outstanding that I was knocked off my feet'. He told the dancers (who included the legendary Wagaitj dancer and musician Mosec Manpurr)[54] that 'as one dancer to another, I tell you that this is as great dancing as I have ever seen anywhere in my life'.[55]

Other modern artists learned about Aboriginal culture from the writings of anthropological experts, however there was disappointingly little recorded about Aboriginal dance outside its connection with ceremony, and there were no anthropologists trained to record and analyse dance movement. In fact, little serious published analysis of embodied Aboriginal performance was available until recent years.[56] There were few opportunities to view traditional Aboriginal dance performances in settled Australia, apart from the occasional hybrid public performances referred to generically as 'corroborees' (a word from the Darug language of the Sydney region), that White Australian audiences have avidly watched from early colonial times to the tourist presentations of today.[57] Cultural historian Anita Callaway calls these corroborees 'a fitting metaphor for the way in which Aboriginal Australians — indeed all colonised people — must constantly "perform" for their daily survival'.[58]

A corroboree at La Perouse that John Antill witnessed as a boy became wedded to his later study of Baldwin Spencer and Frank Gillen's accounts of Aboriginal traditions in Central Australia, and provided the inspiration for his composition *Corroboree*.[59] The work also suggested the influence of modernist composer Igor Stravinsky's score for the ballet *Rite of Spring* (1913), which was inspired by his nostalgia for Russian peasant life.[60] *Corroboree* became the defining composition of Antill's career and was performed under the baton of English conductor and Australian resident Eugene Goossens at concerts in Sydney, London and the United States to rave reviews. Antill sought to combine modern orchestral styles with Aboriginal idioms of melody, rhythm and percussive sounds to create new musical expressions of Australian identity. He described the ballet suite with its seven themed sections based on mythical figures and dances as a 'typical summary' of types of corroboree.[61]

There were few precedents of settler hybrid performances in Australia for Dean to emulate compared with her home country where there was a long tradition of performers dressing up to 'play Indian' — from the colonists who staged the Boston Tea Party, to the sophisticated interpretations of the American modern dance movement, the costumed hobbyists at weekend powwows in the 1950s and 1960s, the hippies and finally the New Age consumers of today.[62] Of the few documented Australian hybrid performances,[63] the best remembered is choreographer Rex Reid's 1950 interpretation of Antill's *Corroboree* as a vision of primitive savagery. Critic Cornelius Conyn described the 'spectacular tableaux and wild dancing' of the final scene:

> The large torches are ablaze and sway crazily. The air is filled with blazing fragments and thick smoke. The mysterious bullroarer sounds a sinister note. The mass of howling, dancing men grotesquely bedaubed, create an atmosphere that could only be described as fiendish. The curtain falls upon a scene of absolute chaos and prostration.[64]

Obviously this performance of *Corroboree* was not suitable for the new young Queen.

Dean's fascination for Aboriginal performance derived from her interest in American modern dance and the work of its pioneer dancers — Ruth St Denis, her husband Ted Shawn and her student Martha Graham. There was also the example from modern ballet of the Russian dancer and choreographer Nijinsky whose search for a new language of dance took him to French cubist art, which drew its inspiration from African art. Martha Graham saw powerful synergies for modern dance practitioners in 'primitive' dance. She was interested in more than new combinations of the disparate elements of primitive dance; she sought out the profound transformative creative encounters that would energise repressed emotions and unleash what Marianna Torgovnick calls the 'oceanic' dimensions of human experience.[65] To this end Graham undertook first-hand study of Native

American religious ceremonies and shamanic rituals in the American southwest that were incorporated in performances like *Primitive Mysteries* (1931), with pagan and Catholic ceremonies.[66]

The modern dance movement was aligned with the anthropological impetus to salvage, preserve and resurrect 'lost or dissolving styles, techniques and forms'. The interest from the modern dance movement was a positive step but in retrospect can be seen as intrinsically unequal and inevitably exploitative. The dancers' hybrid re-workings and transformations reflected their own artistic, commercial and political interests. In the creative process the original meanings, purposes and histories of appropriated elements and the intentions of their creators and the cultural conventions that guided their practice were overlooked and forgotten. The style and forms of what Michael North calls the resulting 'modern-created-primitive-dialects'[67] were the property of alien artists, anthropologists, critics and audiences. They shaped public imaginings and expectations of primitive performance in ways that challenged the authenticity of works by Indigenous artists seeking to establish their own creative identities.

Dean's early performances

In concerts in the early 1950s Dean and Carell created imaginary fragments of Aboriginal dance which they added to an eclectic concert repertoire that brought together fragments of classical ballet, Spanish, Navajo, Aboriginal and Maori dances and chants, didgeridoo solos, recitations of the poet Kahlil Gibran and solo performances by Carell of operatic arias and Aboriginal-inspired songs by Alfred and Mirrie Hill.[68] Arthur Calwell supported their application to the Australian News and Information Bureau for funds to tour, arguing that 'no one before has ever attempted to portray the art both in song and dance of our natives and, I am sure that what these young people propose to do will be good publicity for Australia, as well as a worthwhile contribution to the cultural and artistic world'.[69]

Billed as *Around the World with Dance and Song* the concert toured the United States, Europe, New Zealand and Australia. A review of the concert in the *Hollywood Reporter* encapsulated its strange appeal: 'nothing has been seen here like this before. The extraordinary vitality of these dances, which has the weird, gone feeling of the Stone Age about them, is fascinating.'[70] While both were dressed to 'simulate the appearance of the Aborigines' — painted, barefoot and wearing a minimum of clothing — it was Dean who attracted the comment in the *New York Times* that 'she covers herself with paint — and not much more'.[71]

In her quest to understand 'primitive dance' Dean studied anthropological texts and viewed the few available films held by the Department of Information. During her concert tour of New Zealand she took the opportunity to learn traditional dance from Maori women. This embodied experience of learning presumably furthered her determination to observe authentic Aboriginal performances first-hand in remote Australia.

At a time when Australian women were hemmed in by whiteness and suburban domesticity, Dean, with her force of personality, physical beauty and exotic appeal and glamour as an outsider American, dancer and minor movie star, challenged conventions of gendered and racialised space. She and her husband joined a small group of mainly white male explorers, missionaries, government officers, anthropologists and fellow artists celebrated for journeying into remote Australia. Direct contact with Aboriginal worlds brought creative success and recognition for many artists, and Dean and Carell's first-hand experience brought valuable cultural capital by bestowing the stamp of authenticity and authority on their creative productions.

In 1953 the couple undertook an eight-month journey that led them up the east coast of Australia, through the country around Darwin, down into Central Australia, then to Adelaide and finally back home to Sydney. Their goal was to observe, record and film Aboriginal dance and ceremonies as part of their preparation for the ballet *Corroboree.* Their journey was ambitious in time and distance travelled, the range of meetings with Aboriginal people and the Aboriginal performances they observed and recorded, which Dean documented in her numerous notebooks now held in the Mitchell Library in Sydney. Along the way they travelled with Pintubi people to Mt Larry in Central Australia to observe an initiation ceremony first hand; it was a unique opportunity that had a strong influence on the final form of the ballet.

In the segregated world of 1950s outback Australia the couple experienced the usual barriers to interaction with Aboriginal people — language, culture and racial barriers and social pressures to mix with white residents — pastoral station managers, police officers and settlement superintendents and their families. The influence of white Territory lore inevitably coloured their perceptions as they travelled.

Dean and Carell documented their journey in the book *Dust for Dancers,* published two years after the trip. The account is a case study in the discourse of cultural extinction — beginning with their meeting with an Aboriginal man near Coffs Harbour who prompted the observation that 'it is amazing to think that in four or five generations these east coast natives have entirely lost their culture ... in the inevitable clash of the two cultures the aborigines suffered the consequence of being the weaker'.[72] In relation to remote Australia they noted that 'most experts agree that the Australian Aborigines are no longer a dying race, for their numbers are increasing. But their culture — their age old beliefs and customs — their dances as part of a living, vital link with their religion, history and country — their totemic stories — their unique drawings and the spirit behind them — all these are dying.'[73] These beliefs were repeated throughout the book, juxtaposed with Dean and Carell's eyewitness accounts of vital performances and ceremonies by strong community groups, and what they described as the 'unbelievably great wealth of artistic endeavour [that] was offered freely to us each night … the dances were excitingly varied, and we were able to see many of the different types'.[74] However, for them there was no real clash with the narrative of cultural extermination — they were the intrepid adventurers who were present to capture the final performances, the last moments of a dying culture. The fact that they wrote of the traditional power of the performances also fitted the narrative's requirement for the authenticity and authority of salvaged cultural practices.

For Dean and Carell the mechanics of cultural extinction were the demoralising effects of 'civilisation' on Aboriginal people and the tensions generated when assimilation trapped 'Stone Age man' between two worlds. There was also what they saw as the irresistible lure for Aboriginal people of alcohol, gambling and licentiousness. Then there was the perceived cultural breakdown when as 'young Aboriginal men come more and more into our "white fellow" ways, they are spending less and less time with the old men of the tribe learning the traditional dances songs and stories that have been handed down through untold generations as the tribes wandered their long walkabouts over Australia'.[75] At one point in the book the couple argued that total Aboriginal segregation was the only solution, squarely contradicting their endorsement of the assimilation of Aboriginal people into modern Australian life. Like many other Australians at the time, they resolved the conflict by insisting that to become responsible citizens Aboriginal people would require long and careful tutoring under government supervision in special segregated settlements. On their brief visit to Darwin they were shocked by what they saw as the demoralised conditions of Aboriginal people living at the Bagot Compound and observed that it 'would be far better to leave them to their ancient laws, to their own wise customs in the bush'.[76] If they had to live in town then, Dean and Carell argued, in words that still resonate with public comment today, they should be shown 'one of the basic axioms of all life — that one must work in order to go forward and retain one's self-respect and dignity'.[77] For Dean and Carell their perceived duty as artists was to 'rescue Aboriginal culture from entire oblivion'.[78] They clearly expressed their intention to promote public respect for the theatre and virtuosity of Aboriginal performance with its creative use of staging, props, lighting, music, dance, body adornment, the compelling atmosphere of dust, smoke and fires and enthusiastic audience participation. They were united in their intention to, as Dean put it, 'call out to a blind and thoughtless world that these Aboriginal dancers and musicians are truly great artists'.[79] Despite their experiences with Aboriginal people they, like their peers, saw no dilemma in appropriating Aboriginal art forms to achieve this goal. Yet they were also quick to point out, reflecting on popular misconceptions of Aboriginal people, especially as represented in Rex Reid's version of *Corroboree,* that they saw 'no quality of savagery, nor any trace whatsoever of a trance-like brutality, such as was presupposed by most Europeans at the time'.[80]

The couple had their first experience of traditional Aboriginal dance at Manbulloo Station near Katherine, where 'house girls' at the station' performed *djarada* ('women's business' dances) for them and a young dancer and didgeridoo player, Gilligan from the same Wagaitj tribe as Mosec, thrilled them with his performances of the short theatrical *wongga* dance style. They observed that his brilliance marked him as 'a great artist among his people … he was a young god … he held us spellbound.'[81] From there they travelled east into Arnhem Land to Beswick Compound (now Beswick [Wugularr] Community), where they watched a series of 'play about dances' and then performances for the Warrangan ceremony that impressed on them the power of the men's 'violent stamping, digging deep and hard into the earth, making it fly up about them, so that they are right in the centre of an eddying dust cloud. They do this because they believe that they are gathering strength from the earth; they feel a joy springing right up from the soil, through their pounding legs into their bodies. And they dance about everything in their life, for, to them, to dance is a joy and a duty. It gives them a sense of fulfilment.'[82] Further into Arnhem Land at the Mainoru homestead they met Remberanga people who performed 'highly exciting' *warma* dances for them 'that tremble the knees or dip and rise like Russian Cossacks'.[83]

In Darwin they saw Tiwi dancers from Bathurst and Melville Island (who worked as labourers for the army at the Larrakia barracks) perform sixteen different dances in an afternoon, including part of the Pukamuni burial ceremony. A. P. Elkin was also present recording ceremonial chants.[84] The couple then drove out to the Daly River where they observed large gatherings performing ritual dances for a girl's initiation.

At Yuendumu they observed Aboriginal people taking their 'first step on the long road toward the education of a Stone Age and nomadic group into our twentieth century civilisation'.[85] Again they watched sacred dances and noted the strict separation of men's and women's performances. Here they met Djungartu (Nosepeg) a Pintubi man whom they described as 'shrewd and observant. Intellectually, he was the superior of most other men of the tribe.'[86] He subsequently performed in a corroboree for the Queen, possibly in Toowoomba in 1954. It was Djungartu who invited the couple to go bush to observe the preparations and performances of dance and chanting for one stage of a boy's initiation ceremony that went on each night over a couple of weeks. Using their own version of Aboriginal English the couple recorded an endorsement for their project in the departing words of a group of Yuendumu: 'might be you show that dance belong us Walbiri longa big city … longa white people we hear all about'.[87]

Dean and Carell's stay at Mt Larry out from Haasts Bluff, apparently with no other whites in the party, was a dramatic experience filled with extremes of noise and excitement, women's wailing, daily preparation for dancing, separation of men and women and then gatherings for communal performances:

> The chanting and dancing went on for a long time, till suddenly, the men made a fierce concerted rush towards the women, screaming at them and threatening them in rough, hoarse tones. For a moment, an atmosphere of all-hell-let-loose prevailed … It was so savage … so complete … so sudden … In the dark the women were all running madly back toward the camp … As they ran, the aboriginal women were screaming and calling out, some of their cries having an edge of real panic. As the women dashed past her, Beth felt a spasm of fear at her heels, and went with them … About her the women were all screaming with an incredible volume of sound.[88]

The remainder of the trip seemed anti-climactic as they travelled to Ayers Rock, to Ernabella, then Adelaide where they met up with 'Monty' (Charles Mountford) at the South Australian Museum. Home in Sydney they threw themselves into the task of creating *Corroboree.*

Creating the ballet

Corroboree was an artistic collaboration forged from the creative imaginings of composer John Antill, choreographer and principal dancer Beth Dean and writer–producer Vincent Carell. The music and dance traditions of Central Australian Aboriginal people — the Arrernte and the Warlpiri — as experienced by Dean and Carell and studied by Antill were particularly influential, although this was barely acknowledged at the time. Other factors too shaped the resulting production — the constraints and requirements of modern ballet — to create a feminised performance suitable for the young Queen and cultured Sydney audiences.

Antill's score was already a hybrid creation of Aboriginal music and contemporary forms of classical music. Carell began by adapting its seven themed sections into a narrative of the stages of an Aboriginal boy's initiation that would also represent a modernist narrative expressing universals of the human condition 'based on the age-old theme of initiation, which is discipline learned through trial by ordeal'.[89] This universalising mirrored the transformation over time of Arthur Boyd's *Bride Series* from paintings originally contemplating the plight of 'half-castes' into a study of 'humanity's suspension between two worlds' and the 'passion play' of love.[90] It seemed that the concerns of 'primitive' people alone were not sufficiently compelling to interest sophisticated Australian and international audiences. In a crucial step in feminising the ballet Dean decided to take the lead role of the male initiate despite the many examples she had observed of the strict gender divisions and prohibitions that characterised Aboriginal performance. At the same time, as Catrina Vignando points out, by including women dancers in the ritual performances she was challenging public ignorance and anthropological assumptions that denied the role of women in the sacred life and ceremony of Aboriginal communities.[91]

Dean later wrote that she worked on the choreography 'in days and weeks alone with the music', and that while she drew on Aboriginal movement and steps she was not creating a corroboree but a 'contemporary ballet' set to sophisticated symphonic music.[92] Technically and conceptually the forms were very different, even the virtuosic performances by male dancers. Djon Mundine[93] writes that most Aboriginal dance is very grounded and low to the earth: '"foot to the earth" as the famous Aboriginal choreographer Stephen Page described it. It's about physical memory — to be able to tell the story by putting yourself into the movement. Women move in a kind of minimalist shuffle (not really a step) with the feet always in the sand; a quiver of the thighs — a skip perhaps … A type of "dance fractal" … interestingly the performer may actually spend a longer time painting up than actually dancing.'[94] The assumption that Dean and her dancers could readily make the transition from the practices of classical ballet inscribed in their bodies to the complexities of Aboriginal performance suggests an assumption of cultural superiority operating even in the sympathetic approach of Beth Dean to her subject.

Dean selected her dancers for their enthusiasm to extend to Australia the 'style called "modern" or "contemporary" dance' and to create 'true theatre — a translation in dance-language from one culture to another'.[95] However she was working with a group who had no previous experience of Aboriginal performance. Dean had asked the Department of Territories for permission to fly Djungartu to Sydney to assist her in imparting Aboriginal performance to the dancers. She had also envisioned an opening scene for the ballet with Djungartu sitting in front of a small fire and then moving discreetly off-stage as the curtains parted to reveal the opening scene of white dancers dressed as Aboriginal performers — a stunningly simple summary of the narrative of Australian colonial conquest and the discourse of Aboriginal extinction. However, her plans fell through when the authorities saw photographs of sacred Aboriginal ceremonies published in an article by Carell in the November edition of *Pix* in 1953. The couple were castigated by the Northern Territory administration and when Carrel responded that the matter was not so serious since the Aboriginal community would not have seen the images they were informed that community members enjoyed looking through popular magazines like *Pix* for photographs of Aboriginal people.[96] Dean was left to conduct the classes in Aboriginal dance movements and 'points of view' that would 'instil the depth and potent emotional beauty of aboriginal dance into people who had never seen an Aborigine; to try to enthuse their will to picture in their minds the excitement of an aboriginal ceremony that they had never known existed'.[97]

For the performance the painter William Constable recreated his bleak landscapes from Reid's *Corroboree* and added an eclectic mix of manufactured Aboriginal objects including a sacred pole, churingas, a sacred ground drawing from South Australia and a Tiwi grave post. He also designed the costumes — dark woollen body tights that exposed only the darkened faces, hands and feet of the white dancers, with body markings depicted by chenille trims and their hair tied back with feathers and fur or covered by elaborate headdresses. These dark 'second skins' were neither convincing nor aesthetic and hinted at cultural superiority and arrogance. While they may have been acceptable to Australian audiences they were viewed scathingly by New York choreographer Trudy Goth who, on viewing similarly costumed dancers in film footage of Rex Reid's *Corroboree*, had asked why the producers hadn't used a 'coloured cast instead of those horrible black tights'.[98]

On the stiflingly hot night of 6 February 1954 in a fanfare of trumpets the Queen arrived at Sydney's Tivoli Theatre and the audience spontaneously rose and burst into 'a flood of song as if their hearts were pouring forth in prayer for the anthem God Save the Queen'. An excerpt from *Corroboree* was the final item on the program and Dean and Carell recalled that they knew when the curtain fell that 'our months of living among aborigines had been the prelude to a great moment of our lives — the corroboree of the blackfellow had become theatre in the true sense of the word. The ballet corroboree is a proudly dignified yet sincerely humble offering of the fruit of years of earnest endeavour to understand the activating spirit of aboriginal lore and to translate it into live theatre for all to share.'[99]

We have no record of the young Queen's response to the ballet. Anthropologist A. P. Elkin wrote, 'I was so interested by the performance that I hardly heard the orchestra and when all was over, I thought but a few minutes had passed.'[100] Certainly the audience had little experience of performances of Aboriginal dance. Sydney Cove may have been the site of full-scale corroborees in early colonial times, but there would have been few present who, like the young John Antill, had even seen the scaled-down live entertainments put on for tourists at La Perouse. A clue to the perceptions of the male elite audience may be gleaned from the activities of the Sydney Savage Club, which attracted its membership from their ranks and included the leading musicians John Antill, Eugene Goossens and Alfred Hill. (Prime Minister Sir Robert Menzies was President of the Melbourne Savage Club from 1947 to 1962.) The Savage Clubs were part of an international men's network founded to escape the 'worries and frustrations of modern life'. The Sydney Club held weekly 'miniature Corroborees' where they discussed 'literature, arts, music, drama, the sciences, original research or discovery' and their annual newsletter *Gunyah Yabba-Yabba* contained text and images that contrasted civilisation and savagery in ways that were seemingly playful but in fact were deeply prejudiced and derogatory.[101]

Today a performance like *Corroboree* that so clearly breached Aboriginal cultural protocols and rules regarding appropriation would have no hope of being presented in any Australian theatre. However 1954 art critics, imbued with Western imaginings and preconceptions about Aboriginal culture and the 'primitive', deemed the ballet to be of world class and the highlight of the Royal Gala performance. Critics lauded Dean's success in creating from the 'elementally Australian' a ballet that 'transcends mere local interest and belongs to the world'.[102] Others lauded the achievement of 'an American who shows, as even our best writers have not been able to do, what is basically Australian'.[103] One critic wrote that Dean had 'crept inside the skin of our aborigines: she knows his mind, his spirit, his beliefs, his customs and his art of dancing',[104] suggesting a new perceived authority for the creative artist: to bestow authenticity on works based on Aboriginal culture.

Good intentions, mixed results

Dean was prepared to break with convention by travelling to Aboriginal communities to view and experience their performance directly, however she could not escape the webs of conformity within which she worked. Her expressed intention was to encourage respect for Aboriginal culture and people and 'help Australian audiences to a wider appreciation of Aboriginal values'.[105] Ironically, one clear (unintended) message of her good intentions was to endorse the official message of Aboriginal assimilation. Her appropriation of Aboriginal forms to represent the modern condition and nationhood in an all-white performance reinforced the impression of Aboriginal cultural extinction and that assimilation was the only way forward. As such Dean's creative work was firmly embedded in ongoing colonial relations of domination and power.

Dean had observed that 'steps devoid of mood, devoid of the aboriginal belief and atmosphere lose their potency and of themselves seem unusual and weird'.[106] The mix of disparate elements from two distinctive aesthetic and mythological traditions produced a work that failed to achieve heights of creative power and expression in either. Its production fulfilled all the elements of Greenberg's 'precondition for kitsch' and no doubt its performance evoked the emotional and visceral responses typically aroused by kitsch — how else to explain the initial acclaim at its premiere and its subsequent rapid slip from the cultural agenda?

During the 1950s excerpts were toured in Australia, but it was not until 1962 that the ballet was performed in its entirety. It was never performed outside of Australia and was not filmed apart from a brief television segment shot for the Dinah Shore Show in the United States.[107] By contrast Sir Robert Helpmann's later metaphorical exploration of Australian identity *The Display* (1964), based on the iconic Australian lyrebird, became a staple in the Australian Ballet's repertoire and was toured extensively in Australia and overseas. Dean's ballet may also have suffered because it did not fit with settler preconceptions of Aboriginal people and culture. Rex Reid's 1950 interpretation of *Corroboree,* inspired by imaginings of wild primitive savagery, met with wider acclaim from Sydney audiences and footage of the ballet was even used by the Australian Trade Commission's 1952 *Australian Aboriginal Art* exhibition in New York.

Still, Dean and Carell were able to draw on the cultural capital of their journey and the ballet, and later wrote that *Corroboree* was 'very important in our lives. It established an aura whose glow has given meaning to so much other work.'[108] They collaborated with Antill on two further Royal events: the 1959 *Burragorang Dreamtime* created for the City of Sydney Civic Welcome for Princess Alexandria and the 1963 *Pageant of Nationhood Royal Performance* before the Queen. They also collaborated on several televised ballets of Aboriginal legends. In 1968 Dean was awarded a gold medal for her choreography of an Aboriginal story adapted by Carell and performed at the Olympic Cultural Games in Mexico by the Ballet Folklorico de Mexico in the *Ballet of the Five Continents*. From 1973 they devoted themselves to producing the *South Pacific Festival of Arts* as Aboriginal performers increasingly replaced the hybrid performances with their own traditional and contemporary forms.

Already in 1963 the Palais Theatre in Melbourne had premiered an all-Aboriginal performance of forty-five dancers and musicians from Bathurst and Melville Islands, the Daly River and Yirrkala in the Northern Territory accompanied by an exhibition of over a hundred bark paintings and woodcarvings from Arnhem Land. The billing of the show suggested new expectations of performances of Aboriginal culture: 'a unique entertainment never previously seen outside northern-most Australia', 'completely authentic', 'natural form' and 'aesthetic and spectacular appeal'. The review in the *Age* referred to the performance as 'genuine art' and 'a memorable experience' but overlooked the many levels of meaning, preferring instead to address the dancers' 'skill in mimicry' and 'highly developed sense of pattern'.[109] Other newspapers focused on the modern/

primitive binary as they described the dancers' day clothes of navy reefer jackets and grey slacks and their encounters with escalators, ten pin bowling and Melbourne shopping. Referring to the emerging Aboriginal equal wages debate, readers were assured that the performers were being paid equity rates for the three-week show.[110]

While it could be argued that hybrid works fulfilled a positive role by locating Aboriginal art and design firmly in the public domain they also created major obstacles for Aboriginal artists emerging during the 1960s. It was not only that Aboriginal culture was fragmented, misinterpreted and misrepresented in their works or that Aboriginal custodians were not acknowledged or compensated for the commercial use of their cultural property. Aboriginal performers also had to compete with non-Aboriginal artists like Dean who, with Antill and Carell, continued to receive commissions to create Aboriginal-derived performances into the early 1970s. They also had to prove to white audiences their ability and authority to perform and the authenticity of their work. Rather than being judged on their own merits, Aboriginal performers had to counter popular modernist interpretations that locked them into the established binary of 'primitive' versus 'modern' and branded them as 'Stone Age' and exotic. Aboriginal artists also had to overcome the prejudices of changing fashion as a new generation of artists and designers turned away from the once popular hybrid works, although the contrast between those tired commodities and the vitality of Aboriginal art and performances now proved to be a distinct advantage with audiences.

The new wave of Aboriginal campaigns for social justice and land rights demanded a move away from exploitative practices and required the creation of a new Aboriginal imagery in the public sphere. This found expression in the surge of Aboriginal artists, performers and writers in the national and international arenas from the 1970s to the present. Leading the charge within government was H. C. Coombs, who acknowledged the 'radical dissimilarity' of Australia's cultural heritages and was determined to keep the arts of Aboriginal people 'alive, not as decaying museum pieces, but as living elements in the social life of these people; and what is perhaps from our point of view more important, as significant threads to be woven into the great fabric of our own national culture'.[111] In 1973 the Whitlam Labor government appointed the first Aboriginal Arts Board within the Australian Council for the Arts, composed only of Indigenous Australians with musician, bark painter and activist Wundjuk Marika as foundation chairperson. The Board's priorities were to encourage communities to develop their own arts practice, then to work with other Indigenous communities and finally to 'address and enrich the rest of Australia and the Indigenous people of other lands'.[112] This was a complete turnaround from the practices of the 1950s and 1960s.

At the same time, Aboriginal artists began to lobby politically and to take action through the courts for copyright protection for their works. The first major case followed the Reserve Bank of Australia's use in 1966 for the one-dollar note, of a design from a bark painting by Arnhem Land artist Dr David Malangi Daymirringu without his permission. The bank acknowledged the error and the artist was compensated. Since then artists have called for an extension of copyright protection from commercial interests to embrace formal acknowledgement of the special features of Aboriginal cultural rights and obligations and their connections with country, spirit and well-being.

Today dance remains a vital part of ceremonial life and public performance for many Aboriginal communities. In 2002 the Garma Festival in northeast Arnhem Land, one of Australia's major Indigenous events, issued the *Garma Festival Statement on Indigenous Music and Performance,* which affirmed the continuing role of cultural performance in Indigenous Australia: 'songs, dances and ceremonial performances form the core of Yolngu and other Indigenous cultures in Australia. It is through song, dance and associated ceremony that Indigenous peoples sustain their cultures and maintain the Law and a sense of self within the world. Performance traditions are the foundation of social and personal well-being.'[113] In the public domain the Bangarra Dance Theatre, once a small Indigenous community dance organisation, leads the way nationally and internationally with works that explore 'the link between Indigenous cultures of Australia and new forms of contemporary artistic expression' while 'maintaining the integrity of tradition [and] exploring the endless inspiration of dance'. In this way Bangarra creates 'theatre of excellence that resonates with people everywhere and speaks with a myriad of voices'.[114] This sounds uncannily like something Beth Dean might have aspired to, but without the commitment to 'maintaining the integrity of tradition'.

9. Fragments

> *This makes for a 'complex fate' — the phrase is Henry James's about Americans — of multiple allegiances to different worlds, multiple tensions between cultures and environments, which Australians need not scramble to unify. Or as Malouf puts it: 'Our answer on every occasion when we are offered the false choice between this and that should be, "Thank you, I'll take both."' Thus 'identity' becomes a confident way of being in the world, rather than some anxious definition, provided mostly by others.*
>
> Ihab Hassan, 2000[1]

It is a further paradox of the discourse of assimilation that rather than rendering Aboriginal and migrant people invisible within the new White Australia, it directed a critical spotlight on their experiences and responses. The government may have welcomed the growing public, media and academic attention but the consequence was that the discourse began to fragment into a myriad of contested points of view. From its very beginnings the policy had been subject to criticism and, as Bain Attwood and Tim Rowse point out, this 'both deepened and gained influence', until by the early 1970s assimilation had become 'something of a dirty word' in the Australian lexicon.[2]

Public interest was directed overwhelmingly at Aboriginal experiences — real and imagined. By contrast the responses of European migrants as represented in government publicity in the 1950s and 1960s seemed too predictable to capture the public imagination. The government's narrative of the 'disappearing migrant' who moved effortlessly into suburban life seemed to fit snugly with the material achievements migrants made towards this goal. Few migrants were willing to speak out in the mainstream media about the poverty and disadvantage they experienced, although the ethnic press ran sympathetic stories, and their situation remained largely unknown to the broader public until the late 1960s.[3] From the perspective of settler Australians they were another wave of migrants, not too unlike themselves. The real unfinished business lay with Aboriginal people and their future place within the nation. Media coverage of international issues of racism, decolonisation and the civil rights movement also directed public attention to consideration of Aboriginal issues. Government efforts to involve settler Australians in Aboriginal assimilation had found expression in a genuine public curiosity about how Aboriginal people were faring in making the transition and a generalised concern that their conditions should improve. At the same time, in a nation so intrinsically defined by whiteness and boundaries of race, assimilation whipped up anxieties about how these changes would impinge on the lives of settler Australians. Citing Homi Bhabha, historian Catriona Elder observes that while they longed to erase Aboriginal difference and desired that Aboriginal people would come to resemble them by assimilating they also feared the implications of this similarity.[4] There were also uncomfortable ambivalences — opposition to racism had become acceptable, but television images of Aboriginal people asserting Black Power agendas and inalienable Indigenous rights raised a shiver of fear in lounge rooms around the nation.

There was much for members of the public to turn their minds to, with opportunities to engage with new official constructions of Aboriginality being remade yet again, as Marcia Langton explains, 'in a process of dialogue, of imagination, of representation and interpretation'.[5] For the vast majority this remained a mediated experience where settler interpretations based on 'stereotyping, iconising and mythologising' shaped their understandings.[6] However, Aboriginal people were becoming an increasingly visible and vocal part of the nation and they were disrupting the discourse of assimilation with their views. We have seen how a closed loop of government officers and anthropologists created public knowledge about Aboriginal people and assimilation in the early 1950s. Now Aboriginal activists were breaking through this circuit with first-hand accounts of their experiences and agendas for reform. It could be argued that after generations of being publicly silenced and rendered invisible in a segregated Australia, the gradual repeal of race laws gave them the opportunity to speak out. Following a Foucauldian argument, in which counter-discourses emerge where 'power relations are at their most rigid and intense',[7] it could also be claimed that assimilation brought a new intensity of oppression that pushed Aboriginal protest into the public domain, as race laws were only gradually repealed while Aboriginal people were pressured to assimilate and punished for failing to conform.

Either way, the contribution of Aboriginal activists at this time should not be underestimated. Aboriginal narratives of the past, present and future were spreading out to Indigenous people in Australia and overseas, to settler Australians, and to concerned governments and individuals in the international arena. This brought vital knowledge to public debate, and perspectives not previously recognised or even understood by knowledge makers and the public, and it seriously challenged the dominant settler mindset that hitherto had explained and justified existing power relations. As distinguished US lawyer Richard Delgado explains, 'counterstories' can 'shatter complacency and challenge the status quo … open a new window onto reality … enrich imagination … [and] show that what we believe in is ridiculous, self-serving, or cruel'.[8] There were also new opportunities for non-Aboriginal activists who were not drawn to charitable volunteerism to engage with Aboriginal protest organisations and to learn first-hand about their reform agendas and, through personal interactions, to modify and explore mutual understandings of each other.[9]

All this assumes that settler Australians were ready to listen and learn. There is no clear evidence of that, but we do know that Aboriginal activism attracted widespread media attention and was highly visible in the public domain. This combination of Aboriginal voices and the clamour of public interest together with emerging academic research sparked the new public knowledges about Aboriginal people and their cultures and histories that emerged from the 1960s. Indeed, historian Jan Kociumbus argues that the burst of government-funded research initiatives at the time were an effort to regain control over public discourse and to rein in the growing Aboriginal influence on public opinion.[10] Shades of this agenda can be discerned in the fallout from the more recent history wars over the Stolen Generations and Australia's colonial frontiers that sought to restore conservative national history to centre stage.

In this chapter we explore the fragmenting of the assimilation discourse from several perspectives, while always keeping the focus on the responses of settler Australians — they retained ultimate power over public discourse *and* they had much to learn about Aboriginal people and what they wanted. First we examine the iconic settler stories from popular culture and the media that explored dramatically different imagined migrant and Aboriginal experiences of assimilation, with particular attention to the paradigm of 'people between two worlds' that provided a profoundly pessimistic view of the outcomes of Aboriginal assimilation. Then we look at the example of a couple who, like Geoff

Harcus working with the Coolbaroo League in Perth, stepped out of the closed loop of white imaginings and assumptions to join Aboriginal activists in their campaign for change. Jack Horner documents his memories of this political involvement as an evolving learning curve as he and his wife Jean gradually came to understand that Aboriginal goals and agendas went far beyond assimilation's call for civil rights and equality — to demand self-determination, land rights, sovereignty, and recognition of customary law.[11] There was equally little active political engagement with migrants outside of union movement campaigning for equal treatment of migrant workers, which was sometimes for reasons of self-interest, to protect existing conditions. Finally we examine the fragmenting discourse of assimilation in the media and academia, and the new sites of research into Aboriginal societies. Of course the government, media, producers of popular culture and academics maintained overall control over public discourses about migrant and Aboriginal cultures and what policy solutions were offered. The ethnic press provided a forum for community discussion about migrant issues but it failed to reach the wider Australian public. With few such outlets of their own, Aboriginal people struggled to influence the way they were represented, but with determination and ingenuity they sometimes won the day.

Imagining assimilation

Government propaganda materials of the 1950s and 1960s represented assimilation as a seamless unilinear path of progress to Australian citizenship and suburban living. We have seen how the narrative of the 'disappearing migrant' who arrived unencumbered and quickly assimilated and disappeared into mainstream Australian life was mirrored in the various migrant success stories fed to the press by the Department of Immigration. In popular culture radically different paths of migrant and Aboriginal assimilation were imagined: migrants were quickly absorbed while Aboriginal people were locked into the pessimistic trope of the individual 'caught between two worlds' who could never become assimilated.

The 'disappearing migrant'

The 'disappearing migrant' Nino Culotta is the hero of the novel *They're a Weird Mob* (1957) by Australian author John O'Grady. This enormously popular book sold 130,000 copies within ten months of its release and achieved almost a million sales by the time of O'Grady's death in 1981, making him Australia's best-selling author prior to the advent of Bryce Courtney.[12] In 1966 a 'smarter, more complex and more sophisticated'[13] film version appeared with Italian star Walter Chiari as Nino. Actor Gregory Peck had noticed the book during shooting of *On the Beach* in Melbourne and handed it on to British director Michael Powell of Ealing Studios. The film too was a commercial success and grossed three million dollars in profit from Australian screenings alone.[14] Although the story line follows Nino's experiences of becoming assimilated, the real subject is Australian masculinity and national character in the 1950s and this, plus O'Grady's blokey humour, were the keys to the film's popularity.[15] The recent successful mockumentary *Kenny* (2006) had a similar appeal with its 'often hilarious and affectionate look at a true blue working class man and blue-collar hero, with a down to earth sense of humour and a colourful turn of phrase'.[16] That there was no lovable migrant character in *Kenny*, however, perhaps points to the current divisive politics over cultural difference and migration in working-class Australia.

Jeanette Hoorn's analysis of the film describes how Nino is 'naturalised' as he progresses through a series of initiations that transform him from an Italian migrant into an assimilated Australian male.[17] 'Act One: Fair dinkum lingo' addresses the vital importance of language for assimilation, a theme taken up again at the end of the book when Nino advises migrants to 'Learn his way. Learn his language … don't be bludgers. Hop in and learn.'[18] While Nino already speaks some English, he has to learn 'Australian', beginning with the word 'bloody' as in 'Kings Bloody Cross'. In 'Act Two: Shouting and Becoming a Bloke' Nino is introduced to pub terminology and the ritual of shouting as a 'key signifier' of Australian mateship. 'Act Three: Baptism on the Beach' is a further stage in the process of being 'disciplined into Australian manhood' where Nino is ridiculed and subjected to 'physical and verbal abuse' in 'a lesson in socially correct beach behaviour'. Nino's experiences have resonances today with complaints made in the lead up to the 2005 Cronulla riots in Sydney of inappropriate behaviour by beachgoers of Middle Eastern appearance. The final spark was the news texted to mobiles around the city of a confrontation between a group of these youths and surf lifesavers — the untouchable white heroes of beach culture. For Nino, having survived his ritual humiliation, there was the consolation of asserting his manhood in another favourite beach activity — courting his future wife, an Australian girl Kate. 'Act Four: "Making a Man" of Nino — Labour and Nation' is a workplace ritual of masculinisation where Nino's effete European body is transformed into that of a 'working bloke' through demanding physical work as a brickie's labourer on one of the hundreds of thousands of suburban home building sites in Australia at the time.

In a concluding scene, Nino eulogises over the joys of his new life as a suburban husband and father. Significantly, in the discourse of assimilation, marriage between a migrant man and an Australian woman was considered a significant predictor of successful migrant assimilation. The government actively encouraged these marriages as a remedy for its earlier practice of recruiting single male workers that had created the phenomenon of migrant 'bachelors of misery'.[19] The *Woman's Weekly* provided advice in its etiquette page for Australian women on how to respond positively to the attentions of migrant men on the road to marriage.[20]

Writing of fictional accounts of migration to Australia in novels and film, Roy Jones claims that they show 'continental European outsiders [becoming] Australian insiders, [making] a home not only in the nation but inside its memory as well'.[21] This was suggested too in a scene in the film showing Nino's planned new suburban home located directly on top of a set of Aboriginal rock carvings; the inference was that new settlers like Nino would replace Aboriginal people on the land as surely as earlier colonists had done.[22] The fact that Aboriginal people were also destined to live in suburbia under the policy of assimilation was not mentioned. Nor was there any reference to the impossibility for Aboriginal people to follow Nino's path to assimilation. In the year the book was published most were still barred from hotels, their movement around urban areas and associations with whites remained under strict surveillance, and those contemplating marriage to a white person could still be instructed to seek permission from the government. Given their economic circumstances there was no chance that they would be able to obtain a loan to buy land and build a new home.

They're a Weird Mob presented a scenario that appealed to settler imaginings of masculinity and nationhood at the time, though its comical path to assimilation would have been alien to most migrant men, let alone women, as it glossed over the many difficulties they encountered — manifested for some in above-average levels of poverty, physical and mental stress and dissatisfaction with Australia expressed in rates of return to their homelands and low take-up of citizenship. Increasingly the government saw this as direct evidence of the failure of assimilation policies to meet the needs of migrant populations and of the urgent necessity to overhaul the policy by moving away from rigid cultural homogeneity to a measure of cultural pluralism.[23]

Between two worlds

From the legendary tales of Cortes' consort and guide Malinche in Mexico to the Tierra del Fuegan native Jemmy Button's experiences in England, and down to the present, there is a long history of fascination in the West with the experiences of Indigenous individuals negotiating the 'uncomfortable bridges between two worlds'.[24] Popular nineteenth-century race theory projected pessimistic outcomes for these encounters. In the United States the 'savagist dogma' argued that *any* mixing between two races 'led to the corruption and degeneration of each and that, an Indian, even an acculturated one, could never belong in civilised society'.[25] When it came to miscegenation and mixed-race progeny, opinion in Australia shifted between the view that 'half-castes' had the potential to assimilate but could always revert to their 'native ways' and the view that saw them as doubly defective, since they 'inherited the vices of both races and the virtues of neither'.[26] Either way they were destined to eke out their days on the margins of society. In colonial metropolitan settings in French Indochina, British India and Burma and the Dutch East Indies this discourse of racial hybridity settled into the 'tragedy trope of Euro-Asian metissage'.[27]

These earlier views continued to shape mid-twentieth century narratives concerning the fate of individuals who crossed the lines of race and culture. In the United States in the wake of the turbulent changes brought by the civil rights movement, public concerns about desegregation, interracial sex and 'coloureds' seeking to pass as whites found expression in works of popular culture that created a space for imagining various permutations and outcomes. The Hollywood western *Broken Arrow* (1950), featuring James Stewart as a US army scout named Tom Jeffords, explored the theme of crossing cultural boundaries from the perspective of Jeffords, who turned his back on his own people to side with the family of his Native

American wife, played by Debra Paget. MGM's *Night of the Quarter Moon* (1959), starring John Drew Barrymore and Julie London, explored race and class prejudice through the story of the trials faced by a society millionaire who married a fisherman's daughter who 'turned out to be quarter caste'.[28] Readers of movie magazines avidly followed the rise and fall of Oscar-nominated black actress Dorothy Dandridge, whose Hollywood career during the 1950s was curtailed by racism and related personal problems. In Australia anxieties about crumbling race barriers and Aboriginal assimilation found expression in the popular narratives of individuals seeking to lead marginal lives 'between two worlds'.

Australia was itself a nation between two worlds in the 1950s as it endeavoured to negotiate its way through the dramatic changes of the post-war period and carve out a new identity. For journalists and creative artists enmeshed in these processes, Aboriginal imagery and culture provided a rich source of inspiration for expressing their own state of mind as they evoked 'a multiplicity of meanings from alienation, annihilation, and victimisation through to voyeuristic sexuality and eroticism'.[29] Arthur Boyd's *Bride Series*, for example, depicted his 'musings' about Aboriginal alienation and also expressed his own 'ambivalence of belonging' between his British and Antipodean heritages as well as broader ponderings concerning the human condition.

In the imagined black/white cultural binary, Aboriginal people had to choose to live in an Aboriginal or a white world. This rigid line of division limited the possibilities for identity for the Aboriginal targets of assimilation and also restricted the possibilities available to the non-Aboriginal community in experimenting with 'other' identities, cultural values, or world views.[30] This place of constraint falls very short of Homi Bhabha's depiction of cultural boundaries as places 'from which *something begins its presencing*'. Citing Martin Heidegger, Bhabha presents a different vision of the 'uncomfortable bridge' as it 'ever differently ... exhorts the lingering and hastening ways of men to and fro, so that they may get to other banks ... the bridge *gathers* as a passage that crosses.'[31] For Bhabha these liminal cultural zones are creative, generative sites; through the cold prism of the pessimistic between-two-worlds narrative they are a toxic no man's land.

In the iconic 'between two worlds' narratives that we examine in this chapter — the media mythologising of the life of Arrernte artist Albert Namatjira, the film *Jedda* by Charles and Elsa Chauvel, and the novel *Fringe Dwellers* by Nene Gare — there seems to be no cultural space or personal identity for Aboriginal people to inhabit, whatever their racial and cultural make-up, their personal capacities or their hopes and dreams. In contrast to the official government message of fairytale endings in comfortable suburban homes or the happy ending for Nino Culotta, these narratives reached the same paradoxical conclusions: that it was impossible for Aboriginal people to become assimilated, that it was impossible for them to remain unassimilated, and that it was impossible for them to live between the two cultures.

These imagined narratives closely resemble the bleak experiences of Jewish people attempting to assimilate into German society documented by Zygmunt Bauman. Jacob Wassermann recalled in his book *My Life as a German Jew* (1934) that 'to assimilate' meant to 'stay, defenceless, under the gaze of others', and while 'self drill' could perhaps erase cultural behaviours, nothing could be done about one's physical appearance. Wasserman concluded that nothing could bring him full membership of the world he aspired to.[32] Instead loneliness became 'the standard condition': 'no individual claimed me as a being akin to him, nor did any group; neither the people of my own blood, nor those whom I yearned to join; neither those of my own species nor those of my choice. For I had at last decided to make a choice; and I had made it. It was my inner destiny rather than a free decision that had brought about my secession from the old circle. The new, however, neither received nor accepted me.'[33] Bruno Bettelheim later wrote that the value system that assimilating Jews borrowed 'not only was never theirs in its entirety, but always contained elements inimical to them. The Germans saw the adoption of it as merely a mask behind which glowered the unregenerate Jew. Sadly, for the German Jew the mask was the only reality.'[34]

Similarly unrelentingly pessimistic were the imagined stories of Aboriginal psychological tension and pain. Written *about* them, by the *assimilators,* these stories expressed little insight and sympathy for their difficulties. Their failure to assimilate was attributed to personal and racial deficiencies while the backdrop of systemic racism and inequality against which the narratives were inevitably played out remained largely invisible. There was little appreciation of the personal enormity of the task: that the process had to begin with the admission of one's own cultural inferiority; that individuals became embroiled in social processes over which they had no control; and that they faced close surveillance and often ridicule by members of the dominant group. Instead tragic personality flaws and weaknesses that were attributed to their racial background drove the plots, obviating any collective sense of responsibility for the characters' fates. While these narratives were so unrelentingly bleak about assimilation they nevertheless concluded that this was the only reasonable life choice for Aboriginal people.

Our three narratives from the 1950s and 1960s explore various assimilation scenarios and motivations but in each case assimilation offers no solution. Working from within the closed circuit of white imaginings it seemed that the only possible outcomes were disappointment and death. Considering such imagined white narratives, Nyungar author Kim Scott advises that if we are seeking 'meaningful answers' then 'it might be wisest to avoid Australian literature, certainly some of its non-indigenous examples' since they do not seek 'engagement with history, or other Aboriginal people, cultural elders or land, but instead rely on mainstream expressions of their identity.'[35] Working with his co-author Hazel Kayang Brown on the book *Kayang and Me,* Scott realised that Kayang and his Uncle Lomas, 'rather than moving from one world to the other — the "us" and "them" — their heritage and sense of place made it one world, and at worst they need only move from one polemical position to the other, even if only to see what it looks like from there'.[36]

Yet the trope of 'between two worlds' still has strong currency today. This was evident in the *Weekend Australian*'s lead article by film director Rolf de Heer in May 2007 about the film career of Yolngu actor and dancer David Gulpilil. The article was titled 'Between two worlds' and the stand-out quote in large red letters followed through with de Heer's words: 'Gulpilil likes to believe he can straddle the two cultures. The truth is that he's caught between them and is comfortable in neither.' De Heer concluded that the 'great warrior, artist and tracker was in no man's land, unable to settle into whitefella's ways and severed, irreparably, from his own'.[37] Like his predecessors and peers de Heer was writing from a binary view of cultural identity and negotiation that undervalues the cultural sophistication of the Other. One wonders how well de Heer would score in a similar interrogation of his ability to straddle Australian society, his Dutch origins and Yolngu culture. While de Heer was no doubt well-intentioned in his opinions — evidenced by his sensitive portrayals of Aboriginal people as director of *The Tracker* and co-director with Peter Digirr of *Ten Canoes* — his article is proof of how this dominant paradigm continues to shape contemporary narratives about Aborigines responding to change.

'Wanderer between two worlds' — the narrative of Albert (Elea) Namatjira

The lives of the gifted and charismatic Aboriginal men who achieved national attention in the arts, sports and popular entertainment, and in political activism during the 1950s and 1960s were avidly followed in the press. Amongst the luminaries were the artist Albert Namatjira, Australian triple-champion boxer Dave Sands, singer Jimmy Little, tenor Harold Blair, actor Robert Tudawali and activist Charles Perkins. The achievements of Aboriginal women were largely ignored, reflecting gender expectations of women as homemakers and mothers. As we saw in the success stories of Aboriginal men in the government's assimilation pamphlets, the reporting was shaped by stereotypes of Aboriginal masculinity and the goals of assimilation with often-voyeuristic curiosity about the men's struggles to succeed. Readers were exposed to the men's personal and family histories of poverty and oppression, although the edge of these revelations was blunted by the use of patronising language and frequent recourse to the trope of the 'man between two worlds'. The iconic example of this approach was the popular media-created narrative of the life of Albert Namatjira, which captured him forever as 'Namatjira: a Man of Two Worlds' whose efforts to follow 'two contradictory ways of life' left him 'broken in two'.[38] This framing of Namatjira's life glossed over the disabling effects of institutionalised racism and endemic poverty on Aboriginal communities in Central Australia and allowed the media, the government and the public to express deep sympathy for Namatjira's 'plight' while largely absolving themselves of any responsibility for his fate.

Albert Elea Namatjira was the first Australian Indigenous artist to achieve popular national success. He was also a sophisticated communicator and negotiator of cultural difference. An initiated Western Arrernte man, he grew up in the Hermannsburg German Lutheran Mission west of Alice Springs. Most of his life was spent with his wife Rubina and kin in his traditional country, but he also travelled to major cities for exhibitions of his work where he met up with other famous Australian artists, politicians, society leaders and Aboriginal people. In 1936 Namatjira began to paint with artist Rex Batterbee and his aptitude in creating watercolour landscapes of the MacDonnell Ranges was such that only two years later he held his first solo exhibition at the Fine Art Society Gallery in Melbourne. His popularity escalated with the influx of visitors to the region during the war — military personnel stationed in Alice Springs and visitors travelling on the new road linking the town to Darwin — and there were further solo exhibitions in the nation's capital cities. By the 1950s reproductions of Namatjira's paintings were hanging in homes, schools, businesses and art galleries around the nation. In 1953 Namatjira was awarded a Queen's Coronation Medal and in the following year was presented to Queen Elizabeth on her first Royal Tour of Australia. In 1956 Namatjira visited Sydney to collect a truck presented to him by the Ampol Oil company and while there he sat for the portrait by William Dargie that took out the 1956 Archibald Prize, Australia's most prestigious portraiture award. Dargie described Namatjira as having 'the most wonderful face for a portrait I've ever seen ... [he] has a tremendous inner dignity'. Such was Namatjira's popularity that the *Woman's Day* magazine published a full-page colour reproduction of the portrait, 'suitable for framing', for its readers.[39]

Despite these national honours and recognitions Namatjira experienced obstacles and frustrations at home: his request for a grazing licence in 1949–50 was denied and two years later he was refused permission to build a house in Alice Springs. However in 1957, after vigorous lobbying by his supporters, Namatjira and his wife — but not their families — were granted a form of citizenship rights when they were exempted from the Northern Territory Welfare Board's Register of Wards of mainly 'full-blood' Aboriginal people. As in the case of Certificates of Citizenship in

Western Australia, such rights were hedged around by qualifications and anomalies that could rebound punitively on the new 'citizen'. In jurisdictions around Australia the most strictly policed and most frequently breached 'right' related to the purchase of alcohol. Namatjira could go into hotels and purchase alcohol but could not share it with his extended family and it was for this breach of the law that he was sentenced to two months detention at the Papunya Settlement in 1959. He died two months after his release and was buried in Alice Springs cemetery.[40] The text chosen for Namatjira's Lutheran funeral service was 'But by the grace of God I am what I am' from 1 Corinthians 15:10.[41] This was an ironic choice of text for the funeral of a man whose rich and successful life has been enshrined in the national memory within the narrow confines of the trope of 'a man between two worlds'.

Namatjira was initially promoted by the government as the public face of assimilation in the documentary *Namatjira the Painter* (1947),[42] made by the Commonwealth Film Unit with funding of £3000 from the Department of Information. Shot on location with Namatjira, the film was principally a vehicle for expounding the policy of assimilation.[43] A 'prestigious and profitable' venture for the government, it was shown widely in Australia and also in New York and London and was later released commercially.[44] As Meaghan Morris points out,[45] this film transformed Namatjira into the star and the symbol of cultural assimilation.[46] However, already the image of Namatjira as a man straddling two distinct worlds was being formed. In 1951 Hermannsburg missionary Pastor Albrecht described him as a 'restless nomad' and 'wanderer between two worlds'.[47] Photographs in popular magazines over the decade increasingly depicted the image of a man of 'sombre, isolated, almost tragic appearance' bewildered by his success and circumstances.[48]

With Namatjira's arrest and detention the press that had 'fanned' the story of Namatjira's 'wonderful achievements' now fed on his 'disgrace'.[49] Already following his arrest the *Woman's Day* had carried the headline 'Namatjira: Tragic symbol of a lost people' and claimed that he had been set the impossible task of 'obeying two contradictory ways of life'.[50] Namatjira's treatment also provided a crash course for the public in the discriminatory legal controls over Aboriginal people and provoked debate over the anomalies of Aboriginal citizenship. Shocked by this new knowledge some Australians demanded the immediate granting of full citizenship rights for all Aboriginal people, but for others Namatjira's plight was proof that strict controls were essential. What was powerfully evident in the debate was the continuing power of race thinking in the Australian psyche. The agents of destruction popularly believed to have driven Namatjira's downfall were Aborigines' assumed susceptibility and addiction to alcohol; the retarding and debilitating influence of Aboriginal culture; and Aborigines' inability to change and become modern people.

Media mythologising went into top gear following Namatjira's death. Historians John Ramsland and Christopher Mooney detail the claims made in the *Bulletin* that Namatjira was 'hounded to death by fame, celebrity, media hype and critical praise; that there was the unbreachable gap between two opposing cultures of black and white; that he lacked understanding of the English language and consequently of the dominant Australian culture; that he was addicted to alcohol which destroyed his health, and that his spirit was irrevocably broken'.[51] *Pix* magazine even referred to the Hermannsburg Mission as 'a compromise between the white man's world of sciences and religion and the black man's needs'.[52] Communist and social realist artist Noel Counihan's linocut print *Albert Namatjira* (1959) depicted Namatjira as a suffering Christ crucified above a city skyline and church tower by white racism. Poet and activist Oodgeroo Noonuccal[53] (then Kath Walker) wrote sympathetically:

What did their loud acclaim avail
Who gave you honour, then gave you jail?
Namatjira, they boomed your art,
They called you genius, then broke your heart.

Namatjira's recent biographers have endeavoured to deconstruct his public image by acknowledging the direct impact on his life of the racial discrimination and economic deprivation that engulfed Aboriginal communities in Central Australia. These included his history of poor health and a chronic heart condition; the sudden deaths of two daughters and his father and a son badly injured; the disappointments and racial insults over his efforts to obtain land and the injustice of his arrest; the chronic poverty in his extended kin network; and his determination to maintain his Arrernte identity and obligations to family and country despite pressures to assimilate.[54] Art historian Alison French argues that the public myths about Namatjira deflected attention from the quality of his work so that it has only been in recent years that researchers have begun to document his central place in Australian art history and the powerful presence of Aboriginal tradition in his work, 'derived from a deeply felt personal engagement with unique aspects of the Central Australian landscape'.[55] Senior Arnhem Land bark painter and Chairman of the Northern Land Council Galarrwuy Yunupingu stated in 1989 that 'what non-Aboriginal people didn't understand, or chose not to understand, was that he was painting his country, the land of the Arrernte people … No one asked him the name of the country he was painting, or the Dreamings that had made that country important. They thought that all the old man needed was money for his paintings, and nothing else. The buyers did not recognise the Aboriginal law which bound him to the land that he painted.'[56] It was not until 2002 that the National Gallery of Australia hosted the first major retrospective exhibition of Namatjira's work — *Seeing the Centre: The Art of Albert Namatjira*

1902–1959. Curator Brenda Croft acknowledged Namatjira's legacy for contemporary Indigenous artists in 'the long shadow of his spirit, cast over their shared history'.[57]

The call of the wild — the film *Jedda* (1955)

The film *Jedda*, directed and produced by the husband and wife team Charles and Elsa Chauvel, made film history by casting Aboriginal actors — Arrernte girl Rosalie Ngarla Kunoth and Tiwi man Robert Tudawali — in the principal roles of Jedda and Marbuck and by its attention to remote locations highlighting the themes of exoticism and primitivism. The Chauvels' hopes that the promotional campaign — the most extensive for an Australian film at the time — would help to achieve the film's success at the box office at home and abroad were realised and *Jedda* appeared at the Cannes Film Festival in 1955 and toured the United States under the name *Eve in Ebony.* As Katrina Schlunke demonstrates,[58] the promotional hype generated for the film billowed out into ever more mythic constructions surrounding its creation and the lives of its principal actors. Probably the most enduring myth following in the wake of the movie was of Robert Tudawali — Australia's first Aboriginal film and television star — as another ill-fated 'man between two worlds'. Only a few months after Tudawali had appeared at the Melbourne premiere of *Jedda* as a resplendently 'proud and beautiful Black Man About Town', the southern press reported that he was living in a hut at Bagot Compound in Darwin with his wife, their-one week-old baby, and six other 'natives' and that he was suffering from tuberculosis. The article in the *Sun-Herald* explained that 'being a black' Tudawali could not qualify for the 'T.B. allowance' and that the Director of Native Welfare had only just received a payment of £120 owed to him by the Chauvels since December 1954 as part of an agreement that he would not appear in other films during the promotion of *Jedda.* No explanation was given for the Chauvels' delay in making the payments. Having withdrawn some of the money to buy blankets and clothes, Tudawali reportedly told the newspaper that 'all I want now is a house and a worthwhile job to carry me over' — the very things guaranteed him under the policy of assimilation.[58] Rather than these injustices, what survives in the public memory of Tudawali's life are the tragic circumstances of his death at the age of thirty-one when he rolled onto a campfire after a night of drinking. Apparently he still had no house to live in.

When *Jedda* premiered in Darwin in 1955 reviewers described it as a moving adventure movie. Charles Chauvel, however, considered it a 'quasi documentary'[60] that brought together stories he had heard in the Northern Territory about the legendary Aboriginal outlaw Namaluk, subsequently described by Ion L. Idriess in the novel *Nemarluk: King of the Wilds* (1958), and of lonely white women on pastoral stations rearing Aboriginal children. The film also represented perspectives on assimilation and the future of Aboriginal people shaped by the Chauvels' many conversations with 'old hands'[61] in the Territory and their reading of texts by anthropologists Elkin and Mountford. While *Jedda* set up different scenarios for its narrative of Aboriginal people caught 'between two worlds', it nevertheless reached the same desperate conclusion as the media mythologising of Albert Namatjira, with the deaths of Jedda and Marbuck pointing once again to the impossibility of assimilation. Its conclusions reflected entrenched imaginings handed down from the nineteenth century about the inevitable reversion of Aboriginal people to 'type' as they heed the call of the wild and flee civilisation.

Jedda tells the story of a station mistress who rears an Aboriginal baby from the 'Pintari' tribe. Although she can make the girl outwardly 'white' she cannot 'erase the tribal instincts that prevail'.[62] Meaghan Morris describes a scene of 'intensely melodramatic emotional saturation' in the homestead lounge room after Jedda was refused permission yet again to 'go walkabout'.[63] Seated at the piano with an Aboriginal shield mounted on the wall behind her she hears two clashing strains of music — her own piano playing and Aboriginal music emanating from the shield — that drive her to bang on the piano in desperation. The war of the two worlds is battled out within her own mind although, as Morris points out, Jedda's anguish is the legacy of generations of white race hysteria.[64] At first it appears that Jedda is destined to marry Joe, the civilised 'half-caste' stockman, but the arrival of the 'wild' Aboriginal outlaw Marbuck puts an end to this when he uses love magic to seduce her. Marbuck flees with Jedda to his own country followed by the police, her white father and Joe in close pursuit. Warned by his people that they will 'sing' him to death for returning with a girl who is forbidden to him by Aboriginal law, Marbuck escapes into taboo country where he is driven mad by the magic. With his pursuers at his heels he finally leaps over a cliff with Jedda in his arms in a desperate act of murder-suicide.[65]

Anthropologist Jeremy Beckett defines a series of positions within the film that explore the feasibility and ethics of the assimilation project.[66] One reflects the views of Territory pastoralists (also repeated by Beth Dean and Victor Carell) that 'full-blood' Aboriginal people should retain their traditional life and not end up like demoralised mixed-race people in the towns. In this construct, station life is romanticised in a colonial fantasy where Aboriginal people are at home in their country, race relations are paternalistic but harmonious, and brutality and violence and the controls and deprivations experienced by Aboriginal workers are invisible. The conclusion for assimilation is that Aboriginal people should continue to practise their traditions and only be gradually exposed to change — in a segregated environment that maintains their social distance from the outside world. One outcome of this of course is that existing exploitative employment relations can continue on.

Another position explores the consequences when this idyll is disrupted by the 'agent of disorder'[67] — the white mother who endeavours to assimilate Jedda. This inserts assimilation into the heart of settler domestic life and introduces gender to the discussion. The domestic interior the women inhabit is the frontier where state policy impacts on the 'psyches of black and white women in a continuous, prolonged abrasion'.[68] These are the meanings explored by Tracey Moffatt in her film *Night Cries: A Rural Tragedy* (1990)[69] in which she recasts the Jedda story by asking what would have happened if she had remained at home with her white mother. However, the complexities and moral issues raised by the settler-mother/Aboriginal-daughter bond were not developed in *Jedda.* Instead the clichéd conclusion is drawn that Jedda cannot escape her Aboriginal instincts and passions: once again assimilation is impossible. Barbara Creed argues that *Jedda* becomes a narrative of 'reverse captivity' where the issue of the stealing of baby Jedda (who is held captive by the 'dominant white culture') is overlooked to follow the classical captivity narrative of 'abduction and seduction'.[70]

Beckett's third position explores the fate of the three young people caught in the film's lovers' triangle. In a conventional nineteenth-century narrative of mixed-races reverting to type (recast to apply to any cross-cultural situation involving Aboriginal people) Jedda is trapped between the worlds of assimilation and 'tribal instincts'[71] — until Marbuck's powerful sexuality and magical powers drive her back to her primitive origins. In dying, Jedda joins a string of tragic fictional characters, the majority of them mixed-race, who live out tragic lives or have to be killed off in keeping with earlier theories of the non-viability of mixed-race people to survive.[72] The 'half-caste' stockman Joe has an ambiguous status, living in the 'marginal zone of the stockyards' with other Aborigines but not really being one of them. Joe is a feminised male character who loses out on love and seems to have no future.[73] Marbuck has a magnetic physical appearance and sexuality that dominates the screen and has the power to lure Jedda to his side. Yet his life seems equally impossible: like the young men Beth Dean described flouting tribal law, he lives as an outlaw on the fringes of traditional life and pastoral society, hounded by the police and his own people until he meets his death.

Conflicting desires — the novel *The Fringe Dwellers*

The trope of living between two worlds was also evident in mid-twentieth century fiction writing. Victor Carell, the husband of Beth Dean, addressed it in a short story in his book *Naked We Are Born* (1960) about the destructive effects of 'civilisation' on a fringe-dwelling Aboriginal family in rural Australia who are unable to break away from the vices they have learned. In the epilogue Carell cites Namatjira as an example of a man who 'attempted to bridge the gap between two cultures' and instead became 'something of a lost pawn on the chess board of modern urban politics'.[74] At the time, the novel *The Fringe Dwellers* (1961) by Nene Gare was attracting popular acclaim with its story of a young Aboriginal girl struggling to negotiate her way through the competing pressures of her desire for assimilation and her parents' resistance. The book had unique claims to authenticity, being based on Gare's observations of Aboriginal life in the mid-North-West and Pilbara regions of Western Australia during the 1950s where her husband Frank Gare served as District Officer with the Native Welfare Department. (In 1963 he was appointed Commissioner of Native Welfare in Western Australia.) Told with humour, the novel was well received and was reviewed nationally and in Britain, had numerous reprints and became a text for high school students. In 1986 it was made into a feature film by Australian director Bruce Beresford, shot on location at Murgon and Cherbourg in southeast Queensland with Aboriginal actors Oodgeroo

Noonuccal, Bobby Randall, Justine Saunders and Bob Mazza. The film was a finalist at the 1986 Cannes Film Festival.

The main character in *Fringe Dwellers* is Trilby Comeaway, a young woman educated at a mission in the south of the state who has returned to live with her family in their camp on the town reserve but who is determined to achieve her vision of assimilation for herself and her family. The novel is a compelling story of the clash between Trilby's determination to change and the pressures for her to conform to the fringe-dwelling way of life. The expectation is powerfully present that young people like Trilby will feel compelled to remodel their families and to carve out a new life for themselves. As a story line this represented a new development since Aboriginal children reared away from their parents were until then expected never to return home. (This scenario would have been familiar to removed Native American children who were reared as agents of assimilation in residential schools then returned to reform their families on the reservations.) The extent to which Trilby had internalised resentment of her own people becomes evident when she attacks her parents: 'Pigs live better than we do. I tell you I hate white people because they lump us all together and never give one of us a chance to leave all this behind. And I hate coloured people more, because most of them don't want a chance. They *like* living like pigs, damn them.'[75] Trilby also rebels against the town's race barriers and white offers of kindly charity and she challenges Aboriginal norms in a multitude of ways: through her speech, body language, style of dressing and her preference for being alone. She also resents visits by her extended family and is disrespectful to the elders at the town camp. She seems a model of 1950s teenage discontent. By contrast, Trilby's sister Noonah is weaving together the old and the new: a trainee nurse at the local hospital, she helps Aboriginal patients and shares her pay with the family, yet her father finds it difficult to accept her ways.

Trilby's main goal is to transform her family into assimilation's promise of a happy nuclear family unit living in a neat home in the suburbs. The pain and tensions that her dream create drive the plot and the novel's eventual tragic outcome. When Trilby finally persuades her family to move to a house in town they enter a world of heightened tensions generated by the minutiae of small town prejudice and misguided charity (represented in the 'good neighbourly' efforts of Mrs Henwood in the house next door) and their own family upheavals. Trilby has her own inner conflicts. She is attracted to the young Aboriginal man Phyllix but is unwilling to stay with him and abandon her dreams of a better life in the city. Then her father gambles away the rent and the family is forced to return to the camp. Trilby's internal conflicts climax in the birth of her baby and its death, whether by accident or driven by her despair. The novel ends with Trilby wrapped in Phyllix's embrace as he begs her to stay with him. She nods but inside she is thinking: 'She wanted to tell Phyllix what she knew he most wanted to hear — that she would stop not for a while but for always. And she could not. The thing that lived in her heart would not let her. So long as she had youth and strength and pride, so long would she seek to escape this life.'[76]

Gare later claimed that the book was 'more a documentary than a novel. It's all true and the characters are based on real people. I had such ideals then. The way those people were treated made me see white heat.'[77] Anthropologists Diane Barwick, Marie Reay and Judy Inglis wrote to Gare in 1963 claiming that after reading the book they felt 'enormously depressed — for what can we say now? … this sort of material, the impact of change on individuals can best be presented in novel form. We say the same things more drearily with Tables, Figures, and Appendices — and say no more about what culture change means.'[78] Yet there were significant misrepresentations and omissions in the book: the family's ease in getting a house in town at a time when this was an almost impossible outcome and their ability to return to the town camp when so many town camps were being bulldozed; the absence of nosy welfare officers and only a single appearance by the police at their house in town; and the glossed-over legal and administrative controls and inferior services provided for Aboriginal families. With these determining forces obscured or absent, the book lost its claim to being grounded in the struggles and experiences of Aboriginal families. Instead they come to resemble stock characters from other worlds: the 'jolly darkies' of nineteenth-century song writer Stephen C. Foster's imagination or, as a reviewer for the London *Observer* pointed out, the 'stock pattern' in 'countless working-class novels of the slightly better educated child … growing up to despise its parents for their slovenly ways and to long for better things', and the hackneyed equations of 'underprivileged = dirty, slummy, feckless but loving and warm-hearted; privileged = clean, careful, loveless and mean', and in this way obscuring the 'real problem in the novel, the problem of colour'.[79]

Australian reviews of *The Fringe Dwellers* provide a sobering insight into the continued influence of concepts of race and blood in discussing Aboriginal people of mixed descent and the potential for their assimilation. Thelma Forshaw wrote in the *Bulletin* that the book 'arouses the suffocating feelings of impotence and futility. It seems it must be so, as long as dark blood is mixed with white.' Trilby's situation was 'caused by the very temperament of the half-caste — good-natured, slack, amoral. Few have the drive or discipline to hurdle the racial barrier.'[80] The *West Australian* noted that 'all her people react in ways we have been led to expect of natives. They are lazy, shiftless, happy within their own environment but hankering for the material things of the white man's world.'[81] Finally, the *Canberra Times* referred to the problems of 'people caught between two ways of life and belonging to neither'.[82]

The great white hope — Aboriginal child adoption and the press

Standing as beacons to an assimilated future in the midst of these gloomy narratives were the popular media stories of Aboriginal children adopted or fostered into suburban white middle-class families. The public imagined that removing Aboriginal babies and children and isolating them completely from their Aboriginal background in this way would lead to positive outcomes for assimilation. For this initiative, introduced from the 1940s, governments targeted 'lighter' children as the most capable of assimilating and recommended that their Aboriginal ancestry be kept hidden from them. The Queensland government stated succinctly in 1959 that 'near white children' should have 'the opportunity of entering into the white community as white girls and boys'.[83] Adoptions and fostering required a new level of professionalism in Aboriginal child removals, with much stricter legal requirements to be followed, including obtaining the permission of Aboriginal mothers for adoptions, which was not always readily given. Governments also sought out prospective carers through advertising and media 'feel good' stories.

The message was that these children were available for the readers' choosing and that they would be better off and happier assimilated into a white world. This new white hope for assimilation starkly contradicted the images of intact Aboriginal nuclear families depicted in official publications. However, they fitted with and, indeed, reinforced, entrenched negative views of Aboriginal family life and continuing official and public commitment to practices of removing children as the optimum way to achieve their assimilation. They also suggested an outlet for public humanitarianism, misguided though it may have been: here was a way that white families could assist directly in the process of assimilation. Few people connected the pessimistic narratives of people living 'between two worlds' with this hopeful new dream of Aboriginal assimilation. Meanwhile, the pressing need to improve the living conditions of the children's families remained unresolved. The 'rising generations' of assimilated children like Trilby and her sister Noonah were expected to achieve these advances through their own efforts.

Governments working in tandem with the media actively promoted the adoption and fostering of Aboriginal children. In 1955 the New South Wales government advertised for foster parents to give 'a loving home' to 150 Aboriginal babies, children and teenagers who were orphaned or neglected.[84] Two short films — *Native Girls Fairy Palace* (1957) and *Native Mission to Melbourne Mansion* (1957) — and newsreel footage *Dreams Do Come True* (1957), were made depicting the fairy tale story of three girls from the Methodist Mission at Croker Island in the Northern Territory adopted by the Deutscher family — 'a happy white family' living in a spacious fifteen-room modern mansion in Melbourne. In a statement to the press Mr Deutscher spelled out the assimilatory intent of such adoptions: 'the way to solve the native problem was to bring [the children] into the homes of white people so that they can be thoroughly acclimatised'.[85] The *Sydney Morning Herald* praised the Deutschers for the 'lesson in assimilation', which set 'a fine community example'. Feminist lawyer and academic Francesca Bartlett describes such films as 'showpieces' of assimilation policy in action, contrasting the unhealthy degraded Aboriginal way of life with the gleaming clean surfaces and commodity-filled spaces of the homes of Australian women.[86] In this way white suburban mothers, like their earlier missionary sisters, were drawn into the process of assimilation and nation building through their contributions to the bettering of Aboriginal children.

Mr Deutscher's sentiments were echoed by adoptive parents around Australia, many of them migrants of Dutch background. Despite legal prohibitions on identifying parties to adoptions, and the normal privacy rules surrounding foster arrangements, reports routinely included names and photographs of the children and their adoptive families. 'We thought we should do something to help those no one else wanted,' one family told the Melbourne *Age* newspaper in 1962.[87] The adoptive mother of the first 'full-blood' Aboriginal child adopted in South Australia had already taken in three children of mixed Aboriginal descent and when asked if a fourth was not too great a responsibility replied 'my only answer is that even if we cannot give them everything, we can give them a normal home life and lots of love'. After the court adoption proceedings were completed the family went to meet Charles Mountford, who had written about the tribal name of the family's newest member.[88] In 1960 in Victoria there were 250 applications to adopt a twenty-month-old Aboriginal girl, including one from an African-American sailor, after her foster mother died and the press reported her dying request that the baby should never be returned to her Aboriginal family.[89]

There were numerous headlines claiming success for the adoption project. The Adelaide *Advertiser* stated that 'adopted into a white home he becomes a member of the family and automatically a member of the white community'.[90] The *Weekend Mail* in Perth wrote, 'Susanna thrives on love. Four white children, one half-caste — all happy. She's one of the family.'[91] In Melbourne the Harold Blair Holiday Scheme, which placed over two thousand children from the bush for holidays with local families between 1962 and 1974, provided an annual photo opportunity for the press of smiling children visiting the beach and the zoo with testimonials from host families such as 'She loved helping me. I only wish I could have kept her.' Newspaper reports about the children going 'back to reality' and 'to their humpies' reinforced preconceptions about the children's bleak home life. Indeed, some families did keep the children, entering into formal fostering or adoption arrangements with state authorities. In a few cases, as Reg Worthy the Director of the newly established Victorian Department of Aboriginal Affairs reported in 1968, billeting families simply failed to return them, an action that seems unthinkable today.[92]

By the late 1960s Aboriginal leaders and their supporters were protesting that adoptions had become 'a fashion'. Activist Charles Perkins claimed that in New South Wales unofficial adoptions were 'as common as the common cold' and in Victoria the Aborigines Advancement League's liaison officer S. Murray warned this 'would mean genocide to the Aboriginal people'.[93] In 1968 Reg Worthy told the press that he had identified over three hundred illegal Aboriginal adoptions in Victoria, some involving children originally from the Northern Territory and North Queensland.[94] Activists Bruce McGuiness and Molly Dyer commented that many people had 'good intentions' but that as the children grew up they became 'self-conscious of [their] colour and racial difference leading to a feeling of inferiority'.[95] This was borne out in findings made by the Victorian Aboriginal Legal Service in the mid-1970s that 90 per cent of family placements failed and that growing numbers of young people and parents were seeking their assistance to reconnect with each other. They also identified a strong connection between child removal and adult incarceration.[96]

The actions of government and white families in adopting and fostering Aboriginal children had the tragic effect of conjuring into reality the trope of suffering individuals trapped in a no man's land between two worlds. A circuit breaker was clearly needed to break both the pattern of Aboriginal narratives imagined by settler Australians and the nature of solutions devised by government officers working in isolation from Aboriginal families.

Activism: the path to political enlightenment

The circuit breaker was the eruption of Aboriginal voices into the public domain, presenting their experiences of assimilation and their demands for change. This brought into sharp focus the diverging differences between the goals of assimilation and evolving Aboriginal agendas. For some settler Australians the opportunity to participate with Aboriginal people in the expanding network of Aboriginal organisations provided a path to enlightenment about Aboriginal conditions and political aspirations — an opportunity previously denied to them by laws enforcing segregation.

Two settler Australians who set off on this path were Jack Horner and his wife Jean who joined the Sydney-based Aboriginal–Australian Fellowship in 1957 and in the following year the national Federal Council for Aboriginal Advancement (later Federal Council for Aboriginal and Torres Strait Islander Advancement). Horner has charted their journey to enlightenment in his book *Seeking Racial Justice: An Insider's Memoir of the Movement for Aboriginal Advancement 1938–1978*, which provides a valuable case study of the dramatic shift in the understanding of white activists as they become more directly involved with Aboriginal leaders and community members articulating their goals. Jack Horner was a third generation settler Australian from a middle-class family who worked in theatre and the arts. His awareness of racial oppression began during a stay in England when he listened to African and West Indian speakers at Hyde Park Corner expressing their 'yearning for independence' in terms of the four freedoms of the 1941 Atlantic Charter — speech and expression, worship, freedom from want, and freedom from fear.[97] However, it was not until 1957, at the age of thirty-five, that Horner first met Aboriginal people. The meeting at the Sydney Town Hall organised by the Aboriginal–Australian Fellowship was the beginning of his crash course in Aboriginal affairs and his introduction to the expanding network of Aboriginal (and other) activists pushing for change.

The Aboriginal–Australian Fellowship was established in 1956 through the commitment of Pearl Gibbs, Faith Bandler and Grace Bardsley, whose names would become synonymous with the drive for Constitutional reform that climaxed in the 1967 Referendum. The goal of the Fellowship as reported at the time in the *Sydney Morning Herald* was 'to promote better understanding between aborigines [sic] and European Australians.' Despite the women's groundbreaking work, it was an Aboriginal man, Kamilaroi leader Herbert Groves who was elected as its first president. The Fellowship had called the meeting at the Sydney Town Hall to raise support for a petition to the federal government to change the Constitution. Present was a veritable who's who of the activist scene and the attendance of over one thousand Sydneysiders — half of them local Aboriginal people — was a clear statement of the mood for change. In the audience was a mix of 'pacifists, concerned churchmen, trade union members, old-style "lefties", Labor Party members and feminists',[98] all with their own agendas but united around the call for reform. Feminist leader and international activist Jessie Street addressed the meeting and Pastor Doug Nicholls spoke to Bill Grayden's film of Aboriginal conditions at Warburton Mission in Western Australia. Also present was Don McLeod, representing the Pilbara strikers. Together with striker Fred Waters in the Northern Territory, McLeod had helped to arouse trade union support — financial and moral — for Aboriginal workers seeking better conditions. A month later Gordon Bryant, a staunch advocate of Commonwealth control and the first federal Minister for Aboriginal Affairs in the Whitlam Labor government, initiated the first major public debate on Aboriginal affairs in the parliament.[99]

When Horner first joined the Fellowship he fully endorsed the policy of assimilation of Aboriginal people into Australian society — opposed to their discriminatory treatment, he assumed that assimilation was the best outcome. However, his views changed dramatically as he listened to Aboriginal leaders and observed Aboriginal conditions first-hand. He gradually learned that issues of civic and civil rights, while essential for change, were just the beginning of the struggle. Working with Herbert Groves he listened to the long history of Aboriginal protest in New South Wales and the leading role played by Bill Ferguson, and this later inspired him to write a biography documenting Ferguson's life as a political activist. Realising his own ignorance about Aboriginal conditions, Horner proposed that the Fellowship collect information about Aboriginal conditions in the state, both to inform non-Aboriginal people and to use in lobbying government. In late 1958 Jack and Jean Horner began their 'journey of discovery through New South Wales'[100] and most Fellowship members made similar trips at the time to keep in touch with the grassroots communities. In this they were following the example of Bill Ferguson and of Melbourne activist Ian Spalding,[101] who was also travelling and documenting conditions in Aboriginal communities. Between them they were setting a pattern for the Freedom Rides of 1965.

It was on one of these trips that Horner felt his first twinges of doubt about Aboriginal assimilation. The couple had arrived in Armidale just in time for the official opening of a home funded by the Armidale Association for the Assimilation of Aborigines and the ceremonial handover of the house key to its first Aboriginal occupants who were the only Aboriginal people present at the ceremony. Previously Horner had believed that a house in town was preferable to segregation and the terrible living conditions on reserves with no rights. Now he wondered how this isolated Aboriginal family would fare and what alternatives there might in fact be to the intentions of the well-meaning town residents who could see no alternative to assimilated living. These feelings resonated with a comment he read in the *Sydney Morning Herald* in 1960 by John Close, President of the Woodenbong (Bundjalung) Aboriginal Advancement Council, who stated that 'what we care about is that we are not allowed to live together and run our lives for ourselves ... We have been talking in adult education classes and we decided that it is no good getting government houses, government water, government managers and government rations. We've had these for thirty years, and they haven't done us any good. We have decided to join together and cooperate, to run our own affairs.'[102]

Visiting Aboriginal communities Horner heard about discriminatory police harassment and imprisonment of Aboriginal people, something that as a white middle-class person he had not previously encountered. However, the conditions of institutionalised children escaped the couple's attention, despite their visit to the Kinchela Boys Home in Kempsey where they noted the 'high standards set for school uniforms, furniture, tableware and so on; and the heavy authoritarian style of the administrative staff'.[103] Back in Sydney in 1959 and working with local Aboriginal people to set up community dances, Horner observed how important it was to leave it 'to Aboriginal people to find solutions to their own problems and to stand back and wait for them to ask for our help if they needed it. This approach would stand us in good stead in the years to come.'[104] Like the Coolbaroo dances in East Perth, these events provided a meeting place for the disparate Aboriginal groups who had migrated to Sydney.

Horner also became involved in the Federal Council for Aboriginal Advancement, established in 1958 to bring the organisations together to 'actively cooperate' and 'to form a united policy'. This grew into the Federal Council for the Advancement of Aboriginal and Torres Strait Islanders, an independent national umbrella organisation that drove the change agenda leading to the 1967 referendum.[105] Horner recalled that at first he did not see the value of developing a national network but he soon came to appreciate the strength of unity developed through sharing experiences, ideas, strategies and perspectives. Initially the Council's leadership was top-heavy with strong non-Aboriginal members — Dr Charles Duguid (the foundation president), Bill Grayden, Shirley Andrews, Gordon Bryant, Don Dunstan, and Stan Davey. Its original principles were listed as equal citizenship rights, equal living conditions, equal pay for equal work, free education, and the retention of Aboriginal reserves. At its first annual conference in 1958 the Council endorsed the Commonwealth taking control of Aboriginal affairs from the states, and adopted the Fellowship's petition — which by then had gathered 25,988 signatures — as the basis for a national campaign.[106] There was also attention to international developments and at the second conference members debated the relevance to Aboriginal Australians of the ILO Convention No. 107. Horner recalls that the conference welcomed the document as a standard against which to judge the practices of Australian governments and as a 'broad plan for progressive action' that reflected Council policies. However, they 'had not observed its weaknesses', which were later recognised as failing to grant Indigenous people authority over their cultures and lands.[107]

Developments during the 1960s further broadened Horner's horizons. Aboriginal leadership roles and participation were expanding nationally so that conferences shifted from 'being a forum predominantly for "white talkers"' to one for 'Aboriginal and non-Aboriginal people acting together'.[108] With this came a new political radicalism and demands for policies that embraced Aboriginal rights to land and culture. At the 1961 conference in Brisbane, delegates discussed abandoning assimilation in favour of integration. In an Eight Point Policy presented to the conference, Council President Charles Leon insisted that Aboriginal people be allowed to run their own affairs and 'keep their group identity if desired'. Leon explained to Horner the interconnectedness of Aboriginal issues of housing, health, hygiene, training, employment and the urgent need for Aborigines to govern their own affairs. He also argued for the importance of cooperatives built on existing family networks to run community affairs in opposition to the government's plans to scatter families under the policy of assimilation.[109] The sharing of experiences and knowledge about racial exploitation and oppression between delegates took on a new militancy at this conference when delegates were provided with an analysis of Queensland's draconian system of administration of reserves and settlements. This led to the motion that all discriminatory state legislation should be repealed and Pastor Doug Nicholls's controversial statement that 'we must abolish apartheid in our own country before the next Commonwealth Prime Ministers' Conference, or we could find ourselves in the same position as South Africa found itself at this year's conference'.[110] It was also at this conference that Horner began to fully appreciate the central significance of land to Aboriginal people after Ian Spalding's impromptu statement that 'we should make an Aboriginal right to own land the main principle of the [Council], integrating the people on their own land. Isn't it time we give up assimilation altogether? It's time we acted on land rights.'[111]

Horner recalls that from this time on, with widespread student and Aboriginal activism supported by the trade unions and the churches,' 'all things suddenly became possible'.[112] Federal and state governments, alarmed by growing international criticism and national protest, busily pursued their own agendas of legislative reform. The Council adopted a more strategic political program and its Aboriginal leaders 'became the front-line force in the fight for Indigenous rights'.[113] However the pace of change was still slow and Aboriginal people were impatient for practical solutions and outcomes to relieve conditions. At the same time Horner was realising 'the enormity of the problems we were trying to resolve' and understanding that regardless of their 'degree of non-Aboriginal heritage' and familiarity with white ways, Aboriginal leaders 'never lost their particular pride in their Aboriginality ... all desired to maintain their Aboriginal identity'.[114]

From 1965 the Council took on a truly national outlook with the participation of Torres Strait Islanders formally acknowledged in the change to its title, now the Federal Council for the

Advancement of Aborigines and Torres Strait Islanders, and initiatives to ensure inclusion of membership from Western Australia and the Northern Territory. This was also the year of the Freedom Rides and the first all-Aboriginal Fellowship conference. The changing agenda was highlighted by Grace Bardsley who told members that 'the whole point of this conference [was] that Aborigines should not hear whites tell them what to do. The Aborigines should be there sponsoring, chairing and speaking. They should have the whole show.'[115] Horner recalled that this 'provoked' him to consider 'whether it was right for a non-Aboriginal person to be the Fellowship's honorary secretary. Should I step down in favour of an Aboriginal person? I thought the time had come.' After resigning gracefully Horner began work on his biography of Bill Ferguson, and later, 'with my book complete, I took a deep breath and braced myself for the referendum'.[116]

Already in 1962 the Council had begun its National Petition program for constitutional reform with the goal of collecting a quarter of a million signatures from around the nation. This went further than legislative amendments and embraced the Commonwealth government assuming responsibility for Aboriginal affairs and making a real commitment to true equality for Aboriginal people. The tempo of action quickened dramatically with its 'Vote Yes' campaign conducted in April and May 1967 in the lead up to the referendum. This met with a burst of public enthusiasm that foreshadowed the unprecedented crowds who flocked to support *Corroboree 2000* and the Walk for Reconciliation held on Sorry Day, 26 May 2000, forty years later. Sue Taffe recounts that 'car stickers, posters and handbills, addresses throughout the country by Aboriginal spokespeople such as Kath Walker, Pastor Nicholls, Joe McGinness and Bill Onus, support by radio stations, newspaper columnists, editorials: all promoted a yes vote as a straightforward and upright way for electors to signal their concern'.[117] Writing in the *Sydney*

Morning Herald Charmian Clift, the popular columnist, concluded an article entitled 'We must not fail them again' with the observation: 'We do so much that is morally dingy it might do us all some moral good to do a thing that is plainly and positively right.'[118] The result was a proud day in Australian history when the greatest majority ever in a national referendum — 90.77 per cent of Australians — voted to amend the 1901 Constitution and remove all clauses that discriminated against Aboriginal people.

A fragmenting discourse

The mid-twentieth century discourse of assimilation, under attack from Aboriginal activism, was further fragmented by the onslaught of a new proactive media and emerging critiques of the policy within academic and government circles. By the late 1960s Aboriginal issues were no longer a 'state secret' but a matter of vigorous public debate that was frequently initiated by Aboriginal leaders. Public opinion appeared increasingly ambivalent as newspapers documented a complex and critical mixture of self-interested opposition, humanitarian concern and serious questioning of the policy's instruments and intended outcomes. These reports pointed to divided community opinion and difficulties in implementing programs of assimilation.

Governments responding to these trends at home also noted the swing against assimilation in the international arena and by the early 1970s the great experiment of post-war assimilation of Aboriginal and migrant people was drawing to a close. Academic criticism of the policy had also escalated during the 1960s. Social scientists in the United States attempted to maintain the model's hegemonic status by adding qualifications and distinctions such as cultural, structural and psychological modes of response, but as condemnation of its inherent ethnocentrism and lack of explanatory power mounted, assimilation was superseded by a loosely defined pluralist model of integration. The participation of Australian social scientists in international forums like UNESCO exposed them to new trends in academic research and government practice, while anthropologists were learning from new research in universities and government research institutes set up during the 1960s. As Tim Rowse points out, a common thread in both fields was that assimilation should not be directed at the individual but should be 'interpreted so as to leave space for group life'.[119] This view also came to dominate migrant and Aboriginal policy and practice, which during the 1970s worked closely with ethnic and Aboriginal community organisations in service delivery and population management.

Media

Steve Mickler's sampling survey of Perth's conservative daily newspapers the *West Australian* and the *Daily News* identified significant changes in their reporting on Aboriginal issues over the decade of the 1960s. Mickler concluded that the state 'lost its monopoly on the production of meaning about Aboriginal affairs' as a body of public opinion emerged that was increasingly 'sceptical, incredulous and hostile to state Aboriginal policy'.[120] As the decade advanced and with the success of the 1967 Referendum there was 'a remarkable transformation in both the issues constituting Aboriginal affairs and the configuration of relations between readers, the state and Aborigines as organised and made available for public consumption in the news'.[121]

For the year 1960 Mickler found a scarcity of entries, suggesting a 'marginal interest' amongst Perth readers. The 'native problem' was depicted as a threat to society and the public was encouraged to support assimilation. Issues of 'health, welfare of people on reserves, government funding, alcohol problems and some criminal matters' were presented from the perspective of the assimilatory imperative for Aboriginal people to acquire 'western industrial skills, social values, behaviours and lifestyles'.[122]

Information for reports was gathered from Native Welfare officers, police, missionaries, politicians and pastoralists. They spoke for and about Aboriginal people. Like the government's campaign pamphlets, the press showed images of white people assisting Aboriginal people, along with appealing shots of Aboriginal babies and children available for adoption and fostering by white families.

A marked shift in news reporting was evident in 1965 with stories that incorporated Aboriginal perspectives appearing at least once a week. The powerful appeal of events like the 1965 Freedom Rides led by Charles Perkins riveted the attention of the nation and indelibly associated the Aboriginal struggle with the civil rights movement in the United States, 'in terms of political objectives (social equality with whites) and methods (media-oriented protests and civil disobedience)'.[123] There were also the growing movements for land rights and equal wages, with the presentation by the Yirrkala people of their bark petition to Federal parliament in 1966 and the strike at Wave Hill in the Northern Territory in the same year. Alongside these powerful stories of Aboriginal political agency ran conventional stories endorsing assimilation. The institutionalisation of Aboriginal children at Tardun Mission was 'exalted' and their lack of rights 'made virtuous' in a report claiming that 'in our Beatle-ridden world they work 16 hours a day, seven days a week without pay'.[124] A further perspective emerging in the press was that assimilation was creating a situation where demands by Aboriginal people — for equal wages in the pastoral industry, for instance — were becoming a serious threat to white interests.

This theme was more pronounced in news reporting for 1967. As assimilation began to impact on country towns in the south of the state, local white residents found that they were expected to treat Aboriginal families as equals when they lacked the necessary economic resources — land, capital, housing and work — to fit in. During the year accounts filled the papers of a crisis in the southern town of Pingelly, attributed to the combined effect of the granting of social security benefits, the repeal of discriminatory legislation including drinking rights, and the growing movement of Nyungar families into town on a permanent basis. Press reports claimed that civil rights were leading to civic disobedience with outbursts of racial conflict, juvenile misbehaviour and petty crime. There were also calls for greater control over social security payments to Aboriginal people — although there were not yet calls to remove these benefits or claims of welfare dependency. There were even demands for 'birching as a deterrent to [Pingelly's] native problems' and renewed calls for the tired old solution of farm training schemes to assimilate Aboriginal people into the community.[125] At the same time the 1967 Referendum was widely reported. The *West Australian*[126] endorsed the vote for an end to discrimination in the Constitution as 'universally acceptable' but reverted to recurring themes in federal–state relations when it expressed concern about federal interference and echoed earlier state calls on Canberra to provide sufficient funding for Aboriginal services.

Anthropology challenges Aboriginal assimilation

During the 1960s a new generation of anthropologists reacted against the dominance of Elkin's model of Aboriginal assimilation, and anthropology departments established at the Australian National University (1949), Western Australia (1956), Monash (1963), and Queensland (1966)[127] began to establish their own approaches to the study of Aboriginal communities. The results of fieldwork in the cities and towns of southern Australia showed an unexpected degree of complexity and variability in assimilation scenarios and obstacles to be overcome. In contrast to the simplistic between-two-worlds narrative, these studies showed that assimilation was impeded by institutionalised racism, legal and administrative controls, white opposition, endemic poverty, limited education, economic adaptations and a strong emphasis within Aboriginal communities on cultural maintenance and solidarity. On the basis of her research in northwestern New South Wales, Ruth Fink (1957) claimed that 'while the caste barrier remains, few of the darker coloured people have any incentive to assimilate themselves, and they prefer to make the best of their lot'.[128] There was a new understanding amongst anthropologists of the significance and extent of kin networks in these communities, and a consensus that they should be supported rather than undermined in the drive to promote assimilation. In her research with Jamadji people in the Murchison district of Western Australia, Ruth Fink found that strong ties of kinship, marriage and socialising linked communities across the region.[129] She concluded that the continuing existence of these links, even amongst the 'detribalised part-aborigines' was proof that anthropologists had been wrong in assuming that assimilation inevitably followed the breakdown of traditional life and she urged government officers to take this into account rather than slavishly follow conventional welfare models developed for disadvantaged white families.

Fink made these comments at a conference of academics at the Australian National University in 1961 called by W. E. H. Stanner under the auspices of the Commonwealth government's new Social Sciences Research Council. The conference launched a major attack on assimilation. Stanner reflected the tone in the foreword to the conference papers published in 1965 when he wrote that there was 'serious questioning' under way of 'the morality, appropriateness and application of the modern policy of assimilation'.[130] The policy had, he argued, become 'part of the whole structure of thought towards the aborigines' but there was little clarity about what could be achieved apart from 'the imagined … future'. 'Our intentions,' he continued, had become 'so benevolent that we find it difficult to see that they are still fundamentally dictatorial.' He pointed out that most Aboriginal people felt that they had never had 'fair return' on the loss of their 'land, labour, way of life, beliefs and, now, works of art', and felt powerless to stop this from continuing. Stanner concluded that assimilation's 'insistence that they must deal on our terms is against natural justice, it will inevitably mean that the worm will be in our conscience as well as in the apple'.[131] West Australian anthropologist John Wilson attacked assimilation for its ethnocentric, conformist and monocultural perspectives, for being out of step with international trends towards integration and self-determination, and for failing to live up to its promises to Aboriginal people. He added, in a comment that still holds for today, that the policy provided governments with 'a convenient justification for existent action' that was typically 'short-term, ameliorative, and reflect[ed] current political pressures and economic allocations'.[132]

While these criticisms challenged Elkin's model of assimilation for Aboriginal people in southern Australia, anthropologists were now united in their opposition to government efforts to force rapid assimilation on Aboriginal communities in remote Australia still following a traditional way of life. Stanner[133] presented a lively attack on the government in his life narrative of the Nangiomeri elder Durmugam whom he had visited regularly in Arnhem Land from the early 1930s until Durmugam's death in 1959. Stanner described a man who had little in common with the subjects of the between-two-worlds narrative. Durmugam retained a strong identification with Aboriginal culture and was a 'unified person who, somehow, could bridge two worlds and, while preferring one, lived with two'.[134] Stanner observed that assimilation 'assumes that the aborigines want, or will want, to be assimilated; that white Australians will accept them on fair terms; that discrimination can be controlled; that, in spite of the revealed nature of the aborigines or their culture, they can be shaped to have a new and "Australian" nature. The chauvinism is quite unconscious. The idea that aborigines might reject a banausic life occurs to no one. The unconscious, unfocussed, but intense racialism of Australians is unnoticed. The risk of producing a depressed class of coloured misfits is thought minimal, although that is the actual basis from which "assimilation" begins.'[135] Commenting on Stanner's observations, Marie Reay noted that 'for Aborigines who are distinctly tribal in their orientations and live in regions where there is no local "white" society of dimensions to absorb them, "assimilation" is an unrealistically remote goal'.[136] She concluded that the appropriate model was the process of education for self-determination followed by the Australian government in its mandated territory of Papua New Guinea.

Despite the increase in anthropology departments in Australian universities other disciplines were making inroads into anthropologists' monopoly of the role of experts advising governments and interpreting Aboriginal culture for the public. Art curators and historians were encroaching on the field and differences of interpretation and approach did not always make for harmonious relations. In 1960 Tony Tuckson invited Ronald Berndt to edit a lavish book based on his 1960 exhibition *Australian Aboriginal Art*, which contained articles by leading anthropologists Elkin, McCarthy, Mountford and T. G. H. Strehlow, as well as Tuckson. However, while the two men were united in their intention to introduce Australian audiences to the meanings of Aboriginal imagery, Berndt was critical of Tuckson for addressing Aboriginal art as art rather than focusing on the anthropological contexts and cut several paragraphs from Tuckson's essay — a liberty that led to enduring acrimony between the men.[137]

The fields of Aboriginal archaeology and colonial history were also drawing in new researchers, some with ties to anthropology and others who would undermine its dominance in interpreting the Aboriginal past. Along with the galleries, the government's research institutions like the Institute of Aboriginal Studies in Canberra were challenging university and museum control.

Archaeologists were establishing Australia's ancient origins through science rather than Aboriginal mythology and in 1956 John Mulvaney of Melbourne University stretched the claims of prior human occupancy of the continent back to 18,000 years before present. With greater professionalisation of the discipline over the years this would be extended to between 40,000 and 100,000 years before present. Despite these vast time spans, researchers began to speak of Aboriginal people as Australia's 'first wave of migrants'. The new Australian Institute of Aboriginal Studies established in Canberra in 1961 strongly supported the quest to study Aboriginal origins and migration to Australia through archaeological research and physical anthropology.[138] Jeremy Beckett observed that during the Institute's first decade it was little more than an 'Institute of Nostalgia' bent on salvaging the last remnants of Aboriginal culture and favouring studies of old typologies in 'archaeology, rock art, linguistics, and films of the "last" performance of this or that ceremony'.[139] It was not until the 1970s, as indigeneity was recognised as 'enduring into modernity rather than vanishing before it', that the Institute began to support studies of 'living cultures' across the continent. This reflected in part the growing active involvement of Indigenous people in Institute activities.

Another new site for research, also based in Canberra, was the Social Science Research Council, funded by the federal government and the Myer Foundation. Former principal of the Australian School of Pacific Administration Charles Rowley was commissioned to head its major project, *Aborigines in Australian Society*, which produced seven volumes covering Aboriginal population trends, attitudes, special conditions, settlements, and plans for integration with three volumes by Rowley on the history of Aboriginal policy and practice.[140] Rowley's trilogy provided a 'relentless' analysis of discriminatory laws and social conditions in the states and territories and linked this to Aborigines' 'deep-seated distrust … of officialdom' that 'for most of this century confined them to dependency and pauperism'.[141] The study stands as a classic history of the destruction and survival of Aboriginal society and is widely recognised as one of the great scholarly and moral achievements of Australia's intellectual history. At the time it 'heralded a flood of new white writing about Aboriginal historical experience'.[142]

Rowley was also an outspoken critic of assimilation. In his 1962 *Oceania* article he argued that the term had come to signify 'a means of disappearance of the Aborigines. It earlier assumed that he would die out and be replaced; in the context of the same popular prejudice the disappearance is now to be of another kind. All will in time come to be exactly the typical Australian.'[143] Rowley compared assimilation with programs operating in the United States between the 1860s and 1934, where government efforts to suppress culture and force assimilation through a process of 'ruthless benevolence and benevolent ruthlessness' served to 'keep alive resentment against whites; and to strengthen the bonds of loyalty within the persecuted group'.[144] The 1934 Indian Reorganisation Act abandoned assimilation for an enlightened program of cultural revival and appreciation and the goal that 'there might be, indefinitely, American citizens with systems of belief and affiliations quite different from those of the majority as long as all were equal before the law'.[145] Rowley looked optimistically to a future where a monolithic white Australia would be replaced by a 'multi-racial Australia with very different problems and opportunities for Aborigines'.[146] His vision of the way forward was through equal rights, a secure social and economic base with land and property, transfer of control to community councils, assistance provided on request, appropriate housing, and managerial skills. Meanwhile welfare authorities should be left to get on with the real job of welfare.[147] Twenty years later Rowley was still venting his wrath on the policy of assimilation. He wrote in a report in 1982 that 'it does seem fitting to remind ourselves of the idiocy of the "assimilation" policy and the rigid control of Aboriginal lives by an officialdom restricted by pious humbugs instead of policies which assume racial equality'.[148]

It was Stanner who famously attacked 'the great Australian silence' about the colonial past and criticised academic historians for relegating Aboriginal people to a 'melancholy footnote' in the nation's history. He noted that 'inattention on such a scale' could not be due to 'absentmindedness' but was a 'structural matter, a view from a window which has been carefully placed to exclude a whole quadrant of the landscape'.[149] It could be argued that assimilation sought to remove even the passing historical footnote by erasing the Aboriginal past, present *and* future. Up to this point anthropologists had dominated Aboriginal history, either by providing historians with the necessary background to inform their research or by writing their own social histories of Aboriginal–white relations, regional studies, analyses of broad historical trends, and micro-histories of individual life experiences. Elkin's stages of adaptation framed most of their accounts of the past.

Academic history may have been gripped by a deep silence, but as we have seen there was a clamour of popular interest in the Aboriginal past. Aboriginal narratives in particular challenged existing paradigms and assumptions and drove the need for new accounts for the past. There was also the influence of international social movements formed around gender, race, class and ethnicity that were generating new knowledges and methodologies within the discipline of history. These new perspectives were brought to bear on the task of uncovering new historical understandings. During the 1970s the new vanguard of 'Aboriginal historians' successfully colonised Aboriginal history. The academic discipline they created, pioneered by historians such as Henry Reynolds and Raymond Evans, for the first time addressed the violence of colonial frontiers and race relations in Australia.[150] This proved to be a highly charged and contested domain: during the 1980s Aboriginal people publicly challenged academic historians' right to represent their past, then in the 1990s the history wars erupted over conflicting versions of frontier and colonial histories.

Once the objective of legislative reform had been achieved in the 1960s the paths of government (state and federal) and Aboriginal organisations diverged sharply as Aboriginal people pushed more radical rights agendas. Frustration within government departments in achieving the goals of assimilation mounted as new reliable statistical data on Aboriginal conditions showed an appalling state of affairs after almost two decades of assimilation policy. The first attempt at a comprehensive National Census in 1966 counted an Aboriginal population of 80,027 making 0.7 per cent of the Australian population. Fifty per cent were under the age of twenty-one, only 27 per cent were in the work force, and 23 per cent of school age children had no schooling compared to 0.9 per cent for the general population. A government report on poverty in 1966 found that 'probably 90 per cent of people of Aboriginal descent in Australia are living in poverty, some to a degree matched only in the most backward of the poverty-stricken areas of Asia, Africa and Latin America.'[151]

Federal intervention and control following the referendum seemed to be the only hope. In 1967 the Holt Liberal government set up the Council for Aboriginal Affairs, with H. C. Coombs, Stanner and former Australian ambassador Barrie Dexter at the helm. Coombs stated in his Walter Murdoch Lecture in 1976 that Council members' consultations with Aboriginal people convinced them that most Aborigines did not see assimilation as 'an attractive or even acceptable future'. 'Tradition oriented communities' wanted to return to 'the simplicity of the old way' while Aborigines in rural and urban areas 'aspired to a separate identity' but also 'wanted roles in its economy which were difficult to reconcile with separateness and independence'. Coombs emphasised that for both traditional and urban groups, assimilation could not replace the 'moral and emotional authority of the Aboriginal tradition'. Based on these findings the Council set out to modify assimilation policy by supporting the right of Aborigines to 'build alternative life styles in which characteristically Aboriginal identity would be possible; in which reasonable economic and social security could be found without subservience; and in which Aborigines could take up self-chosen tasks and challenges with some hope of success'.[152]

In 1972 the Whitlam Labor government was elected with an Aboriginal platform committed to introducing land rights, a land fund, a form of self-determination, anti-discrimination legislation, Aboriginal legal aid, and the legal basis for the incorporation of Aboriginal communities and organisations. Funding was dramatically increased from $44 million in 1973 to $200 million by 1975. In 1975 the Whitlam government passed the *Racial Discrimination Act* and in the following year the Fraser government passed the *Northern Territory Land Rights Act.* However the objective of assimilation was not formally repudiated. According to Coombs the breakthrough moment was the Liberal Country Party Coalition Policy for the 1975 election, which made no reference to assimilation. Instead it stated that 'we recognise the fundamental right of Aborigines to retain their racial identity and traditional life style or where desired to adopt a partially or wholly European life style'.[153] These developments suggested that the assimilation policy was dead and buried and that there was no prospect that it could ever be resurrected. Coombs thought otherwise and concluded that 'it is certain that despite its disappearance from formal statements of policy, "assimilation" remains the unstated and unconscious source and purpose of official actions in many aspects of government action bearing upon Aborigines'.[154]

In the new century the Howard government's agenda has been to instate a form of retro-assimilation that harks back to Hasluck's policy of fifty years ago with its insistence that Aboriginal families in remote, rural and urban Australia adopt the suburban way of life. The national reconciliation program, which acknowledged collective national responsibility for past wrongs and Indigenous self-determination and rights, was scrapped along with the federal Aboriginal and Torres Strait Islander Commission and replaced by the lean backdoor meal of practical reconciliation and shared responsibility agreements and a revived emphasis on Aborigines' responsibilities as citizens. In 2007 their citizenship rights and the protections of international human rights covenants were trampled on by the federal government's unprecedented military-style response to the shocking accounts of Aboriginal child abuse in the *Little Children are Sacred Report* (2007). Politicians used the crisis language of military campaigns and natural disasters like Hurricane Katrina to rationalise the decision, made without any prior consultation, to intervene urgently and forcefully in Aboriginal communities across the Northern Territory. Raimond Gaita has pointed out that no other community of Australian citizens would *ever* be treated with such total disrespect and argues that the heat and passion of political rhetoric about child abuse clouded over the depths of contempt and underlying racism that made possible this unparalleled action.[155] In 1996 the Aboriginal and Torres Strait Islander Social Justice Commissioner Mick Dodson observed in his H. C. (Nugget) Coombs Northern Australia Inaugural Lecture that the measures of assimilation could never guarantee equality for Aboriginal people. He argued that rights of citizenship and international human rights instruments 'did not inherently accrue to [them] but were instead a reward if they had renounced their Aboriginality and embraced the dominant status quo. It was equality based not on respect for racial difference, but on the denial of your race.' Dodson concluded that 'assimilation was then, just as it is now, about what white fellas want. What they want first for themselves, and second, what they want for us'.[156]

Challenging migrant assimilation

The federal government did not produce a strict definition of its policy of migrant assimilation although it was integral to its programs of migrant selection and settlement. Social scientists researching migration issues and advising the government were exposed to new international trends through their involvement with UNESCO projects and conferences, contributing to a more open attitude to change than was evident in Aboriginal affairs. In his report on the UNESCO Havana conference in 1959 Wilfred Borrie had already drawn attention to the global trend towards cultural pluralism. In the same year delegates at the Australian Citizenship Convention unanimously agreed that 'immigration policy should aim at integration of new settlers rather than assimilation' and in 1964 integration became the 'accepted doctrine' of the Department of Immigration.[157] According to Rowse, the social sciences were moving towards a form of 'managed pluralism' that would develop into the policy of multiculturalism that actively encouraged and assisted migrants to maintain their cultural identities, more than a decade before it was formally adopted it as national policy following the recommendations of the 1978 Galbally report.[158]

Borrie also reported in 1959 on international acknowledgement of the importance of ethnic organisations and the tolerance of migrant cultures and networks for successful migration. His colleague Charles Price described the organisations as the 'fortresses erected by immigrants in their fight to adapt themselves to Australian conditions'.[159] In the short term they assisted with adjustment and enhanced the merging of subsequent generations into the Australian way of life. Although the Department of Immigration initially opposed their formation, the organisations developed to fill the gaps in government services and lobbied for improvements. The tide had changed by the late 1960s when the department began to transfer delivery of some services to the organisations and prepared to dismantle the Department of Immigration and mainstream its other responsibilities.

Immigration levels had dropped substantially by 1973 as the Whitlam Labor government responded to the end of the long economic boom and the contraction of the local labour market. Three years later Australia experienced its first net immigration loss in thirty years and thereon annual intakes fluctuated with labor market conditions and political trends.[160] Australia's White Australia policy — reflecting as it did the potential to become assimilated — gave way to universally applied selection criteria based on skills and qualifications and humanitarian considerations of family reunion and refugee status. The infamous Dictation test was abolished in 1958, Turkish and Lebanese migration commenced in the early 1960s, limited Asian entry began in 1966 and the White Australia policy was officially discarded in 1973 by the Whitlam government. In 1975 preferential rights for British, Irish and Commonwealth citizens were removed from the *Australian Citizenship Act.*

In the 1970s and 1980s Australia carefully juggled foreign policy and local political concerns in responding to the urgent need to take in refugees fleeing conflicts in Asia, Africa, Latin America and the Middle East. The government's decision to take in refugees in the wake of the Indochinese refugee crisis from 1975 was a turning point but it was only reached after an 'unseemly display of indifference and buck-passing'.[161] In the following year the government announced Australia's first refugee policy in a statement of principles tabled in parliament by immigration minister Michael MacKellar. This became the basis of Australia's annual refugee program from 1981.

Public concern has continued over issues of assimilability, and concentrations of ethnic communities, multiculturalism and Asian migration remain contentious.[162] From the 1990s mass international population movements of migrants and refugees have impacted on Australia. The treatment of 'boat people' attempting to land on Australian territory and the incarceration and punitive treatment of asylum seekers have divided the nation: the Tampa Crisis in 2001 when a boatload of 433 mostly Afghan asylum-seekers were refused entry to the Australian mainland; the 'Pacific Solution' where refugees were transferred to detention in Nauru; the 'Children overboard affair' also in 2001 when the government claimed that parents on a boat carrying suspected asylum seekers threw their children overboard; and the innumerable instances of complaint and protest at conditions in Australia's immigrant detention centres. Heated public debate settled into a stand-off that continues to divide the nation to this day, between critics who accuse the government of inhumane treatment of refugees, and its supporters who argue the need for a firm position to protect Australia's sovereignty. Arguments for both sides were set out in the pages of the Melbourne newspaper, the *Age,* in 2003 in a clash between historians Stuart Macintyre and Barry York.

Macintyre claimed that Australia's past humanitarian refugee program stood 'in marked contrast to the present arrangements of internment, forced repatriation and separation; of excision of territorial waters and imposition on our neighbours; of turning back frail boats and of lies about children overboard. The contrast is shameful and it debases our public institutions as well as our moral repute.' According to Macintyre the change reflected 'deep rifts within and between nation states, the unprecedented numbers of people who are cast adrift, and the commercialisation of large-scale movements of people across border controls'.[163] By contrast York argued that 'practical concerns' had always determined Australia's attitude to refugees and there was 'no basis for assertions that the present policy is a reversion to racial exclusion, or motivated by fear of "the Other"'. Stressing the need for a 'planned system' he claimed that Australia is doing its share to relieve the world's refugee problem, as one of only nine nations with an annual refugee resettlement program. According to UN statistics Australia's resettlement program of 42 per 100,000 of its population makes it 'the world's most generous nation for resettling refugees', with Canada coming in at second with 33 per 100,000.[164]

While many Australians continue to support multiculturalism, the growing ethnic diversity is drawing strong reactions from some sectors of the population seeking a return to the cultural homogeneity promised by assimilation. Hostility expressed in outbursts of racism, ethnocentrism and xenophobia has been compounded by the fear factor of terrorism. With the intention of restoring the hegemony of settler Australian ideals and culture, the conservative Howard government has devised opportunities to emphasise the alienness of refugees and given its implicit consent to campaigns of demonisation against 'people of Middle Eastern appearance'. Quoting from a 2004 report by the Human Rights Equal Opportunity Commission on 'symbolic and physical violence' against these Australians, cultural studies analyst Joseph Pugliese concludes that the many testimonies of racialised violence in the report 'exemplify the manner in which the civic spaces of our nation — the streets, the schools and so on — are becoming off-limits to particular Australian residents and citizens that have been framed not only as "unAustralian" but as prospective terrorists'.[165]

The Howard government has also revived unifying national ceremonies such as Anzac Day, the teaching of citizenship values in schools, and pressure on new immigrants to take up Australian citizenship — after first passing the prerequisite citizenship knowledge test. In Australian schools, values education promoting 'concern for equity, excellence and the promotion of a caring, civil and just society' is now a core part of the curriculum. Migrants seeking citizenship study the government booklet *Let's Participate: A Course in Australian Citizenship*. In December 2006 the government announced plans to introduce a computer test in

English and to require applicants to sign 'a statement that they understood the values of Australian society, including respect for the freedom and dignity of the individual, sexual equality, freedom of religion, commitment to the rule of law, parliamentary democracy and "a spirit of egalitarianism that embraces mutual respect, fair play and compassion for those in need"'.[166] In 2006 the government announced its intention to drop the term 'multiculturalism' and then in 2007 the Department of Immigration and Multicultural Affairs was renamed the Department of Immigration and Citizenship. Howard explained that 'the policy fundamentals of multiculturalism' would be retained within the framework of 'a shared national identity based on a core set of values'.[167]

'If there is a taste of ashes on the lips of white Australian civilisation,' writes H. C. Coombs, 'it is because while we have mastered a continent and subordinated a proud people, we have remained in spirit aliens and strangers to it and them.'[168] There is also an enduring sense of alienation from the waves of immigrants who did not fit the profile of White Australia. Today we live with a heightened sense of anxiety about strangers, fears of enemies lurking within national borders, and jittery governments forever on the alert — the legacy of a world of terrorism, globalisation and mass population movement. In the 1950s the world devised a seductive solution to global threats: if we all became the same we would no longer be strangers or enemies. Governments spun tempting dreams of universal rights and equality projected through images of family, a common way of life, and shared values. Conform to these ways and you will prosper and find acceptance, was the message. However, the truth was that the prosperous prospered and the rest struggled on, while conflict and threats of conflict continued apace. Enmeshed in today's anxieties we are vulnerable to the same spin that plays on our fears with promises of a safe place where there will be no strangers and the problems of others can slip into the deep recesses of forgetting. This inattention compounds a worsening scenario. Recognising the spin and seeing beyond it might just propel us into the clear light of a better future.

Endnotes

Introduction

1 *Woody Allen Movies: The Films of Woody Allen*, www.woodyallenmovies.com/woodyallenquotes.htm
2 Cited in Jan Lee Martin 2005, *Australian Futures in Community.*
3 Tim Rowse (ed.) 2005, *Contesting Assimilation*, cover notes.
4 Rowse, *Contesting Assimilation*, p. 19.
5 Zygmunt Bauman 1991, *Modernity and Ambivalence*, p. 107.
6 Cited in Marie Reay (ed.) 1964, *Aborigines Now*, p. ix.
7 ibid., p. ix.
8 Makere Stewart-Harawira, 2005, *The New Imperial Order*, pp. 17–18.
9 Patrick Wolfe n.d., *Globally Speaking.*
10 Robert van Krieken 2005, 'Assimilation and liberal government', pp. 43–4.
11 Anna Haebich 2002, 'Imagining assimilation', p. 10.
12 Shih Chih-yu 2002, *Negotiating Ethnicity in China: Citizenship as a Response to the State,* Routledge, London, pp. 14, 16–17.
13 Rowse, *Contesting Assimilation*, p. 19.

Chapter 1

1 Ernst Bloch 1995, *The Principle of Hope Volume One*, p. 3. The book was written in the United States between 1938 and 1947, revised in 1953 and 1959 and first translated into English in 1986.
2 Ghassan Hage 2003, *Against Paranoid Nationalism*, p. 3.
3 Claude Levi Strauss 1968, 'Race and History', in *Race and History The Race Question in Modern Science*, pp. 257–8.
4 Abigail Solomon-Godeau 2004, '"The Family of Man". Refurbishing humanism for a postmodern age', p 29.
5 R. Bessell and D. Schumann 2003, *Life After Death*, pp. 2–3.
6 James Carroll 2006, *House of War*, p. 80.
7 Bessell and Schumann, *Life After Death*, p. 7.
8 Nicholas Brown 1995, *Governing Prosperity*, p. 1.
9 Rosch Krieps 2004, 'The family of man', p. 261.
10 ibid., p. 263.
11 Elizabeth Vassilieff 1959, 'Explaining man to man', p. 38.
12 Cited in Eric Sandeen 2004, 'The show you see with your heart: "The Family of Man" on tour in the Cold War world', p. 103.
13 Sandeen 2004, 'The show you see with your heart', p. 115.
14 Rosch Krieps 2005, *Golden Jubilee of Edward Steichen's Legendary Photo Exhibition The Family of Man.*
15 Sandeen 2004, 'The show you see with your heart', p. 115.

16 Marc-Emmanuel Melon 2004, 'The patriarchal family', p. 69.
17 Andrea Tone 2005, 'Listening to the past', p. 378.
18 ibid., p. 377.
19 J. M. Metzl, 2003, *Prozac on the Couch*, pp. 74–5.
20 Metzl, *Prozac on the Couch*, p. 73; Tone, 'Listening to the Past', p. 377.
21 *Pix*, 7 May 1955, p. 2.
22 Hugh Mackay 1997, *Generations*, p. 61.
23 Sue Taffe 1995, 'Australian diplomacy in a policy vacuum'; John Chesterman 2005, *Civil Rights*.
24 Chesterman, *Civil Rights*.
25 Tim Rowse, 2006, 'Review of *Civil Rights*', p. 218.
26 Editorial *Woman's Day* July 1950, cited in John Murphy 2000, *Imagining the Fifties*, p. 95.
27 Carroll, *House of War*, p. 127.
28 Brown, *Governing Prosperity*, p. 37.
29 Murphy, *Imagining the Fifties*, p. 93.
30 *Woman's Day* July 1950, cited in Murphy, *Imagining the Fifties*, p. 95.
31 L. J. Louis 2001, *Menzies' Cold War*, p. 14.
32 *News-Weekly* cited in Murphy, *Imagining the Fifties*, p. 130.
33 Louis, *Menzies' Cold War*, p. 75.
34 J. W. Knott 1952, 'Events and issues that made news in 1952'.
35 Carroll, *House of War* pp. 201–3.
36 Graham Shirley and Brian Adams 1983, *Australian Cinema*, p. 208.
37 *Pix*, 6 February 1954, p. 2.
38 Jessie Lennon 2000, *I'm the One That Know That Country*, pp. 95–7.
39 Murphy, *Imagining the Fifties*, p. 97.
40 Louis, *Menzies' Cold War*, p. 45.
41 David Hilliard 1997, 'Church, family and sexuality in Australia in the 1950s', pp. 133–4.
42 H. I. London 1970, Non-white Immigration and the 'White Australia' Policy, p. 78.
43 S. Macintyre 1998, *The Reds*, p. 51.
44 Communist Party of Australia 1967, *Full Human Rights for Aborigines and Torres Strait Islanders*, p. 20.
45 Lauren Marsh, personal communication, 2007.
46 NAA A1838 557/2 Part 4.
47 Taffe, 'Australian diplomacy', p. 165.
48 ibid.
49 Cited in Anna Haebich 2000, *Broken Circles*, p. 425.
50 Cited in Taffe, 'Australian diplomacy', p. 162.
51 Cited in ibid., p. 158.
52 NAA A1838 557/2 Part 1, 1956–1960.
53 NAA A1838 557/2 Part 3, 1956–1960. The correspondence is discussed in Chesterman, *Civil Rights*, p. 57; Taffe, 'Australian diplomacy' p. 161; and Jennifer Clark, 1997, '"Something to hide?"', pp. 79–80.
54 NAA A1838 557/2 Part 4, 14/2/1963.

55 Cited in Ann Curthoys 2002, *Freedom Ride*, p. 14.
56 NAA A452/1 1952/403.
57 Rowse, 'Review of Civil Rights', p. 218.
58 Taffe, 'Australian diplomacy', p. 171.
59 Commonwealth Parliamentary Debates House of Representatives 22/11/1946, p. 508.
60 Murphy, *Imagining the Fifties*, pp. 156–7.
61 Susan Sheridan 2000, 'The Australian woman and her migrant others in the postwar *Australian Women's Weekly*', p. 123.
62 Murphy, *Imagining the Fifties*, p. 135.
63 Sarah Scott 2002, 'Imagining a nation', pp. 58, 60.
64 Serim Timur 2000, 'Changing trends and major issues in international migration', p. 165.
65 Alexander Weinstock, S. 1960, 'Review of *The Cultural Integration of Immigrants: A Survey Based Upon the Papers and Proceedings of the UNESCO Conference held in Havana, April, 1956*, by W. D. Borrie'.
66 NAA 1838/1 8622/4/1.
67 Brown, *Governing Prosperity*, p. 33.
68 Mary Ann Glendon 2001, *A World Made New*, p. 233.
69 United Nations Headquarters, www.un.org/Pubs/CyberSchoolBus/untour/subunh.htm.
70 Alastair Bonnett 2000, *Anti-racism*, p. 24.
71 Julian Huxley, cited at www.crossroad.to/Quotes/globalism/julian-huxley.htm.
72 Glendon, *A World Made New*, p. 119ff.
73 Ann-Mari Jordens 1995, *Redefining Australians*, pp. 8–9.
74 Ivan Hannaford 1996, *Race*, p. 372.
75 Julian Huxley and A.C. Haddon 1936, *We Europeans*, cited in Hannaford, *Race*, pp. 372–3.
76 Hannaford, *Race*, pp. 385–7.
77 David Goldsworthy 2002, *Losing the Blanket*, p. 88.
78 Marcia Langton 1999, 'Why race is a central idea in Australia's construction of the idea of a nation', p. 35.
79 NAA A1838 557/2, Part 1.
80 UNESCO 1950, *The Race Question.*
81 Hannaford, *Race*, p. 385.
82 ibid., p. 387.
83 David J. Seddon 1971, 'Review: *Race and Science; Passing for White*', p. 130.
84 Langton, 'Why race is a central idea', p. 29.
85 *United Nations Declaration on the Elimination of All Forms of Racial Discrimination*, Proclaimed by General Assembly resolution 1904 (XVIII) of 20 November 1963, www.unhchr.ch/html/menu3/b/9.htm.
86 Kamala Visweswaran 1998, 'Race and the rise of anthropology', p. 76.
87 Bonnett, *Anti-racism*, p. 46ff.
88 Department of Aboriginal and Torres Strait Islander Policy, *A post-contact history of Cape York: Volume 2.*
89 Haebich, *Broken Circles*, pp. 430–5.

90 Chesterman, *Civil Rights*, p. 53.
91 Cited in Chesterman, *Civil Rights*, p. 53.
92 Ravi de Costa 2006, *A Higher Authority*, p. 70.
93 ibid., p. 70.
94 David Goldsworthy 2005, 'Australian external policy and the end of Britain's empire'.
95 Taffe, 'Australian diplomacy', p. 156.
96 Josef L. Kunz 1954, 'Chapter XI of the United Nations Charter in action', pp. 7–8.
97 Ravi de Costa 2006, *A Higher Authority*, p. 69.
98 Nicholas Brown 1995, *Governing Prosperity*, p. 55.
99 Goldsworthy, *Losing the Blanket*, p. 95.
100 ibid., pp. 23–4.
101 *Pix*, 6 July 1957, p. 6; 6 April 1957, p. 44.
102 *Pix*, 19 July 1958, p. 11.
103 'History of South Africa in the apartheid era', from *Wikipedia*, the free encyclopedia, http://en.wikipedia.org/wiki/Apartheid
104 Wikinews 2005, *Historic summit, commemoration by Asian-African leaders in Bandung April 26, 2005*, http://en.wikinews.org/wiki/Historic_summit,_commemoration_by_Asian-African_leaders_in_Bandung)
105 Richard Wright 1956, *The Color Curtain*, p. 115.
106 ibid., pp. 89–91.
107 *Examiner* 30 December 1954, cited in Wright, Richard *The Color Curtain*, p. 84.
108 Bandung was a significant step towards the first Summit of the Non-Aligned Movement in 1961 with its 100 state membership representing 55 per cent of the world's population. Its influence continues to this day and in 2005 a commemorative Bandung Summit was co-hosted by Indonesia and South Africa with 89 African and Asian countries present to celebrate the 'Bandung Spirit' and its original principles of non-aggression and peaceful friendship. The Summit produced the 2005 Declaration on the New Asian-African Strategic Partnership. http://en.wikipedia.org/wiki/Bandung_Conference; Wikinews Historic summit …
109 Stewart-Harawira, *The New Imperial Order*, pp. 127–8.
110 ibid., p. 77.
111 NAA A1838 557/1 Part 1 1954–1961.
112 Stewart-Harawira, *The New Imperial Order*, p. 77.
113 de Costa, *A Higher Authority*, pp. 70–71.
114 Stewart-Harawira, *The New Imperial Order*, p. 129.
115 Office of the United Nations High Commissioner for Human Rights, *Indigenous and Tribal Peoples Convention, 1989 (No. 169).*
116 Catherine J. Iorns 1993, 'The draft Declarations of the Rights of Indigenous Peoples', p. 1.
117 Working group on Indigenous Populations 1994, *Draft United Nations Declaration on the rights of Indigenous peoples.*

118 ABC News 14 September 2007, antar-news <antar-news@lists.antarqld.org.au>
119 ABC News 15 September 2007, antar-news <antar-news@lists.antarqld.org.au>
120 Human Rights and Equal Opportunity Commission Friday, 14 September 2007, antar-news <antar-news@lists.antarqld.org.au>
121 K. J. Twetchett 1972, 'Review of The United Nations and decolonisation', p. 282.
122 Taffe, 'Australian diplomacy', p. 161
123 NAA A1838 557/2/ Part 4; Douglas Lockwood 1962, *I the Aboriginal*.
124 NAA A1838 557/2/ Part 4, p. 3.
125 NAA A1838 5572/2 Part 1, 1956–1960.
126 NAA A1838 557/2/ Part 4.
127 Cited in Taffe, 'Australian diplomacy', pp. 162–3.
128 NAA A1838 557/2/ Part 4, 1965.
129 Cited in Taffe, 'Australian diplomacy', p. 162.
130 Chesterman, *Civil Rights*, p. 57.
131 NAA A1838/2, 9929/5/3, Part 1.

Chapter 2

1 Michael Ignatieff 1996, 'There's no place like home: the politics of belonging', pp. 97–8.
2 Cited in Matthew Jordan 2006, 'The reappraisal of the White Australia Policy against the background of a changing Asia, 1945–67', p. 231.
3 Cited in Joseph Pugliese 2006, 'I am, you are …', p. 2.
4 Egypt, Iraq and Lebanon quit over the Suez Crisis; the People's Republic of China protested at the presence of the Republic of China; and Netherlands, Spain and Switzerland withdrew following the Soviet invasion of Hungary.
5 http://en.wikipedia.org/wiki/1956_Summer_Olympics
6 Graeme Davison 1997, 'Welcoming the world', p. 74.
7 *Herald and Sun News-Pictorial* 1954, 'The Royal Tour to Australia and New Zealand in pictures', Melbourne.
8 Davison, 'Welcoming the world', p. 73.
9 Suzanne Schech and Jane Haggis 2000, 'Migrancy, whiteness and the settler self in contemporary Australia', p. 234.
10 ANIB 1956, *Australia — Your Host: XVIth Olympiad*, pp. 22, 25, 29, 65.
11 Anthony Moran 2005, 'White Australia, settler nationalism and Aboriginal assimilation', pp. 168–9.
12 van Krieken, 'Assimilation and liberal government', p. 43.
13 Andrew Markus 2003, 'Of continuities and discontinuities', pp. 175–6.
14 Ghassan Hage 2003, *Against Paranoid Nationalism*, pp. 53–4.
15 From Australian politician Sir Henry Parkes' original epigram 'the crimson thread of kinship runs through us all' used by him in addresses to the 1890 Federation Conference in Melbourne: Helen Irving 1999, *The Crimson Thread of Kinship*.
16 A. A. Calwell, *Federal Parliamentary Debates*, 3/9/1948, p. 1060.
17 James Jupp 2002, *From White Australia to Woomera*, p. 12.
18 Andrew Markus 1994, *Australian Race Relations*, p. 110.

19 David Dutton 2002, *One of Us? A Century of Australian Citizenship*, p. 4.
20 Richard Bosworth 2001, 'Post-war Italian migration', pp. 505–6.
21 Peter Kivisto 2002, *Multiculturalism in a Global Society*, p. 29.
22 Ann-Mari Jordens 1997, *Alien to Citizen*, p. 192.
23 Cited in ibid., p. 192.
24 Alistair Davidson 1997, *From Subject to Citizen*, pp. 158–62.
25 Patricia Jenkings 2001, Australian political elites and citizenship education for 'New Australians' 1945–1960, PhD University of Sydney, p. 53ff.
26 Patrick Wolfe 2006, 'Operation Sandy Track', *Overland*, no. 183, Winter, p. 29.
27 Donald Fixico 2004, 'Federal and state policies and American Indians', p. 385.
28 Cited in Haebich, *Broken Circles*, p. 131.
29 John McCorquodale 1987, *Aborigines and the Law.*
30 Chesterman, John and Galligan, Brian 1997, *Citizens Without Rights: Aborigines and Australian Citizenship*, p. 3.
31 ibid., p. 3.
32 Ann-Mari Jordens 1995, *Redefining Australians*, p.4.
33 Davidson, *From Subject to Citizen*, p. 193.
34 Term coined by solicitor Bob Haebich during hearings of the complaints of racial discrimination by payment of under award wages to employees of the Queensland government: *Bligh & Ors v. State of Queensland* (1966) HREOCA p. 28.
35 Philip J. Deloria, 2004, *Indians in Unexpected Places*, p. 28.
36 Peter Read 2005, '"A rape of the soul so profound"', pp. 25–6; Rowse, *Contesting Assimilation*, p. 4.
37 Haebich, *Broken Circles*, p. 259.
38 See Heather Douglas 2004, 'Assimilation, Lutheranism and the 1950s justice of Kriewaldt', p. 12.
39 Michel Foucault 1977, *Discipline and Punish.*
40 See Aboriginal statutes passed in Queensland (1897), Western Australia (1905), and South Australia and the Northern Territory (1911). For annotated list of West Australian legislation see Anna Haebich 2000, 'A chronological list of legislation impacting on Aboriginal people in Western Australia 1841–1972', typescript.
41 Warwick Anderson 2002, *The Cultivation of Whiteness*, p. 40.
42 Conditions were strict: the applicant had to be at least 21 years of age, to have served for three years in the French military or public service, to be able to speak French, be of good character, to have demonstrated meritorious service to France and to have 'sufficient material means of existence'. Successful applicants were required to renounce their local customary status, which could result in loss of traditional rights and isolation from their community. In practice this was a trade that many *indigenes* were not prepared to make, preferring to live instead under the *code de l'indigenat*, which empowered police and administrators to summarily punish them for a host of petty offences by imposing fines, corporal punishment, imprisonment, forced labour or confiscating their property. See Robert Aldrich 1996, *Greater France*, p. 213.
43 See Foucault, *Discipline and Punish*, pp. 195–228.

44 Anderson, *The Cultivation of Whiteness*, pp. 235–6.
45 Catriona Elder 1999, 'What is the white in white Australia? A reading of A.O. Neville's *Australia's Coloured Minority*', pp. 28, 29, 32.
46 Diane Barwick, cited in Anna Cole 2000, The glorified flower: Race, gender and assimilation in Australia, 1937–77, p. 29.
47 A. P. Elkin 1951, 'Reaction and interaction', pp. 164–86.
48 Russell McGregor 1996, 'Intelligent parasitism: A. P. Elkin and the rhetoric of assimilation', p. 123.
49 Cited in Russell McGregor 1999, 'Wards, words and citizens', p. 246.
50 ibid., p. 253.
51 NAA A452 1961/1256.
52 A. P. Elkin 1957, 'Aboriginal policy 1930–1950'.
53 Frederick Alexander 1953, 'The Australian people and the world', p. 150.
54 Schech and Haggis, 'Migrancy, whiteness and the settler self in contemporary Australia', p. 233.
55 Markus, 'Of continuities and discontinuities', p. 180.
56 Alexander, 'The Australian people and the world', p. 149.
57 Gwenda Tavan 2005, *The Long Slow Death of White Australia*, p. 201.
58 Harold Holt 1953, 'Introduction', pp. 1–2.
59 Jordens, *Redefining Australians*, p. 56.
60 Dutton, *One of Us?*, pp. 57–60.
61 Ghassan Hage 1998, *White Nation.*
62 Jean I. Martin 1978, *The Migrant Presence*, pp. 207–8.
63 Emma Greenwood 1995, 'No migrants here: Migrant absence within Australian migrant publicity', p. 113.
64 Gwenda Tavan 1997, '"Good neighbours"', p. 80.
65 Discussion draws on Rowse, *Contesting Assimilation*; Van Krieken, 'Assimilation and liberal government'; and Bauman, *Modernity and Ambivalence*, and their analysis of the role of assimilation in nation-building.
66 Bauman, *Modernity and Ambivalence*, p. 104.
67 Tim Rowse 2005, 'The post-war social science of assimilation 1947–1966', p. 151.
68 Benedict Anderson 1991, *Imagined Communities*; Bauman, *Modernity and Ambivalence.*
69 Alexander, 'The Australian people and the world', pp. 152–8.
70 NAA (n.d.), 'Citizenship in Australia'.
71 Brian Galligan and Winsome Roberts 2004, *Australian Citizenship*, pp. xv–xvi.
72 Cited in Brown, *Governing Prosperity*, p. 185.
73 Susan Keen 1999, 'Associations in Australian history', pp. 642, 655, 658.
74 Cited in Noam Chomsky 1989, *Necessary Illusions*, p. 30.
75 Vance Packard 1962, *The Hidden Persuaders*, pp. 11–13.
76 Clara Zawawi 2000, 'A history of public relations in Australia'.
77 Henry Mayer 1964, *The Press in Australia*, p. 139.
78 ibid.
79 Murphy, *Imagining the Fifties*, p. 37.
80 Mayer, *The Press in Australia*, p. 31.

81 ibid., p. 228.
82 *Australia Today* Newsreel, Australianscreen.com http://australianscreen.com.au/titles/australia-today-australias-5th.
83 J. B. Black 1975, *Organising the Propaganda Instrument*, pp. x–xi.
84 NAA CA 219 ANIB, Canberra (1950–1973).
85 Brown, *Governing Prosperity*, p. 186.
86 Alex Carey 1995, *Taking the Risk Out of Democracy*, p 124.
87 Cited in Packard, *The Hidden Persuaders*, p. 161.
88 Jordens, *Alien to Citizen*, p. 78.
89 Carey, *Taking the Risk Out of Democracy*, p. 27.
90 Richard White 1979, 'The Australian way of life', p. 540.
91 Van Krieken, 'Assimilation and the liberal government', p. 40.
92 James Jupp 1966, *Arrivals and Departures*, pp. 146–7, 178.
93 Rowse, 'The post-war social science', p. 161.
94 White, 'The Australian way of life', p. 536.
95 Cited in ibid., p. 537.
96 Cited in ibid., p. 528.
97 *The Way We Live* 1959, 54 minutes, filmed for the Department of Immigration by Artransa Park Studios under the supervision of the Commonwealth Film Unit. Film Australia's Immigration Home, www.filmaust.com.au/immigration/content.htm.
98 Herbert Evatt 1942–1945, 'The Australian way of life'.
99 Others in the series are on the British, South African, French and Pakistani ways of life.
100 Sir Frederic W. Eggleston, 'The Australian nation', p. 6.
101 ibid., p. 16.
102 John O'Grady 1957, *They're a Weird Mob.*
103 George H. Johnston 1953, 'Their way of life', pp. 154–6.
104 London, *Non-white Immigration and the 'White Australia' Policy*, p. 161.
105 ibid., p. 167.
106 ibid., p. 109.
107 ibid., p. 159.
108 ibid., p. 115.
109 ibid., p. 167.
110 Murphy *Imagining Assimilation*, p. 199.
111 Judith Brett 1993, *Robert Menzies' Forgotten People*, pp. 172–3.
112 ibid., 172.
113 ibid., p. 164.
114 Carol Johnson cited in Sally Young 2004, *The Persuaders Inside the Hidden Machine of Political Advertising*, p. 224.
115 Judith O'Callaghan 1993, *The Australian Dream*, pp. 45–6.
116 Wilfred D. Borrie 1953, 'The family', p. 28.
117 ibid., pp. 36–7.
118 ibid., p. 38.
119 ibid., pp. 24–8.
120 ANIB 1964, *An Everyday Australian.*

121 Mackay, *Generations*, p. 29.
122 Brett, *Robert Menzies' Forgotten People*, p. 254.
123 Chris McAuliffe 1996, *Art and Suburbia*, p. 66.
124 Kristin Ross 1996, *Fast Cars, Clean Bodies*, p. 127.
125 Tim Winton 2004, *The Turning*, pp. 38–9.
126 Cited in McAuliffe, *Art and Suburbia*, p. 67.
127 Brown, *Governing Prosperity*, p. 159.
128 Murphy, *Imagining Assimilation*, pp. 202–6.
129 McAuliffe, *Art and Suburbia*, p. 68.
130 Mark Peel 1997, 'A new kind of manhood: remembering the 1950s', p. 149.
131 Marcia Langton, cited in Meaghan Morris 1993, 'Beyond assimilation', pp. 6–7.
132 Nancy Tuana 2004, 'Coming to understand', p. 194.
133 ibid.
134 Charles Mills 1997, *The Racial Contract*, p. 18.
135 Brett, *Robert Menzies' Forgotten People*, p. 165.
136 ibid., pp. 167–8.
137 ibid., p. 168.
138 ibid., p. 170.
139 ibid.
140 Kevin Gilbert 1988, 'Aboriginal sovereignty'.
141 Pauline Hanson 1998, *Pauline Hanson's Maiden Speech.*
142 Brett, *Robert Menzies' Forgotten People*, p. 169.
143 Geoffrey Partington 1996, *Hasluck versus Coombs*, p. 153.
144 Leigh Dale 1997, 'Mainstreaming Australia'.
145 Cited in Michael Dodson 1996, 'Assimilation Versus Self-Determination', p. 4.
146 Dale, 'Mainstreaming Australia', p. 6.
147 Excerpt from John Howard press conference outside Parliament House, Canberra, January 24 2007, www.pm.gov.au/media/Interview/2007/Interview2339.cfm.
148 Excerpt from Interview with Neil Mitchell, Radio 3AW, Melbourne, 24 February 2006, www.pm.gov.au/media/interview/2006/Interview1788.cfm.
149 Jim Collins 1989, *Uncommon Cultures*, p. 5.
150 Michael Gibbons 2004, 'Engagement with the community'.
151 See Judith Bessant and Amanda Wilkinson 2006, 'Principles for developing Indigenous policy-making'.
152 ibid., p. 104.
153 Kivisto, *Multiculturalism in a Global Society*, p. 27.
154 ibid., p. 29.
155 Rowse, 'The post-war social science', pp. 150–68.
156 Borrie, cited in ibid., p. 153.
157 Rowse, 'The post-war social science', pp. 153–4.
158 ibid., p. 153.
159 ibid., p. 154.
160 See W. D. Borrie 1959, *The Cultural Integration of Immigrants.*
161 Cited in F. W. Rudmin 2003, 'Catalogue of acculturation constructs', pp.

10–11.

162 Thelma Vlahonasiou 1983, 'Annual Citizenship Conventions 1950–1963', p. 131; 1961, pp. 152–3.
163 ibid., pp. 96, 194.
164 Davidson, *From Subject to Citizen,* p. 170.
165 A. P. Elkin 1938, *The Australian Aborigines,* p. x.
166 Tigger Wise 1985, *The Self-made Anthropologist,* p. 238.
167 A. P. Elkin 1944, *Citizenship for the Aborigines,* p. xi.
168 A. P. Elkin 1951, 'Reaction and interaction', pp. 164–86.
169 See Anna Haebich 2005, 'Contested histories'.
170 Miriam Dixon 1999, *The Imaginary Australian.*

Chapter 3

1 Charmian Clift 1970, *The World of Charmian Clift,* pp. 205–6.
2 Philip Deloria, *Indians in Unexpected Places,* p. 11.
3 ibid., p. 230.
4 Catriona Moore and Stephen Muecke 1984, 'Racism and the representation of Aborigines in film', pp. 36–9.
5 Emma Greenwood 1995, 'No migrants here', p. 119.
6 Jenkings, Australian political elites and citizenship education for 'New Australians' 1945–1960, p. 48.
7 Murphy, *Imagining the Fifties,* p. 156.
8 Greenwood, 'No Migrants Here', p. 109.
9 Susan Sheridan 2002, *Who Was That Woman?,* p. 144.
10 Greenwood, 'No Migrants Here', p. 117.
11 Sheridan, *Who Was That Woman?,* p. 144.
12 Sheridan, 'The "Australian Woman" and her Migrant Others', p. 182.
13 ibid., pp. 121–2.
14 Sheridan, *Who Was That Woman?,* p. 151.
15 Murphy, *Imagining the Fifties,* pp. 151–2.
16 Jordens, *Alien to Citizen,* p. 149.
17 Commonwealth of Australia 1986, *Immigration in Focus 1946–75,* pp. 13, 14, 39, 40.
18 *People,* 6 March 1957, p. 41.
19 Greenwood, 'No Migrants Here', p. 117.
20 Shirley and Adams, 1983, *Australian Cinema,* p. 192.
21 *Mike and Stefani* 1952, directed by Moslyn Williams for the Department of the Interior.
22 Greenwood, 'No Migrants Here', pp. 115–16.
23 Albert Moran and Errol Vieth 2006, *Film in Australia,* pp. 147–8.
24 *Double Trouble* 1951, by director Lee Robinson, Australian National Film Board production for the Department of the Interior.
25 *No Strangers Here* 1949, made for Department of Immigration by Dr K. Sternberg.
26 *The Cummington Story* 1945, produced by US Office of War Information.
27 Greenwood, 'No Migrants Here', p. 118.

28 NAA A445 261/5/1.
28 Rowena MacDonald 1995, 'Selling a Dream', p. 26.
30 Ale Liubinas 2003, *Homeland Lost*, p. 238.
31 Liubinas, *Homeland Lost*, p. 233; *The Overlanders* 1946, director Harry Watt.
32 Some were published in European languages — for example, *Beel van een natie* (Portrait of a nation), *Kennen Sie Australien?* (Do you know Australia?), and *Australie ihre Heimat* (Australia your home).
33 Artransa Park Studios with Commonwealth Film Unit, see Film Australia's Immigration Home Website, http://svc002.bne241p.server-web.com/programs/default.asp?sn=547
34 ANIB 1960, *A Look at Australia.*
35 Greenwood, 'No Migrants Here', p. 117.
36 ANIB 1951, *Australia and Your future.*
37 ibid., p. 2.
38 ibid., p. 8.
39 ibid., p. 44.
40 ibid., p. 6.
41 ANIB 1956, *About Australia*, Department of the Interior, Canberra, p. 4.
42 ibid., p. 5.
43 Murphy, *Imagining the Fifties*, p. 161–2.
44 William Dick 1965, *A Bunch of Ratbags*, Collins, London, pp. 66–7, cited in Murphy, *Imagining the Fifties*, p. 161.
45 Martin, *The Migrant Presence*, p. 29.
46 Cited in Catherine Panich 1988, *Sanctuary? Remembering Postwar Immigration*, p. 177.
47 National Archives of Australia n.d., 'Citizenship in Australia'.
48 Deirdre Mckeown 2002–03, *Changes in the Australian Oath of Citizenship.*
49 Vlahonasiou, 'Annual Citizenship Conventions', p. 72.
50 Vlahonasiou, 'Annual Citizenship Conventions', p. 171.
51 Jordens, *Alien to Citizen*, p. 174.
52 Martin, *The Migrant Presence*, p. 29.
53 Jordens, *Redefining Australians*, pp. 79–80.
54 Jenkings, 'Australian political elites', p. 154.
55 Vlahonasiou, 'Annual Citizenship Conventions', p. 1.
56 ibid., p. 85.
57 ibid., p. 60.
58 ibid., p. 79.
59 ibid., pp. 85, 47, 152–3.
60 ibid., p. 409.
61 William H. Cohn 1977, 'Popular culture and social history', p. 175.
62 Vlahonasiou, 'Annual citizenship conventions', p. 350.
63 ibid., p. 352.
64 NAA 453 1963/ 6724; NAA A1838 557/1, Part 1 14/3/1955.
65 ATSIC Public Affairs Office, *NAIDOC Week.*
66 NAA A1838 557/1 Part 1, 1954–61.
67 *Namatjira the Painter* 1947, Stanley Hawes, Lee Robinson (directors),

Production Company Australian Department of Information, Charles Mountford and Ralph Foster (Producers), Axel Poignant (Director of Photography).

68 Roslyn Poignant 1995, *Lost Conversation, Recovered Archives*, Tenth Eric Johnston Lecture, Occasional Paper No. 49.

69 For films, see *Walkabout* (1946) and *Tjurunga* (1946), both made with Charles Mountford, *Namatjira the Painter* (1946), film footage of 1950 Corroboree ballet for New York trade exhibitions; for pamphlet see *Facts about Australia* (1950).

70 Brown, *Governing Prosperity*, p. 33.

71 NAA A1838 557/2, Part 1, 1956–60.

72 NAA A1838 557/2, Part 1, 1956–60.

73 NAA A452/54, 1963/5501.

74 NAA A452/54, 1963/5501, pp. 364–5.

75 NAA A452 1961/216, pp. 173–4.

76 NAA A452 1963/3209 Distribution of *Aborigines and You.*

77 NAA 1960/219; NAA A4940/1 C347.

78 NAA 1838 577/2, Part 4; NAA A452 1960/6963.

79 NAA A452 1963/6724.

80 Tim Rowse 2000, *Obliged to be Difficult*, p. 17.

81 Chris Barker 1999, *Television, Globalisation and Cultural Identities*, p. 80.

82 Stuart Hall 1996, cited in Barker, *Television, Globalisation*, p. 84.

83 Commonwealth Government, Minister for Territories 1962, *Our Aborigines*, p. 5.

84 ibid., p. 4.

85 Commonwealth Government, Minister for Territories 1961, *One People*, p. 14.

86 ibid., p. 24.

87 Anne McClintock 1995, *Imperial Leather*, pp. 81, 82.

88 Kim Greenwell 2002, 'Picturing "civilisation"', p. 4.

89 ibid., p. 3.

90 Hooker Creek settlement (now Lajamanu) was located 580 kilometres southwest of Katherine in the Northern Territory and consisted mainly of Walbiri people forcibly moved there from Yuendumu in the early 1950s during a severe drought. Baptist mission involvement began in 1962. Hooker Creek operated as a welfare settlement into the mid-1970s and is now an Aboriginal community.

91 Deloria, *Indians in Unexpected Places*, pp. 55–6.

92 NAA A452 1957/2672.

93 NAA A452 1957/2672.

94 Carol Johnson, cited in Sally Young 2004, *The Persuaders Inside the Hidden Machine of Political Advertising*, p. 224.

95 Commonwealth Government, Minister for Territories 1958, *Assimilation of Our Aborigines*, p. 1.

96 Commonwealth Government, Minister for Territories 1963, *Aborigines and You*, pp. 31–2.

97 ibid., p. 11ff.

98 Steve Mickler 1998, 'The Perth press and problematising Aboriginal status'.
99 Deloria, *Indians in Unexpected Places*, p. 55.
100 Commonwealth Government, Minister for Territories, *One People*, pp. 27–32.
101 Catriona Moore 1984, 'The guiding hand: Representation and Aboriginal welfare politics', p. 31.
102 Commonwealth Government, Minister for Territories, *One People*, p. 10.
103 Commonwealth Government, Minister for Territories, *Aborigines and You*, p. 6.
104 ibid., p. 9.
105 Anna Cole 2000, The glorified flower, p. 191.
106 See Heather Goodall 1990, '"Saving the children"'.
107 Commonwealth Government, Minister for Territories 1959, *Fringe Dwellers*, p. 29.
108 NAA A1838 557/2 Part 1; Taffe, 'Australian diplomacy in a policy vacuum', p. 167.
109 NAA A1838/2, 9929/5/3, Part 1.
110 NAA A452 1960/6963.
111 NAA A452 1960/6963.
112 NAA A452 NT1964/4392, 1964–65.
113 Department of External Affairs 1964, *The Australian Aborigines*, pp. 7–9.
114 NAA A452 NT1964/4392 1964–65.
115 Produced by Collings Production Company.
116 Produced by Collings Production Company.
117 Sylvia Lawson 1964, 'Miss Denny's Aborigines', pp. 19–20.

Chapter 4

1 Oodgeroo Noonuccal 1981, 'Then and now', p. 91.
2 W. E. H. Stanner 1979, 'Continuity and change', p. 50.
3 W. E. H. Stanner 1979, 'Aborigines and Australian Society', p. 352.
4 James Jupp 1998, *Immigration*, p. 104.
5 Brian Murphy 1993, *The Other Australians*, p. 135.
6 Gary P. Freeman and James Jupp (eds) 1992, *Nations of Immigrants*, pp. 131–2.
7 NAA A432/81 1946/891.
8 Janet Phillips 2005, 'Australia's migration program'.
9 Commonwealth of Australia, Department of Immigration and Multicultural Affairs 2001, *Immigration*, pp. 16–17.
10 Ann-Mari Jordens 2001, 'Immigration since the Second World War', in James Jupp (ed.), *The Australian People: An Encyclopedia of the Nation, its People and their Origins*, Cambridge University Press, Cambridge, p. 63.
11 Cited in Martin, *The Migrant Presence*, p. 30.
12 Mark Aarons 2001, *War Criminals Welcome.*
13 Cited in Matthew Jordan 2006, 'The reappraisal of the White Australia Policy', p. 240.
14 ibid., p. 243.
15 James Jupp 1994, *Exile or Refugee?*, p. 35.
16 Jean Martin 1965, *Refugee Settlers*, p. 5.
17 ibid., pp. 10–11.

18 Ronald Taft 1965, *From Stranger to Citizen*, pp. 21–3.
19 Culotta, *They're a Weird Mob*, p 205
20 Sheridan, 'The "Australian Woman"', pp. 129–30.
21 James Jupp 1994, pp. 131–2.
22 Glenda Sluga 1985, 'Bonegilla Reception and Training Centre: 1947 to 1971', p. 112.
23 Undated press clipping from NAA MP 1308/1 1963/3392.
24 Glenda Sluga in James Jupp (ed.) 2001, *The Australian People: An Encyclopedia of the Nation, its People and their Origins*, Cambridge University Press, Cambridge, p. 73.
25 Jordens, *From Alien to Citizen*, p. 76.
26 Sluga, 'Bonegilla Reception and Training Centre', p. 105.
27 Raymond Evans, personal communication, 2008.
28 Jupp, *From White Australia to Woomera*, pp. 27–9.
29 Sheridan, 'The "Australian Woman"', p. 123; private communication Beth Warth, Wollongong, 2005.
30 Jenkings, 'Australian political elites', p. 12.
31 Cited in Martin, *The Migrant Presence*, pp. 85–9.
32 Martin, *The Migrant Presence,* p. 92.
33 Good Neighbour Council of News South Wales Wollongong Branch 1960, South Coast Regional Conference at Wollongong Town Hall Annex, Saturday, April 2, 1960, The Council, Wollongong, n.p.
34 Jenkings, 'Australian political elites', p. 118.
35 Murphy, *The Other Australians,* pp. 176–7.
36 Martin, *The Migrant Presence,* p. 33.
37 Jordens, Ann-Mari 1997, *From Alien to Citizen*, p. 78.
38 *Pix,* 11 April, 1957, p. 11–12.
39 The Good Neighbour Council was also known as the New Settlers League in Queensland and New South Wales.
40 Cited in Jenkings, 'Australian political elites', p. 198.
41 Jordens, *Alien to Citizen,* p. 165.
42 ibid., pp. 165–70.
43 Murphy, *Imagining the Fifties*, pp. 162–3.
44 Good Neighbour Council of News South Wales Wollongong Branch 1960, South Coast Regional Conference at Wollongong Town Hall Annex, Saturday, April 2, 1960, The Council, Wollongong, n.p.
45 *The Helping Hand* (1963), Australian Commonwealth Film Unit Production, produced for the Department of Immigration by Visatone. Film Australia's Immigration home: www.filmaust.com.au/immigration/content.htm.
46 Jordens, *Alien to Citizen,* p. 165.
47 Ann-Mari Jordens 1995, *Redefining Australians*, p. 87.
48 The Malcolm Fraser Collection: Multiculturalism: Australian's Unique Achievement. Address by the Prime Minister, the Rt Hon. Malcolm Fraser, to the Institute of Multicultural Affairs in Melbourne on 30 November 1981, www.unimelb.edu.au/malcolmfraser/speeches/nonparliamentary/multiculturalism.htmlInaugural

49 J.P.M. Long 1964, 'The numbers and distribution of Aboriginals in Australia', pp. 2–3.
50 ibid., pp. 3–4.
51 Davidson, *From Subject to Citizen,* p. 193.
52 Gordon Rowe 1956, *How Can the Aborigines Be Assimilated?*
53 Cited in Peter Biskup, 1973, *Not Slaves, Not Citizens*, p. 194.
54 A 452 1955/858 — letter 5/9/1950.
55 West Australian Government 1958, 'Report of Select Committee on Native Affairs', p. 15.
56 Biskup, *Not Slaves, Not Citizens*, pp. 227–8.
57 West Australian Government, 'Report of Select Committee on Native Affairs', p. 15.
58 Cited in McGregor, 'Intelligent parasitism', p. 124–5.
59 Robert A. Hall 1989, *The Black Diggers*, pp. 60, 144–5.
60 Cited in Biskup, *Not Slaves, Not Citizens*, p. 210.
61 ibid.
62 Connie Nungulla McDonald 1996, *When You Grow Up*, p. 65.
63 See, for example, Marie Reay and Grace Sitlington 1948, 'Class and status in a mixed-blood community', p. 197.
64 de Costa, *A Higher Authority*, p. 74.
65 W. H. Chafe 1982, 'The civil rights revolution, 1945–1960', p. 73.
66 Cited in Marie Reay 1964, 'Introduction', p. ix.
67 W. E. H. Stanner 1969, *After the Dreaming.*
68 Gallup Polls no. 1066 Dec 1954–Jan 1955 cited in Murphy, *Imagining the Fifties*, p. 172.
69 NAA B331/15 Native Welfare Conference.
70 Cited in Haebich, *Broken Circles*, p. 492.
71 ibid., p. 492.
72 ibid., p. 493.
73 ibid., p. 493.
74 ibid., p. 493.
75 Lynette Russell 2000, 'Going "walkabout" in the 1950s', p. 207.
76 Willis, Anne-Marie 1988, *Picturing Australia*, pp. 120–23. *Pix* was set up during the inter-war years and placed great store on photographs; it showed a strong interest in social issues and played an important role in communicating popular ideas about modernity until after the war, when 'sex and sensation' became the focus. *People* magazine was launched in 1950.
77 *Pix,* 5 August 1950, p. 32.
78 Cited in Geoff Gray, 2000, 'Dissolving difference, p. 75.
79 Sheridan, *Who Was That Woman?* p. 146.
80 ibid., pp. 149–51.
81 Raymond Evans, private communication August 2008.
82 Anna Haebich 1998, 'The formative years'.
83 Cited in United Nations 2005, *60th Anniversary of the San Francisco Conference.*
84 Taffe, 'Australian diplomacy in a policy vacuum', p. 155.
85 Marilyn Lake 2005, 'Paul Hasluck's horror of the two-headed calf', p. 260.

86 Tim Rowse 2005, 'The certainties of assimilation', p. 238.
87 ibid., p. 239.
88 Paul Hasluck 1988, *Shades of Darkness: Aboriginal Affairs 1925–1965*, p. 22.
89 Cited in Rowse, 'The certainties of assimilation', p. 240.
90 Russell McGregor 1999, 'Words, wards and citizens', p. 248.
91 ibid., p. 247.
92 Rowse, 'The certainties of assimilation', p. 241.
93 McGregor, 'Words, wards and citizens', p. 249.
94 NAA A4940 C377.
95 NAA A4940 C377.
96 A. P. Elkin 1951, 'Aborigines and the Ministers Welfare Council'.
97 NAA 452/54 1951/1665.
98 NAA B331 4 545136.
99 See Raymond Evans 2006, *A History of Queensland*, p. 233.
100 Rosalind Kidd 1997, *The Way We Civilise.*
101 Haebich, *Broken Circles*, pp. 502, 528–9.
102 NAA A452 1951/1723.
103 William Roger Louis 1978, *Imperialism at Bay*, p. 564.
104 Lord Macaulay, 1825 quoted from *The Columbia Dictionary of Quotations*, www.positiveatheism.org/hist/quotes/quote-m.htm.
105 WA SRO 993/78/1952; WA PD 6/9/1950.
106 Charles Rowley 1966, 'Causation in relation to Aboriginal affairs', p. 347.
107 Tigger Wise 1985, *The Self-made Anthropologist*, pp. 181–2, 185.
108 ibid., p. 182.
109 McGregor, 'Words, wards and citizens', pp. 253–4.
110 *West Australian*, 7 August 1952.
111 Rowse, *Contesting Assimilation*, p. 10; Haebich, *Broken Circles*, p. 482.
112 Haebich, *Broken Circles*, p. 463.
113 Claire Smith 2004, *Country, Kin and Culture*, p. 66.
114 Haebich, *Broken Circles*, pp. 462–3.
115 Cited in Smith, *Country, Kin and Culture*, p. 66.
116 Tim Rowse 1998, *White Flour, White Power*, pp. 160–62.
117 Cited in Haebich, *Broken Circles*, pp. 471–2.
118 Taffe, 'Australian diplomacy in a policy vacuum', p. 171.
119 J. C. Altman and W. Sanders 1995, 'From exclusion to dependence', pp. 209–11.
120 Mary Anne Jebb 2002, *Blood, Sweat and Welfare.*
121 NAA A452 1961/1256.

Chapter 5

1 WA SRO 993/242/1965.
2 Darryl Kickett 1997, 'It's all about a fair go'.
3 Western Australian Government Department of Native Welfare 1964, *Citizens.*
4 *Bulletin*, 13 June 1964.
5 Chesterman, *Civil Rights*, p. 37.
6 Amartya Sen 1992, *Inequality Re-examined.*

7 WA SRO 993/1120/1948.
8 Biskup, *Not Slaves, Not Citizens*, pp. 230–32.
9 Cited in Anna Haebich 2005, 'Nuclear, suburban and black', p. 207.
10 Western Australian Government Department of Native Affairs Annual Report 1950, p. 5.
11 WA SRO 993/803/1945.
12 Lauren Marsh, personal communication, 2007.
13 S. G. M. Middleton 1986, 'Verbatim transcript of interview', Bill Bunbury (int.), Library Board of Western Australia, p. 7.
14 WA SRO 993/249/1953.
15 Biskup, *Not Slaves, Not Citizens*, p. 241.
16 ibid., p. 251.
17 WA SRO 993/720/1949.
18 WA SRO 993/140/1949.
19 WA SRO 993/569/1950.
20 Middleton, 'Verbatim transcript of interview', pp. 15–16.
21 Tim Rowse, personal communication 30 May 2001 (email).
22 Slavoj Zizek 1997, *The Plague of Fantasies*, pp. 45–86.
23 WA SRO 993/720/1949.
24 Western Australian Government, *Department of Native Welfare Annual Report 1961*, p. 65.
25 Biskup, *Not Slaves, Not Citizens*, pp. 247–8.
26 WA SRO 993 189/1964; WA SRO 993 52/1950.
27 NA 376/1945 cited in Biskup, *Not Slaves, Not Citizens*, p. 233.
28 WA SRO 993/720/1949.
29 Henry P. Schapper 1968, 'Administration and welfare as threats of Aboriginal assimilation', p. 5.
30 The government did not hand over all its duties and responsibilities to the federal government but in creating the Aboriginal Affairs Authority Planning Authority, it maintained a central coordinating role between state agencies, liaison with Commonwealth departments, a community liaison role and controls over Aboriginal land and heritage.
31 WA SRO 993/509/1951.
32 WA SRO 993/623/1947.
33 WA SRO 993/184/1953.
34 Carolyne Dean 2004, *The Fragility of Empathy After the Holocaust*, p. 101.
35 WA SRO 993/140/1949.
36 WA SRO 993/94/1928.
37 Zygmunt Bauman, *Modernity and Ambivalence*, pp. 105–7.
38 Biskup, *Not Slaves, Not Citizens*, p. 251.
39 *Great Southern Herald*, 10 April 1952.
40 *West Australian*, 1 August 1950.
41 Biskup, *Not Slaves Not Citizens*, p. 246.
42 WA SRO 993/219/1960
43 WA SRO 993/43/1959.
44 WA SRO 993/464/1952.

45 David Mercer 2003, '"Citizen minus"?'
46 *West Australian,* 10 October 1952.
47 Biskup, *Not Slaves, Not Citizens,* pp. 258–9.
48 ibid., p. 252.
49 ibid., p. 258.
50 ibid.
51 ibid.
52 WA SRO 993/111/1951.
53 WA SRO 993/569/1950.
54 *West Australian,* 19 August, 1952.
55 WA SRO 993/78/1952.
56 WA SRO 993/78/1952.
57 Western Australian Government 1958, *Report of the Select Committee on Native Matters,* p. 9.
58 ibid., pp. 10–11.
59 ibid., p. 10.
60 ibid., p. 11.
61 Western Australian Government, *Department of Native Welfare Annual Report 1964,* p. 7.
62 ibid., p. 8.
63 *Daily News,* 1 June 1964.
64 Hall, *The Black Diggers,* pp. 30, 191.
65 *West Australian,* 26 July, 1952.
66 Western Australian Government, *Department of Native Welfare Annual Report 1964,* p. 8.
67 *West Australian,* 20 February 1964.
68 *Sunday Times,* 21 June 1964; *Geraldton Guardian,* 27 June 1964.
69 WA SRO 993 126/1964.
70 WA SRO 993/242/1965.
71 WA SRO 993/242/1965.
72 WA SRO 126/64 CNW 22/6/64.
73 J.R. Hall 1965, 'Drinking behaviour amongst part-Aborigines in a Western Australian community', p. 59.
74 *Geraldton Guardian,* 30 June 1964.
75 Hall, 'Drinking behaviour amongst part-Aborigines', p. 44ff; Jeremy Beckett 1958, 'Marginal man', *Oceania,* vol. 29, no. 2.
76 *Current Affairs Bulletin* 1961, p. 29.
77 Hall, 'Drinking behaviour amongst part-Aborigines', p. 72.
78 WA SRO 993/242/1965; *Daily News,* 8 July 1965.
79 WA SRO 993/242/1965.
80 *Daily News* 27–28 June 1966.
81 Dennis Gray and Sherry Saggers 1998, *Dealing with Alcohol,* p. 98.

Chapter 6

1 California Newsreel 2003, *Race — The Power of an Illusion, Episode Three: The House We Live In,* Dalton Conley, Sociologist, Executive Producer: Larry

Adelman, Episode Producers: Christine Herbes-Sommers, Tracy Strain, Llewellyn Smith, Series Co-Producer: Jean Cheng, www.newsreel.org/nav/title.asp?tc=CN0149

2 Produced in 1969 for the Home-Maker Service in the Department of Native Welfare.

3 Badcock, Blair 2000, 'Home ownership and the illusion of egalitarianism', p. 255.

4 ibid., pp. 261–2.

5 Carolyn Allport 1993, 'Nicely furnished cottages', p. 108.

6 Donald Fixico 2002, 'Federal and state policies and American Indians', p. 387.

7 WA SRO 993 509/1951; Western Australian Government 1961, *Department of Native Welfare Annual Report.*

8 Haebich, 'Nuclear, suburban and black', p. 211.

9 Western Australian Government 1958, *Department of Native Welfare Annual Report*; WA SRO 993/111/1951; WA SRO 993/90/1957.

10 WA SRO 993/52/1950.

11 Western Australian Government 1961, *Department of Native Welfare Annual Report*, p. 52.

12 Haebich, 'Nuclear, suburban and black', p. 212.

13 WA SRO 993/118/1963.

14 Western Australian Government 1964, *Department of Native Welfare Annual Report*, p. 10; WA SRO 1724/29/1958.

15 While the *1954 Native Welfare Act* allowed for Aboriginal children to be dealt with under the provisions of the *1947 Child Welfare Act*, the department retained the right to remove children through the Commissioner's powers of guardianship until the *1963 Native Welfare Act* was passed.

16 Haebich, *Broken Circles*, pp. 225–7.

17 This was formalised in the *1954 Native Welfare Act.*

18 Legal opinion provided to him either overlooked or overruled a 1909 regulation allowing police to remove children and then report to the department.

19 WA SRO 993/52/1950.

20 Rene Powell and Bernadette Kennedy 2005, *Rene Baker File #28/ E. D. P.*, p. 44.

21 Western Australian Government 1962, *Department of Native Welfare Annual Report*, p. 12.

22 Western Australian Government 1957, *Department of Native Welfare Annual Report;* Western Australian Government 1960, *Department of Native Welfare Annual Report.* Since no statistical series on removals is available for the Middleton period, only isolated statistics can be presented to quantify the extent of removals.

23 WA SRO 993/189/1964.

24 Western Australian Government 1974, *Report of the Royal Commission into Aboriginal Affairs*, p. 259.

25 See, for example, Elizabeth Sommerlad 1977, *Aboriginal Juveniles in Custody.*

26 Cited in Allport, 'Nicely furnished cottages', p. 108.

27 WA SRO 993/111/1951.

28 Mary Louise Pratt 1992, *Imperial Eyes*, p. 4.
29 Biskup, *Not Slaves Not Citizens*, pp. 245–6.
30 WA SRO 993/111/1951.
31 Western Australian Government 1960, *Official Year Book of Western Australia.*
32 Western Australian Government 1960, *Department of Native Welfare Annual Report*; WA SRO 993/476/1960.
33 George Morgan 2000, 'Assimilation and resistance', p. 192.
34 WA SRO 993/111/1951.
35 Western Australian Government 1957, *Department of Native Welfare Annual Report.*
36 New South Wales Aboriginal Welfare Board cited in Heather Goodall 1995, '"Assimilation begins in the home"', p. 97.
37 Corinne Manning 2005, 'If Aborigines are to be assimilated they must learn to live in houses.'
38 Western Australian Government 1964, *Department of Native Welfare Annual Report*, pp. 10, 62.
39 Western Australian Government 1960, *Department of Native Welfare Annual Report:* Western Australian Government 1967, *Department of Native Welfare Annual Report.*
40 www.berndt.uwa.edu.au/Berndt/action.lasso?-database=Information.FP3&-layout=Show&-token=Allawah&-response=generic.lasso&showSuccesses
41 Rosemary Oxer 1963, 'Allawah Grove', pp. ii–iii.
42 Catherine H. Berndt 1962, 'Mateship or success', p. 79.
43 Oxer, 'Allawah Grove', pp. 185–6.
44 Quoted from Rules of the Allawah Grove Progress Association in ibid., p. 108.
45 ibid., pp. 99–100.
46 Berndt, 'Mateship or success', p. 79.
47 Bropho, Robert 1980, *Fringedweller*, pp. 34–40, 43.
48 ibid., p. 54.
49 Goodall, 'Assimilation begins in the home'; Cole, 'The glorified flower'; Francesca Bartlett 1999, 'Clean white girls'.
50 Goodall, 'Assimilation begins in the home', p. 83.
51 Moore, 'The guiding hand', pp. 52–3.
52 WA SRO 993/464/1952.
53 *Baby's Bath* (n.d.) and *Lilly Feeds her Baby* (n.d.) were held at the Aboriginal Affairs Planning Authority Library which has since been closed down and its contents distributed to other libraries. Western Australia Audio Visual Branch 1969, *Good Food Good Health*, Perth; Western Australia Audio Visual Branch 1969, *A House in Town*, Perth.
54 Meaghan Vaughan 1991, *Curing Their Ills*, pp. 182–5.
55 Wave Productions for the Department of Native Welfare, n.d.
56 Haebich, *Broken Circles*, pp. 611–19, written with Darryl Kickett.
57 Corinne Manning 2004, '"A helping white hand"', pp. 8, 15.
58 Morgan, 'Assimilation and resistance', pp. 192–3.
59 Allport, Carolyn 1993, 'Nicely furnished cottages', p. 121.
60 Western Australian Government 1958, *Department of Native Welfare Annual*

Report, 1957–58.
61 *Westralian Aborigine*, June–July 1956, cited in Michael Rose (ed.) 1996, *For the Record*, p. 47.
62 WA SRO 993/111/1951.
63 ibid.
64 ibid.
65 Kidd, Rosalind 2006, *Trustees on Trial*.
66 Hall, *The Black Diggers*, pp. 25, 189.
67 Cited in ibid., p. 24.
68 WA SRO 993 111/1951.
69 Allan Duncan 1966, 'Training Aborigines for employment in New South Wales', p. 46.
70 ibid.
71 E. P. Miller 1966, 'Factors affecting vocational training for Aborigines in the Northern Territory and Western Australia', pp. 31, 35.
72 WA SRO 993 111/1951.
73 Western Australian Government 1961, *Department of Native Welfare Annual Report*, p. 24.
74 California Newsreel 2003, *Race — The Power of an Illusion, Episode Three: The House We Live In.*

Chapter 7

1 Stephen Kinnane 2003, *Shadow Lines*, p. 341.
2 Interview with Mrs Isobel Bropho, 9 December 1989, by Stephen Kinnane, Saunders Street Community, Perth WA, tape 5, transcript p. 18.
3 Interview with Mrs Isobel Bropho, 7 September 1989, by Stephen Kinnane, Saunders Street Community, Perth, WA, tape 2, transcript p. 4.
4 Interview with Mrs Eileen Clarke, 10 February 1993, Adelaide, SA, by Lauren Marsh and Stephen Kinnane, tape 1, transcript p. 5.
5 WA SRO 1733/1312/1943 East Perth Native Matters, Native Welfare Department, file note McBeath 08/01/1945, folio 7.
6 ibid.
7 Jack Davis 1983, *The First-Born: and Other Poems.*
8 Alice Nannup with Lauren Marsh and Stephen Kinnane 1992, *When the Pelican Laughed*, p. 72.
9 Interview with Mr George Harwood, 8 December 1992, Canberra, ACT, by Lauren Marsh and Stephen Kinnane, tape 1, transcript p. 16.
10 Interview with Mr Geoff Harcus, 11 August 1993, Northam, WA, by Lauren Marsh and Stephen Kinnane, tape 3, transcript pp. 5–6.
11 Interview with Helena Murphy, Frank Alberts and Jim Clarke, 13 October 1992, Darwin, NT, by Lauren Marsh and Stephen Kinnane, tape 1, transcript p. 5.
12 ibid.
13 Interview with Mr George Harwood, 8 December 1992, Canberra, ACT, by Lauren Marsh and Stephen Kinnane.
14 Interview with Geoff Harcus, 11 August 1993, Northam, WA, by Lauren

Marsh and Stephen Kinnane, tape 3, transcript p. 13.

15 Interview with Mrs Helena Murphy, 10 October 1992, Darwin, NT, by Lauren Marsh and Stephen Kinnane, tape 1, transcript p. 1.

16 ibid., p. 13.

17 WA SRO 993 146/47.

18 *Daily News*, 18 March 1947, 'Aborigines, Half-Castes Have Weekly Dance, Social'.

19 WA SRO 993 146/47.

20 Interview with Nora Pickett, 18 October 1992, Broome, WA, by Lauren Marsh and Stephen Kinnane, Tape 1, transcript p. 15.

21 See article, 'Reception For US Dancers', *Westralian Aborigine*, June–July 1955, p. 1.

22 Interview with Geoff Harcus, 3 May 1999, Northam, WA, by Lauren Marsh and Stephen Kinnane, tape 1, transcript p. 15.

23 ibid., p. 5.

24 ibid., p. 6; Geoff cites the incident of Desi Parfitt refused service of a cool drink at a café table in Williams.

25 Interview with Mr George Harwood, 8 December, 1992, transcript p. 8.

26 See editorial, 'Mr Nulsen: A Mass of Contradictions', *Westralian Aborigine*, January 1955, p. 2.

Chapter 8

1 Roman Black 1964, *Old and New Australian Aboriginal Art*, pp. xxi–xxii.

2 ibid., p. xxi.

3 Richard White 1993, 'The shock of affluence', p. 23.

4 Anne-Marie Van de Ven 1993, 'Images of the 1950s', p. 39.

5 S. Barton Babbage and Ian Siggins 1960, *Light Beneath the Southern Cross*, photo facing p. 152.

6 *Pix*, 30 October 1948, pp. 14–17.

7 Grace McCann Morley 1954, 'UNESCO's exchange of exhibitions programme', p. 284.

8 Anne-Marie Willis 1993, *Illusions of Identity*, p. 113.

9 ibid., p. 110.

10 Nicholas Thomas 1999, *Possessions*, p. 12.

11 ibid., p. 11.

12 *Pix*, 27 March 1954, pp. 20–21.

13 Newspaper Reviews, Vincent Carell and Beth Dean Papers, Mitchell Library, Sydney. The collection was in the process of being catalogued when research was undertaken so referencing will not correspond to present cataloguing details.

14 Marianna Torgovnick 1996, *Primitive Passions*, pp. 244–6.

15 Clement Greenberg 1939, 'Avant-garde and kitsch', pp. 34–49.

16 Roger Scruton 1999, 'Kitsch and the modern predicament, n.p.

17 Andrew Lattas 1989, 'Colonising the Other', p. 24.

18 Laura Rosenstock 1984, 'Leger: "The Creation of the World"'.

19 Cited in Kirk Varnedoe 1984, 'Abstract expressionism', p. 619.

20 Thomas, *Possessions*, pp. 12–14.
21 Willis, *Illusions of Identity*, p. 37.
22 ibid., p. 110.
23 Marcia Langton, 1996, 'What do we mean by wilderness?', p. 21.
24 Nicholas Thomas 2001, 'Indigenous presences and national narratives in Australasian museums', pp. 300–01.
25 Willis, *Illusions of Identity*, pp. 111–12; *Walkabout* was produced by the Australian National Travel Association between 1934 and 1970.
26 Pemina Yellowbird and Kathryn Mullin, cited in Lisa Aldred 2000, 'Plastic shamans and astroturf sun dances', p. 334.
27 Renato Rosaldo 1989, 'Imperialist nostalgia', p. 108.
28 Australian Broadcasting Commission 2000, *Radio Eye: Greetings from White Australia*, 22 October, www.abc.net.au/rn/radioeye/stories/2000/202831.htm.
29 Julie Marcus 1999, 'The blackness of the body', pp. 195–6.
30 Virginia Fraser citing Coco Fusco in Marcia Langton 1998, 'The valley of the dolls', p. 104.
31 Ann Stephen, Andew McNamara and Philip Goad (eds) 2006, *Modernism & Australia*, p. 12.
32 Van de Ven, 'Images of the 1950s', p. 38.
33 Richard White 1993, 'The shock of affluence', p. 23.
34 Glenn Cooke 1995, 'Kitsch or kind', p. 14.
35 Stephen, McNamara and Goad, *Modernism & Australia*, p. 13.
36 Bernard Smith 2001, *Australian Painting, 1788–2000*, p. 79.
37 Colin Symes and Bob Lingard 1988, 'From the ethnographic to the aesthetic', pp. 203–4.
38 Karel Kupka 1965, *Dawn of Art*.
39 Arjun Appadurai 1992, 'Museums are good to think', p. 44.
40 Elizabeth Hallam 2000, 'Texts, objects and "otherness"', p. 261.
41 Black, *Old and New Australian Aboriginal Art*, p. xxiii.
42 Fred McCarthy 1941, 'Australian Aboriginal art and its application', p. 355.
43 ibid., p. 355.
44 Thomas, *Possessions*, p. 125.
45 *Australian Aboriginal Culture: An Exhibition Arranged by the Australian National Committee for UNESCO*, 1953, catalogue, p. 1.
46 ibid., various pages.
47 See Max Lamshed 1972, *'Monty'*.
48 C. P. Mountford 1948, *Brown Men and Red Sand*; Mountford, C. P. 1948, 'Exploring Stone Age Arnhem land', *National Geographic* magazine; films *Brown Men and Red Sand* and *Brown Men and Blue Mountains*.
49 Charles P. Mountford 1965, *The Dreamtime*.
50 Margaret McDonnell 2002, 'The colour of copyright', p. 2.
51 Australian Broadcasting Commission, *Radio Eye: Return to Arnhem Land*, 2 June 2007, www.abc.net.au/rn/radioeye/stories/2007/1928445.htm.
52 Thomas, Nicholas 1999, *Possessions*, p. 11.
53 Beth Dean and Vincent Carell 1955, *Dust for the Dancers*, p. 2.
54 Mosec Manpurr (d. 1950) was then living at the Delissaville Settlement (now

Belyuen) on the Cox Peninsula west of Darwin. In 1948 Colin Simpson also saw Mosec dancing a death ritual at Delissaville and commented, 'I don't know if I have ever seen finer dancing in my life.' (Australian Broadcasting Commission 1948, *Australian Walkabout Show*; Colin Simpson 1951, *Adam in Ochre*, pp. 166–80) Fifty years later, anthropologist Elizabeth Povenelli, sitting with Belyuen women during a native title land claim, recorded that the women 'remember Mosec as a *djewalabag*, a "clever man", a man steeped in sacred law. They remembered national and international celebrities travelling to Belyuen to record his singing and dancing. They shared camps, food, argument — history — with him.' (Elizabeth A. Povenelli 2002, *The Cunning of Recognition*, p. 226)

55 ANIB 1947, 'Australian Aboriginal dances', p. 70.

56 See, for example, Sylvia Kleinert and Margo Neal (eds) 2000, *The Oxford Companion to Aboriginal Art and Culture*; R. Henry, F. Magowan and D. Murray (eds) 2000, 'The politics of dance'.

57 For a historical overview, see Michael Parsons 2002, '"Ah That I Could Convey a Proper Idea of This Interesting Wild Play of the Natives"'.

58 Anita Callaway 2000, *Visual Ephemera*, p. 117.

59 See John Antill's biography by Victor Carell and Beth Dean 1987, *Gentle Genius*.

60 Shelley C. Berg 1988, *Le Sacre du printemps*.

61 Cited in Michelle Potter 2004, 'Corroboree'.

62 See Philip J. Deloria 1998, *Playing Indian*.

63 The few local performances included a corroboree inspired ballet written into the 1930s romantic operetta *Collitts' Inn* by Australian composer Varney Monk with music based on an Aboriginal chant from the 'Illawarra tribe' (Jean Garling, 195–, *Australian Notes on the Ballet*, p. 21). The ballet *Terra Australis*, choreographed by Czech-born Edouard Borovansky and performed in Melbourne in 1946 by the Borovansky Ballet School, included three dancers — 'the Explorer', 'the White Woman' (Australia) and 'the Aboriginal' (a painted-up white dancer) — who represented the 'coming of the white man to Australia, and the subsequent tragedy that overtook the aboriginal race' in a performance that 'extravagantly demonstrated the relentless progress towards the promised glorious white Australian future' (Callaway, *Visual Ephemera*, pp. viii–ix; Garling, *Australian Notes on the Ballet*, pp. 31–2).

64 Newspaper Reviews, Vincent Carell and Beth Dean Papers, Mitchell Library, Sydney.

65 Torgovnick, *Primitive Passions*, p. 8.

66 Berg, *Le Sacre du Printemps*, p. 142.

67 Michael North 1994, *The Dialect of Modernism*.

68 Dean, Beth and Carell, Vincent 1983, *Twin Journey*, p. 109.

69 Vincent Carell and Beth Dean Papers, Mitchell Library, Sydney

70 USA press extracts, n.d., Vincent Carell and Beth Dean Papers, Mitchell Library, Sydney.

71 *New York Times*, 9 December 1951.

72 Dean and Carell, *Dust for the Dancers*, p. 22.

73 ibid., p. ix.

74 ibid., p. 58.
75 ibid., p. ix.
76 ibid., p. 75.
77 ibid., p. 114.
78 ibid., p. ix.
79 Dean and Carell, *Twin Journey*, p. 91.
80 Catrina Vignando 2000, '*Corroboree*', p. 218.
81 Dean and Carell, *Dust for the Dancers*, p. 26.
82 ibid., p. 41.
83 ibid., p. 64.
84 ibid., p. 130.
85 ibid., p. 112.
86 ibid., p. 131.
87 ibid., p. 154.
88 ibid., p. 173.
89 Dean, *The Many Worlds of Dance*, p. 15.
90 A. Haebich 1999, 'Irresistible journeys and imaginings: Boyd's *Bride Series* Revisited', p. 117.
91 Vignando, Catrina 2000, 'Corroboree', p. 219.
92 Dean, *The Many Worlds of Dance*, p. 15.
93 Djon Mundine 2003, 'A dance through the desert', p. 68.
94 Dean, *The Many Worlds of Dance*, pp. 11–12.
95 Dean and Carell, *Twin Journey*, p. 146.
96 NAA A452 1952/473.
97 Dean and Carell, *Dust for the Dancers*, p. 169.
98 Vincent Carell and Beth Dean Papers, Mitchell Library, Sydney.
99 Dean and Carell, *Dust for the Dancers*, p. 211.
100 Vincent Carell and Beth Dean Papers, Mitchell Library, Sydney.
101 Savage Club Annual Report 1954.
102 *Sunday Telegraph*, Newspaper Reviews, Typescript, February 1954, Vincent Carell and Beth Dean Papers, Mitchell Library, Sydney.
103 Editorial, *Daily Examiner*, Typescript, February 1954, Vincent Carell and Beth Dean Papers, Mitchell Library, Sydney.
104 Columnist Eunice Gardner; *Mirror*, Newspaper reviews, typescript February 1954, Victor Carell and Beth Dean Papers, Mitchell Library, Sydney.
105 Vignando, '*Corroboree*', p. 218.
106 Dean and Carell, *Dust for the Dancers*, p. 209.
107 Potter, '*Corroboree*'. The ballet reappeared again in 1970 for the Captain Cook bicentenary with African-American dancer Ronne Arnold as principal dancer. Dean lobbied unsuccessfully for *Corroboree* to be added to the national ballet's repertoire and to be included in Australia's 1988 Bicentenary Celebrations. In 1994 a notated record of the ballet was prepared and in the following year Stanton Welch created a third interpretation of *Corroboree* to celebrate the fiftieth anniversary of the United Nations charter, using contemporary dance forms to express a 'generalised ritual'.
108 Dean and Carell, *Twin Journey*, p. 152.

109 *Age* (Melbourne), 15 November 1963.
110 *Age* (Melbourne), 12, 14 November 1963.
111 H. C. Coombs 1969, cited in Tim Rowse 2001, 'The arts advocacy of H. C. Coombs', p. 130.
112 ibid., p. 130.
113 Garma Festival 2002, Garma Statement on Indigenous Music and Performance, www.garma.telstra.com/2002/statement-music02.htm
114 Bangarra Dance Theatre Artistic Vision 2001, www.bangarra.com.au/history/vision.html

Chapter 9

1 Hassan, Ihab 2000, 'How Australian is it?', p. 416
2 Bain Attwood 2005, 'Rights, racism and Aboriginality', pp. 271, 284; Tim Rowse, *Contesting Assimilation*, cover notes.
3 Martin, *The Migrant Presence*, p. 33.
4 Catriona Elder 1999, 'Dreams and Nightmares of a "White Australia", p. 28.
5 Marcia L. Langton 1993, *Well, I Heard It On The Radio*, p. 33.
6 ibid., p. 34.
7 Louise McNay, 1994, *Foucault*, p. 101.
8 Richard Delgado 1989, 'Storytelling for oppositionists and others: a plea for narrative', pp. 2414–15.
9 Marcia L. Langton, *Well, I Heard It On The Radio*, p. 81.
10 Jan Kociumbus (ed.) 1998, 'Introduction'.
11 Kay Schaffer and Sidonie Smith 2004, *Human Rights and Narrated Lives*, p. 102.
12 David Carter 2004, 'O'Grady, John see "Culotta, Nino"', pp. 57, 62.
13 Jeannette Hoorn 2003, 'Michael Powell's *They're a Weird Mob*', p. 160.
14 Shirley and Adams, *Australian Cinema*, p. 228.
15 Hoorn, 'Michael Powell's *They're a Weird Mob*, p. 162; Lindsay Barrett 1992, 'The self-made man, p. 93.
16 Directed by Clayton Jacobson the film won the 2006 AFI Award for Best Lead Actor. Australian Film Critics Association 2006, afca.org.au/kenny.php
17 Hoorn, 'Michael Powell's *They're a Weird Mob*', pp. 164–8.
18 O'Grady, *They're a Weird Mob*, p. 104.
19 Murphy, *Imagining Assimilation*, pp. 164, 165–6.
20 Sheridan, 'Australian Woman', pp. 125–6.
21 Roy Jones 1995, 'Migration to Australia in fiction and film', p. 260.
22 Hoorn, 'Michael Powell's *They're a Weird Mob*', p. 170.
23 Gwenda Tavan 2005, *The Long Slow Death of White Australia*, p. 110.
24 Frances Kartunnen 1994, *Between Worlds*, p. 16.
25 Gordon M. Sayre 1999, 'A bridging between two worlds', p. 493.
26 *Bulletin* 1901, cited in Haebich, *Broken Circles*, p. 135.
27 Centre for Cross Cultural Research 'Pigments of the Imagination' 15–26 November 2004.
28 *Pix*, 20 June 1959, p. 46.
29 Haebich, 'Irresistible journeys, imaginary homelands', pp. 120–21.

30 Lauren Marsh, private communication 2007.
31 Homi K. Bhabha 1993, 'Beyond the pale', p. 66.
32 Cited in Bauman, *Modernity and Ambivalence,* fn 9 p. 115.
33 ibid., p. 117.
34 Bruno Bettelheim 1960, *Autonomy in a Mass Age,* pp. 173–4, cited in Bauman, *Modernity and Ambivalence,* p. 123.
35 Kim Scott and Hazel Brown 2005, *Kayang and Me,* p. 195.
36 ibid., pp. 227, 228, 258.
37 Rolf De Heer 2007, 'Between two worlds'.
38 Cited in John Ramsland and Christopher Mooney 2006, *Remembering Aboriginal Heroes,* p. 47.
39 *Artists Footsteps,* www.artistsfootsteps.com/html/Dargie_namatjira.htm. The *Portrait of Albert Namatjira* (1956) belongs to the Queensland Art Gallery Collection.
40 Sylvia Kleinert 2000, 'Namatjira, Albert (Elea) (1902–1959)', pp. 458–9.
41 E. Leske (ed.) 1977, *Hermannsburg,* p. 73.
42 Roslyn Poignant, *Lost Conversations.*
43 ibid., p. 3. Made by Commonwealth Film Division, based on treatment by Charles Mountford, with filmmakers Lee Robinson, Ralph Foster, Stanley Hawes.
44 ibid., p. 9.
45 Meaghan Morris, 'Beyond Assimilation', p. 12.
46 Poignant, *Lost Conversations,* p. 7.
47 Leske, E. (ed) 1977, *Hermannsburg: a Vision and a Mission,* Lutheran Publishing House, Adelaide, p. 73.
48 Ramsland and Mooney 2006, *Remembering Aboriginal Heroes,* p. 54.
49 Alison French 2003, *Seeing the Centre,* p. 21.
50 Cited in Ramsland and Mooney, *Remembering Aboriginal Heroes,* p. 45.
51 ibid., p. 43.
52 *Pix,* 12 September 1958, p. 35.
53 Kath Walker 1964, *We are Going,* p. 15.
54 Ramsland and Mooney, *Remembering Aboriginal Heroes,* p. 59.
55 French, *Seeing the Centre,* p. 22.
56 ibid., *Seeing the Centre,* p. 27.
57 Brenda L. Croft 2003, 'Albert's gift', p. 145; Australian Broadcasting Commission, 'Albert's gift', *Awaye!,* 29 September 2006, www.abc.net.au/rn/awaye/stories/2006/1748223.htm.
58 Katrina Schlunke 2000, 'Imaging the imaged'.
59 Brenda Croft, n.d., Artists Pages, Niagara Galleries, Melbourne, p. 3.
60 Shane Crilly 2001, 'Reading Aboriginalities in Australian cinema', pp. 336–44.
61 Jeremy Beckett 2000, 'Sarah McMann's mistake', p. 95.
62 ibid., p. 98.
63 Morris, *Beyond Assimilation,* pp. 7–8.
64 ibid., p. 8.
65 Chauvel, Charles and Elsa 1954, *Eve in Ebony … the Story of 'Jedda',* Columbia Pictures, Sydney.

66 Beckett, 'Sarah McMann's mistake'.
67 ibid., p. 97.
68 Morris, 'Beyond Assimilation', p. 9.
69 Tracey Moffatt 1990, *Night Cries: A Rural Tragedy*, Ronin Films, Civic Square, Canberra.
70 Barbara Creed 2001, 'Breeding out the black', pp. 210, 229.
71 Beckett, 'Sarah McMann's mistake', p. 98.
72 ibid., p. 98.
73 ibid., p. 99.
74 Victor Carell 1960, *Naked We are Born*, p. 217.
75 Gare, Nene 1966, *The Fringe Dwellers*, Sun Books, Melbourne, p. 70.
76 ibid., p. 257.
77 *West Australian,* 26 April 1986, p. 36.
78 Nene Gare, *Papers, 1939–1994, Box 12,* NLA.
79 *Observer,* 30 July 1961.
80 *Bulletin,* 2 December 1961, p. 35.
81 *West Australian,* 10 February 1962.
82 *Canberra Times,* 21 October 1961.
83 Haebich, *Broken Circles*, p. 549.
84 *Advertiser* (Adelaide), 21 November 1955.
85 Cited in R. MacDonald 1995, *Between Two Worlds*, p. 58.
86 Bartlett, 'Clean white girls', pp. 64–5.
87 *Age* (Melbourne), 20 September 1962.
88 *Advertiser* (Adelaide), 20 June 1962.
89 *Herald* (Melbourne), 8, 9 February 1960.
90 *Advertiser* (Adelaide), 30 January 1957.
91 *Weekend Mail,* 1 February 1956.
92 Haebich, *Broken Circles*, pp. 440–43
93 Cited in Haebich, *Broken Circles*, p. 579.
94 *Sun,* 25 June 1968.
95 *Advertiser* (Geelong), 22 August 1968.
96 Haebich, *Broken Circles*, p. 601.
97 Jack Horner 2004, *Seeking Racial Justice*, pp. 6–7.
98 ibid., p. 22.
99 ibid., p. 28.
100 ibid., p. 36.
101 Ian Spalding published his findings in the newsletter *On Aboriginal Affairs,* (1962–67).
102 Horner, *Seeking Racial Justice*, pp. 43–4.
103 ibid., p. 47.
104 ibid., p. 51.
105 Sue Taffe 2005, *Black and White Together: FCAATSI, the Federal Council for the Advancement of Aborigines and Torres Strait Islanders 1958–1973*, p. 4.
106 Ibid., p. 85.
107 Horner, *Seeking Racial Justice*, p. 55.
108 ibid., p. 65.

109 ibid., pp. 71–2.
110 ibid., p. 63.
111 ibid., p. 64.
112 ibid., p. 98.
113 ibid., p. 69.
114 ibid., p. 69.
115 ibid., p. 110.
116 ibid., p. 113.
117 Sue Taffe 2005, 'The role of FCAATSI in the 1967 Referendum', p. 296.
118 Cited in ibid., p. 296.
119 Rowse, 'The post-war social science of assimilation', p. 168.
120 Steve Mickler, 'The Perth press', p. 15.
121 Steve Mickler 1998, *The Myth of Privilege*, Fremantle Arts Centre Press, Fremantle, p. 141.
122 Steve Mickler, 'The Perth press', pp. 5, 7.
123 ibid., p. 8.
124 *West Australian,* 11 January 1965, p. 5; Mickler, 'The Perth press', p. 11.
125 Mickler, 'The Perth press', pp. 12–14; *Weekend News,* 22 May 1967, p. 2.
126 *West Australian,* 26 May 1967.
127 Kociumbus, 'Introduction', p. 25.
128 Ruth Fink 1957, 'The caste barrier', p. 110.
129 Ruth Fink 1964, 'Guided social change at the community level', pp. 145, 147.
130 W. E. H. Stanner, cited in Reay, *Aborigines Now,* p. viii.
131 ibid., p. ix-x.
132 John Wilson 1964, 'Assimilation to what? Comments on the white society', p. 151.
133 W. E. H. Stanner 1960, 'Durmugam a Nangiomeri'.
134 Cited in Marie Reay 1965, 'The background of alien impact', p. 390.
135 ibid., p. 393.
136 ibid., p. 395.
137 Stephen, McNamara and Goad, *Modernism in Australia,* p. 745; Tony Tuckson 2006, 'Aboriginal art and the Western world', 1964.
138 NAA A463 1962/2944.
139 Jeremy Beckett 2001, 'Some aspects of continuity and change among anthropologists in Australia, p. 7.
140 Kociumbus, 'Introduction', p. 37.
141 F. Lancaster-Jones, 'Review', pp. 330, 331.
142 Kociumbus, 'Introduction', p. 37.
143 Charles Rowley 1962, 'Aborigines and other Australians', p. 254.
144 ibid., p. 255.
145 ibid., p. 258.
146 ibid., p. 259.
147 ibid., pp. 262–4.
148 Charles Rowley 1982, *Equality by Instalments,* p. 33.
149 Stanner, *After the Dreaming,* pp. 1, 24, 25, 53, 56.

150 See their early works: Henry Reynolds (ed.) 1972, *Aborigines and Settlers*; Henry Reynolds (ed.) 1978, *Race Relations in North Queensland*; Raymond Evans, Kay Saunders and Kathryn Cronin 1975, *Exclusion, Exploitation and Extermination.*
151 Cited in Elizabeth Eggleston 1976, *Fear, Favour or Affection*, p. 7.
152 H. C. Coombs 1976, *Aboriginal Australians* 1967–1976.
153 Cited in ibid.
154 ibid.
155 Gaita, Raimond 2007, 'Comment', in *The Monthly*, August, p. 13.
156 Dodson, Michael 1996, Assimilation versus self-determination: No contest, H.C. (Nugget) Coombs Northern Australia Inaugural Lecture, Darwin, 5 September 1996, p. 1 http://www.hreoc.gov.au/speeches/social_justice/assimilation_vs_selfdetermination.html
157 Tavan, *The Long Slow Death of White Australia*, p. 110.
158 Rowse, 'The post-war social science of assimilation', p. 158.
159 Charles Price cited in Rowse, 'The post-war social science of assimilation', p. 156.
160 Patrick Ongley and David Pearson 1995, 'Post-1945 international migration, p. 766.
161 Barry Wain 1979, 'The Indochina refugee crisis'.
162 Ongley and Pearson, 'Post-1945 international migration', p. 788.
163 Macintyre, Stuart 2003, 'Fear of invasion has given way to fear of the refugee'.
164 Barry York 2003, 'The myth of our humanitarian tradition'.
165 Pugliese, '"I am, you are"', pp. 5–7.
166 *Sydney Morning Herald*, 12 December, 2006, www.smh.com.au/news/national/new-citizens-face-test-on-200-questions/2006/12/11/1165685615942.html
167 Lenny Roth 2007, *Multiculturalism.*
168 Coombs, *Aboriginal Australians*, n.p.

Bibliography

Aarons, Mark 2001, *War Criminals Welcome: Australia, a Sanctuary for War Criminals Since 1945*, Black Inc., Melbourne.

Aldred, Lisa 2000, 'Plastic shamans and astroturf sun dances', *American Indian Quarterly*, vol. 23, no. 3.

Aldrich, Robert 1996, *Greater France: A History of French Overseas Expansion*, Macmillan, London.

Alexander, Frederick 1953, 'The Australian people and the world', in George Caiger (ed.), *The Australian Way of Life*, Columbia University Press, New York.

Allen, Woody n.d., *Woody Allen Movies: The Films of Woody Allen*, www.woodyallen-movies.com/woodyallenquotes.htm

Allport, Carolyn 1993, 'Nicely furnished cottages: Government housing for black and white Australians', in Judith O'Callaghan (ed.), *The Australian Dream: Design of the Fifties*, Powerhouse Publishing, Sydney.

Altman, J. C. and Sanders, W. 1995, 'From exclusion to dependence: Aborigines and the welfare state in Australia', in John Dixon and Robert P. Scheurell (eds), *Social Welfare with Indigenous Peoples*, Routledge, London.

Anderson, Benedict 1991, *Imagined Communities: Reflections on the Origin and Spread of Nationalism*, rev ed., Verso, London and New York.

Anderson, Warwick 2002, *The Cultivation of Whiteness: Science, Health and Racial Destiny in Australia*, Melbourne University Press, Melbourne.

Appadurai, Arjun 1992, 'Museums are good to think: Heritage on view in India', in Ivan Karp, Christine Mullen Kreamer and Steven Lavine (eds), *Museums and Communities: The Politics of Public Culture*, Smithsonian Institution Press, Washington, DC.

ATSIC Public Affairs Office, *NAIDOC Week*, www.abc.net.au/message/naidoc/naidoc2003/history.htm

Attwood, Bain 2005, 'Rights, racism and Aboriginality', in Tim Rowse (ed.), *Contesting Assimilation*, API Network, Curtin University of Technology, Perth.

Australian Aboriginal Culture: An Exhibition arranged by the Australian National Committee for UNESCO 1953, Government Printer, Canberra.

Australian News and Information Bureau 1947, 'Australian Aboriginal dancers', *The Dancing Times.*

Australian News and Information Bureau 1951, *Australia and Your Future*, Department of the Interior, Canberra.

—— 1956a, *About Australia*, Department of the Interior, Canberra.

—— 1956b, *Australia — Your Host: XVIth Olympiad, Melbourne*, produced by authority of the Minister for the Interior, the Hon. Allen Fairhall.

—— 1960, *A Look at Australia*, Department of the Interior, Canberra.

—— 1964, *An Everyday Australian*, Canberra.

Badcock, Blair 2000, 'Home ownership and the illusion of egalitarianism' in P. Troy (ed.), *A History of European Housing in Australia*, Cambridge University Press, Melbourne.
Barker, Chris 1999, *Television, Globalisation and Cultural Identities*, Open University Press, Buckingham.
Barrett, Lindsay 1992, 'The self-made man: Narrative and national character in post-war Australia', *Southern Review*, vol. 25, no. 1.
Bartlett, Francesca 1999, 'Clean white girls', in Belinda McKay (ed.), *Unmasking Whiteness: Race Relations and Reconciliation*, Centre for Public Culture and Ideas, Griffith University, Brisbane.
Barton Babbage, S. and Siggins, Ian 1960, *Light Beneath the Southern Cross: The Story of Billy Graham's Crusade in Australia*, The World's Work, Sydney.
Bauman, Zygmunt 1991, *Modernity and Ambivalence*, Polity Press, Cambridge, UK.
Beckett, Jeremy 1958, 'Marginal man', *Oceania*, vol. 29, no. 2.
—— 2000, 'Sarah McMann's mistake: Charles Chauvel's *Jedda* and the assimilation policy' in Julie Marcus (ed.), *Picturing the 'Primitif': Images of Race in Daily Life*, LHR Press, Canada Bay, NSW.
—— 2001, 'Some aspects of continuity and change among Anthropologists in Australia or "He-who-eats-one-dish-with-us-all-with-one-spoon"', Plenary Address to the 2001 Meeting of the Australian Anthropological Society, www.aas.asn.au/Working%20Papers/Conference%202001/beckett.pdf.
Berg, Shelley C. 1988, *Le Sacre du printemps: Seven Productions from Nijinsky to Graham*, UMI Research Press, Ann Arbor, MI.
Berndt, Catherine H. 1962, 'Mateship or success: an assimilation dilemma', *Oceania*, vol. 33 no. 2.
Bessant, Judith and Wilkinson, Amanda 2006, 'Principles for developing Indigenous policy-making', *Australian Journal of Public Administration*, vol. 65, no. 1.
Bessell, R. and Schumann, D. 2003, *Life After Death: Approaches to a Cultural and Social History of Europe During the 1940s and 50s*, Cambridge University Press, London.
Bettelheim, Bruno 1960, *Autonomy in a Mass Age*, Free Press, New York.
Bhabha, Homi K. 1993, 'Beyond the pale: Art in the age of multicultural translation', in Elisabeth Sussman (ed.), *1993 Biennial Exhibition*, Whitney Museum of American Art, New York in association with Harry N. Abrams Inc. Publishers, New York.
Biskup, Peter 1973, *Not Slaves, Not Citizens*, University of Queensland Press, Brisbane.
Black, J. B. 1975, *Organising the Propaganda Instrument: The British Experience*, Martinus Nijhoff, The Hague.
Black, Roman 1964, *Old and New Australian Aboriginal Art*, Angus & Robertson, Sydney.
Bloch, Ernst 1995, *The Principle of Hope Volume One*, MIT Press, Cambridge, MA.
Bonnett, Alastair 2000, *Anti-racism*, Routledge, New York.
Borrie, Wilfred D. 1953, 'The family', in George Caiger (ed.), *The Australian Way of Life*, Columbia University Press, New York.

—— 1959, *The Cultural Integration of Immigrants: A Survey based upon the Papers and Proceedings of the UNESCO Conference held in Havana in April 1956*, UNESCO, Paris.
Bosworth, Richard 2001, 'Post-war Italian migration', in James Jupp (ed.), *The Australian People: An Encyclopedia of the Nation, Its People and Their Origins*, Cambridge University Press, Cambridge.
Brett, Judith 1993, *Robert Menzies' Forgotten People*, 2nd ed., Pan Macmillan, Sydney.
Bropho, Robert 1980, *Fringedweller*, Alternative Publishing Cooperative Ltd, Perth.
Brown, Nicholas 1995, *Governing Prosperity: Social Change and Social Analysis in Australia in the 1950s*, Cambridge University Press, Melbourne.
Callaway, Anita 2000, *Visual Ephemera: Theatrical Art in Nineteenth-century Australia*, University of New South Wales Press, Sydney.
Carell, Victor 1960, *Naked We are Born*, Ure Smith, Sydney.
Carell, Victor and Dean, Beth 1987, *Gentle Genius: A Life of John Antill*, Akron Press, Sydney.
Carey, Alex 1995, *Taking the Risk out of Democracy*, University of New South Wales Press, Sydney.
Carroll, James 2006, *House of War: The Pentagon and the Disastrous Rise of American Power*, Houghton Mifflin, Boston.
Carter, David 2004, 'O'Grady, John see "Culotta, Nino": Popular authorship, duplicity and celebrity', *Australian Literary Studies*, vol. 21, no. 4.
Chafe, W. H. 1982, 'The civil rights revolution, 1945–1960', in R. H. Bremner and G. W. Reichard (eds), *Reshaping America: Society and Institutions 1945–1960*, Ohio State University Press, Columbus.
Chesterman, John 2005, *Civil Rights: How Indigenous Australians Won Formal Equality*, University of Queensland Press, Brisbane.
Chesterman, John and Galligan, Brian 1997, *Citizens Without Rights: Aborigines and Australian Citizenship*, Cambridge University Press, Melbourne.
Chih-yu, Shih 2002, *Negotiating Ethnicity in China: Citizenship as a Response to the State*, Routledge, London.
Chomsky, Noam 1989, *Necessary Illusions: Thought Control in Democratic Societies*, Pluto Press, London.
Clark, Jennifer 1997, '"Something to hide?" Aborigines and the Department of External Affairs, January 1961–January 1962', *Journal of the Royal Australian Historical Society*, no. 83.
Clift, Charmian 1970, *The World of Charmian Clift*, Ure Smith, Sydney.
Cohn, William H. 1977, 'Popular culture and social history', *The Journal of Popular Culture*, vol. xi, no. 1.
Cole, Anna 2000, The glorified flower: Race, gender and assimilation in Australia, 1937–77, PhD Thesis, University of Technology, Sydney.
Collins, Jim 1989, *Uncommon Cultures: Popular Culture and Post-modernism*, Routledge, New York.
Commonwealth Government, Minister for Territories 1958, *Assimilation of Our Aborigines*, Commonwealth Government Printer, Canberra.
—— 1959, *Fringe Dwellers*, Commonwealth Government Printer, Canberra.

—— 1961, *One People*, Commonwealth Government Printer, Canberra.
—— 1962, *Our Aborigines*, Commonwealth Government Printer, Canberra.
—— 1963, *Aborigines and You*, Commonwealth Government Printer, Canberra.
Commonwealth of Australia 1986, *Immigration in Focus 1946–75: A Photographic Archive*, Department of Immigration and Ethnic Affairs, Canberra.
Commonwealth of Australia, Department of Immigration and Multicultural Affairs 2001, Statistics Section, *Immigration: Federation to Century's End 1901–2000*, Commonwealth Government Printer, Canberra.
Communist Party of Australia 1967, *Full Human Rights for Aborigines and Torres Strait Islanders*, 21st Congress of the Communist Party of Australia.
Cooke, Glenn 1995, 'Kitsch or kind: Representations of Aborigines in popular art', *Artlink*, vol. 15, no. 4.
Coombs, H. C. 1976, *Aboriginal Australians 1967–1976*, Walter Murdoch Lecture, www.murdoch.edu.au/vco/secretariat/records/murdochlectures/MurdochLecture 1976.doc.
Creed, Barbara 2001, 'Breeding out the black: *Jedda* and the Stolen Generations in Australia', *Body Trade: Captivity, Cannibalism, and Colonialism in the Pacific*, Pluto Press, Annandale, News South Wales.
Crilly, Shane 2001, 'Reading Aboriginalities in Australian cinema: From *Jedda* to *Dead Heart*', *Australian Screen Education*, nos. 26–27.
Croft, Brenda L. 2003, 'Albert's gift', in Alison French, *Seeing the Centre: The Art of Albert Namatjira 1902–1959*, National Gallery of Australia, Canberra.
—— n.d., Artists Pages, Niagara Galleries, Melbourne.
Curthoys, Ann 2002, *Freedom Ride: A Freedom Rider Remembers*, Allen & Unwin, Sydney.
Dale, Leigh 1997, 'Mainstreaming Australia', *Australian Public Intellectual (API) Network*, p. 6, http://www.api-network.com/main/index.php?apply=s cholars&webpage=default&flexedit=&flex_password=&menu_label=&menuID =homely&menubox=&scholar=219
Davidson, Alistair 1997, *From Subject to Citizen: Australian Citizenship in the Twentieth Century*, Cambridge University Press, Melbourne.
Davis, Jack 1983, *The First-Born and Other Poems*, Melbourne, Dent.
Davison, Graeme 1997, 'Welcoming the world: the 1956 Olympic Games and the re-presentation of Melbourne', in Judith Smart and John Murphy (eds), *The Forgotten Fifties*, Australian Historical Studies, no. 109.
de Costa, Ravi 2006, *A Higher Authority: Indigenous Transnationalism and Australia*, University of New South Wales Press, Sydney.
De Heer, Rolf 2007, 'Between two worlds', *Australian Weekend Magazine*, 5–6 May, p. 17. Reprinted from *Griffith Review 15: Unintended Consequences*, ABC Books, Sydney.
Dean, Beth and Carell, Vincent 1955, *Dust for the Dancers*, Ure Smith, Sydney.
—— 1983, *Twin Journey: To Sing, to Dance, to Live*, Pacific Publications, Sydney.
Dean, Carolyne 2004, *The Fragility of Empathy After the Holocaust*, Cornell University Pres, Ithaca, NY.
Delgado, Richard 1989, 'Storytelling for oppositionists and others: A plea for narrative', *Michigan Law Review*, vol. 87, no. 8.

Deloria, Philip J. 1998, *Playing Indian*, Yale University Press, New Haven.
—— 2004, *Indians in Unexpected Places*, University Press of Kansas, Lawrence, KA.
Department of Aboriginal and Torres Strait Islander Policy, *A Post-contact History of Cape York: Volume 2*, www.communities.qld.gov.au/community/publications/documents/pdf/capeyork.
Department of External Affairs 1964, *The Australian Aborigines*, Information Handbook no. 1, Commonwealth Government Printer, Canberra.
Dixon, Miriam 1999, *The Imaginary Australian: Anglo-Celts and Identity, 1788 to the Present*, University of New South Wales Press, Sydney.
Dodson, Michael 1996, 'Assimilation Versus Self-Determination: No Contest', H.C. (Nugget Coombs) Northern Australia Inaugural Lecture, Darwin, 5 September 1996. www.humanrights.gov.au/speeches/social_justice/assimilation_vs_selfdetermination.html - 49k
Douglas, Heather 2004, 'Assimilation, Lutheranism and the 1950s justice of Kriewaldt', *Australian Journal of Legal History*, vol. 8, no. 2, http://138.25.65.50/au/journals/AJLH/2004/12.html
Duncan, Allan 1966, 'Training Aborigines for employment in New South Wales', in Ian G. Sharp and Colin M. Tatz (eds), *Aborigines in the Economy: Employment, Wages and Training*, Jacaranda, Brisbane.
Dutton, David 2002, *One of Us? A Century of Australian Citizenship*, University of New South Wales Press, Sydney.
Eggleston, Elizabeth 1976, *Fear, Favour or Affection: Aborigines and the Criminal Law in Victoria, South Australia and Western Australia*, Australian National University Press, Canberra.
Eggleston, Sir Frederic W. 1953, 'The Australian nation', in George Caiger (ed.), under the auspices of the Australian Institute of International Affairs, *The Australian Way of Life*, Columbia University Press, New York.
Elder, Catriona 1999a, 'What is the white in white Australia? A reading of A. O. Neville's *Australia's Coloured Minority*', *Olive Pink Society Bulletin*, vol. 11, no. 1.
—— 1999b, Dreams and Nightmares of a "White Australia": The Discourse of Assimilation in Selected Works of Fiction from the 1950s and 1960s, PhD Thesis, Australian National University, Canberra.
Elkin, A. P. 1938, *The Australian Aborigines*, Angus & Robertson, Sydney.
—— 1944, *Citizenship for the Aborigines: A National Aboriginal Policy*, Australasian Publishing Co., Sydney.
—— 1951a, 'Aborigines and the Ministers Welfare Council', *The Australian Quarterly*, vol. 23, no. 4.
—— 1951b, 'Reaction and interaction: a food gathering people and European settlement in Australia', *American Anthropologist*, vol. 53, no. 2.
—— 1957, 'Aboriginal policy 1930–1950: Some personal associations', *Quadrant*, September.
Evans, Raymond 2006, *A History of Queensland*, Cambridge University Press, Melbourne.
Evans, Raymond, Saunders, Kay and Cronin, Kathryn 1975, *Exclusion, Exploitation and Extermination: Race Relations in Colonial Queensland*, Australia and New Zealand Book Co., Sydney.

Evatt, Herbert 1942–1945, 'The Australian way of life', New York, Australian News and Information Bureau.
Fink, Ruth 1957, 'The caste barrier — an obstacle to the assimilation of part-Aborigines in North-west New South Wales', *Oceania*, vol. 28, no. 2.
—— 1964, 'Guided social change at the community level', in Marie Reay (ed.), *Aborigines Now: New Perspectives in the Study of Aboriginal Communities*, Angus & Robertson, Sydney.
Fixico, Donald 2002, 'Federal and state policies and American Indians', in Philip J. Deloria and Neal Salisbury (eds), *Companion to American Indian History*, Blackwell, MA.
—— 2004, 'Federal and state policies and American Indians', in Philip J. Deloria and Neal Salisbury (eds), *A Companion to American Indian History*, Blackwell, Oxford.
Foucault, Michel 1977, *Discipline and Punish: The Birth of the Prison*, trans. Alan Sheridan, Pantheon Books, New York.
Freeman, Gary P. and Jupp, James (eds) 1992, *Nations of Immigrants: Australia, the United States and International Migration*, Oxford University Press, Melbourne.
French, Alison 2003, *Seeing the Centre: The Art of Albert Namatjira 1902–1959*, National Gallery of Australia, Canberra.
Galligan, Brian and Roberts, Winsome 2004, *Australian Citizenship*, Melbourne University Press, Melbourne.
Gare, Nene 1966, *The Fringe Dwellers*, Sun Books, Melbourne.
Garling, Jean 195-, *Australian Notes on the Ballet*, Legend Press, Sydney.
Gibbons, Michael 2004, 'Engagement with the community: The emergence of a new social contract between society and science', Community Engagement Workshop, Griffith University, South Bank, www.griffith.edu.au/er/newss/2005_1/michael_gibbons.html.
Gilbert, Kevin 1988, 'Aboriginal sovereignty: Justice, the law and land', www.aiatsis.gov.au/lbry/dig_prgm/treaty/t88/m0066865_a/m0066865_p4_a.rtf " Kevin Gilbert
Glendon, Mary Ann 2001, *A World Made New: Eleanor Roosevelt and the Universal Declaration of Human Rights*, Random House, New York.
Goldsworthy, David 2002, *Losing the Blanket: Australia and the End of Britain's Empire*, Melbourne University Press, Melbourne.
—— 2005, 'Australian external policy and the end of Britain's empire', *Australian Journal of Politics and History*, vol. 51, no. 1.
Goodall, Heather 1990, '"Saving the children": Gender and the colonisation of Aboriginal children 1788–1990', *Aboriginal Law Bulletin*, vol. 2, no. 4.
—— 1995, '"Assimilation begins in the home": The state and Aboriginal women's work as mothers in New South Wales, 1900s to 1960s', in Ann McGrath, Kay Saunders and Jackie Huggins (eds), Aboriginal Workers, special issue of *Labour History*, no. 69.
Gray, Dennis and Saggers, Sherry 1998, *Dealing with Alcohol: Indigenous Usage in Australia, New Zealand and Canada*, Cambridge University Press, Melbourne.
Gray, Geoff 2000, 'Dissolving difference: The day may come when Australia will be a land of half castes', in *'A Race for a Place': Eugenics, Darwinism and Social*

Thought and Practice in Australia, Proceedings of the History & Sociology of Eugenics Conference, University of Newcastle, 27–28 April 2000, Faculty of Arts and Social Science, University of Newcastle, Newcastle.

Greenberg, Clement 1939, 'Avant-garde and kitsch', *Partisan Review*, vol. VI, no. 5, www.sharecom.ca/greenberg/kitsch.html.

Greenwell, Kim 2002, 'Picturing "civilisation": Missionary narratives and the margins of mimicry', *BC Studies*, no. 135, Autumn.

Greenwood, Emma 1995, 'No migrants here: Migrant absence within Australian migrant publicity', *Antithesis*, vol. 7, no. 2.

Haebich, Anna 1998, 'The formative years: Paul Hasluck and Aboriginal issues during the 1930s', in Tom Stannage, Kay Saunders and Richard Nile (eds), *Paul Hasluck in Australian History: Civic Personality and Public Life*, University of Queensland Press, Brisbane.

—— 1999, 'Irresistible journeys and imaginings: Boyd's Bride Series Revisited', in Richard Nile and Michael Williams (eds), Imaginary Homelands: The Dubious Cartographies of Australian Identity, *Journal of Australian Studies*, vol. 61.

—— 2000a, 'A chronological list of legislation impacting on Aboriginal people in Western Australia 1841–1972', typescript.

—— 2000b, *Broken Circles: Fragmenting Indigenous Families 1800–2000*, Fremantle Arts Centre Press, Fremantle.

—— 2002, 'Imagining assimilation', in Joy Damousi (ed.), Challenging Histories: Reflections on Australian History, Special Edition, *Australian Historical Studies*, vol. 33, no. 118.

—— 2004, 'A long way back — reflections of a genealogical tourist', *Griffith Review*, no. 6.

—— 2005a, 'Contested histories: The battlefields of Australian Aboriginal history', in Martin Lyons and Penny Russell (eds), *Australia's History: Themes and Debates*, University of New South Wales Press, Sydney.

—— 2005b, 'Nuclear, suburban and black', in Tim Rowse (ed.), *Contesting Assimilation*, API Network, Curtin University of Technology, Perth.

—— 2007, 'Retro-assimilation', *Griffith Review*, no. 15.

Hage, Ghassan 1998, *White Nation: Fantasies of White Supremacy in a Multicultural Society*, Pluto Press, Sydney.

—— 2003, *Against Paranoid Nationalism: Searching for Hope in a Shrinking Society*, Pluto Press, Sydney.

Hall, J. R. 1965, Drinking behaviour amongst part-Aborigines in a Western Australian community, BA thesis, Department of Anthropology, University of Western Australia, Perth.

Hall, Robert A. 1989, *The Black Diggers: Aborigines and Torres Strait Islanders in the Second World War*, Allen & Unwin, Sydney.

Hallam, Elizabeth 2000, 'Texts, objects and "otherness"', in Elizabeth Hallam and Brian V. Street (eds.), *Cultural Encounters Representing 'Otherness'*, Routledge, New York.

Hannaford, Ivan 1996, *Race: The History of an Idea in the West*, John Hopkins University Press, Baltimore.

Hanson, Pauline 1998, Pauline Hanson's Maiden Speech, One Nation the Voice of

the People NSW Division, www.nswonenation.com.au/parliamentryother-speeches/paulinhansosnspeech.htm
Hasluck, Paul 1988, *Shades of Darkness: Aboriginal Affairs 1925–1965*, Melbourne University Press, Melbourne.
Hassan, Ihab 2000, 'How Australian is it?' in Peter Craven (ed.), *The Best Australian Essays*, Schwartz, Melbourne.
Henry, R., Magowan, F. and Murray, D. (eds) 2000, The Politics of Dance, *The Australian Journal of Anthropology*, vol. 11, no. 3.
Hilliard, David 1997, 'Church, family and sexuality in Australia in the 1950s', in Judith Smart and John Murphy (eds), The Forgotten Fifties, *Australian Historical Studies*, no. 109.
Holt, Harold 1953, 'Introduction' in H. Holt et al., *Australia and the Migrant*, Angus & Robertson, Sydney.
Hoorn, Jeannette 2003, 'Michael Powell's *They're a Weird Mob*: Dissolving the "undigested fragments" in the Australian body politic', *Continuum: Journal of Media and Cultural Studies*, vol. 17, no. 2.
Horner, Jack 2004, *Seeking Racial Justice: An Insider's Memoir of the Movement for Aboriginal Advancement 1938–1978*, Aboriginal Studies Press, Canberra.
Howard, Michael C. 1981, *Aboriginal Politics in Southwestern Australia*, University of Western Australia Press, Perth.
Ignatieff, Michael 1996, 'There's no place like home: the politics of belonging' in *The Age of Anxiety*, Sarah Dunant and Roy Porter (eds), Virago Press, London.
Iorns, Catherine J. 1993, 'The draft Declaration of the Rights of Indigenous Peoples', *E-law*, vol. 1, no. 1, www.murdoch.edu.au/elaw/issues/v2n1/humphry21.htmlE.
Irving, Helen 1999, 'The Crimson Thread of Kinship', Henry Parkes Foundation Launch, New South Wales Parliament House. www.parkesfoundation.org.au/Irvingspeech.htm.
Jebb, Mary Anne 2002, *Blood, Sweat and Welfare: A History of White Bosses and Aboriginal Pastoral Workers*, University of Western Australia Press, Nedlands, WA.
Jenkings, Patricia 2001, Australian political elites and citizenship education for 'New Australians' 1945–1960, PhD thesis, University of Sydney.
Johnston, George H. 1953, 'Their way of life', in Ian Bevan (ed.), *The Sunburnt Country Profile of Australia*, Collins, London.
Jones, Roy 1995, 'Migration to Australia in fiction and film', in Russell King, John Connell and Paul White (eds), *Writing Across Worlds: Literature and Migration*, Routledge, London.
Jordan, Matthew 2006, 'The reappraisal of the White Australia Policy against the background of a changing Asia, 1945–67', *Australian Journal of Politics and History*, vol. 52, no. 1.
Jordens, Ann-Mari 1995, *Redefining Australians: Immigration, Citizenship, and National Identity*, Hale & Iremonger, Sydney.
—— 1997, *Alien to Citizen: Settling Migrants in Australia 1945–75*, Allen & Unwin in association with the Australian Archives, Sydney.
—— 2001, 'Immigration since the Second World War', in James Jupp (ed.), *The*

Australian People: An Encyclopedia of the Nation, Its People and Their Origins, Cambridge University Press, Cambridge.

Jupp, James 1966, *Arrivals and Departures*, Cheshire/Lansdowne, Melbourne.

—— 1994, *Exile or Refugee? The Settlement of Refugee, Humanitarian and Displaced Immigrants*, Australian Government Publishing Service, Canberra.

—— 1998, *Immigration*, 2nd ed., Oxford University Press, Melbourne.

—— (ed.) 2001, *The Australian People: An Encyclopedia of the Nation, its People and their Origins*, Cambridge University Press, Cambridge.

—— 2002, *From White Australia to Woomera: The Story of Australian Immigration*, Cambridge University Press, Melbourne.

Kartunnen, Frances 1994, *Between Worlds: Interpreters, Guides and Survivors*, Rutgers University Press, New Brunswick, NJ.

Keen, Susan 1999, 'Associations in Australian history: Their contribution to social capital', *Journal of Interdisciplinary History*, vol. XXIX, no. 4.

Kickett, Darryl 1997, 'It's all about a fair go', *Sunday Times* (Perth), 7 December 1997, p. 47.

Kidd, Rosalind 1997, *The Way We Civilise: Aboriginal Affairs — the Untold Story*, University of Queensland Press, Brisbane.

—— 2006, *Trustees on Trial: Recovering the Stolen Wages*, Aboriginal Studies Press, Canberra.

Kivisto, Peter 2002, *Multiculturalism in a Global Society*, Blackwell, Oxford.

Kleinert, Sylvia 2000, 'Namatjira, Albert (Elea) (1902–1959)', *Australian Dictionary of Biography*, vol. 15, Melbourne University Press, Melbourne.

Kleinert, Sylvia and Neal, Margo (eds) 2000, *The Oxford Companion to Aboriginal Art and Culture*, Oxford University Press, Melbourne.

Knott, J. W. 1952, 'Events and issues that made news in 1952', National Archives of Australia, Cabinet Records, www.naa.gov.au/the_collection/cabinet/1952_cabinet_notebooks/1952_events_issues.html.

Kociumbus, Jan (ed.) 1998, 'Introduction', in *Maps, Dreams, History: Race and Representation in Australia*, Sydney Studies in History No. 8, Department of History, University of Sydney, Sydney.

Kovacs, Martin and Cropley, A. J. 1975, *Immigrants and Society: Alienation and Assimilation*, McGraw-Hill, Sydney.

Krieps, Rosch 2004, 'The Family of Man: A photographic world-document as beacon for the future of mankind', in Jean Beck and Viktoria Schmidt-Linsenhoff (eds), *The Family of Man 1955–2001*, Jonas Verlag, Marburg.

—— 2005, *Golden Jubilee of Edward Steichen's Legendary Photo Exhibition The Family of Man*, Luxembourg American Cultural Society, www.luxamcc.org/id42.html

Kunz, Josef L. 1954, 'Chapter XI of the United Nations Charter in action', *The American Journal of International Law*, vol. 8, no. 1.

Kupka, Karel 1965, *Dawn of Art: Painting and Sculptures of Australian Aborigines*, Angus & Robertson, Sydney.

Lake, Marilyn 2005, 'Paul Hasluck's horror of the two-headed calf', in Tim Rowse (ed.), *Contesting Assimilation*, API Network, Curtin University of Technology, Perth.

Lamshed, Max 1972, *'Monty': The Biography of C. P. Mountford*, Rigby, Adelaide.
Lancaster-Jones, F. 'Review', *Population Studies*, vol. 26, no. 2.
Langton, Marcia 1993, *Well, I Heard It on the Radio and I Saw It on the Television: An Essay for the Australian Film Commission on the Politics and Aesthetics of Filmmaking By and About Aboriginal People and Things*, Australian Film Commission, Sydney.
—— 1996, 'What do we mean by wilderness? Wilderness and terra nullius in Australian Art', *The Sydney Papers*, vol. 8, no. 1.
—— 1998, 'The valley of the dolls: Black humour in the art of Destiny Deacon', *Art and Australia*, vol. 35, no. 1.
—— 1999, 'Why race is a central idea in Australia's construction of the idea of a nation', *Australian Cultural History*, no. 18.
Lattas, Andrew 1989, 'Colonising the other: Dreaming, Aboriginal painting and white man's search for a soul,' *Olive Pink Society Bulletin*, vol. 1, no. 2.
Lawson, Sylvia 1964, 'Miss Denny's Aborigines', *Nation*, 14 November.
Lennon, Jessie 2000, *I'm the One That Know That Country*, Aboriginal Studies Press, Canberra.
Leske, E. (ed.) 1977, *Hermannsburg: A Vision and a Mission*, Lutheran Publishing House, Adelaide.
Levi Strauss, Claude 1968 'Race and History', in *Race and History: The Race Question in Modern Science*, Columbia University Press, New York.
Liubinas, Ale 2003, *Homeland Lost: An Autobiographical Novel*, Sid Harta Publishing, Hartwell, Victoria.
Lockwood, Douglas 1962, *I the Aboriginal*, Rigby, Adelaide.
London, H. I. 1970, *Non-white Immigration and the 'White Australia' Policy*, Sydney University Press, Sydney.
Long, J. P. M. 1964, 'The numbers and distribution of Aboriginals in Australia', in Ian G. Sharp and Colin M. Tatz (eds), *Aborigines in the Economy: Employment, Wages and Training*, Jacaranda, Brisbane.
Louis, L. J. 2001, *Menzies' Cold War: A Reinterpretation*, Red Rag Publications, Melbourne.
Louis, William Roger 1978, *Imperialism at Bay: The United States and the Decolonization of the British Empire, 1941–1945*, Oxford University Press, New York.
MacDonald, R. 1995, *Between Two Worlds: The Commonwealth Government and the Removal of Aboriginal Children of Part Descent in the Northern Territory*, Institute of Aboriginal Development Press, Alice Springs.
MacDonald, Rowena 1995, 'Selling a dream', *Weekend Australian Magazine*, 4–5 November, p. 26.
Macintyre, S. 1998, *The Reds*, Allen and Unwin, Sydney.
Macintyre, Stuart 2003, 'Fear of invasion has given way to fear of the refugee', *The Age* (Melbourne), 20 June 2003, www.theage.com.au/articles/2003/06/19/1055828433377.htm
Mackay, Hugh 1997, *Generations: Baby Boomers, Their Parents and Their Children*, Pan Macmillan, Sydney.
Manning, Corinne 2004, '"A helping white hand": Assimilation, welfare and

Victoria's transitional Aboriginal housing policy', *Labour History*, no. 87, www.historycooperative.org/journals/lab/87/manning.html.

—— 2005, 'If Aborigines are to be assimilated they must learn to live in houses: Victoria's transitional Aboriginal housing policy', in Tim Rowse (ed.), *Contesting Assimilation*, API Network, Curtin University of Technology, Perth.

Marcus, Julie 1999, 'The blackness of the body', in *A Dark Smudge Upon the Sand: Essays on Race, Guilt and the National Consciousness*, LHR Press, Canada Bay, NSW.

Markus, Andrew 1994, *Australian Race Relations*, Allen & Unwin, Sydney.

—— 2003, 'Of continuities and discontinuities: Reflections on a century of Australian Immigration control', in Laksiri Jayasuriya, David Walker and Jan Gothard (eds), *Legacies of White Australia: Race Culture and Nation*, University of Western Australian Press, Nedlands.

Martin, Jan Lee 2005, Australian Futures in Community: Inayatullah, The Futures Foundation, www.futuresfoundation.org.au/Future-News/Features:-Applied-Futures/Australian-futures-in-community:-Inayatullah-20050625174.

Martin, Jean 1965, *Refugee Settlers: A Study of Displaced Persons in Australia*, Australian National University Press, Canberra.

—— 1978, *The Migrant Presence: Australian Responses 1947–1977: Research Report for the National Population Inquiry*, George Allen & Unwin, Sydney.

Mayer, Henry 1964, *The Press in Australia*, Lansdowne Press, Melbourne.

McAuliffe, Chris 1996, *Art and Suburbia*, Craftsman House, Sydney.

McCarthy, Fred 1941, 'Australian Aboriginal art and its application', *Australian Museum Magazine*, vol. 7, no. 10.

McClintock, Anne 1995, *Imperial Leather: Race, Gender and Sexuality in the Colonial Context*, Routledge, New York.

McCorquodale, John 1987, *Aborigines and the Law: A Digest*, Aboriginal Studies Press for the Australian Institute of Aboriginal Studies, Canberra.

McDonald, Connie Nungulla 1996, *When You Grow Up*, Magabala Books, Broome.

McDonnell, Margaret 2002, 'The colour of copyright', *M/C Journal*, vol. 5, no. 3, http://journal.media-culture.org.au/0207/copyright.php.

McGregor, Russell 1996, 'Intelligent parasitism: A. P. Elkin and the rhetoric of assimilation', *Journal of Australian Studies*, vol. 50, no. 51.

—— 1999, 'Words, wards and citizens: A. P. Elkin and Paul Hasluck on assimilation', *Oceania*, vol. 69, no. 4.

Mckeown, Deirdre 2002–03, *Changes in the Australian Oath of Citizenship*, E-Brief: Research Note no. 20, 19 November 2002, Research Note Index 2002–03, Politics and Public Administration Group, Parliamentary Library, Parliament House, Canberra, www.aph.gov.au/library/pubs/rn/2002–03/03rn20.htm

McNay, Louise 1994, *Foucault: A Critical Introduction*, Polity Press, Cambridge.

Melon, Marc-Emmanuel 2004, 'The patriarchal family: Domestic ideology in The Family of Man', in Jean Beck and Viktoria Schmidt-Linsenhoff (eds), *The Family of Man 1955–2001*, Jonas Verlag, Marburg.

Mercer, David 2003, '"Citizen minus"?: Indigenous Australians and the citizenship question', *Citizenship Studies*, vol. 7, no. 4.

Metzl, J. M. 2003, *Prozac on the Couch: Prescribing Gender in the Era of Wonder Drugs*, Duke University Press, Durham, NC.

Mickler, Steve 1998a, *The Myth of Privilege*, Fremantle Arts Centre Press, Fremantle.

—— Steve 1998b, 'The Perth press and problematising Aboriginal status', website of the Centre for Research in Culture and Communication, Murdoch University, wwwmcc.murdoch.edu.au/ReadingRoom/impi/articles/press.html.

Miller, E. P. 1966, 'Factors affecting vocational training for Aborigines in the Northern Territory and Western Australia', in Ian G. Sharp and Colin M. Tatz (eds), *Aborigines in the Economy: Employment, Wages and Training*, Jacaranda, Brisbane.

Mills, Charles 1997, *The Racial Contract*, Cornell University Press, Ithaca, NY.

Moore, Catriona 1984, 'The guiding hand: Representation and Aboriginal welfare politics', in Sex, Politics and Representation, *Local Consumption Series 5*, April.

Moore, Catriona and Muecke, Stephen 1984, 'Racism and the representation of Aborigines in film', *Australian Journal of Cultural Studies*, vol. 2, no. 1.

Moran, Albert and Vieth, Errol 2006, *Film in Australia: An Introduction*, Cambridge University Press, Cambridge.

Moran, Anthony 2005, 'White Australia, settler nationalism and Aboriginal assimilation', *Australian Journal of Politics and History*, vol. 51, no. 2.

Morgan, George 2000, 'Assimilation and resistance: Housing Indigenous Australians in the 1970s', *Journal of Sociology*, vol. 36, no. 2.

Morley, Grace McCann 1954, 'UNESCO's exchange of exhibitions programme: The first circulating exhibition', *Museum*, vol. 6, no. 4.

Morris, Meaghan 1993, 'Beyond assimilation: Aboriginality, media history and public memory', *Rouge*, www.rouge.com.au/3/beyond.html.

Mountford, C. P. 1948, *Brown Men and Red Sand: Journeyings in Wild Australia*, Robertson & Mullens, Melbourne.

—— 1949, 'Exploring Stone Age Arnhem land', *National Geographic Magazine*, vol. 96, no. 6.

—— 1965, *The Dreamtime: Australian Aboriginal Myths in Paintings by Ainslie Roberts*, Rigby, Adelaide.

Mundine Djon 2003, 'A dance through the desert', in *Dancing Up Country: the Art of Dorothy Napangardi*, Museum of Contemporary Art, Sydney.

Murphy, Brian 1993, *The Other Australians: Experiences of Migration*, Cambridge University Press, Melbourne.

Murphy, John 2000, *Imagining the Fifties: Private Sentiment and Political Culture in Menzies' Australia*, University of New South Wales Press, Sydney.

Nannup, Alice with Marsh, Lauren and Kinnane, Stephen 1992, *When the Pelican Laughed*, Fremantle Arts Centre Press, Fremantle,

National Archives of Australia n.d., 'Citizenship in Australia' in *A Guide to Commonwealth Government Records*, http://aa.gov.au/Publications/research_guides/guides/ctznship/chapter2.htm.

Noonuccal, Oodgeroo 1981, 'Then and now', in *My People: A Kath Walker Collection*, Jacaranda, Brisbane.

North, Michael 1994, *The Dialect of Modernism: Race, Language, and Twentieth*

Century Literature, Oxford University Press, Oxford, 1994.
O'Callaghan, Judith 1993, *The Australian Dream*, Powerhouse Publishing, Sydney.
O'Grady, John 1957, *They're a Weird Mob*, Ure Smith, Sydney.
Office of the United Nations High Commissioner for Human Rights, Indigenous and Tribal Peoples Convention, 1989 (No. 169), www.ohchr.org/english/law/indigenous.htm.
Ongley, Patrick and Pearson, David 1995, 'Post-1945 international migration: New Zealand, Australia and Canada compared', *International Migration Review*, vol. 29, no. 3.
Oxford American Dictionaries On-line 2005, Oxford University Press, New York.
Oxer, Rosemary 1963, 'Allawah Grove: An experiment in assimilation', BA Honours thesis, University of Western Australia, Perth.
Packard, Vance 1962, *The Hidden Persuaders*, Penguin, Harmondsworth.
Panich, Catherine 1988, *Sanctuary? Remembering Postwar Immigration*, Allen & Unwin, Sydney.
Parsons, Michael 2002, '"Ah that I could convey a proper idea of this interesting wild play of the natives": Corroborees and the rise of Indigenous Australian cultural tourism', *Australian Aboriginal Studies*, no. 2.
Partington, Geoffrey 1996, *Hasluck versus Coombs White Politics and Australia's Aborigines*, Quaker's Hill Press, Sydney.
Pearson, Noel 2007, 'When hope is lost we must imagine a future', *Inquirer, The Weekend Australian*, 5–6 May, p. 28.
Peel, Mark 1997, 'A new kind of manhood: Remembering the 1950s', in Judith Smart and John Murphy (eds), *The Forgotten Fifties*, Australian Historical Studies no. 109.
Phillips, Janet 2005, 'Australia's migration program', Research Note no. 48 2004–05, Social Policy Section, Parliamentary Library, Parliament of Australia, www.aph.gov.au/library/pubs/RN/2004–05/05rn48.htm.
Poignant, Roslyn 1995, *Lost Conversations, Recovered Archives*, Tenth Eric Johnston Lecture, Occasional Paper No. 49, www.ntl.nt.gov.au/__data/assets/pdf_file /0015/5262/occpaper49_ej10.pdf.
Potter, Michelle 2004, 'Corroboree', *National Library of Australia News*, vol. XIV, no. 6, www.nla.gov.au/pub/nlanews/2004/mar04/article3.html.
Povenelli, Elizabeth A. 2002, *The Cunning of Recognition: Indigenous Alterities and the Making of Australian Multiculturalism*, Duke University Press, London.
Powell, Rene and Kennedy, Bernadette 2005, *Rene Baker File #28/ E. D. P.*, Fremantle Arts Centre Press, Fremantle.
Pratt, Mary Louise 1992, *Imperial Eyes: Travel Writing and Transculturation*, Routledge, New York.
Pugliese, Joseph 2006, '"I am, you are …": the cultural politics of unAustralian', paper presented at the 2006 Ideas Festival, Brisbane.
Ramsland, John and Mooney, Christopher 2006, *Remembering Aboriginal Heroes: Struggle, Identity and the Media*, Brolga Publishing, Melbourne.
Read, Peter 2005, '"A rape of the soul so profound": Some reflections on the dispersal policy in New South Wales', *Aboriginal History*, no. 7.
Reay, Marie (ed.) 1964a, A*borigines Now: New Perspectives in the Study of Aboriginal*

Communities, Angus & Robertson, Sydney.
—— 1964b, 'Introduction', in Marie Reay (ed.), *Aborigines Now: New Perspectives in the Study of Aboriginal Communities*, Angus & Robertson, Sydney.
—— 1965, 'The background of alien impact', in Ronald M. Berndt and Catherine M. Berndt (eds), *Aboriginal Man in Australia: Essays in Honour of Emeritus Professor A. P. Elkin*, Angus & Robertson, Sydney.
Reay, Marie and Sitlington, Grace 1948, 'Class and status in a mixed-blood community', *Oceania*, vol. 28, no. 3.
Reynolds, Henry (ed.) 1972, *Aborigines and Settlers: The Australian Experience, 1788–1939*, Cassell, Melbourne.
—— (ed.) 1978, *Race Relations in North Queensland*, James Cook University of North Queensland, Townsville.
Rosaldo, Renato 1989, 'Imperialist nostalgia', *Representations*, no. 20, Spring.
Rose, Michael (ed.) 1996, *For the Record: 160 Years of Aboriginal Print Journalism*, Allen & Unwin, Sydney.
Rosenstock, Laura 1984, 'Leger: "The creation of the world"', in William Rubin (ed.), *'Primitivism' in 20th century Art: Affinity of the Tribal and the Modern*, Museum of Modern Art, New York.
Ross, Kristin 1996, *Fast Cars, Clean Bodies: Decolonialization and the Reordering of French Culture*, MIT Press, Cambridge.
Roth, Lenny 2007, *Multiculturalism*, Parliament of New South Wales Briefing Paper No. 09/2007, www.parliament.nsw.gov.au/prod/parliament/publications.nsf/0/F6EEFB50EFBD5F17CA257309001E18B7
Rowe, Gordon 1956, *How Can the Aborigines Be Assimilated?*, n.p.
Rowley, Charles 1962, 'Aborigines and other Australians', *Oceania*, vol. 32, no. 4.
—— 1966 'Causation in relation to Aboriginal affairs,' in Ian G. Sharp and Colin M. Tatz (eds), *Aborigines in the Economy: Employment, Wages and Training*, Jacaranda, Brisbane.
—— 1982, *Equality by Instalments: The Aboriginal Householder in Rural New South Wales 1965 and 1980*, Australian Institute of Aboriginal Studies, Canberra.
Rowse, Tim 1998, *White Flour, White Power: From Rations to Citizenship in Central Australia*, Cambridge University Press, Cambridge.
—— 2000, *Obliged to be Difficult: Nugget Coombs' Legacy in Indigenous Affairs*, Cambridge University Press, Cambridge.
—— 2001, 'The arts advocacy of H. C. Coombs', in Tony Bennett and David Carter (eds), *Culture in Australia: Politics, Publics and Progress*, Cambridge University Press, Melbourne.
—— 2005a, 'The certainties of assimilation', in *Contesting Assimilation*, API Network, Curtin University of Technology, Perth.
—— 2005b, 'The post-war social science of assimilation 1947–1966', in Tim Rowse (ed.), *Contesting Assimilation*, API Network, Curtin University, Perth.
—— 2006, 'Review of *Civil Rights: How Indigenous Australians Won Formal Equality* by John Chesterman', Work and Leisure, *Australian Historical Studies* vol. 37, no. 127.
Rudmin, F. W. 2003, 'Catalogue of acculturation constructs: Descriptions of 126 taxonomies, 1918–2003' in W. J. Donner, D. L. Dinnel, S. A. Hayes and D. N.

Sattler (eds), *Online Readings in Psychology and Culture*, Unit 8, Chapter 8, Centre for Cross-Cultural Research, Western Washington University, Bellingham, www.wwu.edu/~culture.

Russell, Lynette 2000, 'Going "walkabout" in the 1950s: Images of "traditional" Aboriginal Australia', in Julie Marcus (ed.), *Picturing the 'Primitif' Images of Race in Daily Life*, LhR Press, Canada Bay, NSW.

Sandeen, Eric 2004, 'The show you see with your heart: 'The Family of Man' on tour in the Cold War world', in Jean Beck and Viktoria Schmidt-Linsenhoff (eds), *The Family of Man 1955–2001*, Jonas Verlag, Marburg.

Sayre, Gordon M. 1999, 'A bridging between two worlds: John Tanner as American Indian autobiographer', *American Literary History*, vol. 11, no. 3.

Schaffer, Kay and Smith, Sidonie 2004, *Human Rights and Narrated Lives: The Ethics of Recognition*, Palgrave Macmillan, New York.

Schapper, Henry P. 1968, 'Administration and welfare as threats of Aboriginal assimilation', *Australian Journal of Social Issues*, vol. 3, no. 4.

Schech, Suzanne and Haggis, Jane 2000, 'Migrancy, whiteness and the settler self in contemporary Australia', in John Docker and Gerhard Fischer (eds), *Race, Colour and Identity in Australia and New Zealand*, University of New South Wales Press, Sydney.

Schlunke, Katrina 2000, 'Imaging the imaged: Stories of *Jedda*', in Julie Marcus (ed.), *Picturing the 'Primitif': Images of Race in Daily Life*, LHR Press, Canada Bay, NSW.

Scott, Kim and Brown, Hazel 2005, *Kayang and Me*, Fremantle Arts Centre Press, Fremantle.

Scott, Sarah 2002, 'Imagining a nation: Australia's representation at the Venice Biennale, 1958', *Australian Studies*, 17 (2).

Scruton, Roger 1999, 'Kitsch and the modern predicament', *City Journal*, Winter, n.p., www.city-journal.org/html/9_1_urbanities_kitsch_and_the.html.

Seddon, David J. 1971, 'Review: *Race and Science; Passing for White*', *Man*, New Series, vol. 6, no. 1.

Sen, Amartya 1992, *Inequality Re-examined*, Russell Sage Foundation & Clarendon Press, Oxford.

Sheridan, Susan 2000, 'The Australian woman and her migrant others in the postwar *Australian Women's Weekly*', *Continuum: Journal of Media and Cultural Studies*, vol. 14, no. 2.

—— 2002, *Who Was That Woman? The Australian Women's Weekly in the Postwar Years*, University of New South Wales Press, Kensington.

Shirley, Graham and Adams, Brian 1983, *Australian Cinema: The First Eighty Years*, Angus & Robertson and Currency Press, Sydney.

Simpson, Colin 1951, *Adam in Ochre: Inside Aboriginal Australia*, Angus & Robertson, Sydney.

Sluga, Glenda 1985, Bonegilla Reception and Training Centre: 1947 to 1971, Master of Arts thesis, University of Melbourne.

Smith, Bernard 2001, *Australian Painting, 1788–2000* with additional chapters by Terry Smith and Christopher Heathcote, 4th ed., Oxford University Press, Melbourne.

Smith, Claire 2004, *Country, Kin and Culture: Survival of an Australian Aboriginal Community*, Wakefield Press, Kent Town, SA.
Solomon-Godeau, Abigail 2004, 'The family of man: Refurbishing humanism for a postmodern age', in Jean Beck and Viktoria Schmidt-Linsenhoff (eds), *The Family of Man 1955–2001*, Jonas Verlag, Marburg.
Sommerlad, Elizabeth 1977, *Aboriginal Juveniles in Custody: Report Arising from a National Symposium on the Care and Treatment of Aboriginal Juveniles in State Corrective Institutions*, Australian National University Centre for Continuing Education, Canberra.
Stanner, W. E. H. 1960, 'Durmugam a Nangiomeri' in J. B. Casagrande (ed.), *In the Company of Man*, Harper, New York.
—— 1969, *After the Dreaming: Black and White Australians — an Anthropologist's View*, Australian Broadcasting Commission, Sydney.
—— 1979a, 'Aborigines and Australian Society', in *White Man Got No Dreaming: Essays, 1938–1973*, Australian National University Press, Canberra.
—— 1979b, 'Continuity and change', in *White Man Got No Dreaming*, Australian National University Press, Canberra.
Stephen, Ann, McNamara, Andrew and Goad, Philip (eds) 2006, *Modernism & Australia: Documents on Art, Design and Architecture 1917–1967*, Miegunyah Press, Melbourne.
Stewart-Harawira, Makere 2005, *The New Imperial Order: Indigenous Responses to Globalisation*, Zed Books, London.
Symes, Colin and Lingard, Bob 1988, 'From the Ethnographic to the Aesthetic', in Paul Foss (ed.), *Island in the Stream*, Pluto Press, Sydney.
Taffe, Sue 1995, 'Australian diplomacy in a policy vacuum: Government and Aboriginal affairs 1961–62', *Aboriginal History*, vol. 19.
—— 2005a, *Black and White Together: FCAATSI, the Federal Council for the Advancement of Aborigines and Torres Strait Islanders 1958–1973*, University of Queensland Press, Brisbane.
—— 2005b, 'The role of FCAATSI in the 1967 Referendum: Mythmaking about citizenship or political strategy?' in Tim Rowse (ed.) *Contesting Assimilation*, API Network, Curtin University, Perth.
Taft, Ronald 1965, *From Stranger to Citizen: A Survey of Studies of Immigrant Assimilation in Western Australia*, University of Western Australia Press, Perth.
Tavan, Gwenda 1997, '"Good neighbours": Community, organisations, migrant assimilation and Australian society and culture, 1950–1961', *Australian Historical Studies*, vol. 28, no. 109.
—— 2005, *The Long Slow Death of White Australia*, Scribe, Melbourne.
Thomas, Nicholas 1999, *Possessions: Indigenous Art/Colonial Culture*, Thames and Hudson, London.
—— 2001, 'Indigenous presences and national narratives in Australasian museums', in Tony Bennett and David Carter (eds), *Culture in Australia: Politics, Publics and Progress*, Cambridge University Press, Melbourne.
Timur, Serim 2000, 'Changing trends and major issues in international migration: An overview of UNESCO programmes', *International Social Science Journal*, no. 52.
Tone, Andrea 2005, 'Listening to the past: History, psychiatry, and anxiety',

Canadian Journal of Psychiatry, June.
Torgovnick, Marianna 1996, *Primitive Passions: Men, Women, and the Quest for Ecstasy*, University of Chicago Press, Chicago.
Tuana, Nancy 2004, 'Coming to understand: Orgasm and the epistemology of ignorance', *Hypatia*, vol. 19, no. 1.
Tuckson, Tony 2006, 'Aboriginal art and the Western world', in Ann Stephen, Andrew McNamara and Phillip Goad (eds.), *Modernism in Australia: Documents on Art, Design and Architecture 1917–1967*, Miegunyah Press, Melbourne.
Twetchett, K.J. 1972, 'Review of The United Nations and decolonisation: The role of Afro-Asia by Yassin el-Ayouty', *International Affairs* (Royal Institute of International Affairs 1944–), vol. 48, no. 2.
UNESCO 1950, *The Race Question*, http://en.wikipedia.org/wiki/The_Race_Question
United Nations 2005, *60th Anniversary of the San Francisco Conference*, www.un.org/aboutun/sanfrancisco/history.html.
Van de Ven, Anne-Marie 1993, 'Images of the 1950s: Design and advertising', in Judith O'Callaghan (ed.), *The Australian Dream: Design of the Fifties*, Powerhouse Publishing, Sydney.
van Krieken, Robert 2005, 'Assimilation and liberal government', in Tim Rowse (ed.), *Contesting Assimilation*, API Network, Curtin University, Perth.
Varnedoe, Kirk 1984, 'Abstract expressionism', in William Rubin (ed.), *'Primitivism' in 20th century Art: Affinity of the Tribal and the Modern*, Museum of Modern Art, New York.
Vassilieff, Elizabeth 1959, 'Explaining man to man', *Overland*, vol. 14, Autumn.
Vaughan, Meaghan 1991, *Curing Their Ills*, Polity Press, Cambridge.
Vignando, Catrina 2000, '*Corroboree*: Aboriginal inspiration in contemporary Australian ballet', in Julie Marcus (ed.), *Picturing the 'Primitif': Images of Race in Daily Life*, LHR Press, Canada Bay, NSW.
Visweswaran, Kamala 1998, 'Race and the rise of anthropology', *American Anthropologist, New Series*, vol. 100, no. 1.
Vlahonasiou, Thelma 1983, Annual Citizenship Conventions, 1950–1963 (An analysis of the background against which the Education for a Multicultural Society is to be seen), Master of Education, University of Melbourne.
Wain, Barry 1979, 'The Indochina refugee crisis', *Foreign Affairs*, Fall, www.foreignaffairs.org/19790901faessay8212/barry-wain/the-indochina-refugee-crisis.html.
Walker, Kath 1964, *We are Going*, Jacaranda, Brisbane.
Weinstock, Alexander S. 1960, 'Review of *The Cultural Integration of Immigrants: A Survey Based Upon the Papers and Proceedings of the UNESCO Conference held in Havana, April, 1956*, by W.D. Borrie', *The American Journal of Sociology*, vol. 66, no. 2.
West Australian Government 1958, 'Report of Select Committee on Native Affairs', *Western Australia, Votes and Proceedings*, vol. 3, Government Printer, Perth.
—— 1960, *Official Year Book of Western Australia*, Government Printer, Perth.
—— 1974, *Report of the Royal Commission into Aboriginal Affairs*, L. C. Furnell, Government Printer, Perth.

Western Australian Government Department of Native Welfare 1964, *Citizens*, Government Printer, Perth.

White, Richard 1979, 'The Australian way of life', *Historical Studies*, vol. 18, no. 73.

—— 1993, 'The shock of affluence' in Judith O'Callaghan (ed.), *The Australian Dream*, Powerhouse Museum, Sydney.

William, Dick, 1965, *A Bunch of Ratbags*, Collins, London.

Willis, Anne-Marie 1988, *Picturing Australia: A History of Photography*, Angus & Robertson, Sydney.

—— 1993, *Illusions of Identity: The Art of Nation*, Hale & Iremonger, Sydney.

Wilson, John 1964, 'Assimilation to what? Comments on the white society', in Marie Reay (ed.), *Aborigines Now: New Perspectives in the Study of Aboriginal Communities*, Angus & Robertson, Sydney.

Winton, Tim 2004, *The Turning*, Pan Macmillan, Sydney.

Wise, Tigger 1985, *The Self-made Anthropologist: A Life of A. P. Elkin*, Allen & Unwin, Sydney.

Wolfe, Patrick n.d., *Globally Speaking: The Politics of Globalisation Program 4: Where to Australia?* www.abc.net.au/global/radio/radio04.htm

—— 2006, 'Operation Sandy Track', *Overland*, no. 183, Winter.

Wright, Richard 1956, *The Color Curtain: A Report on the Bandung Conference*, World Publishing Company, Cleveland and New York.

York, Barry 2003, 'The myth of our humanitarian tradition', *Age* (Melbourne), 27 June 2003, www.theage.com.au/articles/2003/06/26/1056449364608.html.

Young, Sally 2004, *The Persuaders: Inside the Hidden Machine of Political Advertising*, Pluto Press, Melbourne.

Zawawi, Clara 2000, 'A history of public relations in Australia', in Jane Johnston and Clara Zawawi (eds), *Public Relations Theory and Practice,* 2nd ed., Allen & Unwin, Sydney.

Zizek, Slavoj 1997, *The Plague of Fantasies*, Verso, London.

Acknowledgements

Spinning the Dream is based on research completed while I was an Australia Research Council QEII Fellow and Co-Director of the Centre for Public Culture and Ideas at Griffith University. This research is woven together with insights from decades of previous study and my own experiences growing up in a migrant community and living with my partner Darryl Kickett as part of an extended Nyungar family. Working on this book was a far more desk-bound and introverted process than any of my previous books, so I am thankful to Griffith University and the Centre for providing me with a nurturing intellectual home where I could pursue my passion for cross-disciplinary research and cultural history. I am also grateful to the Australia Research Council for funding me to research and write this comprehensive cultural history of assimilation in Australia.

For bringing my unruly manuscript to order I am indebted to the forensic editing of Janet Blagg at Fremantle Press. Susan Jervis added necessary final edits. Ray Coffey at Fremantle Press managed the entire enterprise with aplomb and pushed through a speedy publishing schedule. Working on Chapter Seven with Lauren Marsh was a collaborator's dream. My Research Assistant Jodie Taylor brought intelligence, grace and friendship to her tasks and Andrew Walker, Heather Anderson and Jill Jones provided generous assistance. Raymond Evans read and commented on the manuscript. The Warth and Mataitis families shared migrant stories that fed my imagination and Jack Horner agreed to my request to use his story. Darryl Kickett added many personal insights to my research. David Dare Parker made available his great photograph for the book cover. Danny Ford helped with access to a vital set of images. Colleagues who provided advice and encouragement include Tim Rowse, Peter Read, Fiona Paisley, Jay Arthur, Anna Cole, Ann Curthoys, Pat Grimshaw, Matt Trinca, Julianne Schultz, Marilyn McMeniman, Pat Hoffie, Terri Ann White, Kay Ferres, Terry Maybury, Wayne Hudson, Jim Walter, Louise Denoon, Mary Anne Jebb, Malcolm Albrook, Sarah Yu and Mark Finnane. My sincere thanks also to staff at the Griffith University Library, National Archives of Australia, National Library of Australia, Battye Library, and the West Australian State Records Office.

Finally, my heartfelt appreciation to my family and friends who sustained me with laughter and ideas and overlooked my anti-social tendencies: Darryl, Rikia and Latisha Kickett; Joan, Derek and Daniel Curtin; Bob Haebich; Yvonne Schaffierius; Rowena and Geoff Newton; Steve Kinnane; Helen Cattalini; Georgina Murray and David Peetz; Diane Moon; Hedley and Carolyne Pearson; and my dear dad Bert Haebich.

Some material used in the book has appeared in earlier publications. Extracts from Haebich, Anna 2007, 'Retro-assimilation', *Griffith Review* are included in the Introduction and Chapter Three, which also includes material from Haebich, Anna 2002, 'Imagining assimilation', in Damousi, Joy (ed.), Challenging Histories Reflections on Australian History, Special Issue, *Australian Historical Studies.* Chapters Five and Six contain edited material from Haebich, Anna 2005, 'Nuclear, suburban and black: Commissioner Middleton, Aboriginal families and assimilation', in Rowse, Tim (ed.), *Contesting Assimilation. Histories of Colonial and Indigenous Initiatives.* Part of material from Chapter Eight previously appeared in Haebich, Anna 2006, 'Assimilation and Hybrid Art: Reflections on the Politics of Aboriginal Art', in Foley, Fiona (ed.), *The Art of Politics, The Politics of Art.* Chapters Five, Six and Nine contain material from Haebich, Anna 2000, *Broken Circles. Fragmenting Indigenous Families 1800–1990.*

Index

First published 2008 by
FREMANTLE PRESS
25 Quarry Street, Fremantle
(PO Box 158, North Fremantle 6159)
Western Australia.
www.fremantlepress.com.au

Consultant Editor Janet Blagg
Production Editor Ray Coffey
Cover Designer Tracey Gibbs
Cover photograph courtesy David Dare Parker
Printed by Everbest Printing Company, China.

National Library of Australia
Cataloguing-in-publication data

Haebich, Anna.
Spinning the dream: assimilation in Australia 1950–1970.

ISBN 9781921361074 (pbk.).

1. Assimilation (Sociology) — Australia. 2. Minorities — Government policy — Australia. 3. Aboriginal Australians — Government policy — Australia. 4. Immigrants — Government policy — Australia. 5. Australia — Cultural policy. 6. Australia — Social conditions — 1945– . I. Title.

303.48294

Publication of this title was assisted by the Commonwealth Government through the Australia Council, its arts funding and advisory body.